RESOUNDING THE RHETORICAL

COMPOSITION AS A QUASI-OBJECT

BYRON HAWK

University of Pittsburgh Press

Published by the University of Pittsburgh Press, Pittsburgh, Pa., 15260
Copyright © 2018, University of Pittsburgh Press
Manufactured in the United States of America
Printed on acid-free paper
10 9 8 7 6 5 4 3 2 1

ISBN 13: 978-0-8229-6541-1

Cataloging-in-Publication data is available from the Library of Congress

Cover art: Bobby Hill's set up, MOM² performance at Conundrum Music Hall.
Photo by Brian Harmon.
Cover design by Jordan Wannamacher

CONTENTS

ACKNOWLEDGMENTS

I WOULD LIKE TO thank my many composition and rhetoric colleagues at the University of South Carolina—Kevin Brock, Erik Doxtader, Gina Ercolini, Mindy Fenske, Christy Friend, Pat Gehrke, Chris Holcomb, John Muckelbauer, Bill Rivers, Hannah Rule, and Dan Smith—along with Greg Stuart from the School of Music. Being here with them greatly influenced my thinking in many ways that made it into the project. Thanks to all of the graduate students in the New Material Rhetorics and Sonic Rhetorics seminars at USC, particularly students and former students who gave me feedback on chapters during the process—Casey Boyle, Justine Wells, Mary Fratini, and Anthony Stagliano (not to mention the many conversations with Casey Boyle). Special thanks go to Brian Harmon for all of his hard work filming and editing, which made the research possible; Rhetoric Society of America Summer Institutes at Lawrence, KS, Madison, WI, and Bloomington, IN, for having me colead workshops on New Material Rhetorics and Sonic Rhetorics that were formative of the project, especially Thomas Rickert and Jonathan Alexander for making those experiences rigorous and productive; and colleagues at Indiana University—John Schilb, Scot Barnett, and Justin Hodgson—who invited me to give a talk on campus that jump-started the project.

Many thanks go to Josh Shanholtzer, David Bartholomae, and Jean Carr of the University of Pittsburgh Press and the outside reviewers for letting and guiding another quirky project through the pipeline, especially Josh for his limitless patience. Their support over the years has meant a great deal. Thanks to Cheryl Ball for coediting the *Computers and Composition* sound issue with me, which really started turning my thinking in this direction; Christian Smith for coauthoring a piece with me in *Currents in Electronic Literacy's* "Writing with Sound" issue edited by Diane Davis; the many colleagues who host and regularly attend the Rhetorical Theory Conference, the Western States Rhetoric and Literacy Conference, and the Indiana Digital Rhetoric Symposium, where I presented pieces of the manuscript in conference paper form; all of the many scholars who are starting to make sonic rhetorics happen, in particular Steven Hammer, Steph Ceraso, Jon Stone, and Eric Detweiler for interviewing me about the book in his podcast *Rhetoricity*; Tim Mayers and Paul Kameen both for help on *Counter-History*; all of my former colleagues at George Mason University; "The Arlington School" and its many associates for informing much of what follows in these pages; and Sid Dobrin for inviting me to write chapters for edited collections that became the bases for book chapters. And to Pre/Text, Utah State University Press, and Routledge for reprint rights to material from previously published articles and chapters.

I would especially like to thank the amazing artists who gave me some of their time and let me pop into little slices of their lives for the sake of some obscure academic project: Jim King at Sonic Dropper Studios; Jacob Aaron, James Guajardo, Bob McCrary, and Bryan Patrick of New Magnetic North; Thomas Stanley, Bobby Hill, and Luke Stewart of Mind over Matter, Music over Mind (MOM²) ; Ned Durrett of Ned and The Dirt; and Boyfriend and her DJ Earl Scioneaux III. Thanks also to Tom Law and Cecil Decker at Conundrum Music Hall for all of the work that went into Conundrum and supporting music in Columbia, SC, and to the University of South Carolina for the research funding that allowed me to travel to or pay the travel for the artists that drove the project.

Finally, and maybe most of all, I would like to thank my family—Susie, Alex, and Aidan—for tolerating all of the things that go along with academia and supporting what has been a crazy ride so far.

RESOUNDING THE RHETORICAL

INTRODUCTION

RE-SOUNDING

RESOUNDING THE RHETORICAL brings together two emerging trends in composition and rhetoric—the developing interest in sound studies and the turn toward new materialisms. In 2006 Cheryl Ball and I coedited a special issue of *Computers and Composition* on "Sound in/as Compositional Space: A Next Step in Multiliteracies." The issue began with the premise that multimodal composition should start taking notice of sound. Just as the field shifted from linguistic to visual "meaning making" in the 1990s and early 2000s, the next logical move would be to include other modes such as audio—music, sound effects, voice-overs, samples, and amateur field recordings (263). While many of the articles emphasized music in addition to voice-overs and sound effects in film and multimedia texts, sound is still something to examine in addition to texts and images. The issue showed that this attention to sound was "possible within composition studies," and the field has since slowly attended to sound in addition to texts and visuals as part of an overall meaning-making enterprise (263).[1] In his book *Sonic Persuasion* (2011), for example, Greg Goodale shows how dialect, accents, and intonations in presidential speeches; ticking clocks, rumbling locomotives, and machinic hums in literary texts; and the sound of sirens and bombs in cartoons and war propaganda all function persuasively along with words and images. But he maintains that a significant hurdle for sound's wider inclusion in rhetoric is that it is difficult to *read*. So Goodale develops a series of close readings to show that sound can be interpreted on par with words and images. However, his take on rhetoric is largely traditional. Rhetorical concepts such as the enthymeme and identification are predominant in his examples, and his sense of criticism is grounded in interpretation based on historical context and close reading for meaning with the goal of critical awareness. What is compelling about sound is the potential to develop newer rhetorical concepts and theoretical models grounded in affect, material engagement, and emergent methods. While Goodale hints at this potential,[2] his interpretive practice doesn't necessarily take us to these diverse places.

The field's emerging interest in sound studies, however, is starting to progress beyond sound as an additional mode of composition or object of study for the interpretation of meaning. In 2011, Diane Davis edited a special issue of *Currents in Electronic Literacy* on "Writing with Sound." Citing Simon Reynold's turn away from rock and lyrics toward rave and rhythm, she frames the work in the issue as a shift from interpretation to performativity, asking not "what the music 'means' but how it *works*" (Reynolds qtd. in Davis). Persuasion, she argues, doesn't just aim to mean but to "entrain, to engender a kind of rhythmic sync-up . . . between the body and the music." The various interviews, articles, and media projects in the issue attempt to draw out and in some cases enact sound's materially performative operations.[3] Similarly, Steph Ceraso's article "(Re)Educating the Senses" (2014) calls for a shift toward embodiment because listening is a multisensory act. Sound isn't experienced through a single sense: we hear it with the ear, feel it with the body, and see it with the eyes, all as functions of listening. But when listening is taught, all of the emphasis is on hearing, meaning, and interpretation. "In addition to teaching students what sound means," she writes, "it is critical to teach them how sound *works and affects*. . . . [T]houghtfully engaging and composing with sound requires listeners to attend to how sound works with and against other sensory modes to shape their embodied experience" (102–3). As an embodied event, sound modulates feelings and behaviors in ways that aren't always immediately clear or tied to particular meanings. As her analysis of deaf percussionist Dame Evelyn Glennie shows, a good deal of persuasive work is happening through the body's capacity to feel vibrations and the eyes' ability to see objects vibrate, both of which inform understanding and ground interpretation.

These turns toward affect and embodiment are at root turns toward the materiality of sound, the physical force of sound and its affectivity. A few scholars in composition and rhetoric have recently begun to examine this connection between sound and materiality and what it might do for developing sonic rhetorics. In "Toward a Resonant Material Vocality for Digital Composition" (2014), Erin Anderson argues that digital composition hasn't fully embraced sound, continuing to use it predominantly for rhetorical analysis, multimodal composition, or as an analogical method for writing. And to the extent that composition has attempted to take up the materiality of sound, it has left voice on the side of meaning, tied to its human origins and the concepts of authorship, identity, and agency. But for Anderson, the conceptual fidelity to a past human source ignores the voice's present digitally embodied materiality and its vibratory, effective, and affective impact. Auditors experience sound waves in the present, not some originary moment in the past, which impacts bodily affect, current interpretation, and any future effect. This affect- and effect-ability gives recorded sound itself its own agency separate from the human agent and opens up potential collaborations. Once recorded, digitally mediated sound is an independent "sonorous body" that pushes the limits of human embodiment and agency. It has an increased capacity for storage and circulation that makes it more available and accessible; an increased digital fidelity that allows it to be replicated in multiple configurations; and an increased flexibility that allows it to be more manipulable and adaptable to various rhetorical aims. In short, it has the "vibrational potential to act and affect in its own right."

Three works in the field extend Anderson's call to further examine the materiality of recorded sound. Jonathan Stone's "Listening to the Sonic Archive" (2015) explicitly takes up recorded sound's increased capacity for storage and circulation. Through an analysis of John and Alan Lomax's archived recordings of African American folk songs, Stone shows how recorded voices work through "modes not generally foregrounded in scholarly discourse: simultaneity, dissonance, and multiplicity." In addition to voice being a "creation of the shape of one's skull, sinuses, vocal tract, lungs, and general physique," it is also a function of "age, geography, gender, education, health, ethnicity, class, and mood" (Peters qtd. in Stone). And once the voice has been recorded, the recording itself has a grain of its own, which embodies the shift in temporality from all of those historical conditions to the particular moment of recording up through subsequent listenings. The recording articulates resonances and dissonances among these multiple differences simultaneously, both embodying the communal experience and decontextualizing it though individual performance and wider cultural and historical circulation. Lead Belly's performances, for example, called forth a historical, collective suffering but did so through his own individual virtuosity and creativity. And while Lomax wanted to preserve the emerging African American culture and bring it to the attention of white audiences, the wider circulation created a series of new cultural and genre expectations that would eventually turn into tropes and essences and fold back to impact the reception of the recordings and limit what the culture could become. This paradox, for Stone, is one way that sonic rhetoric *works*. Rather than operate through a form of direct persuasion, it works through, in both senses, these paradoxical dynamics of difference.

In "Glenn Gould and the Rhetorics of Sound" (2015), Jonathan Alexander examines recorded sound's capacity to resonate in multiple configurations. Gould's work with voice and recording techniques emphasizes the material in addition to linguistic aspects of voice. Voices have their own "substance, . . . intensities, and intimacies" that can be highlighted through the recording and mixing process and layered into sonic compositions (74). Gould's many musical recordings layer in his own voice in the background not as a predominant singing voice but as another instrument or sonic element. And in his radio documentaries on living in the extreme environment of the Arctic north, Gould splices interviewee voices together to complicate their multiple perspectives, from rugged individualism to the necessity of interdependence in order to survive the harsh climate, and mixes them with ambient sounds of the environment such as trains heading north, Arctic winds, bits of music, and dense sounds of ice breaking and colliding. Gould called these overlapped multiple voices "contrapuntal radio"—a "fugal" set of sonic materialities that "resonate with and at times contradict one another" (83). This approach, for Alexander, is "less argumentative and more concept building" (83). The repeated and remixed motifs function more as affective soundscapes than discursive statements and put the audience in a space of active listening and coparticipantion in the conversation. For Alexander, this is composition as an activity, performance, and mode of inquiry that can extend voice in mul-timodal composition beyond its inclusion as linguistic content and provides another example of how sonic rhetoric might embody and enact multiplicity.

Michelle Comstock and Mary Hocks more explicitly see sound's material-ity in relation to new materialism and work through the increased flexibility of recorded sound that makes it adaptable to various rhetorical aims.[4] In "The Sounds of Climate Change" (2016), they examine the work of sound artists Susan Philipsz and Bernie Krause as alternatives to visual accounts of environ-mental change through photography and data charts. Their sound installations reveal the surface time of sounds emerging and decaying in an environment and the deep time of species coming and going from the earth. Through technology and sonic manipulation, Philipsz and Krause can make these larger temporal-ities perceptible, showing how sound doesn't just document the environment but also "reshapes our very sense of time, place, and self as environment" (166). For Comstock and Hocks, this coproductive aspect of sound helps listeners imagine and experience what Stacy Alaimo calls "trans-corporeality"—where "the human is always intermeshed with the more-than-human world" and is "ultimately inseparable from 'the environment'" (Alaimo qtd. in Comstock and Hocks 167). Krause, for example, recorded Lincoln Meadow in the Sierra Nevada mountain range before and after logging to highlight human impact. Initially, he recorded a full range of voices in the ecosystem—birds, bugs, frogs, wolves, owls—to situate the human listener in an "idealized natural space" (172). Then he recorded the meadow after logging and staged a stark juxtapo-sition of the soundscapes to show that, despite the company claims that their technique wouldn't impact the environment, the soundscape had changed dra-matically—most of the voices had vanished. Like Gould, these recordings aren't simply representations. Comstock and Hocks note that Krause's "microphone replaces the microscope" to coproduce a version of the ecosystem that brings the human impact on the environment into view in a new way (172). For them, Krause's work highlights human entanglement with the environment through recorded sound—it enacts a particular rhetorical aim by actively coproducing the material conditions for experiencing an issue.

Resounding takes up and extends this emerging sonic + material turn as a re-sounding of rhetoric after a long detour through print culture and argues that its implications go even deeper into challenging and changing the field itself. If sound is not just another mode to add on to the practice of composition or just another object for the application of rhetorical theory, then it forces a more substantial rethinking of our object of study—considering how sound works forces us to reconsider what composition proper might be. By pushing composition to study the processes of a variety of modes and media as material practices, sound pushes the field more explicitly toward new materialist perspectives that see all of these modalities as functions of larger processes, ecologies, and mediations. It pushes the field more toward composition in general as a series of processes not tied to any medium in particular—whether textual or visual, print or digital—and instead concerned with anything in the process of being composed. Once detached from a particular medium, the field's object of study, I argue, is more profitably understood as a quasi-object. *Quasi*, as a nontechnical term, means being partly or almost, partially or to a certain extent. For example, everyday objects like a rock or a chair can have temporary stability, boundedness, and force and can be understood from a commonsense notion of objects and a technical sense of affordances. But they aren't simply static: they are also partially moving, emergent, composed events that are slowed down or sped up by relational forces into something stable enough to be perceived or engaged directly. They are to a certain extent objects but are also a function of material relations, encounters that leave their unique marks on the objects, changing them in every iteration. Even everyday objects, in other words, are quasi-objects in the process of being composed by geological forces into a rock or manufacturing processes into a chair and simultaneously being decomposed into dirt or scrap lumber.[5] And ultimately what material relations slow down into what humans perceive as stable objects are emergent vibrations and energies in complex processes of becoming composed.

Sound itself, even more explicitly than an everyday object, is fundamentally a quasi-object. "Sound is vibration that is perceived and becomes known through its materiality" (Novak and Sakakeeny 1). It is a process of emergence from energetic movements that generates a material encounter, emits a vibratory wave of force, and is then experienced by and extended through other bodies—energy circulating through my body rises up to force my hands together, generating a wave through air molecules that is then experienced by another body, everything from skin and ears to walls and electronics. These material relations can then be transformed into larger relational practices, whether musical, social, or cultural. Sound is part energy, part material force, and part relational exchange. Through a close reading and interpretation of Michel Serres's quasi-objects and Bruno Latour's extension of it into actor-network theory, I argue that quasi-objects are bound up with the energies that drive them, the ecologies that coproduce them, and relations that sustain and transform them. When seen as quasi-objects, objects of study are likewise a function of these material and ontological processes of vitality, ecology, and relationality. Quasi-objects of study are sometimes slowly, sometimes quickly composed, sometimes in an infinitesimal scope, sometimes across a global sphere, but always emerge as functions of circulating energy and coproductive activity, and our research into them coparticipates in these composing processes.

In order to trace these kinds of composing processes to see how sound as a quasi-object works, I take up musical composition as my quasi-object of study. Music, as the organization of sound by pitch or rhythm,[6] goes beyond composing the abstract structure of a song or fixing this structure into notation, sheet music, or a score. Matt Sakakeeny argues that music, as "an idea not just a form," includes objects of *inscription*: the science of sound waves, mathematics of pitch, and the recording technologies to capture them; sets of *performative* acts: the aesthetics of style and genre and the practices and skills to enact them; and participatory modes of *listening*: the social and cultural forms of response from musicians, audiences, critics, and academics, all of which affect what counts as being sonically "organized" and fold back to influence inscription and performance (113).

Similarly, in *How Music Works*, David Byrne looks for patterns in how music is written, recorded, distributed, and received. He writes, "How music works, or doesn't, is determined not just by what it is in isolation, . . . but in large part by what surrounds it, where you hear it and when you hear it. How it is performed, how it's sold and distributed, how it is recorded, who performs it, whom you hear it with, and, of course, finally, what it sounds like" (9). Byrne argues that music is composed mostly tacitly up through these forces, unconsciously tailored to the venues and conditions made available. Punk made at CBGB, for example, fit that sonic space. The club was modeled on a small country and bluegrass venue in Nashville, but this low-reverb environment was also perfect for noisy punk, which would sound like reverberating mush in a larger hall. The small space and tight acoustics meant that every sound would be heard. Similarly, he argues, African drums and complex polyrhythms work perfectly in open outdoor spaces but would become indistinguishable noise in a larger, reverberating hall; and the acoustic space of medieval cathedrals, which have sustained reverb of up to four seconds, made the slow, drawn-out notes in a single key of the Gregorian chant almost a necessity. In short, music doesn't progress technically or in terms of complexity; it evolves and adapts to fit material conditions and sonic spaces, which include technologies and audiences. Frank Sinatra and Bing Crosby's low-volume crooning style would have never been heard in venues without the microphone, the guitar would have never become a lead instrument over the louder banjo without amplification, and jazz improvisation developed to extend a song's main groove section that got people dancing or moving. For Byrne, music works when sounds best fit their contexts and conditions and when this adaptation strikes an audience, moves them, or resonates with them emotionally, which prompts the continuation of the compositional practice.

While Byrne's approach to musical situation is fairly reminiscent of Bitzer's rhetorical situation grounded in the notion of a fitting response, the appeals to adaptation, evolution, and feedback in the larger compositional processes outlined by Sakakeeny and Byrne come closer to models of rhetorical ecology. Following this lead, I characterize composing practices in the world of popular music as spanning recording, performance, promotion, and distribution—a much larger sense of composing than composition and rhetoric often addresses.[7] Music composition is the broader material practices of gathering technologies, spaces, and relations to coproduce sound waves that are translated into a recorded format such as an MP3 file, performed live, promoted via social networks, and then distributed across the Internet, ultimately to be recomposed along the way into sound waves that gather a whole host of technologies, people, genres, and practices in every coproductive moment of reception. As a heuristic beginning for writing an account of these kinds of composition, I imagine the circulatory life of an MP3 file and the networks it gathers through the sound waves that emanate from its circulation. To examine these movements, this book works through four specific cases— composition practices in a recording studio that use the built ecology of the studio to produce, circulate, and capture sound waves; studio and live performances that use human gestures to open and close circuits for the circulation of sound up through the emergence of genre; the promotional use of social media to compose small-world publics through circulation; and an analysis of an underground album that became a classic almost fifteen years after its release due to the persuasive affects and effects of its distributed circulation online in excess of original authorial intent.

Sound in music composition operates as a quasi-object through these larger composing processes. In "Object Lessons" actor-network theorists John Law and Vicky Singleton outline four types of objects that can help illustrate how this works. *Regions* are temporarily stable, bounded objects, typically at a human scale, such as a guitar or an effects unit, which have the capacity to generate and manipulate sound waves and their translation between electrical energy and sonic waves. *Networks* are extended sets of activities and relations that coproduce a region, both making it possible and temporarily stable. For a guitar, this includes the glue and screws holding it together and its strings, pickups, and hardware but also the cables, stomp boxes, amp, speakers, microphone, sound-proofed studio walls, soundboard, computer interface and hard drive that are entangled through cables and also sound waves, not to mention the activity of the company that built it, shipped it, and sold it, or the person actively playing it—all of this and more make up its actor-networks. These actor-networks are grounded in action at varying rates of speed. *Fluid* objects change slowly, parts of them staying more constant while other parts change sporadically in relation to shifting activities and networks. The recording studio seems like a fairly stable entity, but it is regularly undergoing slow transformations of regions and networks—recording equipment heating up and/or wearing down through use; the engineer swapping out old equipment for new versions; new sound-absorbing and deflecting mechanisms being built into the walls, not to mention new groups coming in to record, setting up, performing, and moving out—without changing what is typically seen as the stability of the studio itself. *Fire* objects participate in fast, intense change through bursts of energy—a gust of air that lifts a plane but isn't simply a part of it; a fire that jumps a road and can't be contained; a disease that suddenly breaks out and spreads. In a musical performance, the electrical energy from the grid, the flash of reverberation or feedback generated by sonic energy, the human desire or striving that sound can affectively engender are all vital to any musical performance in the studio or concert hall and extend through all potential multisensory acts of reception. Such an extended sense of musical composition is a quasi-object: the relational activities of such networks and the fluid changes that they undergo, the capacities of the regions that these networks and transformations cocompose, and the energies that drive the networks along with the changes that they undergo and their entanglement in future acts of reception and coproduction.

This specific account of composition drawn from larger composing processes behind music production and circulation comes with a few conceptual starting places. First, thinking about the formation and circulation of an MP3 file generates an abstract diagram for the case chapters to follow—recording, performance, promotion, and distribution. I don't trace one MP3 file across all the various domains. Instead I examine different cases to draw out common functions without reducing circulation to a single phenomenon: different, as well as multiple, types of circulation are operative in each case and in each moment of the diagram. An abstract diagram is a description of relations, forces, and functions. Foucault's description of the panopticon in *Discipline and Punish*, for example, is a set of relations, forces, and functions detached from any particular prison. As Deleuze notes in *Foucault*, a diagram is "a function that must be 'detached from any specific use,' as from any specified substance": it is "the presentation of the relations between forces unique to a particular formation; . . . the distribution of power to affect and the power to be affected; . . . [and] the mixing of non-formalized pure functions and unformed pure matter" (72–73). But as an abstract diagram it contains its own force, its own power to affect material relations, and carries with it new potential sets of relations. In short, it is a description of how a process works and carries with it the capacity to reenact a version of those forces. Consequently, I focus on how this larger sense of music composition works, what it does, and what it produces in excess of what it means, even as meaning can never be detached from these processes.

Second, the theoretical basis for the book does not enact a theory/application method of criticism. Theory functions as a relay for the invention of new insights, and the cases serve as a basis for inventing new theories. Or, in more common argumentative language, the theoretical bases function as warrants that implicitly ground the examinations carried out in the cases rather than as theory to be explicitly applied to generate supports for the theory. I draw on Serres's use of the model as relay, and ultimately Deleuze's concept of the virtual, to disrupt the method of theory/application more common in traditional rhetorical criticism. For Serres, a model or example is not meant as something to be emulated or copied but as a transformative encounter that produces something new that couldn't have been produced without the particular encounter. In *The Process That Is The World*, Joe Panzner puts this concept in the context of music. Any performance, even of a strictly delineated score, repeats the score with a difference. Panzner writes: "As opposed to . . . 'copies of copies,' . . . they are copies without a model, actualizations that overturn the very validity of the model-copy distinction. Each actualization relates difference to difference without the mediation of a model that could be used to determine a fixed, timeless identity" (57–58). Similarly, Serres's model as relay disrupts a traditional sense of model-copy. Ultimately it is a series of copies that always enacts new transformations in every iteration and folds back to change the model or how it is enacted in the future. Model as relay is at root a process of transduction, allowing me to draw a method out of the material functions of sound. Sound and music, then, are not add-ons to the field or something that preexisting rhetorical theories get applied to: they are things that fold back and impact those theories. The diagram of recording, performance, promotion, and distribution, in other words, is not a model to produce copies: it is a relay for enacting copies of copies.

Finally, my turn to examine music as a version of composing with sound allows me to trace the emerging compositions of quasi-objects and myself as a quasi-subject. Every encounter is driven by circulation, entangles its interlocutors, and coproduces ecologies. Each of the ecologies I investigate, each moment of the diagram, is a relay tied up with me personally, both as a coparticipant and a researcher. All of these examples are cases in which I am already a part of the ecology—a musician and friend from my youth who has a recording studio, an artist and friend from my former university, a former student who started a band and moved to Los Angeles, an artist I became a fan of through a friend of a friend online, and a band that I've followed for years. I was already caught up in their circulations as a coparticipant and function as a quasi-subject to their quasi-objects. Latour sees in Serres's take on quasi-subjects a process that makes it "impossible to define the human by an essence" (*We Have Never Been Modern* 136). Humanism has imposed action, will, meaning, and speech on human bodies to invent the subject, but quasi-subjects don't possess a stable form. Material forces and formations continually generate quasi-subjects as functions of their processes, which then fold back to coproduce versions of those systems by repeating them with a difference. The abstract diagram of the panopticon, for example, coproduces the formation of a prison and the quasi-subjects of particular guards and prisoners, who through the practices partly established by the diagram enact the particular formation of that prison. For Foucault, then, formations don't exist prior to the subject but exist in excess of it, creating the grounds for the subject who coparticipates in producing a version of the formation. What Foucault found so fascinating about processes of subjectivation is that they make the body an instrument-effect—both an effect of the system but also simultaneously its instrument that enacts the system from the "capillaries," ultimately coproducing it otherwise by never faithfully doubling it. The subject, then, is a quasi-subject. Partially a part of the formation and coproduced by it, and partially a distinct repetition of it that operates in excess of its determinations. Now I am folding back as a researcher to rearticulate each of these personal encounters, open them up to further circulations, ultimately coproducing a new version of them and extending them as quasi-objects while remaking myself as a quasi-subject in and through these composing processes.

When understood through sound as a quasi-object, composition and rhetoric's objects of study are not simply random whims of particular researchers but are all complex processes of composing.[8] And seeing our collective object of study from this light can have an impact on how scholars see key concepts in our field. This approach allows me to remake key terms in composition theory across the chapters—composition, process, research, collaboration, publics, and rhetoric—to coproduce *one version* of what composition might look like if the discipline's primary object of study were taken up as a quasi-object. Each key term is engaged through another concept or practice, following Serres's relay as a form of transduction and Heidegger's as-structure as a form of resonance. Interpretation is never of a bare object or entity but one that is already structured within a totality of relations, both material and conceptual. This process shows a movement from tacit understanding through involvement with a particular ambient environment to the more explicit interpretation of its potentialities toward some future: humans experience a room *as* equipment for residing, or a table and chair *as* a place to sit and eat or a place to sit and write, and through this involvement disclose a world. As a form of transduction and layered resonance through involvement, the act of interpretation produces not just means—as an activity it opens up possible worlds and potential lines of flight. Each of the book's engagements with a term, case, or practice is another transduction, transformation, or version.

What this process produces is a reorientation of the field through the iteration of the key term. Each chapter starts out with a redefinition prompted by sound as a quasi-object and its forms of musical composition and ventures into the complexities of its processes of composition. In the case chapters, a concept in the field is examined, a practice grounded in the diagram is traced, and the implications are worked through. Each case shows how living in the world cocomposes a particular version of it and enacts potential resonances through the reader's involvement when juxtaposed with the other chapters. Composition is this broader material process; researchers are a part of that process; and that process is coordinated, public, and rhetorical.

Toward this end, the book is broken down into three groups of two chapters each with emphases on conceptual bases, practices of making, and public circulations. Chapters 1 and 2 form the conceptual basis for the book. Chapter 1, "Composition as Quasi-Object," argues that composition is a function of circulation and the ecological coproduction of quasi-objects—a loosely or tightly knit network composed through a series of circulatory movements and actions. The chapter extends Sirc's composition in general and Shipka's composition made whole by establishing Serres's quasi-object as a primary model for composition and rhetoric's object of study and elaborating on it through Latour's actor-network theory with an emphasis on vibration and energy. It develops an approach to new materialism that combines relationality, ecology, and vitality as the conceptual basis for the book and establishes sound as a function and emergent outcome of these three materialities. Chapter 2, "Process as Refrain," is grounded in this version of new materialism and the three aspects of quasi-objects—vital, ecological, and relational—rather than traditional models of social practice. Through Deleuze's refrain as a model, the chapter develops an approach to postprocess that reorients Thomas Kent's model—writing is public, interpretive, and material—into a sense of enfolded processes that understands Deleuze's vitalism, Heidegger's ecology, and Latour's relationality as functions of quasi-objects and establishes entanglements of situatedness, interpretation, and publics as groundings for the next four case chapters. As an object of study for the field, process would have to emerge from specific cases of circulation that coproduce and are coproductive of these entanglements. This sense of process doesn't dissolve or devalue the human as much as articulate the human as operative in, with, and through these processes in the traditions of Alaimo's trans-corporeality, Foucault's instrument-effect, and Serres's quasi-objects—or what I characterize as the parahuman.

Chapters 3 and 4 delve into the practices of musicians in the process of generating sound and making music through recording and performance. Chapter 3, "Research as Transduction," turns toward the expansion of quasi-objects rather than their explanation and coproduces a version of the object of study particular to that project. Responding to Clay Spinuzzi and others, the chapter emphasizes the circulation of sound waves and their inscription as the basis for understanding research and method as coparticipants in the production of quasi-objects. In other words, research doesn't just examine or study quasi-objects but necessarily coproduces them through its varied practices. Through a case focused on the production, manipulation, and circulation of sound in the recording studio, the chapter shifts Barad's model of diffraction from light waves to sound waves and situates the researcher as cocomposer of the quasi-object of study. My research practice is a transduction of energy that coproduces another version of the studio and extends its circulation and translation of energy as it coproduces me as a quasi-subject. Chapter 4, "Collaboration as Coordination," sees collaboration through quasi-objects and circulation, which is gathered and coproduced through material performance and enaction. The chapter traces models of ecology in composition and rhetoric from Marilyn Cooper and Karen Burke LeFevre to Louise Wetherbee Phelps and Margaret Syverson in order to turn human collaboration toward emergent forms of coordination, which happens in music composition through but in excess of human gesture. In cases focused on both studio and live performance, invention is traced as a form of improvisation through circuits of gesture up through conceptions of genre, extending circulation beyond the confines of traditional performance spaces to see gesture ecologies as the basis for genre ecologies.

Chapters 5 and 6 examine what happens when this music is promoted and distributed through digital means, extending it as a quasi-object. Chapter 5, "Publics as Spheres," characterizes publics as spheres that emerge and decay through the relational and circulatory coproduction of online and off-line networks. Extending Michael Warner's sense of publics with Jenny Rice's distant publics, the chapter turns from the notion of the public sphere to sphere publics in order to show how circulation coproduces publics on the model of quasi-objects. In cases focused on two aspiring artists' use of social media to circulate their music and develop a fan base, it shows how ecologies generate multiple sphere publics through emergent, contingent feedback loops over time—a variable ontology that strings together sphere publics as the "virtual proximity" of digital networks and "actual proximity" of local music scenes intertwine. Finally, Chapter 6, "Rhetoric as Resonance," argues that rhetoric is a coproductive function of circulation that operates in conjunction with but also in excess of human intention, which collapses rhetoric and persuasion into "the rhetorical." Entangling Diane Davis, Thomas Rickert, and Laurie Gries, the chapter shows how publics are quasi-objects coproduced through the relationality of rhetoricity, ambience, and circulation. Through a case focused on a band that gained worldwide cult status fifteen years after breaking up, it establishes how the distributed album coproduces publics through a version of Heideggerian worlding. Over time and through continual digital circulation, the album produced a new musical world for its own material reception.

The book concludes by arguing that "resounding" is the overall process of circulation, transduction, and resonance that functions as a metaphor for the kinds of composition in general examined in the book. Resounding as a key term evokes the re-sounding of rhetoric, or bringing sound back from orality and putting it into electracy. But this reclaiming can't simply go back to orality; it can only go forward into the sonic and the sustained reverberation of its vibratory force. This future orientation, while somewhat latent throughout the chapters, is a vital aim. Resounding suggests that the materiality of past conditions, embodiment in present listening practices, and the future impact on other bodies and ecologies is all a part of the same process. All of these are tied up in every act of the rhetorical and set the conditions for new potential futures. By using "the rhetorical" as a noun that collapses rhetoric and persuasion not just an adjective that modifies a noun, I'm situating rhetoric as an ongoing series of actions that continually modulates and modifies—a series of *suasive* vibrations that speed up, slow down, rearticulate, and invigorate ecologies of composition and their futurities. A sonic approach to rhetoric, then, would mean that the rhetorical is at stake in every circulation of energy, every material encounter, and every unfolding future.

ONE

COMPOSITION AS QUASI-OBJECT

COMPOSITION IS A QUASI-OBJECT. A materiality. A loosely or tightly knit network stitched together through a series of movements and actions. A function of circulation and ecological coproduction. Composition and rhetoric has always had an uneasy relationship toward defining its object of study. With the rise of specialization and disciplinarity in the nineteenth century, disciplines were charged with the task of identifying their unique objects of analysis. In composition and rhetoric's predisciplinary development, its object was construed generally as teaching or the teaching of writing, which the field continued to identify with up through the 1950s as it established both CCCCs and CCCs. But the beginnings of composition and rhetoric as a distinct research discipline in the 1960s and 1970s up through the development of more PhD programs in the 1980s saw a range of objects competing for the field's attention: an early 1960s appeal to social science methodologies with composing processes behind texts ultimately emerging as the field's unique object of study; a mid-1960s appeal to the history of rhetoric with the object of study in some cases being texts or in other cases rhetorical theory itself; and, starting in the later 1960s, an emphasis on students as our object of study, coming, in part, out of educational theories and practices in the UK and ultimately centered on the student's thinking processes. Each of these approaches was meant to provide both a unique object for the discipline as well as a measure of disciplinary authority, with appeals to science, history, or eventually politics as the emphasis on student thinking moved into critical thinking and student subjectivity. By the end of the 1980s and into the 1990s, a combination of rhetorical and literary theory and an emphasis on student ideologies emerged as the field's predominant objects. Within the past fifteen years, however, we've seen a period of fragmentation, with each of these strands developing into major subfields and technology emerging as a significant area of concern, though one that also encompasses many perspectives and approaches. As the social turn has given way to the material turn, no single object of study is currently available to the field.[1] Could composition and rhetoric, however, have an object of analysis that is paradoxically specific and unbounded, expansive while at the same time still being a unique object of study?

Geoffrey Sirc's composition in general and Jody Shipka's composition made whole have both expanded the field's object of study by engaging with material aspects of composition from a found-art perspective. Sirc's *English Composition as a Happening*, for example, called for a radical specificity to practices of composing and an expansion of the discipline of composition and rhetoric into composition in general through an encounter with modern art. The book moves through the material practices and theoretical concerns of visual artists such as Marcel Duchamp and Jackson Pollock and musicians such as John Cage and Johnny Rotten. Sirc examines the gestures of Pollock and the environmental design of Cage as alternatives to the emphasis on written compositions in standard academic genre. This move shifts the object of composition to the materials of designing spaces and their production of intensities. Following Duchamp and ready-made composers, Sirc argues that the materials of found art are "chosen from a vaster field than the disciplined one—a generic one, where all parameters dissolve, opening onto a flat, breathtaking landscape" (47). And invoking Cage, he argues that composers must be open to this more expansive terrain for composition in general: they must listen to the open spaces to recognize they aren't silent and see their potential for composition. In Sirc's earlier article "English Composition as a Happening II, Part One," he explicitly frames his project as a "materialist history," one that can be read as both a realist materialism of the gathered objects of found art and the built environments of sound artists and pedagogues and as a phenomenological materialism of the intensive and affective experiences produced through these compositions. Composition as a quasi-object extends the scale of Sirc's composition in general but also shifts its emphasis on the human to include ecological coparticipation in composition and adds another postphenomenological layer onto the compositional work of intensities.

More recently, Shipka's *Toward a Composition Made Whole* sees composition as a process of communication that can be expressed through any number of media as paths to meaning making. She takes up Sirc's call for the ongoing "discovery of new processes, materials, and products" as the aim of composition (4) and follows Kathleen Yancey and Johndan Johnson-Eilola in seeing "the integration of words, images, sounds, and movements" afforded by emerging digital technologies as driving the need to expand disciplinary notions of composition (5). But for her, focusing predominantly on screen-based technologies continues to limit composition to traditional 2-D forms. Rather than restricting composition to print or even digital technologies, Shipka's practice of composing with found objects pushes us to recognize material composition as a legitimate and significant aspect of our field and pushes our 2-D biases into the 3-D world. Shipka takes up Yancey's definition of these emerging forms of digital technology as "a composition made whole by a new coherence" (qtd. in Shipka 8) but recognizes in it no necessary 2-D limit. Yancey writes, "A composition is an expression of relationships—between parts and parts, between parts and whole, between the visual and the verbal, between text and context, between reader and composer, between what is intended and what is unpacked, between hope and realization" (qtd. in Shipka 9). Nothing here forecloses on material composition and in fact almost invites it as a further movement in the expansion of composition to any set of emerging relations. Shipka's pedagogical practice includes "writing on shirts, purses, and shoes, repurposing games, [and] producing complex, multipart rhetorical events" all the way up through "creating and sustaining the conditions for engaging in these activities" (9–10). While Shipka's theoretical framework is very much committed to theories of mediated action—specifically those of social anthropologist James Wertsch along with activity theories in work such as David Russell's—much of her pedagogical interest focuses on human choices, meaning making, and affects along with a more or less realist ontology. But more recently in "Transmodality in/and Processes of Making" she extends her work more explicitly into the material turn invoking

Jane Bennett's version of vitalism as "the curious ability of inanimate things to animate, to act, to produce effects in dramatic and subtle ways" and distribute agency across a heterogeneous field (Bennett qtd. in Shipka 253). Ultimately both Sirc and Shipka look to situate expanded versions of composition itself as the field's central object of study.

Sid Dobrin's book *Postcomposition* also tackles this issue of the field's object of study by extending the object of composition to writing itself—a Derridean sense of writing not as subservient to human speech, universal concepts, or objective presence but as a general form of activity, what Derrida calls "arche-writing," that produces speech, concepts, and presencings through articulating difference and deferring closure. Dobrin sets up distinctions among writing, composition, and rhetoric in order to make his case, arguing that composition is too focused on the student subject, as an extension of earlier pedagogical work in the field's history, and that rhetoric is too focused on identifying parts of systems, through a focus on theory in the older neo-Aristotelian traditions of our field's history. For Dobrin, both of these approaches tie composition and rhetoric to literary studies and its emphasis on reading subjects and hermeneutics, broadly defined. Instead he follows ecological and complexity theories, such as Mark C. Taylor's, and connects them to writing through Derrida in order to carve out a distinct disciplinary object for the field.[2] "Writing itself," as the movements, emergences, and articulations of systems, is both a distinct object of study separate from composition and rhetoric and a process that "writes it-self," where the student subject or subjectivity of the writer plays a much smaller coproductive role, and theory is a function of the system that folds back on itself. In short, Dobrin is interested in having particular political effects on the discipline's pedagogical and administrative practices by blending "disciplinary critique" with the development of an "ecological/networked theory of writing" (4), and his divisions are a rhetorical means to these ends. But even though he is expanding the field's object of study into broader senses of process, he is doing so by seeing writing a la Derrida as the more expansive term and keeping composition and rhetoric at arm's length.[3] Composition, for example, becomes a term limited largely to first-year pedagogy and student writing. Following Shipka, however, writing in a more everyday sense of words on paper can be seen as the limiting term and composition the potentially more expansive (*Toward* 14). This perspective suggests taking up Latour's sense of composition rather than

Derrida's sense of writing to show that composition, and ultimately rhetoric, can also be a function of circulation and emergent ecologies.

But to fully draw out Latour's expanded notion of composition and what it might do to and for the field as its object of study, it needs to be understood as a quasi-object rather than through a generic notion of networks. In *Ambient Rhetoric*, Rickert contrasts his Heideggerian take on ambient rhetorics with the network model of Mark C. Taylor developed by Dobrin. Ambience is the active role that material and informational environments play in human action and culture. Ultimately ambience dissolves the division between passive material environments and active human doing in favor of emergent entanglements that tacitly coproduce dwelling. In these entanglements, there are various levels of tacit attunement and active attention. The caves at Lascaux, for example, have certain spatial affordances and acoustical properties that support the ritual roles of the caves' paintings. The reverberation of sound waves and reflection of light waves make the rituals experts now believe occurred there compelling and affective, regardless of whether the humans who designed the paintings and conducted the rituals understood those material properties actively. Ambience, Rickert writes, "melds the materiality of the cave with its other properties, and all become integral to the achievement of the whole, from the base material structure to the achievement of the design to the feelings and thoughts that are evoked" (6). The human design is inseparable from the affordances of the cave that attune the painters to its ambience, to the "ensemble of variables, forces, and elements that shape things in ways that are difficult to quantify or specify" (7). In contrast, Rickert reads Taylor's approach to networks as "link driven" or based on "connections among already established points or nodes" (122). Similarly, he characterizes Latour as advocating a "simple assemblage of 'that's just what's there' givens" (280). But Latour says specifically "the network does not designate a thing out there that would have roughly the shape of interconnected points much like a telephone, a freeway, or a sewage 'network'" (*Reassembling the Social* 129). In his reading of Taylor and Latour, Rickert sidesteps the question of where the supposedly "preexisting" nodes came from and whether or not they were transformed through the encounter. For Latour, they are never preexistent in any autonomous or essential way but are temporary stabilities of ongoing emergent movements; they are functions of earlier ecological and ambient processes.

When understood from a basis in quasi-objects, Latour's concept of actor-networks forms an integral coproductive part of an ecological or new materialist ontology that is vital to ambience and how it functions persuasively and rhetorically. For Latour, at least, composition isn't about simply linking two preexisting things but about the actions and movements that coproduce the things that they encounter, which in turn change the lines and capacities of those actions and movements. Actor-networks are not preexisting things or links between preexisting things but traces left by the actions of networks, the coproductivity of mediation, and the accounts of these encounters. Even if we see writing as arche, the grounds of the system, it can't be disarticulated from the postprocesses that also articulate both practices of composition and their rhetorical enactments. Likewise, the relational aspects of ambience can't be disassembled from the networked complexity that Dobrin calls for. An ecological model of mutual coproduction is central to Serres's concept of quasi-objects, which shows why these things can't be disentangled. In many ways *Resounding* is an attempt to show that the turn toward networks and the turn toward ambience aren't antithetical to each other but rather that both are coproduced through composition—the actions, articulations, gestures, movements, and energies of ecologies understood as quasi-objects.[4] It provides one version of what it might look like to extend the discipline's primary object of study beyond its traditional focus on the written composing process and the student subject as critical thinker through an extension of Sirc and Shipka's material composition. Paradoxically, perhaps, I suggest that the field can embrace its contemporary fragmentation and dissemination by adopting a single object of study—quasi-objects coproduced through perpetual movements of composition. *Resounding* considers the possibility that our shared object of study might be such a paradoxical object that is not simply an object. It is the composition of any quasi-object, *any* process of being put together, from the smallest circumference to the broadest scale.

QUASI-OBJECTS AND NOISE

Michel Serres hasn't had the uptake in composition and rhetoric that Latour and new materialists such as Jane Bennett and Karen Barad have had, but his concept of quasi-objects brings together much of this work that is often seen to be at odds. I read Serres's "Theory of the Quasi-Object" through his essay "Noise" to produce a version of quasi-objects that entangles relationality, ecology, and vitality. This reading argues that these three materialities are continually in play and are coproductive of each other. Arguments that favor or highlight one over the others are only seeing one part of the larger composing processes of quasi-objects. This new materialist line of thought is grounded Serres's brief essay "Theory of the Quasi-Object" from his book *The Parasite*. The essay is perhaps lesser known in composition and rhetoric but is important for understanding more contemporary thinking surrounding new materialism that disrupts a more traditional realism/phenomenology binary. Serres sets out to undo, or at least problematize, the beings versus relations dichotomy and does so through the figure of his larger inquiry—the parasite. Lawrence Schehr, translator of the 1982 John's Hopkins edition of *The Parasite*, notes in his preface that the term *parasite* in French has three meanings: a biological parasite, a social parasite or guest, and static or noise. Schehr writes in his introduction,

> The parasite is a microbe, an insidious infection that takes without giving and weakens without killing. The parasite is also a guest, who exchanges his talk, praise, and flattery for food. The parasite is noise as well, the static in a system or the interference in a channel. These seemingly dissimilar activities are, according to Michel Serres, not merely coincidentally expressed by the same word (in French). Rather, they are intrinsically related and, in fact, they have the same basic function in a system. Whether it produces a fever or just hot air, the parasite is a thermal exciter. And as such, it is both the atom of a relation and the production of a change in this relation. (x)

The word *hôte* in French includes both host and guest, whereas the English word *host* does not (vii). But perhaps more importantly, the English term loses this last meaning, noise; static in a system that is fundamentally generative.

In *The Parasite*, Serres is working through all of these meanings, but the parasite has yet to be explicitly defined in the book as relational or real—purely a social relation or a distinct biological entity—and the goal of "Theory of the Quasi-Object" is to work this out through an analysis of three key terms: quasi-object, parasite, and demi-quasi-object. A *quasi-object* is primarily relational; it is largely constituted via social relation and circulation. Serres's two primary examples are a ball and money. A ball, he writes, "is not an ordinary object, for it is what it is only if a subject holds it. Over there, on the ground, it is nothing; it is stupid; it has no meaning, no function, and no value" (225). To be a function of a game as a collective enterprise, the ball must circulate, and the best players facilitate this movement. In games such as football, soccer, or rugby, the one with the ball garners all of the attention and becomes the player to be stopped in order to stop or redirect the circulation. The ball marks the player as a subject and becomes a quasi-object through this circulatory function. *But* as a quasi-object, the ball is *also* a quasi-subject, "since it marks or designates a subject who, without it, would not be a subject" (225). In doing so, the ball becomes the quasi-subject and the player the quasi-object. "The ball is the subject of circulation; the players are only the stations and relays" (226). The best players subordinate themselves to the ball's circulation or become a "ball hog" that works against the flow of the game. The material specificity of the ball and the players are secondary to this relational circulation: balls and players are substituted regularly in games such as football or basketball, for example. The game and its quasi-objects-subjects are constituted by "the set of speeds, forces, angles, shocks, and strategic thoughts" that produce its "network of passageways" (226). This movement "weav[es] the collective, virtually putting to death each individual" (227). In this movement, the purely individual subject or object is abandoned for circulation grounded in enaction. As such, quasi-objects produce a decentering through speed and circulation, turning being toward relation (228). Money, for example, makes it even clearer that the specific body or form matters less—money can be paper, coins, or 1s-0s, because it is almost entirely constituted through circulation and social relation.

The *parasite*, however, evolves to fill a specific niche in an ecology: its body and its specific material configuration matter—a tick can't function as a parasite if it is on a rock or tree instead of a biological host. The most important characteristic of the biological parasite for Serres is its specificity. For a biological adaption to function it must be "carried by a certain vector" or "fit on its wavelength" (230).[5] A dollar bill or coin is a substitute, a stand-in for a relational function. A biological parasite or host can't simply be substituted with any other body. Humans, however, function ecologically in a different manner than fleas and ticks—we have a specificity that is both material and cultural. Materially, we are parasites on the land and each other: the farmer parasites the land, and then the tax collector parasites the farmer. What we end up with, for Serres, is a chain of parasitism as a taking without giving with the goal of being in the last position of the ecological chain (Brown 15). Culturally, there is both a social and linguistic form of parasitism. The social parasite is an uninvited guest who makes an unequal exchange of tall stories for food. For Serres, human relations depend on this kind of material-cultural exchange, which also grounds our relation to language. Language is both host and parasite. On the one hand, language as a system is the most general quasi-object, relational and completely substitutable—as Saussure argued in *Course in General Linguistics*, there is little natural reason why a particular sign should be attached to a particular concept, often leaving meaning to be derived through the difference in sounds. On the other hand, language as pragmatic is articulated through a parasitic body as a specificity: it is specific to that niche in the ecology, that relational exchange, that body, and that moment of rhetorical reciprocity—we might think of Malinowski's example of language use in the scene of fishermen shouting out directions to each other as they are pulling in a net. Culture and language, then, participate in both the relational movements of quasi-objects-subjects as well as the specificity of material configurations. The logic of relation and the materiality of bodies—relation and being—are locked in a process of exchange that coproduces a specific enaction.

For Serres, this model of the parasite turns his initial understanding of quasi-objects and their circulation toward what he calls *demi-quasi-objects*. "Our quasi-objects," he writes, "have [this] increasing specificity" (232). "Demi" in French means half. Quasi-objects, then, like parasites, are half material and half social; have increasing material specificity but are still relational, fractal, complex, and coproduced by circulation and chance; are individual in terms of specificity but not in terms of an isolated or autonomous being apart from relations that coproduce them. His analogy for the circulation of demi-quasi-objects is with the tessera, an individual tile used in creating mosaics. Early mosaics used colored pebbles, but as early as 200 BCE stones were being cut to make tiles. Later glass was cut, and metal or gold leaf was sandwiched between two pieces of glass to give it a richer or more luminous effect. The tessera is something that the host and parasite "share by breaking. They break the tessera and produce a memorial. . . . The breaking of the tessera is not a clean break; it is somewhat fractal, complicated in any case, so random that it is an individual, so serrated and notched that it is unique. The tessera is an individual; it is chance; it is complex; it is a memorial. Who am I? Unique, filled with lots of information, complicated, unexpected, thrown in the whirlpool of the aleatory, my body is a memorial" (233). The host and guest each keep a piece of the tessera, having coproduced it in the breaking (of bread, of language, of social relation). They travel, love, die, and hand the tessera down to their children as a memorial of these travels, movements, and circulations. Serres writes, "Through time and space, the one who has it in his hand will recognize his exact other by this sign, this specific, adapted interconnection. There is no other possible key for such a look, thanks to *stereospecificity*" (233; emphasis mine).[6] This stereospecificity is central to what it means to be a quasi-object. We might think of a retired ballplayer, for example, as a tessera, marked, battered, materially changed after years of circulation and encounter through the game but always tied to the games, players, fields, and balls whose circulations coproduced the player's specific marks and notches. Such a quasi-object is at root a demi-quasi-object—a function of both relations and beings. Quasi-objects are both materially adapted to the ecologies that cut them but also specific material embodiments of their relational circulations—a trace of these coproductive encounters, and, as Serres's etymology of parasite indicates, a trace of the noise, multiplicity, and accidents out of which their specificities emerge.

Serres doesn't emphasize this third meaning of parasite, noise, as much in "Theory of the Quasi-Object," but it is central to the overall theory and is what drives circulation within the system. Relations and beings emerge from and are fed back into a ground of multiplicity, chaos, and noise that coproduce them. To work this out I turn to his essay "Noise," where Serres continues with etymology as a mode of operation, noting that in the Old French, *noiseuse* means both noise and quarrel. "English keeps the sound, and French, the fury" (50). Noise, nausea, nautical, and navy have the same etymology, so we shouldn't be surprised that the best place to hear "white noise" is at sea, which becomes his primary metaphor. The sea is a horizontal plane of exchange between stable and unstable flows of water. Its space is completely invaded and occupied by its white noise. Serres writes,

> Perhaps white noise . . . is at the heart . . . of being itself. Perhaps being is not at rest, perhaps it is not in motion, perhaps it is agitation. White noise never stops, it is limitless, continuous, perpetual, unchangeable. It has no grounding

> ...itself, no opposite. . . . Noise is not a phenomenon, all phenomena arise from
> it . . . as any message, cry, call, signal, must each separate from the hubbub that
> fills the silence, just to be, to be perceived, sensed, known, exchanged. As soon as
> there is a phenomenon, it leaves noise, as soon as appearance arises, it does so by
> masking noise. Thus it is *not phenomenology* but being itself. (50; emphasis mine)

Noise is both the condition for subjects and objects to emerge at all but is also
in subjects and objects, observers and observed. Noise passes through obser-
vation and its channels, whether they are material, linguistic, or logical. It
pushes the very limits of physics—surrounds it, underlies it, takes all forms,
materials, and substances as manifestations. Noise is agitation, interruption,
"turbulence, quarrel, *sound*" (51; emphasis mine). Phenomena are relational
circulation, motion; beings are temporarily stable or at rest; and being is noise,
agitation, the vitality of life itself.

As is typical of Serres's writing, he uses the myth of the sea-god Proteus to
work through noise as grounding potential. Proteus exists in stereo, in a series
of doubles—he is a stereospecificity. He can be an element or animal, water or
fire, inert or alive, possibility or phenomenon, concealing or revelation. As a
prophet, he functions like an oracle, responding to questions, but never really
answering directly. When asked a question, he turns into a lion, or a snake, or
a tree, or a river. Bound by a question, an interruption, he is a chain of phenomena. Unbound, or loosely bound, he is chaos, possibility, white noise. For
Serres, this gives us an epistemology, one that is "not given in a language that
is all distended by rigor but through a channel full of noise, sound, and images"
(51). Proteus hides his answers in infinite amounts of information that when
broken into, interrupted, channel his potential into possibility. In Serres's
reading, the story of Proteus doesn't tell us about the relation between chaos
and form. "Who is Proteus," he asks, "when he is no longer water but not yet a
panther or a boar?" (51). The key to every metamorphosis is that it is an answer
to a question, a response to a disturbance, one that is both "an answer and a
lack of an answer" (51). The question or disturbance cuts into the agitation
and noise of virtual potential, diffracts it, producing sound. "The intermediate
stages of Proteus are the roar of the ocean being made. The beautiful *noiseuse*
is agitated. She must be recognized amidst the swelling, splashing, breaking
of forms and tones, in the unchaining of the element divided against itself"
(51). Sound is produced by an encounter, a disturbance, a clash with noise, and

is diffracted as it resonates throughout space—ontologically forming sound as material waves, epistemologically channeling noise into the phenomena of listenable information.[7]

Noise, then, is the ground of creativity and invention. Serres switches metaphors from the sea to rivers. Instead of waves and white noise, his stereospecificity comes through forking and branching. The time of phenomena, form, and mortality flows down the river. All of the chaos, the multiplicity of creeks and tributaries, flow into the river, forming a single line to the sea. The time of creative work, however, goes back up the river, tracing it back to its sources in multiplicity. "The Junction," he writes, "is no longer a synthesis but a high opening that leads to other openings upstream" (53). This high path multiplies its branches "like a bush, an arborescence, a head of hair, a fibrous network of veins and fibrils, an endless network" (53). Creativity functions through this countermovement. The master artist seeks out this source, this abundance, and operates through the "intermediate interstices" among all of the manifestations of a work. Serres writes, "No one produces a work if he doesn't work in this continuous flow whence comes all form. One must swim in language, dive in as if lost, for a weighty poem or argument to arise. The work is made of forms, the masterpiece is the unbound fount of forms; the work is made of time, the masterpiece is the source of time; the work is in tune, the masterwork shakes with noises. . . . The masterwork unceasingly makes noise and sound" (53). This multiplicity is not the same as strength or power. For Serres it is a capacity, a potentiality, possibility itself. "The multiple is open and from it is born nature always being born" (56). Humans can't know this capacity through calculation or rigor, can't know how multiple conditions exist in relation or predict the futurity of its emergent paths. They can only tap into its infinite base—cut into it, disturb it, fork off a branch. This is the primary role of the philosopher, for Serres, or for us the rhetor or composer or writer: to cultivate the possible and cross over its multiple varieties. The philosopher is no longer concerned with right and truth but instead seeks to "allow the possible to be free, . . . to keep the branching and forking open" (57). The philosopher seeks the places where branchings multiply, where there are torrents and turbulence. Importantly, however, multiplicity is not an original source in the past. For Serres multiplicity is "of the possible here and now. It is the intermediary between phenomena, the noise between the forms that come out of it" (57). There is a continuum, a permanent flow, among noise, sound, and music: "Noise is always there to invent new music" (58). The role of the composer, then, is to "listen to the noises," straddle the possible "like a living network," and break into it to coproduce the material waves of sound and the cultural phenomena of song (58).

Following this relationship between quasi-objects and noise, I see the stereospecificity of relationality and ecology in relation to a vital ground of multiplicity and noise.[8] The relational functions of host and guest, both biological and social, operate in a system of feedback and coproduction with the vitalist energy of noise, which adds difference to the relation, prevents it from becoming fully static, and injects creativity into the system. *Quasi*, as a nontechnical term, means being partly or almost, partially or to a certain extent. Quasi-objects, then, are part relation and part material specificity. They aren't simply static or preexistent—they are partially moving, emergent, composed events that are slowed down and partially stabilized by relations. They are to a certain extent realist but also a function of relations, which leave their unique marks and traces on the objects, changing them in every iteration. And what is it that relations slow down into what we perceive as stable objects but the emergent vibrations, energies, and resonances of the virtual in the complex process of becoming actual. One implication of Serres's insight, when read through his poetic style and the juxtaposition of "Theory of the Quasi-Object" and "Noise," is that arguing for one over the others—relationality, ecology, or vitality—misses their coproductivity. Each feeds back to coproduce the others, forming an ontological system. None of them should be understood in isolation from the others. It is the grounding energy derived from the food, water, and air of the earth that drives circulation, the capacities of the ballplayers' bodies adapted to this environment that allows them to draw on its energy, and the relations and encounters of the game that makes the players and the ball and the game fully quasi-objects.

SOUND AS QUASI-OBJECT

Sound is a paradigmatic example of a quasi-object understood in this larger sense of an overall materialist "theory of the quasi-object"—it is relational, ecological, and vital. In sound studies, most scholars orient themselves by locating their work in relation to the founding debate between realism and phenomenology, or the reality of acoustics and a phenomenology of listening. But many are increasingly doing so through a more new materialist orientation grounded in vibrational energy. In their introduction to *Keywords in Sound*, for example, Novak and Sakakeeny define sound as "vibration that is perceived and becomes known through its materiality" (1). Sound is vibration of a certain frequency in a material medium before it sets to any ear. As a vibrational force, it is a series of "impulses that move particles of air and travel through bodies" (1). The reverberation of these waves resonates in space as a nonsemantic expression of a material environment. As vibrational matter, sound is a function of the bodies that produced it, but it is also a "basic part of how people frame their knowledge about the world" (2). Once in relation with an ear, the material properties of sound ground perception and experience through embodied listening and only through this embodiment can become a semantic object of language and culture. Through sound as matter, people feel their bodies vibrate empathetically (embodiment); locate themselves in an environment via reverberation (spatial orientation); analyze speech and language via phonemes (communication); and capture and distribute sound via technological mediation (music). Meaning, ultimately, is a function of how sonic processes work and the terms people use to describe and highlight aspects of those material processes. Sound, then, is a stereospecificity of realism and phenomenology, but one that is grounded in the generative principle of noise, the circulating energy that drives the system. Sound is ultimately a function of all three materialities—the relationality of waves, ecologies of embodiment, and the ontological vitality of noise.

Many sound studies scholars locate themselves theoretically through a specific emphasis on relationality, ecology, or vitality. In *Humanesis: Sound and Technological Posthumanism*, David Cecchetto outlines a materialist orientation toward sound that is more strongly relational. For him sound is differential, relational, and multiplicitous. First, to hear sound is to experience a shift in air pressure. Ears don't hear air pressure; they experience the change in pressure over time. To hear is simply to experience this relational difference, this movement. Second, sound resists any visual ontology, which for Cecchetto makes it relational as well as differential. When a spotlight is shown on a stage, for example, eyes can pinpoint where light waves stop because the light goes dark(er). But ears can't pinpoint the origin or limits of sound waves in the same way. Sound "is emphatically not where it sounds like it is . . . (i.e., coming from the loudspeakers) because it only comes to be at all through the differential act of hearing, which is the very act that would place it where it isn't" (2). This difference constitutes it as relational through a specific material encounter. It is coproduced by the speakers, the walls and the ears in that moment of circulation. Third, sound also "consist[s] of an infinite number of higher frequencies, with each successive frequency a determinable multiple of the basic frequency of the sound" (3). This multiplicity of overtones is what makes the same pitch sound different when played on different instruments. The relative intensities of the series of overtones create the "timbre" or "color" of a sound. As Cecchetto puts it, "The reason why this is multiplicitous rather than simply multiple is that the infinite nature of this sequence— coupled with the environmental contingencies that are constitutive of any wave behavior—means that the original sound can never be perfectly reverse engineered from its constituent frequencies" (3). Sound is an emergent relation among frequencies that can never be a unity determined through linear causality. It is a singularity that is differential, relational, and multiplicitous. In short, hearing is an encounter with the room-technology-instrument-ear assemblage and its modulation; it is an experience of being a coparticipant in the ongoing movements of circulation and the relational production of a quasi-object.

Similarly, in *Background Noise*, Brandon LaBelle shows how sound is fundamentally material but more ecologically specific than relationally deferred. LaBelle outlines three key takeaways from his ecological approach to sound as dynamic enactions of spatiality—sound is multiple, social, and public. First, "sound is *always* in more than one place" (x). If you clap your hands, the sound is always there at the point of contact. But it is also, and practically simultaneously, in the room, up in the corners, and reverberating back. Sound as an acoustical event is parasitic on its environment—the configuration of the room shapes the contours of the sound, its trajectories of reflection and absorption, reverberation and resonance. This dynamism disrupts reliance on a single viewpoint: sound emerges from multiple locations—the clapping hands, the wall, the floor, the ceiling. Sound circulates and is charged with the energy of the environment. Second, "sound occurs among bodies . . . the acoustical event is a social one" (x). By multiplying and expanding space, sound generates or produces listeners. A body within reach of the wave is called to the event, necessarily made a part of it as it both absorbs and reflects sound—

hearing-impaired bodies can also feel the vibrations and participate materially in the diffraction and coproduction of waves. Bodies, LaBelle writes, "lend dynamic to any acoustical play, contributing to the modulation of sound, its reflection and reverberation, its volume and intensity, and ultimately to what it may communicate" (x). The crowd coproduces sound both materially and socially. Third, "sound is never a private affair" (x). Both multiple and social, the acoustic event is always a public event. As sound moves from a single source and immediately arrives at multiple locations around the room, its movement fills both space and ears. As an intensely public experience that feels intimately private, sound shows that space is more than a rudimentary conception of materiality; that knowledge is much more a chorus than a single voice; and that circulation is fundamentally affective and coproductive. As LaBelle notes, "Like a car speaker blasting too much music, sound overflows borders. It is boundless on the one hand, and site-specific on the other" (xi). In short, for both Cecchetto and LaBelle sound is thoroughly stereospecific, but for LaBelle specific parasitic bodies and their capacities and affordances play a more central ecologically coproductive role.

This materialist orientation to sound also extends to the grounding ontological vitality of noise. In *Sonic Warfare*, Steve Goodman turns the vibrational character of sound waves toward a vibrational force at the source of all matter. An ontology of vibrational force is "below" a physics of acoustics or a phenomenology of sound and aims toward the vibrational process of entities affecting other entities. Audible sound, for Goodman, is simply a small slice of this ontological process that humans and animals are able to hear through their ears. Consequently, he doesn't consider his project a philosophy of sound but instead a "sonic philosophy," because sound becomes a model for deeper ontological processes. An understanding of sound helps him push beyond a reductive materialism that would reduce sound to acoustical physics or quantifiable objectivity; a linguistic turn that would force sound into a carrier of meaning; and phenomenological anthropocentrism that neglects "the agency distributed around a vibrational encounter and ignoring the nonhuman participants in the nexus of experience" (82). Instead, an ontology of vibrational force is concerned with vibration's potential—the in-between of objects and subjects as a virtual space of movement, vibrations, oscillations. "Vibrations," Goodman writes, "always exceed the actual entities that emit them," which constitutes "the mesh of relation in which discreet entities prehend each other's vibrations" (82). Taking from Spinoza, he characterizes this as "an ecology of movements and rest, speeds and slownesses, and the potential of entities to affect and be affected" (83). Importantly Goodman concludes,

> This vibrational ontology begins with some simple premises. If we subtract human perception, everything moves. Anything static is so only at the level of perceptibility. At the molecular or quantum level, everything is in motion, is vibrating. Equally, objecthood, that which gives an entity duration in time, makes it endure, is an event irrelevant of human perception. All that is required is that an entity be felt as an object by another entity. All entities are potential media that can feel or whose vibrations can be felt by other entities. This is realism, albeit a weird, agitated, and nervous one. (83)

Goodman's Deleuzian approach implicitly elaborates on Serres's vibrational agitation and noise as energy stored in potential, which forms the basis for the emergence of subjects and objects and articulates a new materialism grounded in circulation.

Understood through the full theory of the quasi-object, sound circulates up from an ontological basis in potential energy, through embodied material ecologies, and to relational circulations including culture through processes of transduction and resonance. Transduction is the material transformation of energy.[9] As waves of energy, sound is transduced as it circulates through a variety of media—air, walls, antennae, receivers, amplifiers, and ears are all transducers that oscillate, vibrate, and transform waves of energy. Stefan Helmreich argues, "Transduction names how sound changes as it traverses media, as it undergoes transformations in its energetic substrate (from electrical to mechanical, for example), as it goes through transubstantiations that modulate both its matter and its meaning. When an antenna converts electromagnetic waves into electrical signals and when those are converted via loudspeaker into patterns of air pressure, we have a chain of transductions, material transformations that are also changes in how a signal can be apprehended and interpreted" ("Transduction" 222). Julian Henrique, for example, sees the low-end bass of dub and reggae as paradigmatic of the transductions happening through the sound system, room, and body. The human body both feels and hears the waves, literally experiencing transduction. Henrique writes, "My use of the term transduction, as a connection or homology between physical and social circuits, flows and fields, is not intended as any kind of reductionism.... At each point of transduction, electromagnetic, sonic, or cultural, one thing changes into another" (qtd. in Helmreich 224). His point, in part, is that the human body, as a transducer, can convert sonic energy into kinetic energy as dance, a vocal response, or clap of rhythmic participation or applause, a process that cycles upward through culture, not just metaphorically but as a series of material transformations.

As Novak and Sakakeeny argue, Steven Feld's acoustemology, the combination of acoustics and epistemology, completely relies on transduction. Feld's research shows how the Bosavi people of Papua New Guinea compose songs by imitating birds in the region as a means of understanding and navigating their environment.[10] But this knowing via acoustics doesn't happen without the soundscape of birds and waterfalls and the circulating energies that produce them; the listening practices of the Bosavi people that transform the soundscape into songs; and the microphones, records, and speakers that allow Feld to capture the soundscape and songs for further academic study ("Introduction" 4). All of these are transductions of energy grounded in what Goodman calls unsound, vibrations that exist below the threshold of human hearing that are then transformed into birds' songs and transduced again by embodied listeners into relational circulations of cultural knowledge that is expressed sonically. Helmreich wonders if transduction reaches its limit with the phenomenology of Feld. For him, acoustemology marks a distinction between energy and sound. Sound, he argues, doesn't travel—energy or waves travel through media, but sound is an event centered on perception (228). Understanding sound as a quasi-object, however, shows this to be an unnecessary distinction. As an entangled material process, the transduction of sound waves into electrical brain signals forms the basis of knowledge and folds back to contextualize and coproduce further transductions. As Feld puts it, he's interested in "how the dynamism of sound's physical energy indexes its social immediacy," which suggests a continuum more than a demarcation ("Acoustemology" 12).

One of the primary ways transduction performs this operation is through resonance. The term *resonance* comes from the Latin *resonare*, or to resound. In acoustics, resonance refers to the capacity of a material structure, like a wall, to vibrate at a certain frequency. Some of a sound wave's energy gets reflected back into the room as reverb, some of it passes through the wall and is heard on the other side, and some frequencies line up perfectly with the material capacity of the wall and make it vibrate, sustaining and enhancing the original sound wave, layering more vibrations and frequencies in with the initial sounding. This re-sounding is an interlinking via vibrations, a coentrainment or sync through a physics of vibratory matter. Coupled pendulums, for example, acquire opposing motion when placed next to each other on the same surface. Regardless of the direction in which each one started swinging, the two pendulums will eventually settle into this out-of-phase state or coupled oscillation because they affect each other through slight vibrations in the supporting surface. As Veit Erlmann notes, resonance has been picked up as a concept across a variety of scientific disciplines. For physicists this is "when a particle is subjected to an oscillatory influence of such a frequency that a transfer of energy occurs or reaches a maximum" (175). In astronomy, resonance refers to a periodic gravitational influence of bodies on each other. And in chemistry, resonance refers to a kind of multiple object, where instead of being associated with a single atom, electrons are "delocalized" and associate with several "resonant structures" at once (175). Each of these indicates an entanglement of embodied ecologies through circulatory waves of energy and force.

In the humanities, resonance has extended this model of circulation into culture, problematizing any sense of essence and collapsing any materiality-immateriality binary into "a kind of echo chamber together with other things, signs, discourses, institutions, and practices" (Erlmann 181). In the early modern period, theories of hearing used resonance as the term for the way vibrating strings make the physiology of the ear vibrate in kind, which influenced theories of music and the affective nature of major and minor chords or modes. Even though romantic thinkers rejected resonance's correlation between a vibrating materiality and social, moral, and aesthetic concerns, Erlmann argues that they actually strengthened the resonant theory of hearing, sans the term *resonance*. In conjunction with the discovery of fluid in the inner ear, they adopted "a different set of metaphors privileging circulation and flows of energy, electricity, and water" (180). This more complex set of mediations and transductions created a more developed sense of vibratory materiality that grounds cultural takes on resonance. In the mid-nineteenth century, Hermann von Helmholtz extended the resonant model of auditory sense perception, arguing that the senses aren't directly representational in an Enlightenment sense but produce signs that people interpret: people experience material relations and intuitively understand the world through this practical experience, associating the sound of violin strings, for example, with a violin through repeated, embodied listenings. *Resonance*, as a term for this process, was then picked up by twentieth-century phenomenology as a model of being-in-the-world. Ecologies making bodies vibrate in sync demonstrated how people are intuitively attuned to environments. Erlmann argues that in "Heidegger's Ear," Derrida sees Heidegger's "otophilosophy" as a theory of aural resonance: the ear of the other does not demarcate a distinct essential body separated from others but enacts a transformative resonance among beings in the world, linking bodies in an ecological coproductivity. In short, resonance layers and amplifies multiple transductions, entangling them into ecologies all the way up through knowledge production and cultural circulation.

As a quasi-object that encompasses the full theory of the quasi-object and its connections between vitality, ecology, and relationality, sound is fundamentally ontological. Serres's larger point in *Parasite* is that human culture and relations functionally mirror parasitic biological and ecological ones. By being pests, humans inject difference and diversity into a system, which allows new thought to emerge or be created. This extends to quasi-objects and makes them ontological in two senses: noise as ontological ground conditioning the ecologies and relations that emerge from it, and the new future objects, subjects, concepts, and cultures that ecology and relationality coproduce. These quasi-objects become resonant through a series of transductions: the transduction of energy through a series of material and technological mediations (ontological vitality); individual experiences of vibration through the ears and skin that turn resonant vibrations in space into electrical signals in the brain (ecological embodiment); cultural experiences of circulating concepts and practices that are resonant layers of these transductions at another level of scale without ever severing their connection to material transformations—they are resonant epiphenomena of transduction that then feed back into material experience and future transductions (relational circulation). Like sound, all quasi-objects transduce and resonate—sustain and multiply, or resound—as they continue to articulate new versions of themselves through waves of energy that make language, meaning, and culture functions of this materiality and how it works to entangle the world.

COMPOSITION AS VARIABLE ONTOLOGY

This approach to understanding sound positions quasi-objects as a vital concept for a more expansive sense of composition, one based on new materialist ontologies that see composition as a larger material process in constant modes of transformation. While Latour's work has generated a surge of interest in composition and rhetoric in the past ten to fifteen years, his work hasn't typically been read through Serres's quasi-objects, and it has certainly not been read through a version of quasi-objects that emphasizes its grounding in noise. In Paul Lynch and Nathaniel River's collection *Thinking with Bruno Latour in Rhetoric and Composition*, for instance, the term *quasi-objects* only generates two references in the index totaling three pages (*quasi-subjects* gets one reference and page). This isn't altogether surprising since, in *We Have Never Been Modern*, Latour never lays out a particularly close reading of Serres. But Latour's entire book is built on and presupposes Serres's "Theory of the Quasi-Object." In many places Latour refers to quasi-objects and quasi-subjects but later falls into the use of quasi-objects as the shorthand for Serres's fuller theory. When Latour uses the term *quasi-object*, he doesn't simply mean quasi-object in Serres's first relational sense but rather "Theory of the Quasi-Object," which includes all three meanings. If we take Latour's use of quasi-object to mean the "demi" stereospecificity of quasi-objects' relationality and parasites' biological and social ecologies, *as well as* their emergence from an ontological grounding in noise, agitation, and energy, then it becomes even more difficult to read Latour's actor-networks as a simple node and line model, as Rickert and others do. Using quasi-objects as a model for Latour's actor-networks and his sense of composition provides a new way to think about composition that is more complex and ontologically coproductive, which extends composition and rhetoric through the material turn and pushes on the boundaries of what might constitute our disciplinary object.

Serres's tripartite structure provides a way to read Latour's classic diagram of objects (nature, nonhumans), subjects (culture, humans), and networks (translations, transductions) in *We Have Never Been Modern* (11), and perhaps the Viking helmet image that adorns the book's cover—two horns for the poles of stereospecificity emerging from a ground of dark matter.[11] The grounding noise of networks and the ecological specificities that its circulation coproduces is what allows both quasi-objects and quasi-subjects to emerge as relational functions. Latour opens *We Have Never Been Modern* with a series of everyday examples of the kinds of quasi-objects that he argues are proliferating despite the fact that the current modern philosophical regime looks to purify the categories of objects and subjects, nature and society. Latour's examples scale out to global ecologies and in to the smallest notches on a "tessera." The ozone layer, for example, affects the entire ecosystem and scales from the upper atmosphere and global companies such as Monsanto to chemists and meteorologists to refrigerators and the button on aerosol cans to chlorofluorocarbons and molecules. Similarly, the AIDS epidemic scales from a global human population to social institutions to individual human practices to the microscopic virus. None of these things are fully commensurable or incommensurable: they are caught up in the same networks whose movements and circulations coproduce them—cut notches on them as they adapt to the larger ecologies and coparticipate in their production and proliferation. Neither of these examples is a distinct static object but emerges through constant activity and motion. The *modern constitution*—Latour's term for the philosophical and cultural legacy that continues to uphold a strong division between nature and society, subjects and objects—can't fully account for these kinds of quasi-objects. While Kant saw a difference between them that allowed him to theorize phenomena as the meeting point of the two through a cascade of intermediaries, later thinkers created a stronger division that posited a one-dimensional continuum bridging the divide. Subsequent philosophical, theoretical, and methodological positions were always placed somewhere on this continuum in order to situate epistemological debates. Arguments either assumed nature to critique sociologies or assumed society to critique the sciences. Latour's argument that "critique has run out of steam" simply means that scholars have exhausted stasis points along this continuum: the draw of this abstract division, he writes, is so strong that "no new position is tenable" ("One More Turn After the Social Turn" 278), leaving scholars nowhere else to turn.

Latour's solution is to include a vertical dimension to the continuum that cuts down into more layers of complexity and opens up more possible relationships and theoretical models that dissolve the separation between the two. In "One More Turn After the Social Turn," his call for "one more turn" argues that the social turn away from positivism leaves us on the same continuum, just at the other pole, which still presupposes the division and distance between object and subject: in short, it still presupposes that objects and subjects largely preexist their encounter in phenomena, either assuming objects as a cause or subjects as a cause. Latour, however, outlines five modifications to the modern constitution that enact a material turn down into the coproductive space of circulatory networks. The first two modifications make this initial turn toward the energy of noise and emergent ecologies as the conditions of possibility for quasi-objects and quasi-subjects. The first modification implicitly draws on Heidegger's "thrownness." Latour writes, "We live in a Society we did not make, individually or collectively, and in a Nature which is not of our fabrication" (281). Individuals are born into a world not of their own making. Latour reads this as an ontological flattening out. From this perspective, the division between object and subject is moot. Nature and society are equal in that they are both made and fabricated ontologically, and neither is produced by humans as subjective or autonomous agents. The second modification is to shift from either the object or subject as the grounding cause of knowledge to understanding that "the two poles are a consequence of a common practice that is now the only focus of our analysis" (281). This means that scholars have to discard any realist assumptions about nature and society or keep both and remake realism on the basis of this common, emergent, coproductive practice that Latour calls science in action and society in the making. Latour chooses the latter.

The third and fourth modifications establish the fundamentally coproductive nature of this material turn. The third modification makes the point more directly: the common ground between objects and subjects is making, emergence, or coproduction. Latour isn't advocating realism in the old sense. And phenomena aren't just the meeting point of preexisting objects and subjects but the ontological origin of reality in their mutual coproduction in the present. For Latour, gravity waves, air pumps, scallops, microbes are neither objects, nor subjects, nor even a simple mixture of the two. He writes, "This is why after Serres (1987) I call them quasi-objects. It is out of their production and circulation that something originates that looks somewhat like Nature 'out there,' as well as somewhat like Society 'up there'" (282). The focus of any scholarly or philosophical work should be "down there" in the agitation of noise and its emergence into coproductive ecology and relational circulation. The fourth modification shifts the emphasis from the dominance of science at one pole of the modern constitution and sociology at the other to the fields of history and anthropology as more predominantly concerned with making or composing. Under the modern constitution, history and anthropology are forced into presupposing a position on the continuum, trying to be objective or accepting a subjective stance. But this new common ground in the vitality of noise puts history and anthropology at the center of academic or knowledge work, at the center of these compositions that are fundamentally historical. Latour writes, "Now, on the contrary, it is an *experimental scene* that produces and shapes our new actants that then increase the long list of ingredients that make up our world. Historicity is back and it flows from the experiments, from the trials of force" (283; emphasis mine). In short, epistemology and ontology are collapsed—research produces new actants rather than reports on preexistent objects or subjects. Microbes, for example, are neither timeless entities discovered by Pasteur nor political entities produced in a lab. "They are a *new social link* that *redefines* at once what nature is made of and what society is made of" (283; emphasis mine). A microbe is a quasi-object, an emergent agency that reconstitutes objects and subjects in every moment of circulation. It produces and is produced by a series of coproductive encounters. A link in an emergent network, then, is not simply something that attaches to a preexisting node that remains unchanged: it is the active process of remaking and coproducing versions of those very nodes through collective relations, driven by the constant activity of the system that engenders the encounters—energy, ecology, relations.

The fifth modification takes the ontologically inflected meeting point or origin of phenomena and explodes it into the multiples and multiplicity of a variable ontology. Rather than having to force agency into one of the two poles, Latour argues that there are as many poles as there are actants. This irreductionist move means that entelechies, monads, fields, forces, networks all now have ontological status as world-making mediators. Every action collapses objects and subjects into quasi-objects that are historically emergent and coproduced through every encounter. Rather than the division between passive things-in-themselves and active subjective agents that requires layers of intermediaries to transmit their causal forces unchanged, everything becomes a mediator of everything else, becomes a new social link in the network that is constantly remaking, recomposing, the network. This produces what Latour calls variable ontology, which is absolutely central to understanding his position. In this emergent model, actants are lines, not points. As quasi-objects, any actant exists at any moment on the horizontal continuum of nature and society and on the vertical line from chaos to stabilization. Latour writes, "Boyle's air pump, Pasteur's microbes, Millikan's electrons, do not have to be defined as points in the one dimensional diagram but as trajectories in the two dimensional one" (286). The "same" microbe could be more like an object, more like a subject, more stable, or more distributed "depending on its history" (286). The same entity can occupy many states, can be made and unmade, can be more transcendent and more immanent. The key to this variable ontology is to accept that any actant will have multiple versions: "You will have as many 'microbes' as there are points along the trajectory" (286).

Again, such a position significantly problematizes the claim that Latour's networks are simply links between preexistent entities. The point-line model is clearly problematized when every actant becomes a line, when all points bleed together into the lines and trajectories of mutual coproduction and the circulation of quasi-objects—actor-networks are coproductive entanglements of these emergent lines.[12] Latour notes that many theorists have put forward terms for thinking about these trajectories: Serres calls them quasi-objects; Callon, actor-networks; Shapin and Schaffer call them forms of life; Lynch, experimental practices; and Latour has put forward many additional terms—*allies, collective things, entelechies, actants, networks,* and *modalities* (286). Latour argues that all of these terms will be misunderstood if they are only seen from the one-dimensional continuum rather than the two dimensions of variable ontology. "As soon as they are meant to designate points, they become meaningless" (287). Latour's material turn asks scholars to swerve from temporarily stable entities or regions down into the instability of the variable, emergent chaos and noise that produce them and back up into what Latour calls "the co-production of collective things" in order to trace the movements of these entanglements—these networks (287). An actant, then, is both multiple and a multiplicity. Synchronically, it stretches down into the multiplicity of networks that coproduce it, support it, and stabilize it. Diachronically, it stretches out and is remade into multiple versions, sometimes changing slowly, at other times being rapidly recomposed.

Networks, in other words, are never simply there; they only exist through continual enactments, mediations that transduce and transform everything in each case. In many of his works, Latour goes to great pains to make the distinction between intermediaries and mediators. In "The Berlin Key," for example," Latour notes that intermediaries do nothing but "carry, transport, shift, incarnate, express, reify, objectify, reflect" (18). If the key were an intermediary that preexisted the relation, it would only faithfully transmit the meaning of the request and provide a mirror of its social relations. But there is no simple transmission of or linkage to something simply preexisting the relation. Mediators make the actions of these requests and relations possible and are coproduced through the process. "[T]he meaning is no longer simply transported by the medium but in part constituted, moved, recreated, modified, in short, expressed *and* betrayed" (19; emphasis mine). The key might get stuck, not open the door, or break off. The lock might slowly wear down from use and no longer link the person-key-lock-door actant. Each use makes additional notches on the key and lock as tesserae, coproducing new versions each time.

Rickert particularly looks to problematize Latour's notion of politics as simple democratic representation of preexisting humans and nonhumans, or an intermediary. But as early as the beginning of *We Have Never Been Modern*, Latour notes that this is a typical misunderstanding. Politics is not simply the intermediary of science, nor is science reduced to politics. Science studies, Latour writes,

> are talking not about the social contexts and the interests of power, but about their involvement with collectives and objects. The Navy's organization is *profoundly modified* by the way its offices are allied with its bombs; EDF and Renault take on a *completely different look* depending on whether they invest in fuel cells or the internal combustion engine; America before electricity and America after are *two different places*; the social context of the nineteenth century is *altered* according to whether it is made up of wretched souls or poor people infected by microbes; as for the unconscious subjects stretched out on the analyst's couch, we *picture them differently* depending on whether their dry brain is discharging neurotransmitters or their moist brain is secreting hormones. . . . The context and the technical content turn out to be *redefined every time*. (4; emphasis mine)

Any articulation, assemblage, or actor-network is coproduced in every articulation through a series of mediating actions. Any representation, then, is not an intermediary but full-blown mediator operating through a variable ontology.

It is important, however, to see these emergent trajectories as resonant temporalities rather than through a linear, modernist, or progressive sense of time. In *We Have Never Been Modern*, Latour posits a much more complex sense of time that he draws, in part, from Serres. Latour argues against the linear "flow" of time because it presupposes that everything is a part of the same moment if it falls on the same calendar day and tick of the clock. Only then could there be distinct categories like premodern, modern, postmodern (72–73).[13] However, quasi-objects are more like turbulent whirlpools, or even slow-moving tidal pools that hover, than a linearly flowing river. Is something like the Islamic Revolution purely of the past, present, or future? Outmoded, up to date, or atemporal? The symmetrical flow of time "is disturbed once the quasi-objects are seen as mixing up different periods, ontologies, and genres. Then a historical period will give the impression of a great hopscotch. . . . Time becomes reversible instead of irreversible" (73). If time is a more like a whirlpool or spiral, then some bands will reach back to the past while others will spin out to the future. The past would not simply be surpassed but revisited, repeated, recombined, reinterpreted and brought closer to the present. Similarly, contemporary elements might be slung out to remote possibilities. Latour offers some simple examples: "I may use an electric drill, but I also use a hammer. The former is thirty-five years old, the later hundreds of thousands" (75). His activity contains both temporalities, his habits a few days old to a few thousand years old. His body may contain "genes [that] are 500 million years old, others 3 million, others 100,000" (75). At the same time, it may contain a mutation that is singular to his body but will in the future become distributed throughout the species. So for Latour, "Every contemporary assembly is poly-temporal" (74). This, then, is how to understand the variable ontology of quasi-objects—*as simultaneously the multiplicity of networks, the multiples of lines, and the spirals of temporalities*—simultaneously horizontally multiple, vertically a multiplicity, and temporally a spiral.[14] Any simplistic notion of networks as nodes and lines or composition as a linear process should be set aside to see if we can think the thought of composition as a quasi-object and coproduce an account of what such compositions might do.

Serres's quasi-object is not only a model for Latour's networks but also a potential model for composition. In "An Attempt at a 'Compositionist Manifesto,'" Latour builds his concept of composition on multiple associative meanings: (1) to put things together; (2) an attitude of holding it together, or composure; (3) to compromise, or be prudent; and (4) compost, decomposition, or a material and ecological breaking down. Composing never results in a unified, stable nature or society but in a world that is always in process. "The world," Latour writes, "has to be built from utterly heterogeneous parts that will never make a whole, but at best a fragile, revisable, and diverse composite material" (474). Every act of composition, then, coproduces versions of the worlds it enacts and carries along with it both political means and rhetorical functions. Latour's examples operate in the liminal phase between solid-single-isolated objects and a unified or holistic nature. A phone, for example, is not simply an identifiable object but instead an open network that is both its condition and extension. Taken out of its digital network the phone is a different object that doesn't have the same capacities. Climate change isn't a preexistent reality or matter of fact to be proven or disproven. It is a matter of concern that is ontologically composed through a series of complex actions: human scientists scrambling to gather data; refining instruments to make the climate "speak"; building data sets and trying to make them speak; scrambling to procure grant money; and managing, writing, correcting, and rewriting texts and articles (478)—all in a series of compositions with material agencies and global economies. Only someone operating through an assumption that nature is a preset reality to be proven or disproven could be outraged at this very typical construction of the world that scientists cocompose every day.

Instead composition fills the gap between macro and micro, nature and culture, with compositions of animals, plants, soils, chemicals, friends, enemies, assemblies, websites, blogs, demonstrations. "Red tuna," for example, includes a networked chain of predator and prey (an entire ecosystem), Japanese consumers, activists, president Sarkozy, Mediterranean fishing fleets, and sushi bars across the planet ("An Attempt" 480–81). Latour's version of composition shows how the world is put together in every act, in every movement, in every moment as an "entangled pluriverse" of emergent material, social, and linguistic compositions that capture, remake, and deploy "the creativity of all agencies" (484). The actions of Latour's actor-networks are processes of composing. Run through the model of quasi-objects as a relay, composition is always involved in the vital energies, ecologies, and relations that compose *through* a heterogeneous set of emergent assemblies that are always in the process of being reassembled.

For Steven Brown, Serres's models function as relays that enact both communication and invention. As the objects of study encounter the model they enact a process of translation that forges passageways between the two domains and establishes a channel for communication. But like Latour's mediation, it is repetition with a difference—to forge the channel that makes communication possible is to produce a new articulation, to carve traces, the unique scars of the tessera, onto the models being composed *and* the ideas, things, people, and resources that the model gathers. For actor-network theorist Michael Callon, the act of deploying a model as a relay is an act of composing "something new," whether that is "the discovery of an object or the formulation of a theory," through "the forging of novel relations" (Brown 6). Communication, therefore, presupposes invention through the encounter. As Serres makes clear, there is no simple binary between communication and miscommunication, signal and noise. Noise is both the source of invention and produced through the course of transmission. Importantly, the process composes a new version of the model as well as the object of study; it changes both in every rearticulation. "Theory of the Quasi-Object," for example, is a version of the parasite model that is put to work in a different constellation, but its deployment is grounded in the original model. And quasi-objects grounded in noise is a version of Serres's quasi-objects that is both redeployed and impacts "Theory of the Quasi-Object" and *Parasite*. Models as relays are a series of coproductive mediations. Each relay or version stays connected to the model and deepens or thickens its meaning and connectivity, strengthening the model's affectivity as a more global motif (Brown 3–4). The parasite as a model, then, is both remade and enhanced through its associations with the image of the tessera, the myth of Proteus, or the Balzac story "The Unknown Masterpiece" that opens Serres's essay on noise. Each allows Serres to connect the parasite to information theory, philosophy, myth, and the creative arts and extend the efficacy of the model across a variety of practices. In short, a model is a quasi-object.

Alternately, I take quasi-object as a model—one that builds connections, thickens descriptions, and mobilizes invention—to coproduce a version of composition. When I run the model of quasi-objects through my own analysis, I get a particular version that emphasizes noise; when I run that model through sound I get a different copy that emphasizes transduction and resonance; when I run that model through Latour I get another version that highlights coproduction and variable ontology.[15] This drift or difference is not simply a lack of methodological or representational fidelity but a function of the emergent composing processes of quasi-objects. So when I run this model through the key terms of composition and rhetoric, new versions of the concepts emerge that expand and strengthen the quasi-object of study. Composition, then, is a process that assembles, but as it accumulates versions it strengthens the global models. This is the paradox of quasi-object as an object of study: it is both specific and unique to its vertical moment of articulation *and* connected to and coproductive of a more horizontal network of disciplinarity and its spiraling temporality. Quasi-object as a model gets stronger as it accumulates operational versions along its trajectory. Perhaps the same holds for composition as a quasi-object of study. In order to extend composition in general and composition made whole into material practices, processes, and systems, I situate composition as a quasi-object as the field's object of study. This provides ways of expanding the field's object of study, whether it is conceived of as composition, writing, or rhetoric, into various layers and levels of systems that compose a more complex, shifting, unbounded object, which becomes more deeply intertwined with sound and its analogs such as transduction and resonance, ultimately strengthening our disciplinary ecology.

On the one hand, this is not necessarily a radical move but a coparticipation in the typical movements of disciplinarity. In their book *Engaged Writers and Dynamic Disciplines*, Chris Thaiss and Terry Zawacki quote then-Dean of Arts and Sciences at George Mason University Daniele Struppa on the tendencies of disciplinary change: "[E]ven the very traditional disciplines constantly evolve towards a breaking of boundaries, towards an enlargement of their objects, and essentially, towards a more interdisciplinary view" (Struppa qtd. in Thaiss and Zawacki 43). Even though Struppa is a mathematician by trade, he is one of the more interdisciplinarily learned people I've been interviewed by, so I take this experience and his role as dean to evaluate work across the arts and sciences as grounds for reading his comment as more than simply anecdotal. There is a sense in which my project is only playing out this disciplinary logic, moving from the historical and institutional need to identify a disciplinarily specific object in the nineteenth and early to mid-twentieth centuries to the expansion of that object in all of its permutations in the early twenty-first century. Or to put it ahistorically, it is moving from the need to identify a disciplinarily specific object when establishing a new discipline to the expansion of that object as the discipline matures and engages more of its rhetorical situatedness. On the other hand, it is a slightly more radical move ontologically. To expand disciplinary objects in scope also means expanding conceptual models as well as increasing iterations of the discipline. The expansion in scope means extending realist and phenomenological ontologies into the vital practices, processes, and systems that go beyond the creative arts and into the ontological coproduction of quasi-objects.

TWO

PROCESS AS REFRAIN

PROCESS IS GROUNDED IN a materiality that encompasses the three aspects of quasi-objects—vital, ecological, and relational—rather than a traditional model of social practice. And as an object of study for the field, it would also have to emerge from specific cases or locations of circulation and produce multiplicities. Lisa Ede, in *Situating Composition*, argues that the writing process movement never took place as a unified or coherent paradigm. Just as current-traditional rhetoric was produced as a generic paradigm by people who wanted to argue for writing as a process, such as Maxine Hairston and Richard Young, the writing process movement was created as a generic paradigm so that advocates of social processes, which is how Ede reads Marilyn Cooper, and postprocesses, such as Thomas Kent, can propose new theories. No one who practiced current-traditional rhetoric called it that or advocated for it. It was only outlined as a paradigm in retrospect in order to identify typical practices for the purpose of critiquing them and inventing new ones. The process movement that emerged in response was a set of diverse practices and theories, not a coherent or unified paradigm. Teachers and scholars focused on the specifics of their teaching and research and not on the period, movement, or paradigm. At best, for Ede, process was a trope that allowed for the production of this diversity. Similarly, the writing process movement as a unified paradigm was created in retrospect for the purpose of critique and production. Critics—from Susan Miller to Sharon Crowley to Thomas Kent— construct an overly general model that never really stood for the field's diversity of practice, or even diversity of theory, in order to build a straw paradigm as a foil, making it look more unified and coherent than was historically the case. This allowed postprocess theorists a similar kind of inventional productivity but had little to do with the process movement as a historical phenomenon. Cooper and Kent, among others Ede outlines, typically assume that their readers already know what the process movement is, primarily only providing a nod to the cognitive processes of individuals (48, 62–64). For Ede, the process movement is far from obvious, and its history has largely never been written in a way that accounts for its large body of scholars, its wide array of practices and institutional locations, its wide range of agents, and its more complex chronology.[1]

Ede sees using overly generic categories for the purposes of critique as a function of the field's professionalization and warns scholars of the pitfalls of this approach even as they utilize its affordances. The need for disciplinary status drove the production of the composing process as a unique and unified object of study in the face of the field's clear diversity in both theory and practice. But this abstract unity did provide a basis for the production of an increasing diversity of new theories in the field, which disciplines need in order to thrive (66–67, 74). Professionalization, then, is both limiting and productive. Ede's solution to this paradox is to always emphasize location, or the *material sites of practice* where theory gets used and produced, such as the classroom. A materially grounded history of the writing process movement for her would use documents from years of teaching to see how theories played out and changed in practice and show that "the writing process movement was hardly the singular engine of composition's disciplinary success and that composition's professionalization was the result of multiple forces—multiple movements . . ." (43). Attentiveness to locations of practice keeps scholars from making overly general paradigmatic claims about the field, such as a movement into postprocess, that cover over practices such as the continued use of writing process pedagogies. Ede argues, "Despite claims that composition is post-process, signs of an ongoing commitment to process are everywhere evident" (64). Seeing a generic writing process as composition and rhetoric's primary object of study makes it too easy to see process as something in the past, something we've moved beyond instead of something that continues today in a variety of forms and practices. Not unlike Latour's sense of temporality, Ede's method problematizes a narrative of progress that sees writing process as old and postprocess as new. Instead Ede sees the activity of building and building upon our objects of study as an ongoing disciplinary process that continually brings the past into the present and both inhabits and disrupts disciplinarity.

The production of a generic version of the writing process plays out in Thomas Kent's introduction to *Post-Process Theory*. As Ede notes, writers typically assume readers know what the process paradigm is and only offer readers a thumbnail sketch of the writing process movement. Kent states explicitly in his first sentence, "I suspect that the readers of this volume already know the central tenets of the writing process movement about as well as they know the letters of the English alphabet" (1). Then Kent devotes half a paragraph to its general assumptions: writing is a process that is generalizable and recursive, and teachers can intervene in it as expert writers. But he also gives a similarly general account of postprocess theory grounded in three main assumptions—writing is public, writing is interpretive, and writing is situated—organized as a movement, from public to interpretive to situated. His notion of the public is based on human-to-human communication via language. For Kent, writing "automatically includes other language users" and "must be accessible to others" who can understand what is written (1). These publics have knowledge of conventions, genres, and words from specific languages that facilitate this communication but cannot determine the outcomes of communication. Since writers can't predetermine these public encounters, writing requires ongoing interpretation. To "enter into a relation of understanding with other language users," writers must interpret readers' situations, motives, and genres with "uncodifiable moves" in an "attempt to align our utterances with others" (2–3). Kent calls these moves "hermeneutic guesswork" (3). Since this process can't be predicted, writers can only map out the process they used in retrospect in an attempt to get better at guessing future outcomes. But when employing these maps, writers will still make wrong guesses and misunderstand the other and will have to continually test their hermeneutic guesses in particular situations. Kent argues, "When we write, we elaborate passing theories during our acts of writing that represent our best guesses about how other people will understand what we are trying to convey, and this best guess, in turn, will be met by our reader's passing theories that may or may not coincide with ours" (4–5). Since no two people can really share the exact same discourse community, writers have to see how others will respond to their utterances in each case. In short, Kent's theory relies on a dialogic exchange among humans who must overcome their difference through hermeneutic guesses that are continually tested on humans in particular social situations.

Kent's model leaves writers caught in a kind of hermeneutic circle, struggling to understand and interpret the contingency of their world: they never seem to be fully connected to others or the world, and there isn't a sense of how this detachment would produce a basis for rhetorical enaction beyond hermeneutic guessing and testing.[2] As Stephen Yarbrough argues in *After Rhetoric*, Kent's notion of hermeneutic guessing promotes a reified notion of language use by positing "the strategies we always use to get everything done" (222). For Yarbrough, "As Kent's theory stands, all the advice it could offer . . . is a set of formal 'strategies' used by others" (222). If his primarily contingent guessing game is the dominant mode of language use, then teachers are only left discussing their guesses that have worked in past situations and proposing those as possible strategies for students to employ in similar situations—ultimately generalized heuristics in the tradition of Richard Young, Janice Lauer, and James Berlin.[3] In *After Pedagogy*, however, Paul Lynch argues that Kent's call for a radical contingency—a more complete reinvention of the wheel for every situation—problematically leaves him to conclude that teaching writing is impossible since prior theories really have no connection to future situations. Kent follows Donald Davidson's distinction between "prior theories," the theories a listener brings to an utterance, and "passing theories," the theories that the listener actually uses to interpret an utterance. For Davidson, communication works because listeners toggle back and forth between the two to produce interpretations or better guesses about the meaning of the utterance (89, 142n6). But for Lynch, Kent places too much emphasis on a narrow sense of the passing moment that is more detached from prior theories than Davidson contends. Kent draws on John Dewey as a transactional thinker who would see writing as too situated to understand in an abstract way. But again for Lynch, Kent ignores Dewey's work on education that argues people can learn from experience. Kent casts invention as nonrenewable, but for Dewey "such experiences do not disappear so much as become available means for the shaping of future practice" (90)—"The 'new' is, in all cases, relatively not absolutely new" (Dewey qtd. in Lynch 90).[4] Kent's radical contingency shortchanges Dewey's work that shows how experience and the accumulation of experience via material ecologies allow our "hermeneutic guesswork" to actually get better over time and our generalizations to become more effective even if still contingent. For Lynch, Dewey counters the desire for systematic approaches with embodied experience rather than disruptions and contingencies.

This kind of more radical contingency that breaks with the past grounds paradigmatic arguments about the move from process to postprocess. But, as Ede argues, a paradigmatic break doesn't necessarily exist between the two. Through looking at the ways past practices continue under present theories—a position that again resonates with Latour's sense of temporality—she begins to see writing processes, social processes, and postprocesses as blurring together and evading clear breaks. Even early on in the field's history, the concept of process allowed the work of many people to be collected together even as their projects and practices varied widely—Emig, Flower, Elbow, Lauer, Macrorie, Murray, Perl, Shaughnessy, Young (*Situating Composition* 71). From this perspective, postprocess is a continuation of process, not a break. Ede opens process up to larger ecologies, moving from writing processes through social processes to material processes.

But this expansion can't be limited to specific cases only. It also has to be entangled with an emergent conceptual basis. In *Composition as a Human Science*, Louise Wetherbee Phelps unpacks this broader and more complex sense of process, arguing that the turn from product to process was clearly successful but naïve because scholars "didn't see that process was a concept rather than an object to study" (42). As an object of study, writing was taken up as a literal act, and the composing process was seen as its underlying psychology, which gave the field a positivist ontology and a behaviorist psychology that largely called for empirical description. But this left process as a concept underdeveloped and composition "without systematic definition or philosophical formulation" (42). For Phelps, the underlying tenets of process as a concept connect it to postcritical thought more than its early adherents realized: it moved from language as system or structure to an act; it focused on writing as a temporal event; restored the act to a thinking, feeling, agential subject; it turned to actual experience of concrete individuals in social settings; and it remade composition into "a vital, intellectually open system" (44).[5] Phelps looks to unpack a number of the connotations surrounding process—"event, act, activity, interaction, transaction, open system, relation, ecology" (46)—and assimilate them to a worldview that she calls contextualism.[6] For Phelps, none of the terms alone will suffice. They are all root metaphors of reality, like process, that come with their own complications. But in searching for a root metaphor for the field, two key factors come into play. First, following Peirce and Derrida, compositionists have to let terms or themes proliferate—become "signs that refigure and resymbolize the key term in a process of 'unlimited semiosis'" (46). There will never be an ultimate God term, only a shifting and emergent series of concepts that develop a worldview. Second, these terms have to come from "our own subject matter," which was the original intent of the "composing process" (46). Even though process as an object of study failed at this on its own, the conflicts and connections made possible through the process movement compel Phelps's search for "productive abstractions that do not simply designate phenomena" but redescribes them in a way that allows for "reconceiving facts in fresh and surprising ways" (47). Process as a concept, for her, becomes a transitional term that facilitates this ongoing movement.

Taking quasi-object as a model instead of Phelps's contextualism as a worldview leads to an ulterior conceptual basis for composition and rhetoric. The paradox of quasi-objects means that it is both model and enactment, a concept and an object of study. Ede is on the right track with her solution to turn theory toward practice in specific locations, but with quasi-object as an object of study multiple versions fold back into the model as an ongoing process, practice, and movement: the model *is* the versioning; or, the process of versioning is the ongoing coproduction of the model. Instead of Kent's radical contingency that disconnects moments from any prior theory and future enactments, a variable ontology shows how a model can resonate with multiple enactments, strengthening it as a model and a movement. The move, then, is not to oppose process but to extend and entangle it—produce other versions through particular compositions or locations. Postprocess doesn't mean doing away with process, just as posthuman doesn't mean doing away with the human. Posthumanism questions the autonomous human self as the primary site of agency, coherence, and meaning by seeing the human as a function of larger systems that coproduce it but without overdetermining it. Postprocess examines composing processes as functions of larger social and material processes in ways that problematize reducing the writing process to an autonomous human agent. They are not after humans or after process in a linear sense but rearticulate them into new future assemblages. As Ede notes, there was never really a fully stable or unified process movement, just as Latour argued that we've never been modern because it was never a discrete historical period. Instead, every articulation is a quasi-object—a network of multiplicities, multiples, and swirls that materially entangle pasts, presents, and futures.

Extending process through composition as a quasi-object rearticulates it through the material turn just as postprocess rearticulated process through the social turn. Rather than follow Kent's model that is grounded in social construction and hermeneutics, which moves from public to interpretive to situated, I take a countermovement that inverts Kent's social process to emphasize materiality, starting instead from situation (Deleuze's vitality), moving through interpretation (Heidegger's ecology), and ultimately into forging publics (Latour's relationality). Bodies coproductively emerge from material situations that are in constant motion, interpret those encounters through bodily knowledge and expression as much as language, and contribute to those assemblages by participating in their public gathering. These three moments are movements of Deleuze's refrain. They are emergent, coresponsible, and happen in the ongoing entanglement of past, present, future in every quasi-object. If composition and rhetoric were to articulate a model that goes beyond a linear process as well as human scale, this is a place to start—the emergent movements among vitality, ecology, and relationality. Humans don't just test their theories on other humans: their engagements emerge from circulating energy that expresses worlds and assembles publics. Such an approach isn't based on conscious debate about effective guesses but on embodied enactions with a complex, evolving world that includes innumerable quasi-objects at various levels of scale. Rather than being grounded in a human world of guessing or heuristics, reassembling postprocess theory articulates a parahuman world of the refrain, open invention though the expression of worlds where the quasi-object of composition is the network that inscribes the subject as the subject scribes the network.

SITUATED—DELEUZE'S VITALITY

While Kent clearly stresses the importance of situated rather than formal models of communication as well as the provisional nature of any interpretive encounter, he doesn't go beyond human dialogue and interpretation to account for material aspects of situatedness and the complex processes of change that are a part of these situations. Deleuze and Guattari, however, include material processes of all kinds as functional actors in the coproduction of situatedness. Deleuze is a process philosopher. In his early works such as *Difference and Repetition* and *Logic of Sense*, he develops a model or diagram for processes of change in material systems. For Deleuze, virtual conditions are engaged by intensive processes to produce actual entities and assemblages. The virtual is a field of stored energies that have not been expended, potential degrees of freedom within a system, and a collective capacity of life to induce differentiation through the transduction of this energy within the system's range of potential. Intensive processes are forces such as temperature, pressure, and density; capabilities to fold, stretch, or bend; and capacities to shift between functions and structures that draw on this store of energy and actualize its potential. The actual is the collective entities and assemblages that emerge from these self-organizing material processes. For example, differences in temperature or thermodynamic intensity are capable of driving fluxes or changes in a population of molecules, such as a boiling pot of water. Water, if heated from the bottom, has differences of temperature between the top half and bottom half, which reaches an intensive threshold where the entire pot of water is the same or average temperature but then reaches another threshold that is a phase transition where the water transforms into steam. Energy transfer enacts motion in the system and ultimately a transformation in actual state. These movements from the virtual to the actual are processes involving differing elements, relations, and singularities. A hurricane, for example, involves elements such as intensive differences of temperature and pressure; relations between these elements link air and water currents and create shifts in their velocities, which then produce a particular storm as a singularity that emerges from these differential conditions. This is a self-organizing system with no controlling agent—multiple processes of air and water movements propelled by differences in temperature and pressure drive emergence or actualization through flows of energy and matter. As a process thinker, Deleuze gives primacy to process not to any imagined or assumed unity, agent, or state but to the vitality of open systems.

In his later work, especially *A Thousand Plateaus* with Guattari, Deleuze shows how this movement from the virtual to the actual plays out in particular biological, social, and historical systems through another version of the diagram called the refrain. For Deleuze and Guattari, actual assemblages and ecologies are situations composed through virtual intensive processes that are never static but operate through continual movements of reterritorialization—the development of particular embodied habits that establish a territory—and deterritorialization—the breaking of those habits and establishing of new ones (*A Thousand Plateaus* 311-25). The refrain is a general rhythmic pattern to life embodied through these collective habits in relation to a milieu that organizees three kinds of territorial movements within and among assemblages:[7]

1. one that demarcates an assemblage in relation to the chaotic milieu around it;
2. one that organizes the internal assemblage once it is distinguished from its milieu; and
3. one that opens the assemblage back to the outside world in order to make new connections with it (311-12).[8]

Rather than linear moments in a chain, however, "They are three aspects of a single thing, the Refrain" (312). The refrain is any recurring pattern of sounds, gestures, actions, and qualities that simultaneously mark a territorial center from its outside, internally organizes the assemblage, and opens it to other functions and assemblages. A monk's chant, for example, is a sonic intensive process that separates his space for meditation from the outside world; organizes his thoughts and regulates his body's position, heart rate, and blood pressure; and coproduces a different plane of organization than other enactments of the refrain such as running a marathon or teaching a class. The monk's chant functions to gather and transduce bodily energy in order to shift assemblages in a particular way.

Importantly, enactments of the refrain aren't restricted to human activity. Each morning the brown stagemaker (a species of bowerbird native to

Queensland, Australia) establishes a territory for its own activities (feeding, courting, nesting) that is distinct from other bowerbirds in the area. The stagemaker drops leaves from its tree and then turns them upside down around the tree so the lighter sides contrast with the ground (315). Such a practice demarcates the territory from its milieu by reflecting the sun's light, which creates distance between two stagemakers, sets the grounds for organizing the bird's own intra-assemblage, and opens spaces for the assemblages of other species—various insects whose population exceeds the single stagemaker's nutritional needs can fill ecological niches at other levels of scale around the tree because they now have a space safer from other stagemakers and other predators (319–20). A variety of these refrains are then assembled into a "full song." The wren family, for example, assembles a whole set of territorialized functions: "The male takes possession of his territory and produces a 'music box refrain' as a warning to possible intruders; he builds his own nests in his territory, sometimes as many as a dozen; when a female arrives, he sits in front of a nest, invites her to visit, hangs his wings, and lowers the intensity of his song, reduced to a mere trill" (323). This collection of sounds, gestures, actions, and qualities performs a "nesting function" that establishes the male's territory in distinction from other males, but it also performs a "courtship function" that opens the territory to various females by changing the song's intensity. These intensive processes hold together materials, colors, sounds, odors, and postures as intra-assemblages while simultaneously opening the assemblage to other functions and configurations.

In addition to operating simultaneously, a single refrain from one assemblage can also change to perform another function in a different or new assemblage. For example, "When the male does not make the nest and confines himself to transporting materials or mimicking the construction of a nest (as in Australian grass finches), he either courts the female holding a piece of stubble in his beak (genus *Bathilda*), uses the grass stem only in the initial stages of courtship or even beforehand (genera *Aidemosyne* and *Lonchura*), or pecks at the grass without offering it (genus *Emblema*)" (324). In its transition among these different practices and subspecies, the rhythmic relation to the grass stem is not simply a leftover of nesting behavior. It is a practice that passes from the territorial assemblage to the courtship assemblage and is expressed differently in each case. It becomes what Deleuze and Guattari call an "assemblage converter," functioning as a structural component in territorialization and as a gestural component in courtship. It opens a space for the male's song to take on a stronger territorial role, which produces two distinct assemblages instead of simultaneous overlapping ones (325). The rhythmic enactment of the refrain is a mediating transducer that transfers energy among multiple assemblages or alliances along with the grass stem, the beak, the song, the flapping of wings, the nest, the tree, the female, other males, and more. These movements and performances aren't rituals in the traditional, human sense but habitual rhythms within the material emergence of situations out of milieus.

The rhythmic movements of the refrain enact processes of transduction by tapping into a milieu's virtual potential, which becomes the conditions for further transformations. As Deleuze and Guattari characterize it, "Transduction is the manner in which one milieu serves as the basis for another, or conversely is established atop another milieu, dissipates in it or is constituted in it" (313). Amoebas, for example, are produced and sustained through a surrounding liquid (external milieu), their organs (internal milieu), exchanges between inside and through a cell membrane (intermediary milieu), and their relation to sunlight, food, and other energy sources (annexed milieu). The amoeba is a focal point of transduction in relation to annexed energy from an external milieu that is circulated through the system. Deleuze and Guattari write, "[The refrain] acts upon that which surrounds it, sound or light, extracting from its various vibrations, or decompositions, projections or transformations. The refrain also has a catalytic function: not only to increase the speed of the exchanges and reactions in that which surrounds it, but also to assure indirect interactions between elements devoid of so-called natural affinity, and thereby to form organized masses" (348). The stagemaker, for example, takes the leaf as a component of the milieu and converts it into a quality by diffracting the energy of light waves as a signal to other birds. The stagemaker, however, doesn't act with the intention to produce qualities. Instead this action is the milieu's becoming-expressive as a territory—it is the ecology that acts, not the isolated bird. The rhythmic pattern itself is a differential relation that coproduces a set of qualities, demarcates a territory, and names its occupant. As Ronald Bogue notes, this "is not a pre-existing subject; rather, the . . . subject and the territory are both constituted at the same time through the delineation of an expressive quality" (*Deleuze on Music* 20). Any particular rhythmic movements are not a matter of an individual or artistic signature but a style of territorialization. The territorializing process as an autonomous refrain sings through the bird and expresses the milieu's potential as a territorial ensemble.

Deleuze and Guattari's refrain shows how vitality—the potential and activity of life—actualizes ecologies. One of their key sources, Jakob von Uexküll, is considered the founder of ecology. Uexküll supposed an infinite variety of worlds for each species of animal that were separate but linked together to produce functional relations with an environment. Each animal type has a body with specific capacities for particular relationships with its milieu, or what Uexküll calls "carriers of significance."[9] Two of Uexküll's examples are the spider and the tick. The spider and the fly don't know each other, they don't communicate directly, but the spider's body builds a web perfectly to trap the fly—the spiderweb is constructed at a level of scale that the fly's eyes can't detect and is constructed with the right amount of play and tension to keep the fly's body from escaping. They communicate by proxy through their interconnected bodily capacities, virtual conditions of potential, and the vibratory signals reverberating through the spider's web. Similarly, the tick's body has the capacity to experience three primary carriers of significance: touch, odor, and temperature. Ticks are eyeless. They find their way to braches by the sensitivity of their skin to light, being drawn up the stalk toward the warmth of light waves. They have no ears but can smell the butyric acid emitted by mammals. When they smell it, they drop off their perch. If a tick manages to fall onto a mammal, it has an organ that perceives the mammal's precise temperature. In short, the tick is the intensive relationships its carriers make possible: the tick is a coproductive mediator of its ecology's energy. Uexküll was investigating "the communicative unity of the organism and the world sensed by it" (Rüting 66) and can be read as articulating an ecology in which life communicates with itself.

Rather than understand these relationships as a series of mechanistic stimulus responses, or see animals as captured in a closed-off world through their limited carriers of significance or bodily capacities—a kind of absolute territorialization[10]—Deleuze and Guattari see these same carriers as converters that also have the potential to deterritorialize, opening the bodies to other reterritorializing assemblages. They follow Uexküll's treatment of milieu components "as melodies in counter-point, the one serving as a motif for the other, and vice versa: Nature as music" (A Thousand Plateaus 314). Their rhythmic melodies are entangled through vibratory waves of energy. Just as a tick functions in relation to light waves, and spiders function in relation to vibrations along their webs, bats function in relation to sound waves as a kind of melodic counterpoint to butterflies. Not only does the bat operate through sonic reverberation to navigate at night, but certain nocturnal butterflies that are its primary prey also possess a sonic apparatus that can only hear a narrow bandwidth that corresponds to the bat's cry. The same sound has a different function or carrier of significance for each species, functioning as sonar for the bat and signaling "enemy" to the butterflies. The layers of milieus and assemblages function more like modes stacked on a melody than a single line of response. As Bogue notes, "The stem of a wildflower is a different object for the tick that climbs it, the girl who plucks it, the locus larva that pierces the stem and extracts the sap, and the cow that eats it. The same components, which in the stem of the flower belong to a precise plane of organization, separate into four milieus and with the same precision join four totally different planes of organization" (Uexküll qtd. in Bogue, *Deleuze on Music* 59).

The refrain, however, doesn't operate like a formal harmony that determines relations. These layers develop through the tension and release of multiple counterpoints, processes of territorialization and deterritorialization that can join in compositions with other bodies through transductions that build resonance. Resonance results from vibrations aligning along waveforms, different notes in the same key (or the same note at a different octave). It enables organization into an identifiable song, or territorialization. Dissonance results from vibrations that are out of key, or deterritorializations of traditional keys. Sometimes the waves of dissonant notes (mis)align in ways that cancel each other out; sometimes dissonant notes affect to repel; and sometimes dissonant notes resonate in new, pleasurable, or productive ways (e.g., "off" notes in music such as the blues note, chromatic scales, or "eastern" scales). These intensive processes are the very basis of life. The refrain, then, is another version of Serres's quasi-object that coproduces subjects, objects, and ecologies through circulations and relations that emerge from the energetic agitation and vitality of noise.

Rather than a kind of cause-and-effect behaviorism or a form of naïve vitalism that sees vitality in mysterious substances or a panpsychism, Deleuze and Guattari understand vitality as emergent attunements of life.[11] The virtual is not a cause but a set of potential effects that Deleuze calls "quasi-causality."

The virtual does not cause the actual: it is the range of potential effects and the complex interplays that induces their emergence through processes of self-organization. The virtual is not a logical form that prefigures and is copied by the real. It sets the potential conditions for real emergence (*Logic of Sense* 6, 33, 95). Vitality is the force of these intensive processes modeled on sound as a quasi-object. Sound is produced by gravity, friction, atmospheric pressure, an emergent and coproductive series of movements and materialities that cut into the virtual, activate it, intensify it, modulate it. Sound is nothing if not these movements, transductions, and resonances. When people in composition and rhetoric think of materiality, they often think of objects or bodies. But sound waves, light waves, or functions are also material, and are the bonding elements, or connective tissue, of an emergent situatedness—aspects of materiality that establish the transduction of energy and resonant relationships across distances via sight and hearing. These vitalist rhythms of life are self-organizing and self-differentiating forces that are continually actualized through concrete emergent processes that make novelty in a system of actual assemblages possible. The refrain, then, is a virtual idea or abstract machine, much like Serres's model, that is never separate from its actualizations in assemblages and that provides a very different model for postprocess theory, one that converts process from social construction into new materialism.

INTERPRETIVE—HEIDEGGER'S ECOLOGY

If composition and rhetoric is to ground process in such a complex model of situatedness, then a more traditional model of interpretation as human guesswork about language and intent also has to shift. Even though Kent touches on Heidegger in his discussions of interpretation, a closer, more detailed examination of Heidegger's embodied model of interpretation moves beyond human guesswork toward a richer engagement with emergent ecologies. For Kent, writers communicate "only because we hold a cohesive set of beliefs about what other language users know and about how our beliefs cohere with theirs" ("Introduction" 3). Humans already have to have these beliefs to produce guesses about the way other humans will respond to their utterances. But Heidegger is interested in how interpretation emerges through the codisclosure of a world, through understanding that is only possible by being an embodied part of the world in the process of disclosing itself. Kent opens up this direction for postprocess by constructing his take on guess-work from Heidegger's fore-having. In Kent's "Paralogic Hermeneutics," he seeks to describe his notion of hermeneutics in relation to Davidson, Derrida, and Heidegger, drawing a connection between guessing and habit from Der-rida's "displacement" and a sense of how-to knowledge or skill from Heide-gger's "fore-having" (28–29). Heidegger's model of interpretation, however, includes fore-having, fore-sight, and fore-conception, and a fuller analysis of his model shows how interpretation might work in a more expansive sense of material situatedness, not unlike Deleuze and Guattari's. Heidegger too draws on Uexküll's notion of ecology and how humans habitually operate in relation to the material ecologies around them. While Heidegger draws a more defini-tive line between animals and humans, a human lifeworld can be qualitatively more expansive than a tick's without there being a categorical divide between the two.[12] Even though humans have more potential affects than ticks, they are still a function of the ways they can be affected or not affected by the intensive processes of the ecologies they are embedded in. Heidegger's project, early on especially, is about mapping out these potential affects, which can be seen as extending Serres's ecological sense of the parasite into the human world. Any kind of improvisational performance is embodied and tacit, a parasitic func-tion of its material and musical ecology.

In his tool analysis, Heidegger examines tools in the context of their par-ticular relations to ecologies, activities, and possibilities. Heidegger's premise is that any tool is always experienced in terms of its belonging to other equip-ment: "ink-stand, pen, ink, paper, blotting pad, table, lamps, furniture, win-dows, doors, room" (*Being and Time* 97). Such tools are never distinct objects: they are only experienced in relation to other entities arranged in complex assemblages to form particular environments. What human bodies encoun-ter is the room in its totality, which is not simply a geometrical space but is experienced ecologically "*as* equipment for residing" (98; emphasis mine). The overall assemblage sets the actual conditions of possibility for particular acts, processes, or products, which in this case is experienced as equipment for writing. This understanding emerges from two things: a tool's "specific manipulability" and an environment's "manifold assignments" (98). What shows up in the use of a tool is its specific manipulability, a material capacity integral to it. When picked up and used, a hammer's material structure allows it to hammer a nail into a board in a way that a drinking glass doesn't. But a hammer only enacts this possibility within a larger environment. Within this totality of equipment there are manifold assignments, or the possible paths of future action and development produced by all of the interrelated specific manipulabilities within the situation. A hammer's specific manipulability may allow it to drive in a nail, but a hammer by itself doesn't carry the possible line of development, or assignment, for a house in the way a hammer, saw, nails, wood, a plane, a blueprint, multiple human bodies, and a sturdy, level plot of earth create the material conditions of possibility for a house. Like Deleuze and Guattari, Heidegger's analysis isn't deterministic in a simple cause-and-effect way. Rather than objects causing effects or subjects determining ends, they combine with many other capacities in the environment to create actual conditions that enable the emergence of possible futures, not necessary ones—if one piece of the assemblage is taken out, changed, or added, possible futures are changed. All of the "tools" for building a house might be assembled, but if funding falls through it won't be built.[13]

This ecological model of situatedness that extends the virtual into the actual creates the need for an understanding of interpretation beyond human language, beliefs, and intents. Heidegger makes this clear in his discussion of the fore-structure of understanding and the as-structure of interpretation later in *Being and Time*. He writes, "Whenever something is interpreted as something, the interpretation will be founded essentially upon fore-having, fore-sight, and fore-conception" (191). Fore-having is the totality of equipment that exists before and grounds any interpretation and recedes from our conscious, explicit recognition but sets the material and habitual conditions for thought and action. Fore-sight unveils aspects of this tacitly understood world through acts of appropriation. It is an initial point of view or future purpose that "takes the first cut" out of what is understood in fore-having in a way that sets the conditions for how fore-having will be interpreted (191). Fore-conception is the imposition of established concepts on our interpretation. Whether these are concepts of the entity at hand or other concepts that interpretations "force the entity into," fore-conception has a set way of grasping the object—"it is grounded in something we grasp in advance" (191).[14] In short, interpretation is never of a bare object or entity but one that is already structured within a totality of relations, both material and conceptual. The as-structure of interpretation is grounded in the fore-structure of understanding—fore-having, fore-sight, and fore-conception show a movement from tacit understanding through embodied involvement with a particular ambient ecology to the more explicit interpretation of its possibilities toward some end: humans experience a room *as* equipment for residing, or a table and chair *as* a place to sit and eat or a place to sit and write, and through this involvement disclose a version of the world.

Kent's emphasis on fore-having as tacit skill cuts interpretation off from this larger fore-structure and its emergent, coproductive movements. Because the as-structure of interpretation is immersed in an ambient ecology, it can't be broken up into a linear process or individual elements separate from the whole. For Heidegger, a human's primary task is to work out these fore-structures in relation to ambient ecologies and their conditions of possibility rather than simply accept or interpret assumed ideas, beliefs, or opinions about objects cut out of the world. As a part of these ambient ecologies, humans contribute to understanding, but fore-having, fore-sight, and fore-conception should never be controlled by "popular conceptions" (195). This kind of understanding is a human body's "specific manipulability"— humans are built to engage understanding through interpretation and turn it into meaning. To blindly accept a popular opinion or even a narrower scientific definition of an entity is to be cut off from ambient ecologies and the understandings and interpretations that continually integrate fore-having, fore-sight, and fore-conception. Popular opinion overemphasizes fore-conception and scientific models cut objects out of fore-having, removing them from their totalities of involvement. By emphasizing fore-having as skill and seeing interpretation as focused on human intents and beliefs, Kent makes postprocess theory perform a similar cut or reduction. Interpretation, in Heidegger's broader sense, attempts to articulate all of the elements of the fore-structure, connecting them through the as-structure. Humans can interpret a hammer *as* a tool for building houses, which would functionally situate it in relation to a particular totality of equipment. But in a different material ecology they could interpret a hammer *as* a tool for cracking nuts or any number of other possible uses as various assemblages shift its potential functions. Interpretation isn't simply about shared meaning but about capacities for situated activity. Tacit, embodied understanding grounds more explicit temporal interpretation, which gets turned into meaning that can then be shared or communicated and contribute to future fore-conception.

While the emphasis is on interpretation as a function of the human body's specific manipulability, Heidegger's model is a more parahuman function of ecology than Kent's model where humans make guesses about the thoughts and intents of other humans.[15] In "Letter on Humanism," Heidegger argues that all –isms, such as humanism, take reductive or narrow cuts out of Being— out of the emergent coproduction of past, present, and future that grounds the fore-structure. Humanism draws a division between subjects and objects, makes human subjectivity primary, and leaves the earth, animals, and often other humans to the processes of objectification (197).[16] For Heidegger, how-ever, Being is primary and originary, not human subjectivity. Fundamentally temporal, Being is the emergent disclosure of a world from its past condi-tions of possibility, in its present mode of relations, and toward its possible futures.[17] Being is the encounter of past, present, and future in any coproduc-tive moment that makes the human possible and presides over human rela-tions to Being. Instead of human subjectivity, Heidegger puts forward Dasein, being-there, as the form of human being that disrupts human-centeredness. In "Building, Dwelling, Thinking," Heidegger is perhaps his clearest: "When I go toward the door of the lecture hall, I am already there, and I could not go to it at all if I were not such that I am there. I am never here only, as this encapsulated body; rather, I am there, that is, I already pervade the room, and only thus can I go through it" (157). Humans are immersed in ambient ecol-ogies and the coproductive movements of past, present, and future. They aren't simply the center of action—here. They are decentered and distributed throughout both space and time—there. This materiality and temporality are prior to, or more originary than, any subject/object division and are funda-mental to Dasein. Being-there is a working through of this temporality and a movement toward possible futurity that allows Dasein to "pervade the room" and live more expansively in a world. Dasein is thrown into a world, a factic-ity of being-already-in the emerging past; fallen into a specific set of relations and specificities, an immersion in coping with or being-amid the present; and a projection into future possibilities, an always being-ahead-of-itself or being-there toward the future. Just as the refrain is a model of territorialization and deterritorialization, this structure of temporality is a model for every moment of disclosure or the emergence of Being.

What is more qualitatively distinct about Dasein is the greater poten-tial capacity to understand and interpret this movement of temporality and become more aware of its own coparticipation in Being, which disrupts subject/object instrumentalism. Rather than subjectivity as the center of action and control over beings, Dasein is grounded in an ethic of care for Being. Care is Dasein's awareness of its coparticipation in Being through ecological involvements—projects, inclinations, insights, or activities—and its concern for other people, animals, and things. Care is being attentive in every moment and relation to the ways Dasein is coresponsible for how the world and its beings show up. In *Being and Time* Heidegger writes, "In the disclosedness of the 'there,' the world is disclosed along with it. The unity of significance—that is, the ontological make-up of the world—must then likewise be grounded in temporality.... The horizon of temporality as a whole determines that *whereupon* factically existing entities are essentially disclosed. . . . In so far as Dasein temporalizes itself, a world *is* too" (416–17). Heidegger makes it clear that entities are already there as a function of the past in fore-having but that Dasein also codiscloses them through its enactment of temporality and thus coproduces a *version* of the entities in that new constellation. Whether any entity is preestablished *or* coproduced is a false dichotomy. It is always both, entangled in emergent temporality. Care is not any direct or linear cause-and-effect responsibility—it is a coresponsibility for emergence. Care calls Dasein to specifically attend to the ways that it always coparticipates in bringing entities, the world, and Being into temporality and is thus coresponsible for how they show up—something the metaphysics of humanism does not ask humans to do. Morality as a function of philosophy since Plato calls for abstract, preestablished rules for how humans ought to live. But Heidegger goes back to the pre-Socratics, before the advent of humanism, and draws an ethics out of ethos as dwelling. The everyday atmosphere and ecology that surround Dasein is where Being is disclosed, making care an "original ethics," an attunement to temporality, coproduction, coresponsibility, codisclosure prior to any metaphysical rules ("Letter" 234–35).[18]

Heidegger's analytic of Dasein provides a more in-depth understanding of how interpretation is parasitic on its ecology and operates prior to or below the metaphysics of representation. Public opinion and cultural commonplaces take a narrow slice out of Being and represents it with a concept or a more fully developed metaphysics like humanism. This abstracted representational logic uses language to pre-understand objects or subjects and removes interpretation from its basis in embodied understanding. Kent's representative guesses based on sets of beliefs about audiences and their prior knowledge would do much the same. Heidegger writes, "Communication is never anything like a conveying of experiences, such as opinions or wishes, from the interior of one subject into the interior of another" (*Being and Time*, 205). Instead, it is a mutual coemergence with the world. As one part of the fore-structure and the as-structure, language codiscloses Being through Dasein, not because of Dasein. In such a scenario, Dasein's role is listening to language's coparticipation: "It is a listening not *while* but *before* we are speaking" (Heidegger, "The Way to Language" 123). Listening accompanies and surrounds speaking and writing: "Whenever we are listening to something we are letting something be said to us, and all perception and conception is already contained in the act" (124). When speaking or writing, Dasein hears language in the mind's ear that split second before speaking or typing. What is heard is language as a function of ecological embodiment in that emergent moment. Rather than abstract meaning imposed on a being, language is speaking through and alongside this embodied experience of the world. Steph Ceraso argues in "(Re)Educating the Senses" that listening is ultimately an embodied act that isn't limited to sound waves entering the ears. For her, listening is as much about feeling and experiencing sound waves hitting the body as it is about the ears and brain processing signals. Heidegger pushes this further to say that listening should be Dasein's primary orientation to the body's immersion in its ecology if interpretation is going to be grounded in understanding rather than divorced from it.

Interpretation, then, is more akin to musical improvisation than guessing about a subject's intents or public beliefs. In any act of musical improvisation, players hear a melody, a riff, or a beat in their minds the split second before they play it. Listening to this moment gives Dasein broader access to the temporality that grounds the fore-structure. That split second emerges out of the ecology of performance through the embodied temporality of improvisation: all of the ecology's material conditions up through the player's past experience, practice, and learning that coproduce tacit understanding; the development of the musical piece in that particular present performance; and the momentary glimpse of where that piece could go, the line of flight that opens a space and creates the possibility for that melody, riff, or beat to emerge out of potentiality. Like the refrain, this temporality isn't simply linear but emerges together—the past, present, and future are there in every moment of improvisational embodiment and the act of listening and being open to these unfoldings.

In this context, acts of interpretation are centered more on what they do and produce than what they mean, even as meaning emerges with these activities and folds back into coproduction. As Hubert Dreyfus notes, Heidegger's approach is typically called "hermeneutic phenomenology." But seen in the context of Deleuze and Guattari's refrain as a model of situatedness, it might be better characterized as Jeffrey Nealon's "hermeneutic of situation." For Nealon, new criticism in literature was obsessed with meaning—often *the* meaning—or *what* the text says. Postmodernism blew this up into endless interpretations. Contingency turned the work of literature into endless multiple readings (via in part reader response) and emphasized the *how*, or methods and theories for producing meanings. In *Post-Postmodernism*, Nealon argues that meaning is not the question to ask, especially for music or art or sculpture or architecture. Postmeaning is thinking in relation to, about, or through a world of infinite relations—a Deleuzian becoming-molecular (141). He calls this post-post move a shift from hermeneutics of meaning and a hermeneutics of suspicion to "hermeneutics of situation" (169). While Heidegger still includes meaning, it has to emerge up through, with, and alongside a situated world of infinite relations to have any efficacy and open up possible worlds with care. Understanding, interpretation, and meaning are functions of material ecologies and the temporality of improvisation, a ballplayer's constant shifting in response to the game play as a function of listening to the fore- and as- structures. Any model of process that takes complex material situatedness into account has to correspondingly expand interpretation to this larger world of embodied ecologies.

PUBLIC—LATOUR'S RELATIONALITY

If postprocess is to be understood through the embodied interpretation of actual material assemblages driven by virtual potential, then, again, composition and rhetoric's sense of publics also has to participate in this shift. Kent's model of the public is a medium for the communication of human intents, opinions, or assumptions that are then confirmed or denied—the public sphere is still the traditional agora of the citizen. Deleuze's model of situatedness and Heidegger's model of interpretation, however, open up the possibility for a rearticulated sense of publics put forward by Bruno Latour. In "From Realpolitik to Dingpolitik or How to Make Things Public," he works to build an alternative way to consider public "matters." Rather than press forward with the more traditional concept of "realpolitik"—"a positive, materialist, no nonsense, interest only, matter-of-fact way of dealing with naked power relations"—he adopts the neologism "dingpolitik"—"a risky and tentative set of experiments in probing just what it could mean for political thought to turn 'things' around and become slightly more realistic than has been attempted up to now" (14). Following the invention of "object-oriented" programming languages, he wonders what an object-oriented democracy would look like, an image that goes beyond public deliberation, traditional public spaces, and a generic public sphere to a model of publics that contributes to expressing a milieu, codisclosing a world, and making a public.[19] Any becoming-public is grounded in the vital and the ecological and emerges through circulation and relationality like the ball in Serres's game. Not only are the ball and player functions of circulation, which continually converts them into quasi-objects and quasi-subjects, but the game itself is enacted through this circulatory and relational system. "Dingpolitik" is not "realpolitik," in other words. Latour's materiality is constantly shifting and on the move and based in circulation and emergent relationality.

To outline "object-oriented" politics, Latour interrogates the multiple meanings and etymology of key concepts, initially focusing on representation. In addition to the two traditional meanings—the legitimate procedures for gathering the right people around an issue (politics) and the accurate portrayal of what is at issue (science)—he wants to add a third. While the former signifies a sanctioned gathering, a council or congress, and the latter creates a focus on the facts that are at issue, the third he draws out of the cover of Hobbes's *Leviathan*: how to represent the emergent relationality of a body politik—how to represent people and issues through what medium (rhetoric)? The interesting thing for Latour in Hobbes's original book cover and in Shapin and Schaffer's revision is the composite of objects assembled. The body politik is not only made of people: "They are thick with things: clothes, a huge sword, immense castles, large cultivated fields, crowns, ships, cities and an immensely complex technology of gathering, meeting, cohabitating, enlarging, reducing and focusing" (16). For Latour, this crowd of objects is "a whole new ecology loaded with things" that is never integrated into the definition of representation or politics (17). His representational strategy is to pack things in the spaces that were once only imagined with people and issues and put them in relation. An object-oriented politics would bring together things, people, and issues to express, disclose, or coproduce the material conditions that make politics possible. In short, what this third meaning brings to the assembly is "rhetoric" (18): beyond the laws of participation and the representation of facts is the concern for the methods of bringing proof to the debate and the willingness to conclude a dispute with disputable assertions. Rather than trying to establish WMDs as matters of fact with a few slides and the power of authority to force consensus and sidestep debate, a la Colin Powell, a "dingpolitik" would bring together complex assemblages of concrete things, humans, and discourse around matters of concern, debate, and difference. In short, this "new eloquence" is fundamentally relational and plays a key role in the assembling or gathering of emergent publics (17, 21).

The turn to a new eloquence is based on a sense of language more in line with Heidegger's disclosure, so Latour's refigured model of rhetoric draws explicitly on Heidegger's etymological reorientation of the German word for "thing," *ding*.[20] In Heidegger's attempt to move away from the object as a presence-at-hand that is isolated from other objects as matters of fact, he takes up the alternative term *thing* as something that gathers other things around it: the hammer "gathers" wood, nails, people, blueprints, because their collective specific manipulabilities create capacities for functional, ecological relationships. Latour taps into the political meaning of this term as well in order to similarly move away from a realist politics based on objectivity toward a materialist politics based on relationality. Many Nordic and Saxon languages still use variations of "ding" or "thing" to designate forms of political assembly. Latour writes, "Long before designating an object thrown out of the political sphere and standing there objectively and independently, the Ding or Thing has for many centuries meant the issue that brings people together because it divides them" (23). The etymology includes the people who assemble, the place they gather, the issue or division that creates their mutual concern, and the things that create the division.[21] Instead of seeing common ground or unity as the centering force around an issue, he sees issues as "objects" that gather sets of differences—"passions, indignations, opinions" (15). Latour doesn't limit or privilege what can gather or be gathered. He would include "the

objects of science and technology, the aisles of supermarkets, financial institutions, medical establishments, computer networks—even the cat walk of
fashion shows," all of which "offer paramount examples of hybrid forums and
agoras, of the gatherings that have been eating away at the older realm of pure
objects bathing in the clear light of the modernist gaze" (23–24). Each object,
each thing, each issue, gathers a different assembly of concerned parties and
coproduces a different set of relations, different versions of the objects, and
different conditions for emergence.[22] A "dingpolitik," then, is grounded in the
gatherings and movements of assemblages and enacted through the manifold
assignments of the objects gathered and the human, interpretive involvement in this disclosing of a world—the expression of voices, differences, and
complexities.

This third sense of representation as rhetoric assembles differences, forging new relations among differences rather than unifying a common public
sphere. Representation in this sense, of course, is never an intermediary but
instead a mediator that gathers and transforms an ecology of interests with
more and more elements taken into account, considered simultaneously,
side by side, in coproductive relation.[23] Rhetoric would no longer follow the
matter-of-fact power points of Powell's WMDs or the interpretive guesses
of human beliefs and opinions but would now rely on "a delicate aesthetic of
painting, drawing, lighting, gazing, convening . . ." (23). The explosion of the
space shuttle Columbia is offered as an example:

> "Assembly drawing" is how engineers call that invention of the blueprint. But
> the word assembly sounds odd once the shuttle has exploded and its debris
> has been gathered in a huge hall where inquirers from a specially designed
> commission are trying to discover what happened to the shuttle. They are now
> provided with an "exploded view" of a highly complex technical object. . . . How
> sad that we need catastrophes to remind us that when Columbia was shown on
> its launching pad in its complete autonomous objective form that such a view
> was even more of a lie than Mr. Powell's WMD. It's only after the explosion that
> everyone realized the shuttle's complex technology should have been drawn
> with the NASA bureaucracy inside of it in which they too would have to fly. (24)[24]

Rather than citizens speaking their minds through common sense and
guessing about each other's intents, Latour's version of eloquence is more

"indirect, distorted, inconclusive" (30). This kind of public rhetoric does not revolve around policy—solutions to problems—but the articulation or assembling of the conditions for the emergence of solutions. The engineer's assembly drawing is an example of rhetorical practice that coproduces an emergent assemblage in a specific space around a matter of concern. The solution is still unclear, open to debate, and requires the gathering and mapping of a vast array of different people, disciplines, institutions, and technologies through the assembly drawing. About these kinds of discursive enactions, rhetors should ask, "How do they manage to bring in the relevant parties? How do they manage to bring in the relevant issues? What change does it make in the way people make up their mind to be attached to things?" (34). Making things public, in other words, opens them to other assemblages, relations, and functions, opening them to new potential and possible futures, to becoming-possible.

Language in these processes of assembly not only participates in the disclosure of a version of the world but also functions pragmatically, similar to language use in Deleuze and Guattari. It assembles via enunciation and shifts functions among assemblages. In *A Thousand Plateaus*, Deleuze and Guattari provide one of their classic examples—the feudal assemblage: "[W]e would have to consider the intermingling of bodies defining feudalism: the body of the earth and the social body; the body of the overlord, vassal, and serf; the body of the knight and the horse and their new relation to the stirrup; the weapons and tools assuring a symbiosis of bodies—a whole machinic assemblage" (89). Among these assemblages of human, animal, and material bodies and their complex relations to tools and the earth are enunciations, death sentences, judgments, proceedings, laws. These expressions do not simply enable human communication or represent material machines but function with/in the assemblages to coproduce their potential for relationality and rearticulation. Deleuze and Guattari continue their outline of the feudal assemblage: "We would also have to consider statements, expressions, the juridical regime of heraldry, all of the incorporeal transformations, in particular, oaths and their variables (the oath of obedience, but also the oath of love, etc.,): the collective assemblage of enunciation" (89). Language is a regime of signs in which signs don't stand on their own any more than tools but operate as variables at the intersection of a machinic assemblage of bodies and an assemblage of enunciation composed of words and gestures.

In an incorporeal transformation, for example, a judge's guilty verdict transforms the defendant's body from an accused person into a criminal. In one sense, it is still the same body, but it now functions differently within an entire disciplinary and discursive regime. The term *guilty* isn't a determinant or something to be guessed about in terms of human intention but a variable that rearticulates the body's position within an assemblage of institutions, laws, and actors, changing it from accused to convict and producing a new articulation or version of that body (80–81). Generating a written account, for Latour, coproduces a version of the object, so circulating the document circulates that object, expanding its capacity for relation, opening it to new possible relations, making it a different kind of functional actor, making it a quasi-object. Publics are functions of these kinds of circulation and therefore can be gathered anywhere discourse circulates.[25]

Not only is Latour's sense of publics not a general or common public sphere, it is not confined to sanctioned public spaces or forums for debate. Dingpolitik moves the assembly from sacred or sanctioned spaces to anywhere processes of assembling gather publics. Enlightenment thinkers wanted to build a space to gather issues—domes, palaces, city halls—but these sanctioned spaces can no longer gather the full scope of dissent and difference of publics in the contemporary global sphere. May 1968 in France, for example, saw the inability of the National Assembly to gather all of the dissenting voices and engage the public's matters of concern. Latour notes that "commentators . . . were amused to see the turbulent demonstrating crowds [pass] by the National Assembly without even looking at it, as if its irrelevance was so great that it could not even invite abuses" (30). For Latour, a new global assembly would have to be expanded to all spaces because any space has the potential to gather matters of concern and coproduce publics through relationality. He writes,

> Scientific laboratories, technical institutions, marketplaces, churches, temples, financial trading rooms, internet forums, ecological disputes . . . are just some of the forums and agoras in which we speak, vote, decide, are decided upon, prove, are being convinced. Each has its own architecture, its own technology of speech, its complex set of procedures, its definition of freedom and domination, its ways to bring together those who are concerned—and even more important those who are not concerned—and what concerns them, its

expedient way to obtain closure and come to a decision. Why not render them
all comparable? (31)

For Latour, all of these assemblages are in constant states of change and
exchange. The temples became churches and then city halls. Heads of states
learn from artists. Products in the marketplace are changed by laboratories.
Supermarkets mirror voting booths. Social theories borrow from physics.
The Internet produces virtual parliaments. Art installations draw from the
sciences. This "constant commerce, the ceaseless swapping, the endless
crisscrossing of apparatuses, procedures, instruments, and customs" is what
the new public rhetoric attempts to gather in all of its potential spaces (34).
These spaces are not the public sphere but are coresponsible for the gathering
of sphere publics—multiple, layered, resonant spheres in constant states of
circulatory and relational transformation.

This movement among situatedness, interpretation, and publics extends
Kent's model of process beyond the limits of his passing hermeneutical theory and into a new version of process that shifts it from the social turn into
the material turn. If, as he says, a passing theory "never 'stops' so that we can
capture some sort of unitary, complete, or determinate meaning, . . . it never
endures, never works twice in quite the same way" ("Introduction" 4), then
rhetors can't see it as a theory applied to a case or as the same theory working
differently in different situations. A new version of the theory emerges with
every gathering. But this doesn't mean everything is purely contingent and
there can be no general model or abstract diagram. For Deleuze, the model or
diagram is a virtual idea, something that exists in potential that is then actualized in systems with measurable variables. Ideas of this type are concrete
universals, fully real but not yet actualized. Deleuze considers himself a "pure
metaphysician" because he develops models or diagrams that function across
diverse material systems and instantiations. But unlike traditional metaphysics, these models or diagrams are not assumed to be ideal forms that are separate from the world and carry more ontological weight or truth value. The
enactment of an ideal form in the world produces a copy of it in reality and
therefore nothing new is ever generated, only a playing out of the preexistent
form. Deleuze is much more interested in theorizing the new. The virtual idea
is not a transcendent form but a set of potential functions that are immanent
to the real, as equally real as the actual and not more true—it is abstract but

real. Virtual models, diagrams, or ideas function across domains and are a real part of the world's actualization, producing versions of the idea in various assemblages. They do not articulate a specific solution in advance but operate as a guideline to establish conditions out of which solutions emerge.

At the end of *A Thousand Plateaus*, Deleuze and Guattari give three meanings for abstract machines. First, abstract machines draw the cutting edges of territorialization and deterritorialization and are singular and immanent. Rather than abstract in the Platonic sense, they operate within concrete assemblages through unformed matter and nonformal functions—the dated and named plateaus in the book are abstract machines in this sense and specific to that assemblage (511–12). Second, there is an abstract machine that serves as "the" model, the very "abstract idea of a Machine." As a Machine the abstract machine organizes assemblage components such as territories, "entangled lines constituting the 'map' of the assemblage," and "relations between the assemblage and the plane of consistency" or virtual potential and intensive processes (512). Third, there are various types of abstract machines: faciality machines, which generate subjectivities; order-word machines; enslavement machines; machines of consistency, of stratification, or overcoding, examples of which are spread throughout the book (513–14). While the refrain participates in each of these meanings, I take it mostly in the second sense as a predominant model or virtual idea for processes that assemble through movements of territorialization and deterritorialization. As the very idea of a machine, however, it produces both specific assemblages and other models of process. It is an abstract machine that exerts force in the world not to produce exact copies but new versions, ontologically different and new but maintaining a tie to the virtual idea both extending and re-articulating it. If the general model is changed in every emergent actualization but still retains its status as a virtual idea, then, as Phelps suggests, process can be both a concept and an object of study.

The movements of the refrain—territorialization, deterritorialization, and reterritorialization—provide a more detailed model for process as a quasi-object through the functions for each movement. A function is a capacity to receive inputs and transduce them into outputs as a way of transforming one domain into another. A milieu, or set of environmentally embedded thresholds for self-organizing processes, is activated by these functions to internally organize assemblages and open them back out to other relationships. The refrain gives this rhythm to Serres's "theory of the quasi-object" as a process:

1. *Situated*—Serres's noise functions as an energy source for the production of actual assemblages. The transduction and circulation of this energy sets lines of potential development for future assemblages and begins the demarcation of a territory in relation to the milieu around it. It is the source of coproduction.

2. *Interpretative*—Serres's parasite functions to draw on this energy and adapt in relation to its ecology. It has the capacity to respond to and translate intensive processes, which deterritorializes or distinguishes its body from a milieu while organizing it in relation to its ecological conditions. Parasitism functions in humans as well, who interpret their ecologies through improvisational performances that resonate with the ecology. It is the enactment of coproduction.

3. *Public*—Serres's quasi-object functions as a public expression of the assemblage that opens it back to the outside world in order to make new transformative relations with it possible, continually enacting the process through circulation and layered resonances that ripple, cascade, and reverberate from it, coproducing quasi-objects and quasi-subjects in their wake. It is the dissemination of coproduction.

Understood through the refrain, this is the larger "theory of the quasi-object" written into a model for processes of change.

And in relation to sound as a quasi-object, this movement among situatedness, interpretation, and publics can also be used as a general diagram for the processes of music production:

1. *Noise*—Sound emerges up through the noise of the virtual as a transduction of its energy that is produced and ultimately recorded in a studio.

2. *Sound*—Music, as the internal organization of sound, emerges up through material ecologies and embodied performance, transducing sound's energy and resonating with its ecologies.

3. *Music*—Publics emerge up through circulation, through promotion and distribution of music, which resonates with audiences, opening to further potential relations that gather publics.

Situated, interpretive, and public ultimately collapse into a model for processes of material composition, which builds, invents, coproduces associations with highly localized sets of practices, agencies, and mediators. For Latour, the production of a model for DNA, for example, didn't define the nature of things once and for all but built a composition with it, one that is continually in the process of being rebuilt, reassembled, and recomposed. Through this conceptual sense of process, compositionists will always be composing versions of their object of study, continually coproducing composition as a quasi-object.

THREE

RESEARCH AS TRANSDUCTION

RESEARCH RESULTS IN THE expansion of quasi-objects, not simply their explanation, and coproduces a version of the object of study particular to that project. Despite the fact that research has been at the center of our disciplinary self-reflection since the early 1960s, it has remained debated and contested.[1] Innumerable courses, presentations, workshops, and manuscripts have yet to solve the conflict between the "two cultures"—quantitative and qualitative, scientific and humanistic. And attempts to break the division through finer determinations or bring in multiple methods and methodologies from various disciplines have made research more complex and, in a word, messy. As John Law notes in *After Method*, "What happens when social science tries to describe things that are complex, diffuse, and messy. The answer, I will argue, is that it tends to make a mess of it. This is because simple clear descriptions don't work if what they are describing is not itself very coherent. The very attempt to be clear simply increases the mess. So the book is an attempt to imagine what it might be to remake social science in ways that are better equipped to deal with mess, confusion, and relative disorder" (2). The positive outcome of this complexity has been greater awareness of the rhetorical nature of research and its necessary embeddedness in rhetorical situations but largely without pushing these understandings beyond research's episte-mological basis in producing knowledge or explaining the world and into the ontological practice of coproducing worlds.

As a discipline, composition and rhetoric has become much more atten-tive to the coproductive interrelationships between theory, methods, and objects of study. Kristie Fleckenstein's co-authored piece with Clay Spinuzzi, Rebecca Rickly, and Carole Papper, "The Importance of Harmony," follows writing as an ecology developed in the work of Marilyn Cooper and Margaret Syverson to argue that the goal of research should be harmony among objects of study, theories or methodologies, and methods. If the object of study is a writing ecology that is always shifting and evolving, then theories and meth-ods don't simply align to a static object. Imposing a theory on an object would form a terministic screen that would reveal only certain aspects of it. And strict adherence to initial methods or techniques would not only restrict the object of study but also limit the capacity to theorize. Instead, object, theory, and method evolve together, resonate, and coproduce each other through the process of research. Without this alignment or resonance, the research risks producing a limited or reductive version of the object of study and with it problematic understandings. Theories and methods have to emerge and coevolve in relation to objects of study, which are complex rhetorical ecolo-gies whose circulations expand, and researchers have to continually seek out resonances with them. Fleckenstein et al. characterize this feedback loop of resonance as a kind of melodic call and response among object, theory, and method. Even if the research is messy and emergent, the constantly shifting relations of harmony and disharmony work object, theory, and method into a resonant research project that has an object, theory, and method particular to it. It is precisely the messy nature of writing as an ecology that makes a reso-nant research project possible.

In "Losing by Expanding," however, Spinuzzi steps back from his collabo-ration with Fleckenstein et al. to argue that expanding objects of study make it difficult to reliably "bound" an empirical case study and to show how this theoretical and material expansion has produced methodologically unsound studies. Spinuzzi agrees with third-generation activity theory that objects of study are cyclically transformed by collective activity and should be the linchpin of analysis. But he proposes a method for constraining the scope of these runaway objects for scholars in professional and technical writing who are less diligent than activity theorists about the outcomes of their methods. If creating reliable empirical studies is the goal, then bounding the object of study would be an important aspect of research methods. But there are many other rhetorical purposes beyond the empirical. In a broader concern for writing as ecology, Fleckenstein et al.'s extension of ecology to research offers a more rhetorical approach: if the object of study is complex, diffuse, or messy, then the research methods should be complex, diffuse, or messy also. A new materialist approach seeks precisely this unbound object as its object of study. In other words, a rhetorical and ecological approach to research more broadly is concerned with coproducing runaway objects rather than corralling them, multiplying quasi-objects rather than bounding them. Fleckenstein et al. argue, following Gregory Bateson, that negotiating the circumference of a research project's object of study is central to an ecological approach. But articulating a circumference to coproduce a version of the object of study is not "bounding" or "corralling" it in order to produce more specifiable results. It coproduces a version of it as a quasi-object.

Latour's variable ontology in relation to objects of study goes at least as far back as Gregory Ulmer's "The Object of Post-Criticism." Ulmer characterizes postcriticism in the context of the postmodern turn as centered on the crisis of representation and its movement from the avant-garde arts into criticism. This turn breaks representation from its realist presumptions that posit a correspondence model of the relationship between the critical text and the object of criticism. Postcriticism, for Ulmer, brings the avant-garde compositional methods of montage and collage into criticism because of their "objectivist impulse" and emphasis on constructivism. Much of cubism incorporated actual objects or fragments of objects into its compositions, blurring the lines between object and representation. Similarly, as Ulmer writes, "Montage does not reproduce the real, but constructs an object (its lexical field includes the terms 'assemble, build, join, unite, add, combine, link, construct, organize'...) or rather mounts a process ('the relation of form to content is no longer a relation of exteriority, the form resembling clothes which can dress no matter what content, it is *process, genesis, result of a work*' ...) in order to intervene in the world, not to reflect but to change reality" (Ulmer, "Object" 86). Ulmer is explicitly out to disrupt models of representation that inform theory/application approaches to criticism.[2] Later in *Heuretics*, Ulmer uses objects as relays to appropriate theory for the production of a method. He writes, "The relevant question for heuretic reading is not the one guiding criticism . . . but one guiding a generative *experiment*: Based on a given theory, how might *another* text be composed?" (4–5; emphasis mine).

Latour's call has much in common with such previous versions of postcriticism,[3] especially in terms of invention and production over negative models of critique. But Latour and other actor-network theorists want to extend our concern with objects and the material world further into constructivist and compositionist practices and interventions. In seeing anthropology and history at the center of academic or knowledge work, at the center of constructivist makings that are fundamentally historical and contingent, Latour extends the invention of texts into the coproduction of objects. Latour writes, "Now, on the contrary, it is an *experimental scene* that produces and shapes our new actants that then increase the long list of ingredients that make up our world. Historicity is back and it flows from the experiments, from the trials of force" (*We Have Never Been Modern* 12; emphasis mine). In short, epistemology and ontology are collapsed—research produces new actants rather than reports on preexistent objects or subjects. This, as Ulmer suggests, puts a particular emphasis on material intervention and change, but disrupts a progressive model of research that seeks specific, predetermined outcomes. As a function of experimentation, the outcome is always variable within a range of possibilities. As Simmons, Moore, and Sullivan argue, Latour's approach is grounded in uncertainties and researchers should "resist articulating methods that either trap us in their certainties or draw overly stable portraits" ("Tracing Uncertainties" 276). The goal is not to produce reliable conclusions but to engage in experimentation and coproduce a version of the object of study.

Katrina Powell and Pamela Takayoshi's introduction to *Practicing Research in Writing Studies* aims for a more open orientation to research into composition and rhetoric but without this emphasis on ontology. On the one hand, they are no longer trying to stabilize the discipline as Stephen North did by breaking the quantitative/qualitative divide into experimental, clinical, formal, and ethnographic practices. They look to broaden the concept of research and call to be more self-reflexive about how composition and composition scholarship might impact not only our academic discipline but also the communities our research engages. On the other hand, while Powell and Takayoshi invoke Karen Barad's diffractive methodology, they don't draw out its fuller implications. Much of the collection hangs on critical self-reflection of research practices and the ethics of engaging research subjects without extending diffraction into the coproduction of research objects. This continued emphasis on conscious critical awareness and self-reflexivity keeps them from going all the way into ontology with Barad, which is precisely what is at the heart of Barad's notion of diffraction.

Barad grounds her approach, not unlike Ulmer's, in a practice of juxtaposition and invention. She writes, "Based on a 'diffractive' methodological approach, I read insights from . . . different areas of study through one another" (*Meeting the Universe Halfway* 25). What is critical, however, is that this model of relays doesn't stop at epistemology or the productions of texts, ideas, or concepts. This research method "suggests a fundamental inseparability of epistemological, ontological, and ethical considerations" (26). Barad is explicitly arguing against representationalism that posits a separation between subjects and objects of study, the one reflecting on and properly representing the other. Instead, she opts for a performative understanding of research that focuses on conditions and effects of "practices, doings, and actions" (28). Research produces performative accounts that are not separate from the objects of study but entangled with them. Barad juxtaposes the physical aspects of diffraction with her approach to method to produce an account of it. She writes, "Diffraction is a phenomenon that is unique to wave behavior. Water waves exhibit diffraction patterns, as do sound waves, and light waves. Diffraction has to do with the way waves combine when they overlap and the apparent bending and spreading out of waves when they encounter an obstruction" (28). The simplest image of this phenomenon is ripples in the water that disseminate, overlap, break, and dissipate. What is central for Barad is seeing this behavior as fundamental to all matter. Light waves, for example, act as waves under certain conditions of diffraction and as particles under others. The same goes for electrons. The takeaway is that conditions of diffraction coproduce a version of the electrons or light waves, which is the ontological basis of reality in performativity—conditions and effects through practices, doings, and actions.

Barad turns this paradox of matter into an approach to methodology, contrasting it explicitly with reflection. Reflection or reflexivity "is about mirroring and sameness, diffraction attends to difference" (29). Reflection assumes a fixed position from which to envision, critique, and represent. Diffraction attends to the processes of small differences that entangle concepts and materials, both displacing and coproducing that researcher's position at any given moment as particle or wave and doing the same for the object under examination. A diffractive methodology, in other words, is more attuned to the entanglement of epistemology and ontology. In *Aircraft Stories*, Law takes up both reflexivity and performativity in relation to a planned aircraft that was never built. He argues that the plan nevertheless "performed social distributions" (7). In contrast to models of representation, he writes, "The alternative is to imagine, reflexively, that telling stories about the world also helps perform that world. This means that in a (writing) performance reality is staged. And such a staging ensures that, everything else being equal, what is being performed is thereby rendered more obdurate, more solid, more real than it might otherwise have been. It becomes an element of the present that may be carried into the future" (6). Any moment of reflexivity or reflection coproduces both subject and object in any performative moment of circulation. Research and writing all help perform the aircraft and all of its distributed effects, producing a version of the object of study as a quasi-object.

Just as Serres's model functions as a relay, theories, methods, and objects of study all function as coproductive mediators in relation to each other. Research under such a model would look to trace these transductions. But it is also a mediating translation that both transduces and diffracts as it records traces in new media, expanding and extending new versions of the object of study. Following this circulation looks like Jenny Rice's rhetorical life of an ecology. In "Unframing Models of Public Distribution," she argues that rhetorical ecologies are spaces where affective and embodied experiences circulate and operate as an emergent system—like the weather they can be predictable in some ways but unpredictable in others because they are in a continual process of change and every encounter with other variables changes the conditions of possibility of the system throughout the life of a text's circulation. Her case study, the "Keep Austin Weird" campaign, started as a bumper sticker to support local businesses; then migrated to T-shirts of other businesses; transformed over the course of a number of years to pledging campaigns for public radio, various tote bags, mugs, and billboards; and then it began to shift to other causes—becoming a central focus of a white paper on city politics; functioning in support of UT liberals arts; and by the end of its circulatory life, ironically ending up as an advertising slogan for Cingular Wireless. Following Deleuze and Guattari's conceptual metaphor of a virus migrating between baboons and cats and evolving in an aparallel manner, she argues that what is carried through the rhetorical life of "Keep Austin Weird" is not the same text "but certain contagions and energy" (14). Rice brings to light multiple eventual encounters that coproduce and transform the text and its shifting materiality, the difficulties any author would have producing consistent effects, and, by implication, the complexities researchers cut into in order to trace these transductions and produce an account.

Starting with composition in a recording studio, I trace the circulation, transduction, and diffraction of sound waves and the inscriptions they coproduce as the basis for understanding research and method as coparticipants in the production of quasi-objects grounded in the energies of the virtual. For Deleuze and Guattari, "recording" is something that happens all the way through a process, not just at the end. The engagement of virtual potential by intensive processes produces traces, inscriptions, leaving records of their transduction and coproduction (*Anti-Oedipus*, 10–16). To record—through the studio or through research—is to coproduce these traces, marks on the tesserae, mediations that continually generate new versions of the objects of study. Using Latour's key terms from "Mixing Humans and Nonhumans Together" as "descriptive tools" for this process—scripts, descriptions, inscriptions, prescriptions, preinscriptions, and chreods—the researcher's primary role becomes to record further inscriptions, and ultimately generate one that resonates with the object of study, coproduces another version of it, and opens it to further modes of relationality.

PREINSCRIPTIONS—TRANSLATION AS TRANSDUCTION

In order to trace these transductions, Brian Harmon and I traveled to Dallas, Texas, and spent five days in Sonic Dropper Studios documenting the band New Magnetic North as they began a recording session along with interviewing Jim King, the owner of the studio and the album's producer. The trip was an experiment in deploying the practices of documentary filmmaking as a research method for investigating sound recording as a form of material composition. There is a burgeoning maker culture that ran through everything about the sessions, from the world of boutique electronics—studio rack effects, guitar effects pedals, and guitar amps—all the way up to independent studios themselves like Sonic Dropper. In our daylong interview with King, he walked us through his ongoing project of building the studio—the physical acoustics, the architectural construction techniques, and the electrical engineering behind his efforts. If someone wanted to build a studio in past decades, they would have hired a person with a degree in architecture and a specialty in acoustics to design and build the studio, along with a series of contractors. Today, with the decline of corporate money in the recording industry and the rise of digital technologies for recording, building studios is largely becoming a DIY-maker effort. There is a big market for learning how to do this—books, manuals, websites, blogs, and YouTube video tutorials.[4] Most of King's knowledge comes from years of practice and experience recording and extensive independent research online and through books. This *ethos* extends to the recording itself. The premise behind the studio's construction is to achieve the best raw analog sound as possible through the sound of the room, the guitars, amps, and drums themselves, along with various specialized microphones, and to manipulate the signals with boutique, analog studio effects rather than plug-ins—digital programs that simulate analog effects—before the tracks go into the digital recorder.[5] This production, circulation, and manipulation of sound in a recording studio coproduces relations among sound waves, electronic circuits, walls, and sound's reverberation on a model of Latour's translation of energy, force, or action through mediation. The studio is built solely to produce the preinscribed conditions of possibility for such a series of transductions.

In "Mixing Humans and Nonhumans Together," Latour offers a research method and vocabulary for tracing the compositional practices and processes of an office space that provides a model for researching the recording the studio. Latour examines the office as an actor-network by focusing on a door closer as a coproductive mediator. He traces the conditions of possibility for the door closer from the building of walls, to the cutting of holes in the walls for access, to the invention of doors to shift between wall and hole, to the invention of the hinge and pin to transition more easily from hole to wall, to the concierge who makes sure the door is consistently opened and closed, to the addition of a spring on the door to automatically pull it shut, and finally to the hydraulic door closer that absorbs the *energy* produced when humans open the door and then slowly releases it to close the door. For

Latour, this shift from maximum to minimum effort is a form of *translation*, circulating energy back and forth through human and nonhuman actions.[6] In order to trace these translations, he proposes a double-entry notebook as a basic research method: in the left column, list the work needed in order to accomplish the task without the door closer; in the right column, list the work needed with the door closer. The notebook is used to trace these actions and follow the reversals of forces in order to understand the social context of the office as an actor-network. The door produces an "obligatory passage point" that does not rely on what humans feel or think but on the material persuasion that channels humans through the door's pathway multiple times a day to give it their energy (302). This series of delegations of action through various actors such as hinges, springs, and hydraulic pistons circulates energy that coproduces material networks and grounds social action.

In addition to the double-entry notebook, Latour provides a series of key terms to use as "descriptive tools" for tracing these networks: *scripts, descriptions, inscriptions, prescriptions, preinscriptions*, and *chreods. Scripts* are the typical protocols embedded in or made possible by a scene or scenario in which translations are played out by humans and nonhumans. Most of these scripts are silent: intrasomatic like Foucault's discipline or extrasomatic like Heidegger's conditions of possibility. *Descriptions* are the retrieval of the script, path, or protocol from the scene by a researcher, which is not a neutral representation of the scene but a de-*script*ion that produces a version of the script via discourse. These descriptions are neither a function of the author nor the scene but are also actors in a series of translations—they define actors; endow them with capacities or affordances; make them do things; and evaluate their effects and affects. *Inscriptions* are the translations or transfers of the script from a provisional, less reliable version or medium to a longer-lasting or more durable one—a user manual for a practitioner, or a traffic light for a policeman, or a door closer for a concierge, or ultimately a book for a researcher. *Prescriptions* are whatever the scene prescribes for the actors—like "roles" in sociological theory but built materially into the scene. Latour's examples are the functions of perspective in Renaissance painting prescribed by intersecting lines; traffic lights that prescribe traffic rhythms; or computer users who are free to surf the web but prescribed through protocols. Prescriptions are not necessarily determinate: both humans and nonhumans might not follow the script, like hackers or a broken door closer. *Preinscription* is "all of the work that has been done upstream of the scene, and all of the things assimilated by the actor (human or nonhuman) before coming to the scene" (307). Preinscription *necessarily* includes both human and nonhuman. A researcher can always zoom in to only look at human-human or nonhuman-nonhuman prescriptions, but scaling out preinscription always encounters the mixing of humans and nonhumans.[7] Finally, the entire range of preinscription's tacit setup forms *chreods* or "necessary paths"—a gradient of aligned arrangements that endow scenes with the preinscribed capacities to find their users: people effortlessly flow through the door and energy regularly circulates through the door closer hundreds of times a day. Latour writes, "The result of such an alignment of set-ups is to decrease the number of occasions in which words are used; most of the actions become silent, familiar, incorporated (in human or nonhuman bodies)" (308)—they become tacit habits of a refrain.

Latour's "Door-Closer" provides a model for mapping the actions and relays of forces in the studio as translations of energy. Preinscriptions, chreods, and prescriptions are what Latour follows in order to produce descriptions of scripts that function as new inscriptions—versions of the script that translate material relations of actor-networks into a new medium—such as academic research. Latour's translation of energy is precisely what happens with the circulation of sound waves in the studio, where mediation is a form of material persuasion that channels and transforms the flows and transductions of energy. A big part of the *script* or protocols for this transduction emerges through building the studio and assembling electronics as a part of *preinscription* that produces *chreods*. King's experiential history of performing, recording, and engineering, and all of the work gone into designing and building the studio as a containment shell of walls and diffusers for sound should be understood as preinscriptive work upstream of the recording. Once the studio is built it is filled with amps, mics, cables, a soundboard, and a computer as pathways or *chreods* that the sound waves follow for their mediation, translation, and diffraction, all of which set the conditions of possibility for enaction—the band setting up to perform, doing sound checks, and recording tracks. Initially the *prescriptive* role of nonhumans in the studio could be seen as opening circuits, and the role of humans as to completing circuits—from the circuits made possible through the networks of cables and technologies to the gestures of humans that connect them through performance. But the slightest notion of feedback can flip these roles into a recognition that the role of mediators—human and nonhuman—is to both open and close circuits in a network, transducing energy like the opening and closing of the door. *Inscription* is ultimately what recording does: it translates the energy of the waves and inscribes it into a newer, sturdier medium—a digital version of sound that eventually gets translated into a file format such as an MP3. These four aspects of the network together produce the *script*, but researching in the studio during this process breaks into this energy flow and coproduces an ulterior inscription: a *description* is coproduced that generates a new version of the production, circulation, and diffraction of sound, a version of the studio as a quasi-object.

Preinscription in studio construction creates the conditions for the transduction of wave energy. Sound collapses matter and energy into a wave that moves through the air, and studio design is geared toward containing these waves and reducing the vibrations they create. In our interview, Jim notes that the first aim in studio acoustics is to control the sound with a "containment shell" to keep the sound of the instruments from going out of the room. When building a home studio, such as Jim's, designers especially want to keep the sound from getting to the neighbor's house, but in all studios the sound needs to be kept from traveling room to room: the tracking room, the main room for drums and performance; the control room, the room where the engineer mixes the tracks; and isolation booths, rooms for isolating guitar amps and vocal performances. In addition to keeping the sound in the room to avoid recording ancillary noise, containment shells are built to reduce structure-borne vibrations. "It's all about energy," Jim says. "Sound is a form of energy, . . . and when the sound hits the wall it excites it [Jim makes a back-and-forth movement with his hand] especially low frequencies, and that's mainly what we are trying to contain. Low frequencies get things moving in a microscopic way, you don't see it happening." There is a difference between reverb, where higher frequencies reflect back from a surface such as a wall, and resonance, where lower frequencies vibrate an object such as a wall, reiterating, amplifying, or extending the vibrations. Jim notes, "Sound is the excitation of molecules going through the air. The air is not traveling through the wall. [The wall] is re-radiating [the excitation]. It's more like the wall is becoming a speaker." Depending on the material qualities of an object or surface, especially its structural capacities for movement or vibration, sound will be filtered out and reflected back into the room, or the wave will move the material and activate its own natural capacity for vibration, its *becoming-speaker*, which creates a resonant, sustained "ringing" of the original tone or frequency.

Jim uses a comparison between acoustics and optics to explain how sound responds differently to three different types of surfaces that designers use to build containment shells.[8] First, hard surfaces—drywall, glass, wood, tile, stone—are specular reflectors. The sound waves bounce off them just like light waves. Jim explains, "The way sound behaves at higher frequencies is very much like light. So, if the 'angle of incidence' is coming in at a 30-degree angle at this [hard] surface, and you take a perpendicular plane, when it hits that point it will bounce away at a 30-degree angle." Studio designers actually use flashlights to literally see where the sound waves are going to be deflected. This helps control the sound qualities by directing the waves away from key areas of the room where performers or engineers need optimal sound. Too much uncontrolled reflection sounds too noisy or chaotic; too little reflection makes the room sound unnatural, as if the listener is in a vacuum. Second, soft surfaces absorb sound. Insulation, foam, or fiberglass boards all absorb and dampen sound waves. The compressed fiberglass often includes resin, which makes the boards denser so that they absorb more of the waves' energy and less gets deflected back into the room. Increasing the mass of both hard and soft surfaces is critical for more absorption. Unlike light and higher frequencies, Jim notes, "Low frequency wave forms are so huge that they have the tendency to engulf everything or go around anything. That is why you hear people in their cars blasting boom bass. The lower frequencies aren't deflected. They just roll on through." Since low frequency waves are so long, it takes more mass to absorb them. Third, striated or staggered surfaces diffuse sound. Again, like light, sound waves can be broken up so that they don't reflect back in a specific path, which creates a softer, ambient quality to the sound rather than a harsher ringing. Diffusers are often large, shallow boxes that can be hung on walls or used as mobile walls strategically placed around a room. One-dimensional diffusers have multiple vertical or horizontal planes running across them. Two-dimensional diffusers have vertical and horizontal planes to create a grid of smaller boxes, each with varying depths to create more diffusion.

In Sonic Dropper, Jim utilizes all of these containment strategies and types of surfaces in both the tracking room and, more importantly, the control room. In the main tracking room—the living room of the house he is turning into a studio—Jim contains sound with a combination of mass and air space. People playing in their garage often put up foam on the walls, which will dampen some high frequencies but will let the low end of the kick drum or bass guitar go right through. So in his studio, Jim added mass to the walls. He took down the original one-half-inch drywall, since the house was built in the 1940s, and put up a new layer of five-eighth-inch drywall. Jim continues, "Then I used a product called Green Glue. . . . This is called a 'viscous elastic damping compound.' Basically, this is like rubber cement that never dries. . . . It is very low viscosity. But when it cures and dries it stays like a rubber cement. It's really flexible." The Green Glue goes on the backside of a second layer of five-eighth-inch drywall and further dampens or reduces structure-borne vibrations. It essentially adds more mass while using less material and taking up less space.[9] The windows are harder to add mass to, but if the walls are built for containment and the windows aren't, the sound waves simply go out the window. To add more mass, Jim built his own window frames so he could set two pieces of glass in them. The outside panes are traditional glass, but the inside panes are laminated safety glass—two pieces of quarter-inch glass glued together with a clear vinyl membrane in between them. The safety glass will break if hit hard enough but won't shatter. Jim explains, "The lamination is basically a vinyl film that is like double-sided tape that [is used] to glue glass together. So, the more times you do that, the more density you get, and the deader it is." While created for safety reasons, safety glass also has sound properties. When hit, the safety glass makes a thud, whereas traditional glass makes a ping. The vinyl lamination adds mass to the hard surface of the window and creates a duller sound.[10]

Managing the air space between walls, panes of glass, and fiberglass boards is also a critical technique in terms of isolation. When designers build commercial studios in larger spaces, they typically build double walls. They put a wall in each room and make sure there is an inch-and-a half or two-inch space between them so they don't touch and vibrate each other. This is called "decoupling." While Jim's studio is too small to apply this principle to the walls, he does use it on the windows and bass traps. The double-paned windows allow him to control the amount of air space between them and reduce their transfer of wave energy. Bass traps—in Jim's studio, tall, thin, ten- to twelve-inch padded, triangular fiberglass boxes that fit into the corners of the tracking room behind the drums—also use air space to trap waves. Jim explains:

> Bass trapping works like a vacuum cleaner. It helps suck up and absorb low-end frequency energy.... The thicker it is, the lower the frequency it will absorb. One of the huge things that they discovered is that if you space the stuff off the wall ... the bass frequencies are going through the fiberglass, hitting the wall, and then coming back out.... It's passing through the fiberglass two times by putting an air gap behind it. So, you're getting double the absorption or trapping. If it didn't absorb it, then the low end would just be booming in the room. The sound waves wouldn't have anywhere to go.

When combined with fiberglass boards on the walls and diffusers around the room, the tracking room is a solid containment shell that keeps the sound in the room and produces quality sound for the performers.

It is most critical, however, to manage sound waves in the control room, where the sound engineer sits in front of a mixing board, computer interface, and two speaker monitors and needs to hear the best possible version of the sounds being generated in the tracking room. If the engineer only hears a jumble of sound waves bouncing all around the control room, then there would be too much noise to hear the music properly and create a quality mix for the final inscription into a CD or MP3. Designers want to deflect, absorb, and diffuse most of the sound waves reverberating and resonating through the room to create a "reflection-free zone" or "sweet spot" in front of the mixing board. The tweeters from the control room speakers are aimed at this spot to create a "direct path" for the music from the speaker to the engineer, which produces the best conditions for making judgments about mixing the song. The main thing designers want to get rid of is the "first reflection path." Sound waves pass by the sweet spot, hit the side or back walls or the ceiling and bounce back to the sweet spot. The direct path from the speaker might be eight feet. The first reflection might travel twelve feet to the wall and another six feet to get back to the sweet spot. The different distances mean that the waves are arriving at different times. Because sound is a wave with a positive and negative point (a peak and a depth), arriving at different times—even only milliseconds—can get the waves out of phase. When the same sound arrives at different times, one at the top of its wave and the other at the bottom of its wave, they cancel each other out, producing a very unnatural sound—with no reverb in the room at all, the music would sound like it is happening in a vacuum. Too much sound bouncing back to the engineer from around the room will disrupt

FIGURE 3.1.   Jim King in the control room's "sweet spot."

the sound coming out of the speakers directly, but if all of the reverberation is completely eliminated, then this isn't a good environment for mixing either.

So, sound designers often splay or angle the walls in a control room to deflect the sound to the back of the room and create the reflection-free zone. Since Jim's control room—built into a smaller bedroom—isn't splayed, he primarily relies on absorption and diffusion to manage the control room.[11] For high-end frequencies, the front of the room is heavily treated with fiberglass boards and dense cloth for absorption, and the back wall has a large, vertical one-dimensional diffuser. This allows the sound to stay in the room rather than pass through the walls, but it no longer directly reflects back to the "sweet spot" in front of the board. Engineers in the mix position get a direct, clean sound from the monitor speakers, while diffused and diffracted waves behind them arrive later from a number of different directions, which creates an almost pleasing, natural ambient sound. Low frequencies are, of course, a different matter. On low frequencies such as twenty or thirty hertz, wavelengths are ten and twenty feet long, often longer than a small control room, so bass waves are more likely to pass right through the walls. The low frequencies that do stay in the room tend to build up in the back of the room, so Jim set up bass traps in the corners of the ceiling made of fiberglass with dense insulation in the middle. Designers also use "limp mass membranes" for more bass absorption and energy transfer. This is a rubber membrane suspended loosely in a framework behind the wall that is easily excited by low frequencies. Jim explains further:

> If you've ever taken a piece of sheet metal and held it up and banged on it, it sounds like a thunderstorm, but it also has a lot of low frequencies in it too, like a low thunder rumble. There is a lot of internal, natural low-frequency resonance within it. If you take that metal plate and get it excited by these low frequencies, it's going to vibrate. If it is vibrating, it is basically transferring energy. . . . It is basically converting that energy into heat. . . . It transfers it from acoustic waves to heat and that's how it absorbs it.

Suspending the rubber membranes inside a wall absorbs and dissipates the long bass wave, allowing less of its energy to pass through or be reflected back into the room. And the material properties of the membranes also reduce the internal wall resonance, the properties of the wall itself that allow it to vibrate with energy. Each of these encounters between a wave and a surface absorbs and releases energy—like the door closer—in order to control noise in the studio. Noise is ultimately the basis of the studio's preinscription, which is set up to transduce noise into sound up through to its transduction into a recorded inscription and, in this case, eventually into a researcher's account.

CHREODS—DIFFRACTION AND CIRCUITS

Once the containment shell is built, it also has to be filled with electronics to further narrow sound's possible pathways. The sound waves circulating through the studio are changed with every deflection, resound, or absorption, altering the structure of the wave and the qualities of the sound, which are especially at play as the waves are translated into electronic signals, channeled through the chreods or pathways assembled in the studio, manipulated with electronic processors and effects, and combined or layered through the mixing board or digital interface. This process is what Karen Barad calls diffraction. In *Meeting the Universe Halfway*, Barad uses diffraction in three ways: literally as an aspect of quantum and physical reality, metaphorically as a theoretical concept for engaging arguments in science studies and cultural theory, and methodologically to develop her own approach to research. In terms of physics, diffraction is an important phenomenon in both the classical and quantum paradigms. Diffraction appears in classical physics through research on light waves and in quantum physics in the wave versus particle debates on the nature of light and matter that remake the classical model. Diffraction in the classical paradigm deals with "the way waves combine when they overlap and the apparent bending and spreading of waves that occur when they encounter an obstruction" (74). Barad gives three basic examples: water, sound, and light. When ocean waves hit a breaker, such as a wall with a hole or wedge in it, the energy of the wave is channeled through the hole, and the parallel wave emerges and spreads out from the hole in a fan-like pattern of concentric half circles. Similarly, when a person speaks into a cardboard tube, the sound waves emerging from the other end spread out in all directions, filling the room in an overlapping pattern of waves. And when passing through a slit in a wall or partition, light waves bend, producing a pattern of alternating bright and dark lines, which people don't always recognize in everyday contexts because light sources such as a bulb create multiple diffusion patterns that overlap, canceling out the dark lines to create softer ambient light.

Importantly, classical physics makes a distinction between particles and waves. Particles are material entities that occupy a point in space. Waves are disturbances through a medium—water, air, electromagnetic fields—that cannot be localized in the same way. Unlike particles, waves can overlap on the same point in space, combining their amplitudes to compose a different waveform or diffusion pattern. Waves can combine at their peaks, producing a larger wave with more energy and intensity; or, as Jim discussed with sound waves getting out of phase, they can combine at a peak and a trough and cancel each other out into relative calm with low to minimal intensity; or a crest and trough can meet successively, producing alternating waves in a classic diffraction pattern. Standing on a pontoon dock, for example, a person could feel the strong wave, the milder calm, or the oscillating waves. Barad notes the example of a two-slit experiment with monochromatic light: one barrier with a single slit and a second barrier with a double slit. The light projected on the back screen exhibits a similar diffraction pattern with alternating bands of bright and dark areas, where the bright areas are two waves meeting at a peak and the dark areas are two waves canceling each other out. The intensity of the waves concentrates at the center of the screen and fades away toward its edges. The patterns produced through these kinds of experiments depend on specific features such as wavelength, width and number of slits, and the distance between slits or partitions.[12] In each case, the result is the sum of the effects of each wave, a combination of their disturbances, which is called "superposition" (76)—overlapping entanglement at the same point in space. "Physicists," then, "understand diffraction as the result of superposition or interference of waves" (78–79). Some distinguish between diffraction (the bending or spreading of waves when encountering an obstacle) and interference (when two or more waves overlap). But for Barad, following Richard Feynman, both result in superposition, so she uses them interchangeably.

According to classical physics, only waves produce diffraction; particles do not since they can't occupy the same space at the same time, which is of course problematized by quantum physics. The key turn toward quantum physics was discovering that matter—electrons, neutrons, atoms—could function like waves.[13] Under certain conditions, they produced diffraction patterns. In a two-slit experiment, such as the two holes in the water break, particles hit a back screen in an alternating pattern similar to the bright and dark lines produced in experiments with light. Studies showed that even when particles are let through the break one at a time, they still produce the diffraction pattern (81). Simply put, "diffraction patterns are evidence of superposition" (83), which makes more sense when talking about waves rather than particles. But for Barad, even though further experiments attempted to sort out various aspects of the "wave-particle paradox," diffraction is fundamental to materiality (83). To clarify this takeaway from quantum physics, Barad makes the distinction between geometrical optics and physical optics as analogous to classical and quantum physics. Geometrical optics treats light as a "ray" that only indicates direction and is only interested in charting its path or its optics. The nature of light is "of no consequence" (85). Physical optics is concerned both with the techniques for studying light and light itself: light is both a tool and an *object of inquiry*. Geometrical optics "works well when the wavelength is small compared with the physical dimensions of the objects it is interacting with, such as the size of a slit that the light passes through" (85). If the wavelength is small compared to the slit, the diffraction pattern will be too small to notice. Geometrical optics, in other words, is accurate at a certain level of scale. It becomes a shortcut approximation that is useful when wavelengths happen to be small relative to the dimensions of the experiment. Similarly, classical physics or Newtonian mechanics produces workable results under certain conditions at certain levels of scale. However, if the wavelength is the same size or larger than the slit, the diffraction effects can no longer be ignored and requires the mathematics of physical optics to account for the diffraction. For Barad, quantum mechanics is a fuller theory that, like physical optics, accounts for the phenomena at all levels of scale or wavelength, not just at a certain scale or under limited conditions (85).

Diffraction, in short, is the combination of two or more waves encountering and entangling to coproduce a new wave pattern and redistribution of energy. Barad makes clear, though not necessarily in these terms, that this isn't a Hegelian synthesis into a new entity but that the waves literally overlap in the same space, retaining a version of themselves while coproducing at the same time a version that combines them into a new pattern (Barad 417n7). Following quantum physics and the analogy to physical optics, Barad wants to expand this sense of diffraction as superposition and entanglement to matter itself at all levels of scale and to all material encounters, not just wave phenomena or microscopic particles. In the chapter introducing diffraction, Barad notes that she uses diffraction literally, metaphorically, and methodologically, and it seems clear at this stage of the book that her suggested elevation of quantum mechanics to all levels of scale and ethical aspects of social relations remains metaphorical. The rest of the book, however, is her further development of the concept to increasingly move it from the metaphorical to the literal use at all levels. Barad notes that she is looking to go beyond Haraway's more metaphorical use of diffraction. But the issue is far from settled in the disciplinary world of physicists, many of whom are working on alternate theories and models that will show how classical physics can account for quantum phenomenon or at what level of scale or mass quantum mathematics are no longer predictive and the use of classical physics is required.[14] At its root, physicists can't fully account for entanglement. Their mathematical models can predict how change in one particle can effect another particle at significant distances but can't show the full nature of that relationship through experiments. At the very least, however, diffraction is a better methodological metaphor than reflection or reflexivity. It carries with it the recognition that research is coproductive of reality and allows for a stronger ontological basis and a closer tie to materialist thinking.[15]

Jim's work on the containment shell of the studio diffracts and combines waves mechanically, but all of the electronics assembled in the containment shell transduce the energy into electronic and digital signals that allow for more complex forms of diffraction. For this recording session with New Magnetic North, which is focused on recording drum tracks, there are twenty-one total microphones in the tracking room: two mics on the two guitar cabinets (one in the kitchen off of the main tracking room, and one in the isolation booth); one microphone for vocals; a direct input for the bass guitar; and seventeen total mics for drums: one on the high hat, five on toms (one each), two condenser mics for overhead (stereo cymbals), one for general overhead, two on snare (top and bottom), two on bass drums (inside and outside), two in back of the tracking room, and two around the corner in the bathroom to pick up delayed reverb. Contemporary techniques for miking drums emphasize having direct mics within a few inches of the source—drumhead, cymbal, and so forth. On the snare, Jim has a top mic to capture the "crack" of the snare head and a mic on the bottom to capture the buzz of the wires that run across the bottom of the snare. On the kick drum there is a mic outside on the drumhead and one inside of the drum. The inside mic is capturing the snap of the beater and the outside mic is capturing the boom and fullness of the kick drum. In addition to direct mics, Jim places overheads above the drums, one

FIGURE 3.2. Bass trap, diffuser, and overhead mics in a "cardio" pattern.

main mic and two stereo condenser mics that are predominantly capturing the cymbals but are also capturing an overall stereo mix of the drums—one mic points down to the left side of the kit, the other to the right. Jim explains, "This is what they would call a cone-sided pair of mics—they are relatively close to each other [and make an upside-down V shape to the left and right] so that the multiple sources from each drum arrive at the mics at the same time, which means that they'll have 'phase coherency.'"[16] The mic between the overheads literally fills in the middle of the stereo image. It is set up in a "cardio" or heart-shaped pattern (<3 but like an upside-down V) so that it is open to the sound waves coming from below and rejects the sound waves bouncing back from the ceiling. Jim also has two ribbon mics in the back of the tracking room set up in a "Blumlein array" or figure eight. They are both pointed toward the front corners of the room and the drums and toward the back corners of the room to capture a stereo recording of the drums and the reverb from the back corners.[17]

All of these mics in the tracking room are fed into the control room, which is the heart of the studio: all of the electronic signals from the mics are channeled into the control room, diffracted electronically, and channeled back out into speakers and headphones. The basic signal flow in the control room is into the patch bay→preamp→dynamics processors→analog to digital converter→computer/DAW→mixing board→digital to analog converter→and back out to the speakers in the control room and the headphones in the tracking room. The *patch bay* is an electronic rack mounted unit with a number of jacks, usually of the same type, for connecting and routing circuits and interconnecting devices. Jim has sixteen lines coming from the "snake"—the large collection of all of the cables coming from the tracking room—into the patch bay. Each input can be automatically linked to an internal preamp within the patch bay or channeled out to external preamps or other processors and then back into the patch bay. *Preamplifiers* boost a small electrical signal to prepare it for further amplification or processing without significantly degrading the signal-to-noise ratio. The microphone preamp is necessary because the low voltage output of the moving coil, diaphragm, or transducer on the mics needs to be boosted to a higher amplitude to be processed by other devices and ultimately recorded. After the preamp, for example, Jim routes the signal to an equalizer, which is a form of dynamics *processor*, "to manipulate the sound in the analog domain before it is converted to digital for recording." An equalizer essentially has frequency-specific volume knobs used to adjust the amplitude of audio signals at particular frequencies.[18] Jim notes that other producers will run the signal right out of the preamp and into digital recorders to produce the mix, but he uses external boutique analog equipment to its fullest potential before the signals are digitized.

After analog processing, the signals go through an *analog-to-digital converter* (ADC) that converts a continuous voltage signal to a digital number that represents the volt's amplitude and prepares it to be modified and recorded digitally. The ADC stereo output is connected to a PCI card in the computer, which works with the *digital audio workstation* (DAW). The DAW is a computer software application for recording, editing, and producing audio files with a central interface that allows the user to alter and layer multiple recorded tracks into a final version of the song. Every signal comes into its own individual track that is displayed as a waveform and can be manipulated in the software interface that simulates a traditional mixing board and with various plug-in programs that simulate analog dynamics processing.[19] In addition to the DAW, Jim's studio has a physical mixing board that is locked with the software interface and allows him to control the computer manually.[20] A manipulable control surface has knobs and sliders that allow users to do things more easily than the computer alone or that the computer can't do alone. The mouse, for example, only lets users manipulate one thing at a time. With the mixing board, Jim can move multiple sliders at a time or move sliders and knobs with two hands and various fingers. There are two basic ways to set the DAW to mixing-board interface: one makes the digital console the primary source of the mix, and the software is just feeding the tracks to it; the other sets up the console to simply manipulate the software, leaving the software as the primary source of the mix. Jim primarily does the latter. Otherwise he would have to work the software with the mouse and the keyboard, which is much more cumbersome than the traditional manual interface (especially for people like Jim who grew up using analog technology—he sees this as much more "intuitive"). Finally the signal is channeled to a *digital-to-analog converter* (DAC) that converts the binary digital data back into an analog signal (current, voltage, or electric charge) and runs to the monitor speakers in the control room and to the cue box that allows the volume of multiple headphones to be controlled separately for musicians performing in the tracking room.[21]

This signal flow transduces the energy of the sound waves into electrical signals, channels it through multiple chreods and a series of coproductive diffractions that modulate it through analog and digital means, and releases it back out into sound waves through a final transduction. This basic map of the signal flow belies the potential for additional feedback loops in the signal pathway. Jim initially mixes the signal just after digital conversion using the faders in the DAW to boost the volume levels and digital plug-ins—miniprograms or algorithms that are digital versions of analog effects—to manipulate the sound. But he also channels the digital signal back into analog for further processing. He uses a digital-to-analog converter connected to an analog summing system so he can send the digital signal back to an analog compressor or EQ and then back to the summing system, which converts multiple analog signals back into a two-track digital stereo mix that he can bring back into the digital workstation. Then the two-channel stereo mix can also be processed in a number of ways to produce the final mix.[22] During the final mixdown, Jim takes that stereo mix and runs it through an analog compressor and a Millennia STT—an EQ, compressor, and mic preamp in one unit—that is modified with step "attenuators." An attenuator is a type of converter that is the opposite of an amplifier: it reduces the power of a signal, or the amplitude of a wave, without overly distorting its waveform. He uses these primarily for the stereo EQs and the compressor unit, and then has another rack with an EQ, compressors, and a boutique ADC that digitizes all of that additional sound manipulation so it can go back to the workstation. Jim notes that these feedback loops allow him to mix in a "hybrid analog-digital realm" where he can "utilize...the digital plug-ins in the workstation and send the signals out to these high-end boutique analog processors and combine all of that into a stereo mix" that he can also process.[23]

Analog processors add more sonic complexity to the signal because their circuits are nonlinear and unpredictable. Each particular transistor, capacitor, resistor and the transformer of the analog unit operates uniquely, and each transduction from one to the other operates nonlinearly. As Jim puts it, the sound comes from the "composition of all of it." Even though certain parts of the unit might be static, putting them all together in a certain way creates emergent changes that can't be derived deductively and modeled digitally. Jim recounts, "In the early days of digital plug-ins, it was precisely this nonlinearity that they overlooked. . . . The nonlinear characteristics are in the circuitry of the device. . . . In the last couple of years everybody is waiting on them, all the plug-in creators, to make a better tape machine emulation. And that's a very highly nonlinear system. You've got motors that are speeding up and slowing down, you've got different brands of tape [that have different characteristics]. . . . The technology is changing in those regards all of the time."[24] Jim pulls up a kick drum track and starts playing with the "hum," "hiss," "wow," and "flutter" dials on his tape machine digital plug-in. The flutter in particular tries to model the "waver" of the analog tape machine, speeding up and slowing down. There is even a "tape delay" button. And he can crank up the knobs to try and emulate distortion. "What all of this comes down to," Jim continues, "is the distortion characteristics of the transformers, the tape itself, and the circuits. The distortion and harmonics that are generated by the circuits." Modelers can create a digital EQ that has none of the hiss or distortion of an analog unit, and sometimes that cleanness is desirable. But when all of those digital simulations are added up, they lose the "warmth" of the analog machine and the music doesn't sound as natural as it used to. Distortion, originally, was a function of analog nonlinearity, pushing the tubes and speakers beyond where they were meant to go and getting an unanticipated sound or sonic quality out of it. Analog equipment heats up, and when it does it gets different sounds. The physical change in the technology itself as it heats up through use and the energy circulating through it unpredictably transduces and diffracts sounds.

David King, Jim's brother who owns the boutique guitar amp company Naylor Engineering, outlined these diffractive circuits in the amps he builds. Brian and I spent an afternoon with David in his shop tracing his building process and talking about electronics and analog circuits. David's basic building process is to "populate" the amp's chassis with knobs, pots, and wires; build the circuit board by installing the eyelet, soldering in components (capacitors, resistors), and connecting the soldering with wires; and to wire the board to the chassis and solder them. Finally, he tests everything to see if the voltages and bias work, leaving it for a "burning period," letting it sit and run to make sure the tubes are good. The interesting thing is not just the chreods built into the electronics but what happens to the waves as they are translated and processed. The basic flow through the circuits involves striking a guitar to start the strings vibrating; the pickups then capture that vibrating sound wave and turn it into an electrical current that flows through the circuit paths in the guitar through the pots that alter wave qualities (such as volume and tone), to the guitar cable and through the effects pedals, and out to the guitar amp. Once in the amp, the current hits the series of circuits that affect electrical currents—preamps that boost amplitude, capacitors that act as little batteries, resistors that block and channel flow, converters that split AC/DC volts (some applications or alterations work better with one or the other), effects such as a reverb box—and then out to the main tubes that boost the amplitude and to the transformer that combines currents into a form that can go out to the speaker. Finally, the signal hits the speaker magnetic coil that takes the current and uses it to move the cones, which translates everything back into audible sound waves that are then picked up by the mics in the studio. This basic transductive process can do innumerable things to the waves expressed as currents that affect the quality of sound, and those sound waves bounce around rooms, are picked up again by mics, channeled through the same kinds of pathways in the control room, and pumped back out of speakers to produce sound waves that resonate walls and affect listeners. For David, the key to the boutique trend is looking for "quality" handmade construction that doesn't come from assembly lines or circuits produced by machines. Quality here, I think, is more about "qualities"—the different qualities of sound that these boutique analog builds produce.[25]

All of these transductions are moments of diffraction. Waves are disturbances through a medium—water, air, electromagnetic fields—that, when they encounter an obstruction, they diffract—bend, spread out, overlap, and combine to create resonant relationships among the waves and entangle other bodies in the processes. Specific features of the obstructions that the waves pass through produce different affects or diffractions at different levels of intensity, combining at their peaks to produce more energy or intensity, canceling each other out, or producing unpredictable, nonlinear qualities. What the circuits, transistors, amps, pots, and tubes do, as obstructions, is precisely this diffraction and nonlinear entanglement. These technologies aren't static: they are active emergent coparticipants in the production of sound that also change, evolve, intensify, heat up, or slow down as a part of the transduction process. This nonlinear aspect to the signal flow and circuits contributes to the sound through a type of overlapping superposition, the layering and entangling all of these actions and flows to produce a higher-order version of the sound emerging up from the virtual. Wave energy is translated into electrical impulses, diffracted through breaks or disruptions created by effects and amps to produce new patterns that are then translated back into waves via speakers, coproducing a new version of the sound waves. A version of the wave is retained so that listeners might still recognize it as a trumpet or guitar or voice, but it has been altered through diffraction. And instead of being both wave and particle, the sound is both wave and current: under some conditions expressing as a wave, under other conditions as an electrical current, not only when translated by electronics but also by the ear, which expresses the energy as an electrical current again that circulates through the brain. These encounters produce a new entangled actor-network in the moment of articulation or diffraction that leaves marks on each participant, subsequently changing each one as they resound, disengage, and dissipate. Sound is the nonlinear "composition of all of it" as a quasi-object.

INSCRIPTIONS—RESEARCH AS RECORDING

As a researcher, I've been following the traces of transduction that the preinscription and chreods of the studio enact, which puts me in the prescriptive role of generating a description of the script. Through the process of planning, recording, and analyzing the documentary video, a version of the studio emerged as the circulation of energy, as sound waves circulating through a series of diffractions that generates nonlinear effects such as distortion. A script for this flow of energy in the containment shell of the studio looks something like this: from the vocal chords and instruments that generate vibrations→amps and instrument mics→reverberation off the walls→room mics that translate waves into electrical signals→cables to the patch bay and preamps in the control room that channel and boost the signal→analog dynamics processors that manipulate or diffract the signal→analog-to-digital converter that translates the analog signal into a digital one→computer and recording software→mixing board→digital-to-analog converter that translates the signal back to analog→monitors or speakers in the control room that translate the signal back into sound waves. I asked Jim if he had a more detailed flowchart like this for the studio. He said flowcharts can repeat at the level of the patch bay, since its role is to organize inputs and outputs, but they would always have to be emergent with the studio itself, which is fluid and adaptable, not only from project to project but also from day to day and instrument to instrument.[26] Jim estimates that, at any given time, there are over four hundred cables in the studio connecting all of the amps, microphones, effects, and computer, and that these are in modes of constant rearticulation. The studio operates as an actor-network that researchers can follow initially through the model of the the refrain and the example of Latour's door closer—the studio generates and absorbs energy into its interface, manipulates and translates that energy, and releases the energy back out when it plays the tracks. This process of transduction is enacted in every diffractive encounter in every moment of recording and extends to the inscriptions enacted through research.

In the recording studio, sound entangles all of the walls, instruments, wires, electronics, and people in the room, connects them as part of the circuitry for the flow and transduction of energy and the inscriptions it produces. The technologies themselves are changed through use, through the recording and the performance. For some people, the technologies are dead objects. The song might change through the process, and even the humans might change through the process, but the technology doesn't. However, the technology can break down through use. Or linking effects in a certain line, order, or way, even just with different cables, can affect how they sound. When connected one way versus another, the effect becomes a different version of the object with different affordances. It performs differently. Equipment also heats up and cools down, wearing it in or wearing it down. Drumsticks chip away and weaken. Drumheads get worn out and sound dead. When strings go out of tune, the guitar is materially changed. Perhaps the most famous example is Willie Nelson's guitar. The hole worn into it materially changes it and alters the sound to the point that Willie can't get that sound from any other guitar. These are all inscriptions, marks on the tessera made through the circulation of energy that coproduces new versions of the quasi-objects. Ultimately, all of these transductions and diffractions end up inscribed in an MP3 file that is capable of further circulation, relationality, and inscription.

This process of inscription extends to the writing and recording of researchers. For Latour inscriptions such as user manuals, instructions, and tutorials operate within these processes to similarly facilitate operative flow, redirecting it toward the script if the flow gets off script. But Latour extends inscriptions to inventors in workshops, market analysts or engineers, and of course anthropologists or researchers, including their *thought experiments*—What would happen if X weren't here? What actions would be needed? Research methods, then, are not a set of prescriptions to arrive at systematic, generalizable knowledge but rather aim toward the coproduction of new descriptions. They are more like a "travel guide" for engaging sites of practice such as laboratories or recording studios that "cannot be confused with the territory" (*Reassembling the Social* 17). Methods are neither imposed on the practice nor transparent to its operations but are coparticipants in the deployment of that practice. "Deployment," in Latour's use of the term, means that a research account might increase the number of actors, expand the range of agencies, multiply the objects that are acting in groups, and/or map the controversies over matters of concern (138). In other words, as neither critique nor explanation, "deployment" performs the social, assembling and inventing it in every new case of inscription.

As a method for opening these potential futurities, Latour suggests keeping written notebooks during each investigation as a function of deployment, each with specific aims: (1) documenting everything that happens—mapping networks of mediators, following the actions that flow through them, and tracing the changes these mediations make possible, including those of the researcher; (2) organizing these traces chronologically and categorically—this can be done in medias res or after the fact through analysis of the research notes or through the writing process itself; (3) writing improvisationally during the study for momentary flashes and initial ideas to let the investigation and the network coproduce the writing and offset the imposition of stock theories or assumptions onto the network being coproduced; and (4) tracking the effects or potential effects of the investigation on the participants, the actions coproduced, the mediator's change in functions, or the worlds that are reassembled, all of which are vital to understanding research beyond *mere* description (133–35). Inscription, in other words, can also occur anywhere along the path. During our time in the studio, I followed Jim and the band with notebook in hand, scribbling through versions of these four aims. Through this process, versions of the studio appeared scrawled across the page—an initial map of the script, a sketched out diagram of the control room, furiously scribbled notes about the circulation of energy, the nonlinearlity of distortion, and all of the coproductive changes the studio and its technologies undergo. All of these and more were not simply my inscriptions but further inscriptions coproduced by the studio itself. To record through the studio or through research is to produce these traces, marks on the tesserae, mediations that continually generate new versions of the objects of study.

These inscriptions, of course, extend from the studio itself as a recording device to the various recording devices used in research. As I was following the circulations of the studio, Brian was following the actors with a video camera, recording all of the details my furious scribbles couldn't keep up with. In "Not So Innocent Anymore," Susan Naomi Nordstrom shows how recording devices coproduce the object of study via diffraction. Rather than ignore or dismiss recording devices as intermediaries, she shows how they functioned in her research as mediators. In one interview, it was clear that the participant was uncomfortable gazing at the recording device. Nordstrom tried to hide the device under her arm or in a pocket, but this radically affected the sound and materially altered the event and what she was able to glean from it. In another interview, the participant asked that she turn the recorder off and not record sensitive information about her family. Even though the moment wasn't recorded, it lingers in her memory, and versions of it made its way into her research accounts in significantly different ways than if it were recorded. Another interview started immediately as the participant opened her door, leaving little time for Nordstrom to introduce the study and turn on the recorder. She writes, "I did not have time to . . . use any of the discursive moves traditionally used to bind the interview. . . . The boundaries of the event of the interview became arbitrary" (392). The final instance of mediation showed itself in the sound recording device's limitations. As her participant spoke, she showed Nordstrom objects and photographs of objects that the sound recorder couldn't capture. In each case, diffraction coproduced an event through the recording device.

On the one hand, the recorder arbitrarily bounds any meaning that the device captures. So Nordstrom isn't concerned about objective-realist issues such as bias or validity; she is only concerned about recording the event of the interview, "an articulation of the world formed from 'a vibration with an infinity of harmonics or submultiples'" (Deleuze qtd. in Nordstrom 393). On the other hand, of course, Barad recognizes that apparatuses "are perpetually open to arrangements, rearticulations, and other reworkings" and "enact what matters and what is excluded from mattering" (Barad qtd. in Nordstrom 393–94). The capacities of recording devices enact an agential cut, creating a "provisional boundary for the interview" (394). These boundaries provide a space for the researcher to engage, but they do not sit still. The interview itself makes further cuts that create new diffraction patterns and "materialize different phenomena" (Barad qtd. in Nordstrom 394).[27] Researchers don't simply decide to make these cuts: they happen through the overall enaction of research and the collective capacities of everything entangled in the process. As Nordstrom tried to hide the recorder, it produced a different sonic world outside of her initial intentions; the participant's request to turn the recorder off excluded the account from the record but not from Nordstrom's experience and memory; the inability to set up the interview and turn on the recorder disrupted the intended boundary on the interview but opened a new one; and the inability of the device to capture the complex entanglements on display forced a reassessment of her accounts, both in the transcripts of the interviews and the final manuscript.

Brian and I had quite similar experiences in our research in the studio. The presence of the cameras placed additional pressure on the band by making them more aware of everything they were doing. The camera puts a spotlight on more typically tacit practices and holds them up for potential scrutiny. Something as mundane as not getting a proper signal through an amp, which happens all of the time, suddenly becomes highly noticeable when it is being recorded. In one moment during a late-night interview with Jim in the control room, the spotlight got to me. I asked Brian to turn off the camera before I went into a long-winded attempt to explain the project. Of course, turning the cameras off led to an explanation that I later wished I had preserved, but as with Nordstrom, traces of the explanation stayed with me and filtered into the version I got down on paper and later in the manuscript. And on the first day of recording, I managed to interview Jim's nephew, who does hip-hop, about his composing processes and uses of technology. Brian wasn't in town yet and I was on my own. The result was some less-than-stellar footage in a file I named "suck roll," not because of the content but due to my lack of experience recording. We turned the footage over to his nephew, and I often wonder how he read the designation, how it might have retroactively changed the experience for him. And finally, of course, the transcription process was nothing if not a process of emergent agential cuts. I was completely unable to fully grasp the deluge of material and it was a constant challenge to include detail while focusing on purpose and clarity. For Nordstrom, "the transcripts are contestable performances that are always available to different possibilities. . . . Any knowledge I produce is about opening possibilities and becomings—not closing them down" (396). The version that ends up in this chapter and the next is genuinely one among many potential sets of specificities that could have been actualized from the virtual potentials.

Similarly, Laurie Gries argues that when dealing with such runaway objects of study, bounding the research is inevitable. Researchers bound it through location, organizational activity, function, and genre (*Still Life with Rhetoric* 92). Other research limitations of funding, time, and resources also always come into play, all of which limit research but also coproduce its objects of study. While Gries calls for a certain amount of flexibility and acceptance of uncertainty in dealing with these messy objects-becoming-collectives that are "constantly changing, circulating, and triggering all kinds of collective actions via their multiple, divergent relations" (87), she sees Spinuzzi as suggesting strategies for "appropriately bounding case studies" (93).[28] Reduction is important for scientific disciplines that use it to narrow problem situations, which allows them to develop instruments and paradigms that reveal important material processes. The problem is the philosophical reduction of the world to this very specific scientific practice or mode of relation. For Latour, scientists build small-scale compositions, which is not the same thing as building a cage of nature as a philosophical demand ("An Attempt at a 'Compositionist Manifesto'" 483). "Science" with a small *s* is reductive only in its practice, not in its philosophy. Its philosophy is one of composition, because even in these boundings researchers are also coproducing new versions of the objects of study that extend their circulation and necessarily contribute to their unboundedness—it is the continuous bounding through engagement that produces versions and unbounds the object of study. This is Latour's "irreductionist" move. The move from epistemology to ontology leaves both the sciences and the humanities to take on this openness to experimentation and uncertainty. Revealing global warming as a quasi-object that is inextricably bound to publics as much as scientists and politicians creates the possibility of responding to its proliferation more productively, but it leaves us with no guarantees. The goal is not to produce reliable conclusions but to coproduce quasi-objects. Carl Herndl and Scott Graham write, "The very identity of these quasi-objects is changed through their interaction with the other actants or propositions in the collective. That is, their identity is transformed by the unintended consequences of their associations" ("Getting Over Incommensurability" 49).

Like Nordstrom's recorder, the recording studio coproduces the events it captures, and including researchers recording with video in the recording studio further complicates the boundedness of research and the variation it coproduces. For Brian Massumi, in his brief essay "Undigesting Deleuze," traditional models of critique work to bound and limit in order to produce knowledge. They judge the specific case through a general idea in order to "pin something down, . . . the better to dismiss it." But these critical approaches resist the residual energy and vitality of potential variation. Deleuze, on the other hand, sees a thing as a bundle of tendencies holding virtual potential. Affirmative knowledge production is about drawing out these excluded specificities that categorical thought dismisses and activating them, actualizing them. Massumi writes, "What something 'is' can only be got at by accompanying its process of becoming. This invites experimentation: tweaking the thing into expressing its potential further." Research through this model, then, becomes unbounded. These potentialities can only be drawn out by disclosing the specificities of the object of study that were excluded through categorical boundaries, and they can't be revealed in any other way than through the enactment of research apparatuses that collectively perform versions of the objects of study. This process is messy because it is only bounded by virtual potential and degrees of freedom, which are continually affected by the enactment of research, which cuts into the virtual, activates it, intensifies it, modulates it. In short, the studio territorializes vibrations and is simultaneously territorialized by vibrations. And research, like recording, breaks into this flow and channels the energy through one more circuit of diffraction that nonlinearly produces another inscription, another recording, another version of the event.

This turn toward quasi-objects as a model for objects of study impacts the writing researchers do, not just their methods. Any published accounts of these compositions are also diffractive traces, functions of variable ontologies that are mediations all the way down. Any account coproduces a new version that is added on to the emergent trajectory or line. In *We Have Never*

Been Modern, Latour writes, "When I describe Pasteur's domestication of microbes, I am mobilizing nineteenth-century society, not just the semiotics of a great man's texts; when I describe the invention-discovery of brain peptides, I am really talking about the peptides themselves, not simply their representation in Professor Guillemin's laboratory. Yet, rhetoric, textual strategies, writing, staging, semiotics—all of these are really *at stake*, but in a new form that has a simultaneous impact on the nature of things and on social context, while it is not reducible to the one or the other" (5; emphasis mine). Similarly, for Margaret Syverson, writing is at stake. As a trace of complex systems, writing follows traces and produces traces simultaneously, generating an inscription that folds back to affect its own potentiality. For Syverson, this kind of enaction means that disciplines continually coproduce and are coproduced by their object of study (*The Wealth of Reality* 10, 15–16). And as Louise Wetherbee Phelps makes clear, disciplines only happen through ecologies of practice that resonate across a horizontal field of disciplines and a vertical network of cultural practices and contexts—ecologies of practice co-produce the disciplines that are ecologies for practice (*Composition as a Human Science* 8). These key works in composition and rhetoric resonate with Latour's translation, Barad's diffraction, and ultimately Deleuze's virtual as forms of transduction. Writing, in the context of these circulations and breaks, coproduces the actor-network as it adds on to it, expands it, and extends it, leaving more traces as it speeds up and slows down but never fully stabilizes.

Researchers, then, aren't left with certainties, only the ethical mandate to continue to coproduce more versions that respond to emergent conditions and set potential futures. Research breaks into this flow to produce another inscription, generate another record of the event. But rather than fold back into the studio as part of its coproduction, the final published inscription of research folds out, opens the studio to other possible assemblages; it allows the studio to circulate through other networks and gives it greater capacity for relationality with theorists, researchers, students, conference attendees, publishers, booksellers, libraries, classrooms, and much more. Research puts the quasi-object of study into a different flow of circulation, widens its potential paths and relations, and transforms it and the people and places it entangles, expanding it as a quasi-object. Like the slogan Keep Austin Weird and the emergent ecologies its circulation coproduces and is coproduced by, this account of the studio is still connected to it, contributing to it as a virtual model while continuing to circulate, expand, and transform, enabling new potential enactions and performances and eventually extending it into possible futures.

FOUR

COLLABORATION
AS COORDINATION

COLLABORATION FROM THE PERSPECTIVE of quasi-objects and circulation has to extend beyond the human, which is gathered and coproduced through material performance and enaction. During the 1980s, work on collaboration centered largely on human authors with the goal of producing written texts. In 1984's "Collaborative Learning and the 'Conversation of Mankind,'" for example, Kenneth Bruffee establishes a key pedagogical move in the social turn, linking collaboration in writing instruction to collaborative learning through group work and peer review. Collaboration as a pedagogical method is balanced out by seeing collaboration as an epistemic process in scholarly activity, particularly through collaboratively written texts. Lisa Ede and Andrea Lunsford's "Audience Addressed, Audience Invoked" problematizes the addressed/invoked binary by examining the authors' own more complex situation of writing the coauthored article. They show how audiences shifted, reversed roles, and layered through the life cycle of their idea, its articulation in a text, and its eventual circulation. They write, "But even this single case demonstrates that the term audience refers not just to the intended, actual, or eventual readers of a discourse, but to all those whose image, ideas, or actions influence a writer during the process of composition. One way to conceive of 'audience,' then, is as an overdetermined or unusually rich concept, one which may perhaps be best specified through the analysis of precise, concrete situations" (168). Though they develop a more complex model of audience as a collaborative and shifting coauthor, they don't give up on the centrality of human authorship of written texts.[1] By the 1990s, this humanist version of collaboration runs its course. As the social turn moves away from individual humans and written texts to social structures and discourses, *collaboration* as a key term loses its efficacy.[2] But there is a countermovement in the 1980s that sets the stage for seeing collaboration within a larger system of coordination. While Marilyn Cooper and Karen Burke LeFevre are generally read through the lens of the social turn and Louise Wetherbee Phelps still isn't read particularly widely, their takes on ecology work toward extending collaboration to various scales of cooperative material enactment.

Marilyn Cooper is one of the first people to put forward an ecological model of composition.[3] In "The Ecology of Writing" (1986), she argues that cognitive models based on solitary authors can't account for the collaborative pedagogical practices already underway in the 1980s such as group work, brainstorming collaboratively, discussing readings as a class, and engaging in peer review. Bruffee already shows this intuitively or in practice, but no one had put forward "a new model of writing" that could provide explicit grounds for these collaborative practices. Cooper's ecological model sees "writing as an activity through which a person is continually engaged with a variety of socially constituted systems" (367). Ecology, as the science of natural environments, sees all organisms as both effects and causes of their environments, where organisms and environments are both responses to each other. Cooper is prompted to attend to the dynamic interlocking systems that structure the activity of writing but that writing also coproduces—systems are "made and remade by writers in the act of writing" (368). Writers and texts "both determine and are determined by" other writers and texts in the system in inherently dynamic ways: "Though their structures and contents can be specified at a given moment, in real time they are *constantly changing*, limited by parameters that are themselves subject to change over long spans of time" (368; emphasis mine). These ecological systems are entirely "interwoven" with their effects and manner of operation, which connect writers through "systems of ideas, of purposes, of interpersonal interactions, of cultural norms, of textual forms" (369). Cooper's article goes into an analysis of these five interlocking systems, concluding that "the metaphor for writing suggested by the ecological model is that of the web, in which anything that affects one strand of the web *vibrates* throughout the whole" and provides a way of modeling and engaging "complex situations" (370; emphasis mine).

While she frames her argument in terms of Bruffee and collaboration, Cooper works through an analysis of audience to show how an ecological model can reframe the problem of audience in terms of engagements with these systems. Like Ede and Lunsford, she starts with the opposition of real and imagined audiences but contends that both require writers to produce them as mental constructs. For Cooper, writers don't just address or invoke audiences—they communicate with them through activities very much like Ede and Lunsford's account of their collaboration that cycles through roles as readers, writers, reviewers, and editors, producing a "real" social situation for writing. "Ede and Lunsford," Cooper argues, "know their readers, through real social encounters": the abstract cognitive moves of addressed and invoked are "superfluous" in this case (372). Instead, Cooper sees in their account concrete interactions between readers and writers, dynamically shifting roles, institutional arrangements that facilitate activity, specific practices of collaboration, and the emergent coproduction of ideas and texts. The ecological model puts forward an infinitely expandable social that is connected through systems via practices of writing and collaboration, where "ideas are out there in the world, [in] a landscape that is always being modified by ongoing human discourse" (372): purposes arise through the system, roles are developed through institutional arrangements, and genres emerge through evolving practices. Writing is one of the activities, or *energia*, that locates writers in these enmeshed and coproductive systems that make up the social world. Sounding almost like Latour, Cooper highlights action and construction as ontological. An ecological model sees writing as "essentially social activities, dependent on social structures and processes not only in their interpretive but also in their constructive phases," arguing that "writing changes social reality" (366, 368). Importantly, these systems are specific concrete activities that "can be investigated, described, altered" through writing, which is "both constituted by and constitutive of these ever-changing systems" (369, 373). While Cooper is still tied to the social perspectives of the time, this is a becoming-materialist model that extends collaboration to various levels of a system, putting authors and audiences into coproductive relations with larger ecologies.

When Cooper gets cited over the next ten to fifteen years, it is often in regard to her other works.[4] "The Ecology of Writing" doesn't get much uptake, and to the extent that it does, the emphasis is often on the social rather than ecological. For example, in his foreword to Karen Burke LeFevre's *Invention as a Social Act* (1987), Frank D'Angelo cites "The Ecology of Writing" as one of the current responses to the solitary composer myth. He aligns Cooper's turn to the constructive role of social activities with Foucault's model of the author function to provide a context for LeFevre's book. On the one hand, *Invention as a Social Act* is situated squarely in the social turn, examining the ways that invention is not an individual cognitive process but a social act that is mediated through language. While generating a little more traction at the time than Cooper's essay, it is also typically in relation to the social. On the other hand, LeFevre's book, like Cooper's essay, is about invention as a *collaborative* social *act*, and like Cooper she connects collaborative action to the concept of ecology. LeFevre posits a continuum of social perspectives on invention from an individual or private perspective based on Plato to an internal dialogic model based on Freud, to a collaborative perspective based on George Herbert Mead, and finally to a collective model based on Durkheim. By the end of the book—which in many ways sums up the book and points a way forward—she connects these versions, especially the latter two, through an ecological model. LeFevre writes, "We must reinterpret the history of invention. Borrowing from Harold Lasswell's concept of an 'ecology of innovation,' we should study the ecology of invention—the ways ideas arise and are nurtured or hindered by interaction with social context and culture" (126). LeFevre is interested in studying how the dynamics of group interaction generate inventions, both in present configurations and over historical trajectories, researching "temporary communities that emerge spontaneously" and "communities brought together to solve problems" (127). The theory of evolution, for example, evolved through Darwin's engagements with various ecologies and species on his *Beagle* voyage, through his interactions and collaborations with shipmates, through his correspondence with other experts in England, and the active "scientific life of London and Cambridge" (127). For LeFevre, these kinds of local collaborations and global collectivities are at the heart of understanding invention as a social act through an ecology of invention.

Importantly, LeFevre theorizes this kind of ecological collaboration through Lasswell's concept of "resonance." On the one hand, at a local level,

Lasswell's take is fairly humanist. For him, a resonator is a person who functions as a friendly audience or lends financial or emotional support. Without
the "resonant relationships" that connect them to the social sphere—groups
of students or colleagues that provide supportive grounds for developing new
ideas—innovators are often less successful. For Lasswell, this smaller circle
allows the ideas to circulate and percolate before being challenged in a wider
sphere, making it "possible to consolidate the new departure and improve the
chances of survival" (65). On the other hand, LeFevre complicates his more
self-contained notion of the human. Following Gregory Bateson's "ecology
of mind," which conceives of the self as "not bounded by the skin" but acting
constantly in relation to an environment (qtd. in LeFevre 29), and George
Herbert Mead's model for the emergence of meaning, which happens through
a process of gesture, resultant, and response, she shows that the self is a
coconstitutive effect of resonance. For Mead, an action or gesture generates
an outcome and interpretation of the gesture, which invites a response: "The
response of one organism to the gesture of another . . . is the meaning of that
gesture, and is also responsible for the appearance or coming into being of the
new object—or new content of an old object" (qtd. in LeFevre 62). LeFevre,
perhaps forecasting a more Latourian model of construction over the social
construction of her day, places action over essence, seeing essence as only
possible through action, which makes the self along with its inventions a process rather than an entity. All creation, then, "reveals itself as an encounter":
"All is created dynamically in the 'between'" (63–64). Invention at the local
level of collaboration is not the result of an individual thought but the result
of a resonant, responsive, and coproductive social act.

LeFevre then extends this notion of resonance to more global collectivities in two ways. First, she characterizes resonance as an action, a "*vibration*"
that is "*intensified* and *prolonged*" (65; emphasis mine). Resonance is a collective, affective *environment* that extends beyond Lasswell's human resonators.
Second, she extends this through Silvano Arieti's concept of clustering. Arieti
argues that creative individuals don't appear evenly or consistently throughout history but in certain periods of history and geographical locales. Arieti
follows Charles Edward Gray's model that sees history as "a series of three
concurrent cycles: economic, social, and political. Each cycle in turn has
four stages (formative, developed, florescent, and degenerated), and rotates
through these stages at different speeds. Clusters of creativity will occur when

the developed and fluorescent stages of all three cycles coincide" (66). While LeFevre doesn't vouch for the validity of the model, for her it suggests how creativity is "a process occasioned or enabled by interaction within a social sphere that allows one's thought to resonate" (67). Providing further examples from the history of genetics and literature, she argues that the absence of resonance, certainly social but also historical, has ill effects on invention, frustrating thinkers whose work doesn't circulate and resonate in these environments but also creating the conditions of possibility for future innovation. It's not merely accidental or simply geographical that movements of invention in various fields operate in relation to these resonant clusters (76–77). In her concluding "Implications" chapter, LeFevre suggests, not unlike Cooper, that collaborative practice has been ahead of theory (122). So, the implications chapter, in which Lasswell's model of ecology is proposed, is her attempt to account for the collaborative practices already in play and sets ecology up as the takeaway from seeing invention as a social act. For her, the object of study in composition should be this "larger locus of inventive activity," following Foucault's version of discourse as "an endless potentiality, . . . a process extending over time" (125).

This extension of collaboration into larger systems is developed more fully by Louise Wetherbee Phelps in *Composition as a Human Science* (1988). She uses the concepts of ecology and resonance to organize both her conceptual understanding of composition as a discipline and her phenomenological understanding of composition as a practice. Her first two chapters, collectively titled "Constructing an Ecology of Composition," are grounded in "the concept of *field* as a self-organizing system, a kind of system that is dynamically capable, through its openness to the environment, of innovation and unpredictable evolution" (x). Resonance appears as a key factor in this process of innovation: the resonances between writer and field as they develop symbiotically; the resonances among composition and other fields; and the resonances between writer and life (or world). The problem of inventing a discipline is necessarily tied up within these ecological resonances. Phelps writes, "An ecological perspective treats entities like disciplines as systems within larger systems. An ecology is constituted through interdependence and transactions among all levels of the system both horizontally (the relations of parts within the whole at a given level of organization) and vertically (the relations among elements at different levels)" (3). Developing an ecology of composition as a

discipline, then, requires bringing forth the field as a system through its relations to other fields horizontally and larger cultural movements vertically.
So, rather than shy away from composition's tendency to draw on multiple
theories and methodologies, Phelps draws widely on work in the humanities
and social sciences, from cognitive science, linguistics, education, and psychology to literary theory, philosophy, hermeneutics, and rhetoric to develop
the theoretical and cultural grounds for the advancement of composition as a
distinct field. Of course, this disciplinary ecology of composition only comes
into being through composition as ecologies of practice. Theories and practices must be held in constant relation and tension; their interplay, or mutual
relation and difference, constitutes a field as a self-organizing system. "Such a
system is a dynamic process rather than an equilibrium structure: it maintains
its integrity through continual self-transformation and possesses the capacity
for novelty" (4). The task of an ecology of composition as a discipline, therefore, is to coproduce this continual transformation through resonant ecologies of practice.

Phelps sees ecology as an extension of a more general contextualist hypothesis that draws human motive and physical causality together though "biological, cultural, social, and environmental aspects of human development"
and places them "into one open, interactive system" (31). Contextualism sees
the world as event, combining context and process or change into one movement. For Phelps, "Context (also system, field, whole, ecology, relation) refers
to the total set of relationships from which particular entities and qualities
derive. The whole is, by virtue of the principle of change, in a constant state
of flux, a dance of information/energy patterns that underlies all the apparent stabilities, structures, and laws we experience in nature or society" (32).
All local practices are events that participate in these systemic qualities: they
are temporal, they are configured through fields within fields, their elements
are context dependent, their novelty is inexhaustible, and their meanings and
interpretations are always open to new encounters or coproductions. Resonant with quasi-objects, the contextualist hypothesis is generally relational in
that it "assumes an underlying event flow" separate from human consciousness, "which presents itself to humans living (literally) within its perceptual
horizons as a set of affordances for action"; it is generally ecological in that
humans can only know these worlds through "observations, descriptions,
and engagements" that place structure on them, screen out some possibilities

over others and enact those affordances; and it is generally vitalist in that the system "constitute[es] others from its potential energies" (32). The constant tension and entanglement of these variables produces domains, niches, purposes, and variations. In an ecological paradigm, "All parts are not only interdependent but mutually defining and transactive, so that through their shifting relationships they continually constitute new parts or elements as well as new structures" (32). For Phelps these *trans*actions are embedded at all vertical levels and horizontal relationships, making change circulate, disseminate, reverberate, and resonate through the entire system. At its core, an ecology is these resonances that both connect and coproduce. Her concluding definition of ecology is unequivocal: "This is the full measure of an ecology: a total interrelatedness and reciprocity of change for all parts at all levels. Within such a system emergent novelty, unpredictable new orderliness, becomes possible" (33).

Like LeFevre, Phelps draws on Gregory Bateson, who sees human individuals as multidimensional systems inseparable from social and environmental systems. For Bateson, message, learning, and mind are all functions of the system. Bateson writes,

> In the communicational works, this dichotomy [between inside and outside] is irrelevant and meaningless. The contexts have communicational reality only insofar as they are effective as messages, *i.e.,* insofar as they are represented or reflected . . . in *multiple* parts of the communicational system we are studying; and this system is not the physical individual but a wide network of pathways of messages. Some of these pathways *happen* to be located outside the physical individual, others inside; but the characteristics of the *system* are in no way dependent upon any boundary lines which we may superimpose upon the communicational map. (qtd. in Phelps 34)

As Phelps puts it, "Indeed the individual as such is an open system constantly evolving through the exchange of energies with the world, though *interactions* (the interdependence of relatively distinct entities and processes) and *transactions* (their interpenetration and inseparability)" (34; emphasis mine). Interactions and transactions are not a binary opposition or mutually exclusive but coconstitutional. In a position reminiscent of Cooper's, Phelps argues that composition as a discipline and a practice is "prereflectively" already attuned to this ecological model because this is the larger disciplinary context and cultural ground in which it operates. But the field hadn't engaged this context reflectively or explicitly, which her book sets out to do. Composition needs both the tacit and reflective, the practical and the theoretical, the outside and inside, the vertical and the horizontal to function in cascades of collaboration as operative tension and coordination.

Both LeFevre and Phelps are developing models for how practice at the human level of gesture connects ecologically with larger scales of circulation through coordinated enaction. While much of the discourse of the 1980s on collaboration centers on humans and writing discrete documents, this countertradition in the 1980s already shows that the boundary between humans and environments is breaking down in favor of their resonant, entangled coordination.[5] This more parahuman version of ecology—one that speaks to Serres's parasite and Heidegger's hermeneutics of situation—is largely overlooked during the 1980s and up through the 1990s.[6] In many ways, all three of these calls to see composition ecologically—Cooper's, LeFevre's, and Phelps's—were overshadowed by the domination of the social turn as the field's central paradigm. It took over a decade for various takes on the social turn to play themselves out through the discipline before ecology could reach a more central position of exploration in the 2000s.[7] Being able to see collaboration as a function of ecologies initially occurred outside of what LeFevre characterizes as clusters of resonance, but its vibrations—the affects of its continued circulations—have met and coproduced an ambient environment for ecology's increased uptake and elaboration, making it possible to explore collaboration more specifically through composition as a quasi-object.[8] This ecological turn, however, has not gone back to this countertradition to draw out resonance as a form of systemic coordination and consider it as a basis for collaborative ecological entanglement and emergence.

COORDINATED ENACTION

The intervening years between Phelps's *Composition as a Human Science* and Margaret Syverson's *The Wealth of Reality* (1999) are when the social turn plays itself out in composition and rhetoric, a necessary disciplinary working through before a space can open up for Syverson to return to an ecological model and rearticulate it through an encounter with complexity theories. Like Cooper, LeFevre, and Phelps, Syverson comes to ecology as a way to get past individual models of composing. She develops her ecological model because previous models of composition weren't allowing her to fully answer predominant research questions about composing—some as disciplinarily central as "who wrote this text," "why was this text ineffective," or "how did these authors collaborate."[9] But unlike Cooper, LeFevre, and Phelps, she more explicitly frames her model in relation to an emerging material turn.[10] Even though Syverson continues to emphasize human authors and readers and traditional notions of texts, she makes it clear that the "study of the ecology of a text takes us beyond the social constructivist theory of composing by incorporating the material, physical, processes and structures involved in text production" (74). Syverson disrupts the linguistic and social turns through notions of embodied, distributed cognition. Cognition, she writes, is "a complex ensemble of activities and interactions among brains, hands, eyes, ears, other people, and an astonishing variety of structures in the environment, from airplane cockpits to cereal boxes to institutions. More surprising, to me, was the wide range of cognitive activities that seemed to involve no verbal language at all" (xiv). These larger ecologies are not just social, dialogical, or interactive but operate through an ecology of composition centered on complexity theory's entangled processes of distribution, embodiment, emergence, and enaction. Actor-network theory's emphasis on performativity, and in particular enaction, is what drives Latour's prescriptive roles—in particular, human gestures that physically open and close circuits made possible by the preinscription and chreods, all of which lead to the inscriptions of recorded text, video, and sound. Syverson's ecological version of enaction becomes a kind of collaboration qua coordination of the entire system through performance.

Ecology, for Syverson, is the larger configuration through which multiple complex systems operate, overlap, intermingle, perturb, resonate, and coordinate. Drawing on complexity theory, she develops a heuristic grid or matrix out of four predominant systemic attributes (distribution, embodiment, emergence, enaction) and five central dimensions (physical, social, psychological, spatial, temporal) to provide a framework for understanding composition in her case studies on texts, writers, and readers. Her emphasis, however, is on the four attributes. Complex systems are "*distributed* across space and time in an ensemble of interrelated activities" (7). Navigating a ship involves water, waves, weather, technical instruments, institutions, and language, a whole host of shared and coordinated movements among agents and structures across an environment. Systemic processes are also *embodied* in physical experience and material interactions. Humans' bilateral symmetry, for example, prefigures a tendency toward balance, binary opposition, and symmetrical thinking. The fact that humans have a relatively definitive boundary of skin grounds concepts of inside and outside or thinking in terms of container metaphors. These interconnected systems will inevitably display *emergence.* In closed systems, entropy will eventually shut them down. But systems open to their environments will exchange energy at the local level, which produces emergent self-organization at larger levels of the ecology. Human skin, for example, produces a permeable boundary that facilitates relations with an environment and enables cognition or consciousness at a higher level of organization. Complex systems of distribution, embodiment, and emergence coordinate themselves through *enaction*, the interdependent and interrelated practices and activities that unfold over time.[11] Knowledge, for Syverson, is coproduced through an "ongoing interpretation that emerges through *activities* and *experiences* situated in specific environments" (13). Enaction not only produces knowledge but also "every act of knowing brings forth a world" (Maturana and Varela, qtd. in Syverson 13). These attributes and dimensions, for her, aren't categories or classes but "aspects of every object, process, fact, idea, concept, activity, structure, or event" (22). They can be singled out abstractly for analysis, but materially they are all there in every act and comingle to produce every object or event. Each attribute possesses each dimension, and each dimension encompasses each attribute—distribution is physical, social, psychological, spatial, and temporal, and the social is distributed, embodied, emergent, and enacted, for examples. For Syverson, these attributes and dimensions operate at "every level of scale," from neurons and genetics to geophysics and global economics (23).

This move to complex ecologies necessitates a move from collaboration among individuals to system-level coordination. Syverson writes, "We might think of emergence as a process in which disparate individual entities and relations undergo transformation or deformations that bring them into increasing coordination with each other. The process is not necessarily what we would call collaboration or cooperation, although mutual transformations play a key role; the entities or relations may actually be conflictual or predatory. The system as a whole, however, reflects an emerging, dynamic coordination" (59). Complex systems enact phase transitions where a group of individuals transform into a collective with global properties irreducible to the individuals. This transition is a result of the enactive practices and activities that aren't necessarily determined through conscious collaboration. In her chapter on collaboration, Syverson follows a writing group with the assignment to produce an essay. The group coordinates itself through both intentional practices—the goal to produce an essay, the division of duties, and a perceived need to unite against the common threat of a bad grade—and tacit activities—the use of shared language, inhabiting bounded physical proximity, the use of humor, and sharing experiences.

Coordination, however, is not necessarily adaptation. Adaptation is an enduring structural change in the organism relative to the environment: the sustained ability to write effectively in the institution, for example. But coordination is "any accommodation between an organism and its environment, including both transitory and enduring accommodations" (76). The system may coordinate in order to produce a temporary stability or coherence, but the outcome will not necessarily be adaptation. Conscious collaboration aims at adaptation through coordination, but a whole host of attributes and activities within the system could upend it—students, teachers, textbooks, institutional structures, or the activities themselves. This particular group ended up producing a poor essay. But Syverson argues that teachers can't reduce bad writing to a single thing or human error. All of the things that go into student *performance* are based on variability within this system. Instead of adaptation, coordination produces a form of coadaptation where breakdowns and poor performances are normal aspects of such systems, leading the systems to also adjust to them. Teachers, then, should produce the conditions of experimentation that promote the possibility of coordination (and even potential adaptation) without demanding their necessity and without imposing high penalties on variability.

Jane Bennett provides an example of this kind of coordination in a wider sphere than Syverson's accounts of various writing situations and with an emphasis on energy and circulation. In "The Agency of Assemblages and the North American Blackout," Bennett sees the Earth as a whole in which parts circulate and form assemblages such as the electrical power grid—an affiliation of "charged parts" that constellate "in sufficient proximity and coordination to function as a (flowing) system" (446). The grid is a vast assemblage of transmission lines, power plants, and substations and a volitale mix of actants—coal, sweat, electromagnetic fields, computer programs, electron streams, profit motives, heat, lifestyles, nuclear fuel, plastic, fantasies of mastery, static, legislation, water, economic theory, wires, and wood—that always contains variability and frictions among the parts.[12] These elements emit energies that participate in the whole and exceed it and combine to operate emergently by the assemblage's own rules and protocols that fluctuate indeterminately. Such a system doesn't fit into the "willed intentionality of persons, the disciplinary power of society, or the automatism of natural processes" (446). The grid's distributed agency is a capacity to make a difference, produce an effect, or initiate action, which for Bennett grounds a vitalist ontology. This "enchanted" materialism marks an assemblage's "power of expression." The capacity to engage in and enact new compositions via the circulation of energies forces assemblages to become "otherwise than they are" (447–48). Bennett writes, "There are various sources or sites of agency, including the intentionality of the human animal, the temperament of a brain's chemistry, the momentum of a social movement, the mood of an architectural form, the propensity of a family, the style of a corporation, the drive of a sound field, and the decisions of molecules at far-from-equilibrium states" (447). This is a vibrant, overflowing, material, and energetic "generative mobility" at the heart of the grid's emergence and enaction that coordinates it as a system.

The case of the North American blackout in 2003 is a particularly clear example of this distributed agency that grounds enaction in systemic coordination, even in the face of dissonance and variability. The system always contains frictions among its parts that can bubble up to full-blown "dissonance" so great that "cooperation [becomes] impossible" (448). The blackout was an endpoint of a cascade of voltage collapses, withdrawals from the grid, and counterproductive human decisions. During the 2003 blackout, a brush fire and several wire breaks from fallen trees led to the withdrawal of generators in Ohio and Michigan that shifted the flow pattern of the system, overloading other lines and generators, placing more stress on other parts of the system, and tripping off a cascade of shutdowns. The cascade stopped on its own "after affecting fifty million people over approximately twenty-four thousand square kilometers and shutting down more than one hundred power plants, including two nuclear reactors" (449). No one in the United States or

Canada knows why it stopped, outside of the system's own coordination, but "a variety of agential loci" that set it off were identified: electricity and its active/reactive forces; power plants that were understaffed and overprotective of their systems; transmission wires that have heat limits; brush fires in Ohio underneath a line; First-Energy and other energy-trading corporations that legally and illegally milk the grid without maintaining its infrastructure; consumers and their increasing demand for electricity; and the Federal Energy Regulatory Commission (FERC) and 1992 deregulation act.

Bennett elaborates on the first and last causes: electricity and FERC. Electricity is a stream of electrons moving in a current that is measured in amperes, the force of which is measured in volts. In the North American grid, the amps constantly oscillate with volts like a pair of waves. When they are in phase, they act as an active power; out of phase, as a reactive power. The reactive power maintains the voltage or force of the current through the wires. If too many devices demand power, there is a deficit of reactive power that reduces the current. FERC, as a human-social-institutional actant separated production of electricity from its distribution, allowing companies to buy electricity in one part of the country and sell it in another, increasing the distance electricity has to travel and the load on transmission wires. As transmission wires become loaded, they consume more reactive power needed to maintain volts. Reactive power doesn't travel along wires as well as active power, dissipating over long distances. Power plants can produce more reactive power but don't have a financial incentive to do so, since it reduces more over long distances. Even though the system sets up the possibility for this kind of cascade, deregulators failed to anticipate it. And electricity itself also contributes its own "swerves and quirks" of nonlinearity (451). As a flow of electrons, it is always mobile but not entirely predictable. In 2003, the transmission along the shore of Lake Erie disconnected, leading the power flow to take another path. It "immediately reversed direction and began flowing in a giant loop counterclockwise from Pennsylvania to New York to Ontario and into Michigan" (Power Outage Task Force, qtd. in Bennett 451). Ohio-based company First-Energy, looking to minimize its role, placed blame on the shift in flow that took "a route from producer to buyer different from the intended path" (Wald, qtd. in Bennett 451). Bennett looks to this example to interrogate agency, cause, and, in particular, blame and its political articulation. But for me it is a better example of the systemic, distributed, and emergent enaction than Syverson's examples of typical writing scenarios. It is a clear case of systemic coordination over individual or intentional collaboration.[13]

Musical improvisation puts embodied enaction in these kinds of coordinated systems as entangled functions of their ecological processes. In *Sync or Swarm*, David Borgo reads jazz improvisation through contemporary complexity theory, seeing improvisation, in part, through a model of Ilya Prigogine's dissipative structures, "systems capable of maintaining their identity only by remaining continually open to the flux and flow of the environment" (Briggs and Peat, qtd. in Borgo 123). Improvisation, like the weather, needs to be continually agitated and energized. Weather maintains itself as a system through the movement of Earth's rotation, the forces of gravity, and the energy of solar radiation. Similarly, improvisation functions as a kind of open system that takes in energy and produces entropy—excess or waste products that can function as a form of energy for other systems. For Borgo, everything in improvisation—from the education and experience of the performers to their relations with the acoustic space and from the entanglement and diffraction of sound waves to an audience's attention or boredom—operates through these exchanges of energy and their transduction. Even the waste product of an "unintended gesture or noise . . . may also become grist for the mill of others in the ensemble" (125). These dissipative structures produce syncing, the spontaneous organization of systems that makes life possible such as biochemical reactions, circadian rhythms, and the forces of gravity. Borgo follows Steve Strogatz's outline of three levels at which synchronization operates: the microscopic level of cells with their chemical and electrical rhythms within a particular organ; the body's internal syncing of systems and organs linked to a twenty-four-hour cycle and the processing of energy; and the synchrony between bodies and environments that enact evolutionary processes and ecological feedback. Borgo sees this entrainment, or the "shared tendency of a wide range of physical and biological systems to coordinate temporally structured events," as central to sonic events and experiences. In 1665, Christian Huygens noticed two pendulums syncing together and hypothesized that "vibrations were being transmitted through the wall that physically linked the clocks thereby minimizing their collective energy expenditures" (136). One of Strogatz's primary examples is the synchronized flashes of fireflies. Fireflies contain metronome-like oscillators that automatically adjust their timing in response to the flashes of other fireflies, a process simulated in complexity computer models such as the Game of Life. Music improvisation is similarly synced through the resonance of sonic vibrations and the performers learned processes of enculturation that fold back into a tacit, coordinated attunement.[14]

This coordinated enaction produces a kind of swarm intelligence across musical performers through a system of positive feedback, negative feedback, degrees of randomness or error, and multiple interactive coproductions (143). Positive feedback functions through modes of operation such as recruitment of new members and reinforcement of procedures. Similar to the ways swarms of bees or ants can exchange chemical information about paths to a food source or a danger, musicians can drop musical cues and recruit other players to adopt or maintain their musical expressions and also follow the cues or of other players. Negative feedback counterbalances the regularity of positive feedback as it saturates the system. In improvisation, if the ensemble lingers too long on a single idea or musical structure that seems to be exhausted, then players will start to look elsewhere for musical ideas to explore or start to layer new sonic qualities onto the soundscape to compete with the mundane structures. Randomness, error, excess, and noise are also crucial to this collective practice because they enable the system to discover new solutions to environmental shifts and emerging structures. Unexpected fluctuation in "structural cues, developments, and transitions" can set an ensemble off to explore new "sonic territory, musical techniques, and interactive strategies" (144). Even the screeching sound of a microphone feeding back through a PA system can coproduce the conditions for new sonic exploration. Without this additional counterbalance to positive feedback and stability, improvisation as a practice wouldn't be possible. And finally, there needs to be a minimum density of coparticipants that are responsive to their own activity and the activity of others. A swarm intelligence is possible because there are enough participants to interact—a single firefly won't generate sync. In terms of improvisation, there needs to be enough players and listeners who are "sensitive to the many musical gestures and processes circulating within the playing of each individual (including one's own playing) and between members of the group" (144). Sync and swarm, in other words, go hand in hand. Improvisation in this ecological sense will, of course, "always transcend the full awareness of individuals" (128) and extend through Strogatz's three levels of coordinated synchronization.[15]

A microlevel of electricity, sound waves, and affects, along with a mesolevel of performers, tacit capacities, gestures, and enacted exchanges, and a macrolevel of equipment, architectures, and electronic grids all sync and swarm through the nonlinear dynamic of the system. This emergent coordination through embodiment and enaction folds the distinction between composition, as a planned practice, and improvisation, an accidental practice, into performance as a coordinated system, where system and performance become almost synonymous. Enacted performance draws on both positive and negative feedback in dissipative structures along with timing, body postures, and movements to drive its coordination. Essentially, these syncing energy exchanges make everything a "parasite," on each other and the system itself (Borgo, *Sync or Swarm* 151). In other words, Borgo's discussion of interaction at the mesolevel of performers can only be read in a reductive sense if the other levels are ignored. From the perspective of the system writ large as a quasi-object, it is coproductive intra-action all the way down. It is a performing that is forming, an improvisational practice that is as ontologically inventional as it is phenomenologically interpretive.[16]

Improvisation ultimately is a process of conduction—the performer as an open conduit in the system, as a conductor whose affordances and actions redirect flow, and as a coproducer of ethical conduct.[17] In "Letter on Humanism," Heidegger writes, "Thinking never creates the house of Being. Thinking *conducts* historical ek-sistence . . ." (237; emphasis mine). By folding interpretation into ecologies, Heidegger sees conduction as a form of living authentically in the moment. Authenticity is about being open and attentive to that coproductive moment and conducting oneself ethically in response as a form of care, not some kind of abstract essence. As Heidegger argues in "The Thing," the essence of a jug is in its capacities for action, what it can do—taking in, holding, and pouring out. It is only through the embodied act of pouring that this essence exists, and it is only enacted through a coordinated gesture that gathers and entangles related capacities. Being attentive to the coproductive temporality of these enactive moments—being open to their contingency, complexity, and coordination—requires an ethical listening or attunement to these improvisational moments of worlding and an embodied performer's coproductive role in it. Ethical conduct is not a moralism but an attentiveness to the fact that in every moment a performer is composing a world with others as they are composing the performer and as the world composes the performance. Ultimately, conduction is an improvisational performance that simultaneously coordinates and is coordinated. Coordination opens a space for thinking about the shift from interpretation to improvisation as embodied and enacted forms of composing, with performative gestures coproducing the conductive paths of circulation, connecting the various levels of composition as a quasi-object.

GESTURE ECOLOGIES

This turn toward coordination and distributed agency helps us think differently about musical performance, in both studios and live venues, as energy-infused coordination that is conducted through gesture. All of the walls, cables, and effects units would just be lifeless objects in the same proximity without the energy of the electrical grid to bring them to life, without the energy provided through human enaction to activate them, and without the vibrating energy of the sound waves to entangle it all. This vital materiality enables the system's coordination, with gesture becoming a critical aspect of the overall performance. In *Becoming Beside Ourselves*, Brian Rotman looks to move rhetorical gesture beyond a realist model of representation and a social constructivist model of meaning into what we would now consider a new materialist orientation that sees moments of bodily gesture as forms of coproductive mediation.[18] For Rotman, speech is grounded in emblematic hand gestures and gesticulations up through tongue and facial gestures, but alphabetic writing only manages to remediate a small portion of these movements through punctuation and poetics, excluding the rest. Digital media, he argues, brings back much of these excluded gestures. In addition to extending and distributing the body through standard digital genre and programs (from e-mail and social networks up through GPS apps and ambient technologies), new "gesturo-haptic" technologies capture specific gestures so they can be reproduced exactly and distributed across time and space. Visual, magnetic, aural, or inertial sensors can be attached to points on the body to capture the exact gesture, touch, or force and transmit it to objects or screens that can be manipulated at a distance in real time or recorded and "replayed" later and used as CGI in film, in real-time computer games, or even in virtual surgeries. Rotman argues that these gesturo-haptic movements inform the production of both objects and subjects and become significant outside of any cultural system of meaning or subject in control of its outcome. He writes, "The gesture is not referential, 'it doesn't throw out bridges between us and things,' and it is not pre-determined, 'no algorithm controls its staging.' It would be better . . . 'to speak of a propulsion, which gathers itself up again in an impulse, of a single gesture that strips a structure bare and awakes in us other gestures'" (Chatelet, qtd. in Rotman 36). Rotman gives us a gestural mobility that hasn't been overcoded hermeneutically. Gestures' mode of action is meditational, governed more by protocols and rhythms than standard or recognized forms. Rather than signify meaning, gestures enact intensive processes. They coproduce an improvisational practice that is more ontologically intuitive and inventional than phenomenologically studied and interpretive.[19]

Rotman traces these gesturo-haptic technologies to precursors such as painting, photography, and sound recording. Painting, for instance, records specific hand gestures in every brush stroke. And sound recording captures the vibrations produced by gestures and carves them into vinyl, reproducing those sound waves through the phonograph. Both of these are beyond representation and musical notation: each cuts notches into the tesserae and includes gestures that aren't exclusively human. Rotman acknowledges that these movements include "machines, and animals, and objects: from a chimpanzee's grin or the throbbing of a massage chair, to the movements of a musical conductor's baton, the swing of a golf club, [or] the vibrations of a violinist's bow" (47). In the introduction to *Writing Posthumanism, Posthuman Writing*, Sid Dobrin argues for further blurring this line. The distinction between evolution and technology, for example, is a problematic one: evolution is a technique of self-organization that can be broken into and altered or repeated technologically by humans who are a result of the evolutionary technology that they can now break into. For Dobrin this implodes the distinctions among writing, technology, and subjectivity, but more importantly it exposes writing to circulation and saturates "the very phenomenological encounters all subjects, human and nonhuman, . . . have with the world" (6). One of Serres's larger points in *The Parasite* is that human cultural-biological relations mirror the parasite's ecological ones. The human is always a function of the ecological and draws on its energy. The gesturo-haptic, Rotman argues, makes a turn from the posthuman to the parahuman, "since the condition in question is one of horizontal movement, not upwards or forwards but sideways; not linear or sequential but dispersive and parallel; not going beyond but an expansion, a multiplication, an intensification of what was always there; a new realization of the past and its futures" (103). The process of coordinated performance turns gesture into a mediator that facilitates this lateral circulation and attunes bodies to their ecologies, making them functional actors within the ecology, instrument-effects of the system.

Gesture tacitly and habitually positions bodies in relation to the opportunities available in the surrounding ecology. In "Eco-Logic for the Composition Classroom," Richard Coe notes that ecology is taken from the Greek *oikos*, house, or habitation, and the prefix *eco*, which connotes wholeness. Eco-logic, then, is not a logic that breaks down systems into their component parts. For Coe, discussing subsystems without considering the whole system amounts to a fallacy. His primary example is the Indian tradition of protecting sacred cows. Outside of an ecological understanding, it is easy for a westerner to see this as superstition. But this is an invalid position because it doesn't account for food supply in the larger ecology of India's energy supply. Coe writes, "The main ecological function of Indian cattle is to produce calories, which are utilized by people only indirectly. The cattle transform otherwise useless grass into dung. Most of the dung (80% according to one survey) is eventually collected by peasants. Approximately half of what they collect is used as manure to fertilize their fields; the rest is used as fuel" (234). This amount of energy could not come from wood or petroleum given the Indian economy, at least in the 1970s when Coe was writing, so eating many more cows beyond what India's Muslim community eats would disrupt the ecology and economy. From the perspective of eco-logic, the tradition makes perfect ecological sense. But the Indian people don't necessarily see this as the reason. The energy source entrains their relationship to its potential. It has its own eco-logic that resonates with their bodies and attunes them to its rhythm. Performance in the recording studio is very similar. Electrical energy grounds the system, and it is the whole assemblage, including the grid, that composes through entrainment. But like the door-closer scenario, humans are tacitly called to open it and inject additional energy into the system—including through studio staples such as cigarettes, coffee, and fast food—assemble it and connect its circuits. This collective coordinated performance enacts the circulation of energy that is eventually captured in a recorded form.

By examining motion capture beyond painting and sound recording, Rotman moves quickly to newer gesturo-haptic devices and skips over things like the recording studio writ large that already embed and extend gesture as a distributed ecology beyond the phonograph. The recording studio is a closer analog to the distributed sense of gesture that Rotman is after than the specific act of painting or the playback of a record. It is specifically set up to capture traces of gestural movement that parasitically draws on and transduces energy available to drive its distributed gesture ecology. During our research visit to Sonic Dropper Studios, New Magnetic North—Jacob Aaron (guitar, vocals), Bob McCrary (bass), James Guajardo (drums), Bryan Patrick (guitar)—were preparing to record drum tracks for the song "Elephant in the Room." This assemblage requires a lot of setup, from placing and plugging in equipment to what I call microadjustments—a whole host of modifications from fine-tuning mic placements to tweaking volume levels or EQs. Microadjustments blur the lines between preinscription and performance and are all responses to sound waves: the guitar is connected when sound currents come through as waves; headphone levels are set in response to the sound waves' volume; microphone phase is set in response to the balance of waves; song tempo for the track is set through a series of sonic feedback loops among the grid, walls, humans, and waves, an entanglement that composes part of the track; and the ongoing process of mixing is always a listening back to sounds and adjusting their qualities in response. Performance in the studio, and in the live venue, always requires a high degree of microadjustments that are a mix of enactive gesture and resonant feedback as functions of systemic coordination.

In this early stage of the recording process, the band is laying down drum tracks for the song first. In most contemporary recordings, each instrument is recorded individually so the sound can be isolated and manipulated—for a rock band, the recording sequence almost always starts with drums, then guitars and bass, and finally vocals. Before the band arrives, Jim is adjusting the drum mics—microadjustments such as the angle of the boom stand holding the mic, the angle of the mic toward the drumhead, and the distance of the mic from the head all make a difference in sound qualities. Then Jim starts tuning a drumhead with an app on his phone. He has the phone sitting on a snare head while he's tuning a tom, hitting it with his right hand and turning the key with his left as the app oscillates back and forth. The sound waves are activating the app, and the wave is feeding back through Jim as he tunes each peg to adjust the drumhead. Jim notes that once everything is figured out and set and the band warms up, they will need to go back and check all of the mics, cables, and placements before doing an actual take. When James arrives, he sits behind the kit and starts hitting toms one at a time so Jim can adjust the sound from the control room. One of the main things to adjust on the drums is the phase between the direct mics on each drum relative to the overhead mics above the kit. The microphone preamps in the control room have a phase button for each channel that switches the phase 180 degrees. Jim explains, "It just flips the plus and minus wires. . . . So what I'm doing is going through each mic and flipping the phase on each tom mic and seeing if it sounds better flipped 180 degrees in polarity [relative to the overhead mics]."[20] Both the snare and kick drum have two mics—top and bottom for the snare, inside and outside for the kick. If Jim changes the phase on one mic relative to the overhead, he has to check the other.[21] Finally, Jim has James play a beat to check the overheads against the entire kit and the center overhead mic against the stereo overheads. As James plays the full kit, his hands are moving all around the kit—snare, cymbals, toms. Each adjustment of a mic, flip of a phase switch, and hit on a drum enacts a gestural circuit that coordinates the overall ecology through the resonant feedback of sound waves.

Once the drums are set, the other band members get on their instruments and start their own versions of microadjustments. Even though they won't be recording final takes of their performances, they'll be playing along with the drummer and recording "scratch tracks" that both give the drummer a feel for the overall performance as he plays and allow the group to play back the drum performance and evaluate it relative to the other instruments. In order to isolate the drums, none of the other instruments can have amplification in the tracking room. The guitar cabinets are in a separate isolation booth, and the bass guitar has a direct line into the control room. All of these feeds are channeled back into the headphone mixer in the tracking room. Each player has a separate channel on the mixer where he can adjust the volume and basic tone of the overall mix that he hears in his headphones. Jacob, for example, adjusts his guitar tone relative to the headphone mix. He calls over to Bob, who is adjusting Jacob's Line 6 amp, to bring the mids up, and as he plays a few more chords he has Bob bring up the treble and presence. This casts microadjustments as a version of translation—from Jacob, through Bobby, to the amp out the speakers, to the mic and into the board, and back through the headphones.

Jim walks into the isolation booth where the guitar cabinets are and adjusts the mic on the speaker cabinet. Then the band plays while Jacob tries to adjust his headphone mix. He has to step, lean down, and stretch to reach the mixer while he and they play. Once the guitar volume and presence go up, Bob can't hear the click track in his headphone mix. Jim has everyone play and adjust to Jacob's guitar volume, which he typically wants way up front in the mix during tracking. Bryan, the second guitarist, talks about bringing some other gear

FIGURE 4.1.   Jacob Aaron reaching for the headphone mixer.

to the next session so he can match the volume of Jacob's guitar in the headphones.[22] He also wants to get his guitar amp closer so he can reach it to adjust it as he plays but doesn't have a cable that is long enough to stretch from the isolation booth to the tracking room. When the band breaks after a take of the song, they all remove their headphones. James climbs out from drums. The guitarists take off their guitars. Jacob is caught up in a cable. Bob has to dig up his guitar stand from tangled cables to put his bass down. Literally they have to disentangle themselves. James comments, "Unfortunately, wires are also a part of the composition process." These are the mundane microadjustments that get overlooked when one is thinking about collaboration and composing. Recording really is a coordinated performance of the entire ecology in the resonant process of syncing.

Perhaps one of the main accomplishments in this recording session, in terms of what most people might typically consider composing a track, was setting the tempo for the song and deciding whether to run the click track at quarter or eighth notes. This takes place over an extended part of the session and through various versions.[23] Initially the band decides to try the tempo at 163 beats per minute (BPM) with quarter notes. After a take at 163, they debate whether to try the next pass at 165, 166, or 170 and decide to speed it up to 170 to bring some "energy" to the track. Both Bob and James think this tempo is better, but Jim argues that it is too fast and suggests 168 but with eighth notes instead of quarter notes. As Jim and I listen in the control room while the band works through a take, he notes how in certain sections of the song it seems too fast even though it is slower than the last take. The band comes in to listen to one of the takes at 168 with the eighth note click track. Jacob and James think 168 felt fine, and Bobby thinks the eighth notes are good for the middle section. It is clear from listening in the control room that changing from quarter to eighth notes gives the song a different feel, faster and more intense, even though they pulled the tempo back from 170. Jim is worried that it is still too fast and talks the band into trying 165, which becomes the final tempo. Jim tells me,

> It's pretty typical of what goes on when you come in and do a song. Even if you think you have the tempo right, obviously it is one of the main things I want to evaluate as a producer, tempo and how it feels. And then you know everybody doesn't always agree. What's funny is that we came full circle. I don't know why

they chose 163 to try the first time. They had 165 evidently in their mind as what it should be, but then they wanted to try that higher energy feel, so we went and [tried all of these other options] and after splitting the difference [between 163 and 168] Bob was like "Ya, 165, that's what we were thinking we'd do it at."

If the quasi-object ultimately being composed is sound waves captured in an MP3, then something like tempo is critical to the specificity of that object. Even moving the tempo from 168 to 170 BPM can be an exponential leap. The move from 153 to 155, for example, isn't as much of a jump as 168 to 170. The higher the BPMs, the more a performer and listener "feel" the difference. Even going from quarter to eighth notes on the same tempo changes the feel; 168 at eighth notes feels faster than 170 with quarter notes. The band ultimately decides on 165 and eighth notes for a slower groove with a faster feel. None of this, of course, counts in terms of who owns the copyrights as the composer of the song, but it all coproduces the song in its captured digital version. And it's all made possible not just through the human collaboration that takes place in such debates but through the coordination of the ecology—sound, its energy, and its circulation feeding back through the system and the gestures that enact it.

Just as all of the setup and microadjustments are performances that enact coordination as a form of composing, so is producing and mixing. Jim makes the distinction between setting everything up and getting all the technical aspects of the studio running as the engineer's role, and managing the process, collaborating on the songs, coaching the players, and mixing the tracks as the role of a producer. Much of this drum session involves human collaboration fed back through and coordinated with all of the preinscription. For example, when the band gathers in the control room to hear a take, Jim often takes the lead on providing feedback. At one point he notes, "There is a whole section back there where I really feel like it is losing intensity. Like it was kind of getting tired sounding." Then he spins to the computer keyboard and pops the take in and out of the control room speakers to listen back. "Like right in there. Every one of those has to be right on. . . . Let's do another take for sure." The song is a complex one. Even though it is at a steady tempo, it has multiple parts and sections with a number of demanding drum parts. On the next playback, they get into a discussion of dropping some of the drum fills down to simpler parts. Jim asks if the pattern might change; Jacob suggests that not as many sixteenth notes or triplets in the tom parts might help the groove; Jim proposes dropping out some of the higher toms to help accentuate the low toms and make the overall feel of the song heavier. They listen to some playback and Jim air drums and beat boxes out how it could be done differently. After listening to more playback, Jim stops the tape: "That could be a little more authoritative. . . . Maybe make it more staccato and not as busy." At this point the band and Jim are composing the drum parts collaboratively but through the coordination of the system as it is enacted through gesture. Gesture is central to setting up, performing and recording, and playing back tracks in the control room.

Mixing adds another layer of gesture ecologies to the coordinated performance. In the predigital era, mixing was a performance in and of itself.[24] It often took two to three people to do a manual mix, each being accountable for certain faders and knobs to adjust levels and EQs. They had to make a number of practice passes at the mix before they could record a take of it in real time. Now, *mixing as performance* can be programmed into the computer by a producer and done automatically. With the computer and a few clicks of a mouse, a producer can create "moves" in the mixing board or DAW that remember all of the edits, time codes, volume changes, or pans that in the analog days people would have to perform live with the tape rolling. Interestingly called "moves,"

FIGURE 4.2.   Jim King with the mixing board and computer keyboard.

the computer literally moves the faders and knobs on the manual board. Jim shows us an example: he clicks a write W button for a particular track in the software, changes the pan and the volume, and then clicks out. It now remembers these "moves" every time the track plays back, and the software displays the moves as the waveforms pass by on the screen. But "moves" also has other connotations—movements, motions, actions, gestures. All while Jim is showing us automated gestures his hand gestures are in full motion across the computer keyboard and mixing board. The analog mixing gestures have been translated into the computer through a different set of manual gestures. While the current technology affords more convenience than tape, digital mixing also affords the ability to *manipulate a performance*, such as adjusting the timing or copying/pasting a good section multiple times in a song. The producer can manipulate the timing of a drum performance by selecting an entire section and have the software automatically line up the snare hits with the downbeat; or, if the automatic syncing is still off or sounds too mechanical, the producer can go in and line up the timing of individual drum hits one at a time by clicking on the captured digital hit and moving it manually. If a bass player doesn't sustain a note long enough, the producer can click on the waveform and drag or "time stretch" it. And of course there is Auto-Tune that can manipulate a vocal performance by moving the pitch of a note into a pre-programmed musical key.[25] And finally, digital mixing can also *create a performance*. A producer, for example, can "draw" a drum part in eighth, sixteenth, or thirty-second notes, which can generate something in the extreme that is not even playable by humans, or program a bass line and repeat it throughout a track. Whether through manual or automated mixing, manipulating, or creating a performance, producing is a gesture ecology that entangles layers of performance that are translated through, enacted by, and coordinated across the entire ecology.

For the engineers, producers, and performers, these gestures are almost entirely habitual, enacted and coordinated through a process of entrainment that happens in the studio. Technologies, walls, sound waves, and bodily capacities enact a rhythmic gestural response to the ecology in which humans function as circuit makers and circuit breakers. Knobs and faders are designed to resonate with hands and fingers, calling them tacitly to grasp for them; inputs and cables call to be plugged in. And this is just a fraction of the action, mediation, and gesture that coordinates the ecology at any given time, which can entail clicking foot pedals to switch effects; tuning guitars, from kneeling down to plugging them in to plucking the strings to reaching out to turn the tuning pegs; stepping up and leaning into or away from a microphone; adjusting the snare stand so the drum isn't uneven, leading to rim shots. Even each movement across the strings is a gesture that makes a circuit—it produces different vibrations that run through the cables, effects units, EQs, mixer, and computer to be recorded as an electronic sound wave and ultimately into an MP3 file. In the studio, all of these gestures are taken for granted, and they're all microadjustments in an overall gesture ecology. This is composing. Conscious thought is placed on the song, the performance, the sound, but none of that happens without the gestures that immerse bodies in the ecology, tacitly coproducing the ecology as it guides performative actions. All of the discussions of drum dynamics, groove, tempo, timing, and arrangement are not just the performance of a preexisting song but the composing of a song in the process of being enacted and translated into an MP3, which in the end ultimately becomes the most circulated version of the song. But the process is also an overall composing that gathers and coproduces everything in the ecology. Multiple other smaller and perhaps not so small things will be adjusted before this track gets finished or finalized in a mix and MP3. The recording studio is nothing but an elaborate echo chamber, a resonance machine—it is a gesture ecology for the circulation of sound, which, like writing an account in Latour's *Reassembling the Social*, ties the Gordian knot, entangling the studio as quasi-object.

FROM GESTURE TO GENRE

All of these performative aspects of coordination—circulation of energy, assembling performance space, microadjustments via human gesture, and resonant responses to sound waves—are also central to live performance. Gesture articulates all of the potential conditions from the grid up through the live performance but also all of the future possibilities up through the coproduction of genre. Everything from plugging in cables to twisting knobs on a soundboard gathers materials—digital effects, electrical cables, analog amplifiers, sound waves, walls, human affects, and cultural forms. Gesture completes these material circuits that bring together the analog and the digi-

tal, the past and the future, and the micro and the macro into coordinated relations. Compositional practice, then, becomes most basically a gestural mode
of response in relation to the circulation of energies that enact networks and
coproduce ecologies. These gesture ecologies cut across all forms of material
composition but are a particular feature of live performances, especially in
improvisational sound art. In the fall of 2013, Thomas Stanley and the other
two members of his improvisational ensemble MOM[2] (Mind over Matter,
Music over Mind) came down to Columbia, South Carolina, from Washington, DC, to give a lecture and a performance. Thomas is a professor in media
arts and a sound artist; Bobby Hill is a longtime radio DJ and music archivist in
DC; and Luke Stewart is a young up-and-coming musician in the DC jazz and
sound art scenes. The visit was a chance for me to interview the group, learn
more about Thomas's book, *The Execution of Sun Ra*, and film their performances. Their experimental sound art, even more explicitly than composing
in the studio, shows how the entanglements of performance and the gestures
of compositional practice ground emergence at larger scales of circulation.
If the examination of the recording studio looks back at preinscription as the
conditions for enacting gesture ecologies, the live performance extends this
forward to the emergence of genre from a grounding in gesture ecologies.

The first time I saw Thomas perform and speak, his comments on genre
stood out. In a Q&A after the performance, he argued that young people today
are more often than not continuing to play out the music of their parents—
whether that is hip-hop, rock, metal, or even indie music as an extension of
1980s postpunk. For Thomas and I's generation this was unthinkable. The
entire point was to find and invent our own genre in contrast to what came
before. Just prior to MOM[2]'s visit, Thomas posted this similar sentiment on
Facebook: "Unless we can develop a generation of musicians capable of emu-
lating more than the musical style of these masters (e.g., their uncompromis-
ingly fearless embrace of innovation and discovery) we are truly lost. It's not
about J-A-Z-Z anymore. Genres are dead. All of them. What matters is discovering what music can do for us that has not been done before. And soon." In my
interview with Thomas, Bobby, and Luke, I asked them if they thought sound
art was becoming a genre and presented a basic rhetorical approach: genres
aren't universal forms but emerge through recurring rhetorical situations and
inductive attempts to produce fitting responses to those situations. As the
responses that seem effective get repeated in similar situations, the forms and

rhetorical strategies coalesce into what is then named and considered a genre. And if sound art *is* becoming a genre, I asked, what is the recurring situation that it fittingly responds to? After a long conversation about genre that examined a classic avant-garde position on genre in the context of popular music and our current technological moment, Thomas said that he still wanted to think on it in terms of sound art. Since he isn't in the discipline of composition and rhetoric, this was a fitting response. My question, however, was a genuine one. I'd been interested in sound art and reading more about it since I had first seen Thomas perform. As a practice, it can be traced back at least to John Cage's 4'33" in 1952. But at that time, it was considered experimental *music*. Noise as a genre, as David Novak traces its emergence in *Japanoise*, comes from 1960s Canadian group Nihilist Spasm Band, whose members considered themselves musicians, and its later uptake in Japan in the late 1980s and into the 1990s, which turned its work away from music and further toward noise less attached to recognizable forms. Sound art, as a designation, solidifies circa 2006 with Brandon LaBelle's *Background Noise*, which traces its history and emergence as a significant art form into the 2000s. The move, of course, is away from music and toward the sonic, away from something like a genre that signifies or fittingly responds and paradoxically toward sound art as its own distinctive affective practice that aims toward the future.

Later that night, after their performance at Conundrum Music Hall, as all of the bands were packing up, Thomas leaned over to me and said, "I've really been thinking about your question as I've been watching the other performances tonight, and I don't think sound art is a genre but is instead a set of common gestures." Just as my question sat with him, his response sat with me. The artists that performed that evening—Mind over Matter, Music over Mind; Halverson and Stuart; and about.theWindow—all share compositional practices not typical with other musical genre. Instead of standard instruments such as guitars and drums, sound art and noise performances are more likely to include tables, computers, and a vast array of mixers, turntables, and stomp boxes woven together with what seems like miles of cables. In *Japanoise*, Novak describes the practice:

> Ikeda Keiko . . . is setting up her gear. . . . A two-feet by four-feet waist-high table
> has been brought onto the stage . . . and she is pulling mixers, voltage converters,
> commercial guitar pedals, tape recorders, and homemade metal boxes of wires

and buttons from a small suitcase onto the stage floor. She places the items one by one across the table, throwing the chaos together into a jumble of individual units, each brick-like effect pedal trailing a wire down to a clump of nine-volt power transformers on the floor, stuck like barnacles onto a power strip winding out to the front of the stage.... Bending down to grab a coil of quarter-inch instrument cables, Ikeda quickly connects each piece of electronic gear to the next, plugging the output of a mixer channel into a distortion box, into a digital delay, then into a small graphic equalizer—all of them fed back into her block-like mixer at the center of the table and then back out of the mixer again into another set of pedals—a different distortion, another equalizer, a phaser, a filter, a sampler—as the system builds on itself. (139)

This set of practices, much more than an established musical form, connects a broad array of sound artists and noise musicians. The setup bleeds into the overall performance and sets the conditions for improvisation and emergence—the production of sound through the complex feedback loops made possible by the system, grounded in a set of movements, actions, and gestures.

There is a scene in the video of MOM²'s Conundrum performance where Bobby is just opening a gig bag and pulling out cables in a seamless and flowing set of gestural movements that would rarely be considered a part of composition or collaborative practice.[26] But I see these kinds of gestures as central to the coproduction of ecologies and asked the group if they considered these gestures a part of composing. Bobby notes,

My setup is probably a lot more simple. Lay the turntables down, plug them in, and start playing with my music. I need my boxes and I need my wax, and they produce my contribution to this sound equation that we are trying to create.... I do radio, so I'm always thinking about music and . . . I have a sense of what I own. And everything that I deal with I manipulate in some way, through detuning or the ways that you can adjust sound with the treble, midrange, and bass, and physically manipulating the sound [he gestures to the fading up and down of faders that adjust the volume].

Bobby knows his archive, so he isn't just grabbing a random record from a random crate. He anticipates which snippet from which record in which crate he needs for the emerging composition. But the most interesting thing for me is

FIGURE 4.3.   Bobby Hill manipulating faders and a record.

all of the gestures that go into his practice: his crates of records, that he calls "cells" of related material, have to be placed on the floor within reach; he has to spin back and forth from crate to turntable as he grabs a record from a crate, pulls it from its sleeve, and places it on a turntable. Bobby used to bring the bulk of his record collection to a given performance but would only use maybe 5 percent of it. In order to be more economical, he thinks with more foresight about a given performance and what the situation might call for. Knowing the situation for the performance, he anticipates what "cells" to bring. This "forethought-based composition," as he calls it, allows him to respond to the sounds being coproduced at any moment and reach down to pull out the precise record and snippet of music to manipulate.[27]

All of this setup is parahuman and bleeds into composition. But where to draw the line on this continuum from setup through performance differs with each of them. Like Bobby deciding what crates of records to bring on any given night, Thomas decides what technologies and samples to bring based on the occasion:

> Every time I go out there is at least some slight modification to what would constitute my instrument. My instrument is everything that is on this side of ... my mixing board. So I start picking the things I'm going to use on a particular night based on some kind of intuitive sense of what kinds of sound fields or what kinds

of structures best suit that occasion. The performance space might call for quiet or loud or subtle. You might have to compete with a lot of ambient noise or you might not. So you make decisions based on what kinds of sounds are needed for a particular opportunity.

Thomas sees the gathering and setup of these materials as part of an extended "ritual": "I know they are just pieces of plastic and wire and metal," he says, but "they become rattles and bundles of sage and little feathers . . . and I'm going to . . . get magical things to come out of them."[28] Luke, on the other hand, sees much of these practices as a "pre-ritual," or "making ourselves ready to compose." All of the years of practice it takes to learn an instrument and learn to compose up through considering what to bring and set up are just preparing to compose in the moment. Composition, for him, only happens in that moment of improvisation.[29]

But, following Heidegger, this moment of disclosure includes all of its past conditions and future possibilities. A term such as *ritual* connotes this excess as well as the affective attachment to the process and the technologies as they become more like fetishes than objects. Bobby provides what I think is the key response to the question of coordinated performance:

> But I find in this process that we *also* have the opportunity to let go of that fetish relationship. Because there are times when we are all playing and the cosmic sonic mix gets to doing its thing and you can sometimes lose touch with who is adding that sound, doing that thing, who is making that sound. *And it could be that the three of us are making that new thing that becomes something we can't recognize anymore.* And that's what's so nice about this. There is an element of surprise, amazing invention that comes out of this every time we play, and that's what is special about it.

This futurity is precisely diffraction with sound waves rather than light: sound waves are in superposition over one another in ways that function as an extension of all of the preinscription and in excess of both intention and gesture. The compositional practices of each performer are collectively enacting a combined sound that no one individual is making. Sound waves collaborate to entangle composers, technologies, spaces, *and each other* through coordinated enaction that generates unanticipated compositional results.

FIGURE 4.4.   Luke Stewart working buttons and a knob.

Sound art is not interested in the repetition of a musical genre or common meaning but in an experience of sound that hasn't been fully anticipated by the artists or the audience. Its aim is a kind of coordination through sound waves that affects audiences and produces new conditions of possibility for the listeners. Thomas explains his version of this aim:

> We are sort of teaching the audience how to listen, how to hear, from our very first sound. It builds up slowly. We build up slowly. To get to where we've given you enough information, enough tutoring, so that now you ought to be able to handle this, and now we are going to ratchet it up. My standard is space. To create a credible, supervening, altered space with sound waves that is distinctly different, politically, geometrically, socially from the space you were in before you first heard our sound. And that's always what I'm playing towards.

This change in space is temporary, for that moment, but it should give the audience an example, a hint, that there are ulterior possibilities, the potential for something different. Thomas wants to show the audience that it is possible to do something outside of the given historical conditions or parameters of culture that can translate into the listeners' daily lives. When they go back to work or home, they should be thinking, What are the alternatives for these spaces that I live in every day? What different energy can I inject into these spaces and make them different than they were a moment ago? Luke concurs:

> I really do believe in what Thomas is saying. We are using sound waves to create space. It's almost like we are creating a little world that we see as the way it should be, that is working, that is uplifting for the audience and us—changing our world in that 20, 30, 45, or 60 minutes, however long the performance lasts. When you are present for a performance that is really compelling, those sound waves and the feeling and the energy that lies within those waves . . . are emitted from the performer. I think everybody . . . has had an experience at a live show where somebody hits a note or sings a passage and it just hits you. That's something that is in the sound that you're hearing. [But] there is something extra going on rather than just the frequency, a feeling, there is something extra traveling in the sound that is affecting your ear, that is changing your psyche and body, it's changing you in that moment, and this is a really important aspect of what sound is.

It's hard to imagine a better description of new materialism. Sound waves are materially a part of that space, and the room affects how the sound waves resonate and reverberate, which affects what they can do. The sound waves don't just interact with the space but create that space and are altered in the process. These altered waves then change what other bodies can do, persuading them to listen, to think, to move—an overall process of coordinated enaction.

This approach to their practice is inherently political for Thomas. He picks up a poster for their performance that night and points to the image of a sound wave that runs across it and elaborates:

> The visual depiction of sound waves is map of a territory and the political dimension of our work. If you look carefully there are no flags and there is no money. There's no sovereignty of the nation state within this microcosm. There is freedom, real freedom, because we are not playing culture and we're not playing counter-culture. We are playing right down the middle and in that place all of these other -isms they just start to break apart. . . . There is no content in what we are offering, no ideology. And that's why it will work.

Thomas is reversing Steve Goodman's argument in *Sonic Warfare* that sees sound and the policing of frequency as a mode of control. Goodman writes,

"What if the actual weapon was vibration itself, and its target not the operating systems of robots but the affective operating system of the city's population? This would be a scenario in which that which was being transmitted would be not just information but bad vibes. In this ecology, an event would simultaneously draw in the physics of its environment (its vibrations) and the moods of its populace (its vibes), sending an immense collective shiver through the urban as resonating surface" (76). Reversing these principles of control and domination into a dynamic of release and possibility is at the heart of Sun Ra's "tone science." When Ra says, "Space is the Place," he doesn't just mean outer space. He also means the space being inhabited right now. That is a place that can be changed and altered to produce a new mind-set or perception. This notion is also at the heart of Afrofuturism. When Kowdo Eshun writes about the "futurhythmachine," he is invoking, in part, the ability of pulsating low-end sound waves to momentarily detach the listener from a determined past, immerse and suspend them in the present, and open them to new potential futures (*More Brilliant Than the Sun*). These potential futures can be altered through sound, using vibrations to change the vibes, not ideologically but affectively.

Thomas is fairly adamant about seeing his work as nonrepresentational. Sound art, for him, should be about the force and experience of the sound waves as they entangle the audience in and through the performance, not about the ways sound evokes birds, or trains, or water in a listener. Thomas wants the audience to experience sound—feel the waves hitting them, leaving their mark on the body as a tessera, coproducing their resonating body in that moment, coordinating them with the ecology via sound, and disclosing them differently. But their bodies also change the room, change the way the sound waves get absorbed and diffracted, literally changing the sound and coproducing the "vibe" of the performance. This is not a traditionally rhetorical notion of audience in the discussions of collaboration, one that is either passive humans being moved or conscious coauthors of discourse, arguments, or texts. It is one where circulating sound waves entangle everything into an enactive coordination, making the audience a relay for resounding. Bobby at one point chimes in:

> What I am going to describe isn't true . . . but this is what it feels like. Sound
> waves generally emit out and go endlessly, they just go. But I imagine that when

we play in this space and we play for an audience the sound waves go and get all linked up and they drop in that space and they become for that space at that time. And that's what it feels like for me when we create music. We grab sound waves for us as performers and for the audience as listeners, and we create this thing that is still temporary but it's [also] not for that time.

Bobby is describing how he experiences the space that is opened up through coordination and entanglement. And even though it is of the precise moment in time, or moment of disclosure, it is untimely as well. It zeros in on that moment to exclude or push away all of the flags and territories and ideological positions. A momentary world is materially created, opened up through the vitalist energies of sound, but there is a futurity to it, a virtual potential where the sound waves are both entangling that moment but also creating conditions for unnamed futures. Thomas's book, *The Execution of Sun Ra*, captures this moment of building on the past but opening to the future through the dual meaning of "execute": to kill—exhaust, extinguish, burn as fuel (conceal); to enact—"to put a plan into action," carry out, deploy, play out, spark a transformation (reveal) (1–2). MOM²'s "fitting response" to past conditions is to turn away from that past and reach toward potential futures that may not be fully anticipatable. The gesture ecology executes a past genre as it enacts a set of common gestures and sets the potential for the execution of future genre.

The paradox of execution is that an anti-genre stance can still lead to the enaction of a genre. It's the open approach to futurity that allows a genre to emerge from gesture ecologies of composition and their affects on audiences, not in a specific or predetermined sense but through an overall ecological coordination. Artists can't control what happens as their performances resonate and resound beyond the moment and space of performance. The same kind of entanglement through the circulation of sound waves that occurs in performance spaces also operates at a larger, broader level of scale to inform the coordinated coproduction of genre. MOM²'s discussion of genre stayed pretty tightly to the relationship between the avant-garde and the popular and the current technological moment. But genre labeling has typically been the purview of DJs, journalists, and record company marketing departments rather than artists—*grunge*, for example, was designated by a UK journalist, not musicians from Seattle. But I think Novak's analysis in *Japanoise* takes this conversation to the next level of scale, to "music at the edge of circulation." As Novak makes clear, it is often the staunch attempt to resist preexisting genre that, paradoxically, drives the emergence of new genre. Novak boils down an array of responses from the Noise artists he interviews—some of whom disavow use of the term altogether—to two predominant positions: practitioners that see Noise as an extreme form of rock or electronic music, and those who deny any relationship to music whatsoever and see noise as pure sound that can't be categorized or understood as music. Nevertheless, the terms *Noise*, *Noise Music*, and *Japanoise* always show up through his research as designations for the genre. The total incommensurability between noise and music echoes for him "modernist avant-garde projects of anti-art, which attempt, often vainly, to keep emergent forms of expression from being subsumed into the dialectics of historical categories" (118). But despite this anti-genre position, Noise became a genre through a feedback loop with music. As it proclaimed absolute opposition to music, it was at the same time recorded and distributed in musical formats—LPs, cassettes, and CDs. It functioned exactly like other underground music of its time period that emerged through recorded forms of circulation.

As Novak makes clear, this circulation folds over and extends out to a macrolevel and the emergence of new genre. Noise as a genre, he argues, is produced through circulation and feedback between the scenes in Canada and Japan. Noise artists in Japan imagine Canada as the original Noise scene, heralded by the Nihilist Spasm Band in the 1960s. Through the band's influence, the Japanese artists produced more contemporary versions of Noise in the 1980s and 1990s that circulated back to North America through recordings and fanzines. Consequently, contemporary audiences in North America see Japan as the originators of Noise. Each place imagines this great, originary Noise scene in the other place, which fuels its own invention and production. But the "scene" in each place only consists of a small number of fans, artists, and venues. It's not a San Francisco in the 1960s or Seattle in the 1990s from which a genre is disseminated. As a genre, and a scene, Noise primarily exists though performance and circulation. Its location is not in a single place but in the coordinated movements and feedback loops of gesture ecologies that circulate outward to produce emergence. Genre is more of an epiphenomenon of performance and circulation rather than located in a preexistent place (Canada or Japan). For Novak, "Japanoise . . . could only have been produced through this mediated feedback between Japan and North America. . . . For over two decades, Japan was where Noise stuck—not because Noise was invented here, but because it was driven home in transnational circulations that continually projected its emergence back onto Japan" (16). These "translocal" receptions exist far from any particular live scene and displace them into circulation.[30] Like Bobby's discussion of diffraction, no one really knows who made that genre. Through superposition, the electricity and sound waves enacted through the gesture ecologies of performance circulate at a more macrolevel and coalesce as something in excess of its parts or its origins.

It doesn't take much to see that my initial question based on fitting responses to rhetorical situations might not provide enough grounds for answering it. Since the field's turn toward rhetorical approaches to genre through Carolyn Miller's "Genre as a Social Action," composition and rhetoric has turned again from situations to ecologies. Clay Spinuzzi's *Genre Tracing through Organizations*, of course, makes this move. Rather than looking at one level of interaction, where the text responds to its mostly immediate context or exigence, Spinuzzi expands situatedness across three levels: a macrolevel of an entire organization or activity system; a mesolevel of action at the level of the interface among users, technologies, and texts; and a microlevel of operation focused on nonhuman functions of code up through situated user innovation. Spinuzzi is interested in how each level interacts, how each level coproduces the others, and how innovation at one level affects the other levels (26–27). The macro transpires historically and culturally across days, months, and years, informing the other levels largely unconsciously; the meso emerges over minutes to hours, often through conscious goal-directed human action; and the micro in minutes to seconds through a habitual, tacit unconscious or technical protocols. This model complicates the predominantly deterministic or cause and effect logic of rhetorical situation and its relation to individual genre. Spinuzzi is interested in how historically emergent activity informs human actions through layers of coproductive mediation and moments of operation, which feeds back into the process. The innovative outcome of his version of this messy, emergent system is genre ecologies—not one genre as a fitting response but multiple genre collaborating across levels: official organizational genre such as reports collaborating with public genre such as maps and unofficial genre such as sticky notes. Unique, emerging situations often require this kind of multiplicity as the source of innovation, perhaps not unlike Keith Negus's synthesis of popular genre but more explicitly including a larger set of actions and technologies as coproductive agents that result not in the synthesis of a new genre but in the actor-network of a new "genre ecology."[31]

The gesture ecologies of improvisational sound art function at Spinuzzi's micro-, meso-, and macrolevels of scale but add coordinated aspects of temporality through continued circulation. At the microlevel, the energy of electricity and sound waves emerge up through setup, habit, ritual, and tacit response. At the mesolevel, gesture ecologies are enacted through bodily performance that is partially tacit and partially anticipated in the choices of music and technologies gathered. And at the macrolevel, historical and cultural processes coproduce cultural forms such as new concepts or genre. In terms of temporality, gesture cuts into the preinscriptive energy of the virtual and feeds it forward through the embodied and improvisational enactment of gesture ecologies as instantiations of the past in the present that are open to possible futures such as genre—another version of the refrain as a process of de- and reterritorialization from the vitality and agitation of sound and the coproduction of something new out of its repetition. As LeFevre notes, innovation emerges from the resonant overlapping of conditions that are in excess of an artist's control. Artists work with the conditions in which they've been thrown, and if their work circulates through concurrent cycles of favorable economic, social, and political circumstances, then at a future time and another level of scale innovation emerges and takes hold. And as Deleuze and Guattari's primary examples of bird songs suggest, this is not something humans do intently via collaboration but something the system does through entangled resonance as a part of its own coordination.[32] Coordination is something that happens through but in excess of embodied action, human or otherwise. Genre ecologies, then, are not just the circulation of different written or textual genre connecting the levels but the entire quasi-object from gesture ecologies up through genre ecologies to the genre itself as a quasi-object that includes all the levels of scale *and* all of the variable versions and their ecologies in continuous circulation and coproduction. This is composition as a quasi-object, as an emergent, coordinated ecology.

FIVE

PUBLICS AS SPHERES

PUBLICS ARE SPHERES THAT emerge and decay through the entanglement and circulatory coproduction of online and off-line networks. Over the past fifteen to twenty years, composition and rhetoric has been turning toward a reassessment of publics in relation to rhetoric and especially emerging digital culture, which has problematized a Habermasian view of the public sphere and the corresponding emphasis on rational deliberation. The public sphere for Habermas is a space between the private individual and government authority where people can engage in reasoned critical debate about issues of common public concern. Feudal organization posed no distinction between state and society, but as bourgeois capitalism emerged in the seventeenth and eighteenth centuries, two spaces began to develop a distinct public sphere: the bourgeois family and the world of letters. The bourgeois family was partially sheltered from market forces and free to develop its own rules and purposes for deliberation, one of which was to set rank and status of visitors aside when discussing matters of public concern in the home. Perhaps more important was the emergence of literary journals, local print news to circulate and create public opinion, and salons and coffeehouses as spaces for reasoned debate of these issues. By bracketing off differences for the purpose of rational discussion, the bourgeois public sphere expanded possible topics and perspectives and created common interests.[1] But the emergence of the modern state in the nineteenth and especially twentieth centuries made this version of the public sphere untenable as news media consolidated into national and international conglomerates, which again monopolized thought and created a void of public discourse filled by advertising and passive consumerism. Habermas saw emerging special interest associations as possible grounds for an intra-associational public sphere, but these have yet to coalesce into anything resembling the bourgeois public sphere, which seems increasingly unlikely to be reestablished through digital media, which both further fragments common discourses and trends it toward emotion, prejudice, and conspiracy theories.

Much of the work in composition and rhetoric's response to these conditions follows on the heels of Michael Warner, who focuses on smaller groups that take up publication and publicity for their own modes of identification.[2] In "Publics and Counterpublics," he extends his early work on the production of publics in nineteenth-century print culture to more contemporary settings and discursive practices to establish a set of distinct publics.[3] *The public*, for Warner, is the imagined social totality of a nation or community that depends on rhetoric as transparent, rational, and deliberative; on institutionally sanctioned genre, speech acts, and speech situations; and on a hierarchy that counts some activities as public and others as private. As a result, certain dominant groups of people are more likely to stand in for the social totality as opposed to others (423). *A public*, in contrast, is a concrete audience gathered at a particular time and in a particular place whose boundaries are more or less distinct—an audience for a concert, play, or political rally. *Discursive publics* only come into existence via the circulation of texts. A book, for example, isn't bounded by space and time in the way that *a* public is, and its genre and circulation aren't limited to *the* public. Instead they exhibit seven primary characteristics: they are self-organized, a relation among strangers, both personal and impersonal, constituted through attention, created by the reflexive circulation of discourse, structured according to temporality, and a product of poetic world making (413).[4] *Counterpublics* are special cases of discursive publics that are marked by nondominant discursive practices. Because they don't have access to *the* public and its forms and forums of speech, they run counter to dominant genres and modes of address and often don't translate into the critical or rational models of *the* public. Instead, counterpublics might be hostile or indecorous like punk or might participate in the invention of their own discourses like queer counterculture. As counterpublics, they are socially marked by their participation—"Ordinary people are presumed not to want to be mistaken for the kind of person that would participate in this kind of talk, or to be present in this kind of scene" (424)—and their texts are limited in circulation to "underground" venues and alternative distribution networks; the dominant public is much less likely to pick up a local LGBTQ magazine or buy an indie-label punk CD. It is the continual circulation of these kinds of texts that makes and maintains these counterpublics, which are more emergent and ephemeral but mark the potential production of new worlds.

Composition and rhetoric's focus on classroom pedagogy has taken two general approaches to these publics: engaging students in more public issues and techniques for entering into dominant discourses and making them more inclusive or reasoned, or engaging students in more local spaces to develop multiple counterpublics as alternatives to dominant forms and conversations with an emphasis on making.[5] Christian Weisser's "Subaltern Counterpublics and the Discourse of Protest" provides an example of the first approach. During the 2008 Summer Olympics in Bejing, there were numerous public protests around the globe, calling attention to China's human rights record, rule of Tibet, repression of religious movements, and displacement of people to build Olympic facilities. But dominant media outlets in China and the West aired little to no coverage of them. Weisser reads the protests in terms of Nancy Fraser's subaltern counterpublics, which arise in response to exclusion in an attempt to expand the dominant conversation, affect how these issues are "argued out," and "write themselves back into public conversations" (Fraser, qtd. in Weisser 610–11). Weisser sees this emphasis on rhetoric and persuasion as central to Phyllis Mentzell Ryder's "Multicultural Public Spheres and the Rhetorics of Democracy," to which his essay responds. For Ryder, "The power of dominant discourses is rooted in its large circulation: the public is reinforced through regular *public*-ation of itself: because this version is invoked and adopted by writers and readers in millions of texts daily, it has a powerful presence" (Ryder, qtd. in Wesiser 612). To counter the constant circulation via schools, publishing houses, and mainstream media outlets required to maintain a discourse's dominance and exclude other conventions and viewpoints, counterpublics often have to employ alternative conventions to stand out from the mass or express other positions the dominant discourse can't easily convey. Weisser sees three primary alternative strategies in Ryder: the use of emotions as a tool of engagement, particularly anger, which is a disruption of rational debate but can be necessary to raise awareness; the use of lived experience and personal anecdotes to disrupt accepted private/public boundaries and include more issues in public conversations; and the emphasis on community and interaction through storytelling and audience-rhetor, "call and response" reciprocity to offset individual aims and generate collective participation. Drawing on Fraser's subaltern counterpublics and Gerald Hauser's emphasis on issues rather than identities, these rhetorical practices are connected to the future aims of participating in and altering dominant public discourse.

The second approach, developing multiple alternatives to *the* public, is taken up by Frank Farmer in *After the Public Turn*. Rather than focus on counterpublic relations to *the* public, Farmer is interested in how counterpublics are made. Following Warner more than Fraser, he is interested in poetic world making and what this might mean for composition pedagogy. The emphasis on making and text circulation draws him to punk, anarchist, and riot grrrl zines as archetypal genres produced through acts of bricolage. Following Walker Percy, Levi-Straus, Dick Hebdige, and de Certeau, he develops the concept of bricolage as an artful making do.[6] Percy, he notes, sees resistance occurring, "not in the forum, the streets, or the public square, but rather in the ad hoc, ingenuous, and quotidian strategies that individuals deploy in everyday contexts" (30). Zines are a perfect example of this phenomenon. In the 1980s, punk subculture circulated less through mainstream media outlets and record companies than through zines put together by fans or musicians. Very much into DIY aesthetics, they had random typography, hand-drawn images, and photocopied and stapled pages. And sans any official distribution, they were handed out to friends, left in record stores, and traded through the postal service. They were a celebration of the amateurish, makeshift, and the ephemeral, and their collage aesthetics and anticopyright ethos, especially among anarchist zines, outlined an alternative way to live and a form of micropolitics—a power at the capillaries to articulate the system differently with "whatever tools of textual circulation are readily available. This alternative poetic world, in short, must be built from the street up" (50).

This poetic world making doesn't necessarily take the form of discussion or debate. A queer counterpublic, for example, might value visual style over language and be more geared toward nightclub performances addressed to *a* public that is more likely to inhabit that space and be a part of that community. For Warner and Farmer, this practice is based more on expression and affect than deliberating issues. It enacts a social imaginary through a vision of publicness that doesn't just transform policy—it transforms ways of being in the world and "the spaces of public life itself" (Warner, qtd. in Farmer 63). These counterpublics operate through a self-organizational feedback loop and are "conjured into being in order to enable the very discourse that gives it existence" (Warner, qtd. in Farmer 59). This ethos of "put on a show and see who shows up" is exhibited in zine culture as well—make a zine, randomly circulate it, and see who is hailed by it and decides to show up for a gig, start their own band, or make their own zine. Farmer advocates reading these kinds of zines in composition classes as models for alternative poetic world making through writing that is directed at cultural publics rather than *the* public.[7] Making zines in composition classes also gives students more rhetorical options than learning dominant argumentative or reasoned discourse. It gives them more rhetorical options in relation to the types of publics they may want or need to address and bring into being. It gives students an alternate vision of democratic discourse, a different sense of publicness, and a different form of citizenship grounded in making publics.

Contemporary digital publics, however, don't always operate so neatly in relation to Warner's model. In *Distant Publics,* Jenny Rice examines how contemporary publics are entangled through the circulation of issues and discourses in relation to local ecologies in ways that complicate a clear divide between dominant and counter publics. This entanglement coproduces what she calls the "exceptional public subject" that blurs the line between public and private: it is produced by public discourse but adopts a distant, disengaged ethos, even as its feelings are activated by the issue (5). When the primary relation to a public issue is feeling, it can lead to a form of nonparticipation. Whether the feeling is outrage, sympathy, or ambivalence, the exceptional subject participates in public discourse through that feeling while remaining politically quiet. Today's mode of publicness, especially on social media, produces these subjects who participate in the consumption and circulation of public discourse but don't actively participate in what is generally considered civic politics, perhaps not even voting. But while this might typically be called apathy or cynicism and considered outside of or excluded from politics, Rice sees it as a function of contemporary political discourse, albeit in a "state of exception." Giorgio Agamben's "state of exception" is modeled on the sovereign who can stand outside of the system while still being part of it. Rice's slightly comical example is the sign posted on a glass door that reads "Please do not post flyers on the glass." In announcing the rule, the sign breaks the rule. It exists in a state of exception, both inside and outside the judicial order. What is excluded by the rule is maintained in relation to the rule through a suspension or withdrawal—an "extreme form of relation by which something is included solely through exclusion" (Agamben, qtd. in Rice 67). Even though the exceptional subject is distant or withdrawn, it operates through an identification with public discourse. Apathetic, cynical, or oppositional feelings do not place one outside of publics—feeling distant is still an identification and a function of public discursive practices. So for Rice, to encourage students to become a part of the public sphere is redundant. They already are, just in a quasi-public state of exception, partially public and partially withdrawn.

In terms of pedagogy, then, she calls for a "publics approach" that draws on her work on rhetorical ecologies, circulation, and affect.[8] When the slogan Keep Austin Weird circulates, it is both a catalyst and a symptom of a particular type of subjectivity, which populates, changes, and effects the materialities of Austin and coproduces both activist and corporate versions.[9] In response to Habermas's universal or normative public sphere and Fraser's subaltern counterpublics, Rice follows Gerald Hauser in seeing publics as "active manifestations of talk" (*Distant*, 19). In other words, rather than preexisting publics coming together to deliberate, "publics materialize as clusters of conversations happening at various times, across different places," and through "networks of nonofficial spaces from which discourse on public matters emerges" (19). In the case of Waller Creek and Treaty Oak, she argues that "the publics of Austin's trees are not locatable in any fixed sphere or subaltern counterpublics. Rather, they emerge across ordinary instances of talk that coalesce through texts . . . in active exchanges of discourse": "Letters to newspapers, blogs, informal conversations . . . talk radio calls, online message boards, bumper stickers, flyers, community newsletters, rallies, neighborhood meetings." These are not simply places where publics meet but exchanges that are "(re)creating publics with every moment" (19). The crises, issues, and controversies that Rice engages and wants her students to engage are caught up in these rhetorical ecologies. Rather than focus on students' preexisting passions, feelings, or ideologies that can be turned toward activism, she wants to foster open-ended inquiry that could lead to those feelings and passions through engaging specific issues, which then coproduce public matters of concern along with the students' own concerns. Following actor-network theory, inquiry for her is an endless surveying, tracing, and investigation into these ecologies, how they are composed, how they work, and how they can be performatively enacted differently—a "performative ontology of inquiry" that investigates in order to "occupy a different subject position" (168–69). The inquiry seeks to uncover the "composition of a given scene" and a relational position that isn't restricted to distance. Following Latour, she sees this ethos of inquiry as a momentary association in a network of actions that gather publics together in a new shape.[10] Composition pedagogy as public writing should be grounded in this inquiry-first model to create new "rhetorical vistas" or conditions of possibility for both feeling and ultimately action, which, for her, creates a more sustainable orientation to publics.

Rice's Latourian emphasis on inquiry, emergent approach to publics, and attention to feeling and affect are important for tracing the diagram of the MP3 farther out in its circulation through promotion on social media. Warner speculates in *Publics and Counterpublics* that a public can't emerge through the digital world because circulation happens too fast and too continuously—it lacks a certain form of punctuality that comes from anticipatable publication dates, which doesn't give publics the time to coalesce and become self-reflexive. Since he is basing this claim largely on his work with print culture from the seventeenth through the twentieth centuries, his claim seems almost counterintuitive for those who study digital media—of course all sorts of public cultures and protests have been fostered through the circulation of digital communication.[11] But there are distinctive aspects of digital publics. Tiziana Terranova, for example, in her book *Network Culture* argues that mapping Internet traffic shows distinct hubs of activity and connection. Not just around the megasites such as Google, Facebook, and CNN but also around smaller networked archipelagos of like-minded subsites that connect only to each other and are more ideologically homogenous (48, 149).[12] This counters, for her, early arguments that the web would open users to other worldviews and spread alternative information, the dream of the traditional liberal public sphere. Instead of a more liberal mass culture, it creates "a fractal ecology of social niches and microniches" that "materialize at the intersection of manifold connections" (144–45). Eli Pariser goes even further to argue that search engine protocols, from Google to Facebook to Amazon, are tailoring what users see to such an extent that everyone will be living in individualized information bubbles—what one person sees at the top of a Google search on Egypt could be radically different from others based on previous Internet searches and views, in some cases leaving out politics altogether in favor of travel, for example. Warner's argument about digital circulation and punctuality seems closer to Pariser's individualized information bubbles—in this kind of individualized bubble, search protocols restrict the circulation of discourse and thwart a common or shared punctuality. But his notion of counterpublics is closer to Terranova's collective networked archipelagos, which operate through a different sense of time and thus require a different sense of publics to show how they emerge through contemporary media.

Music subcultures provide particularly interesting test cases in coproducing these emergent publics. Musicians cultivate their digital ecologies in ways that foster newer modes of promotion and circulation in order to develop multiple shared publics. Music in the digital age is fractured, multiple, and poly-contextual. Audio files, images, lyrics, videos, and other texts of various genre such as liner notes circulate through multiple sites on the web and weave together networks of artists, club owners, label executives, band managers, booking agents, and fans that operate in continual modes of rearticulation. It becomes clear through an inventory of the pathways and manifold points of connection and intersection that these ecologies entangle online and off-line networks and that they operate in more open-ended or aleatory ways than Pariser's model of bubbles recognizes.[13] It also shows that the publics emerging out of these ecologies have a different sense of time and punctuality that Warner doesn't account for, which ultimately requires a different model of publicness even beyond Rice's. These publics will be qualitatively distinct from the Habermasian notion of publics that Warner argues against and even the counterpublics that Warner poses as alternatives. Ultimately, they entangle *the, a, discursive, counter,* and *distant* publics into what I am calling "sphere publics." To articulate this difference, I'll draw on Bruno Latour's discussions of networks and spheres, which he develops through Peter Sloterdijk, as a basis for conceptualizing how networks and publics can operate in relation to each other through such digital practices, prompting a move from the public sphere to sphere publics. In cases focused on two aspiring artists' use of social media to circulate their music and develop a fan base, I show how circulation generates multiple sphere publics through emergent, contingent feedback loops over time—a variable ontology that strings together sphere publics as the "virtual proximity" of digital networks and "actual proximity" of local music scenes intertwine.

ECOLOGIES AND PROMOTION

As an undergraduate student at the University of South Carolina, Ned Durrett started out in the alt-folk scene around the Carolinas and has since moved to Los Angeles to pursue music with his rock band The Dirt. Over the years, Ned has used social media and various music-specific sites to promote and circulate his work, which created an expansive digital ecology, at times in excess of his conscious or explicit strategies. In *Steps to an Ecology of Mind*, Gregory Bateson was one of the first to develop a distributed model of mind spread across mental, social, and environmental ecologies. Despite the fact that these three ecologies can be seen as three levels of scale, mind is immanent—it functions through circuits or networks of pathways that translate and circulate information across the ecologies and create feedbacks loops with the environment to support both homeostasis and adaptation. For example, "Consider a man felling a tree with an axe. Each stroke of the axe is modified or corrected, according to the shape of the cut face of the tree left by the previous stroke. The self-corrective (i.e., mental) process is brought about by a total system, tree-eyes-brain-muscles-axe-stroke-tree; and it is this total system that has the characteristics of an immanent mind" (317). Bateson describes information in terms of difference: differences in the tree were relayed through circuits of connection to differences in the retina, then differences in the brain, to differences in the muscles, back to renewed differences in the tree—a feedback loop of information processing, movement, and change. Or similarly consider a blind man with a cane, one of his recurring examples. Where does the blind man end and his cane begin: the tip of the cane; the handle; midway between? This is of course a moot question. The cane is "a pathway along which differences are transmitted under transformation," as are his sense organs and even axon—a long slender projection of a nerve cell that conducts electrical impulses (318). These kinds of circuits or pathways are multiplied tenfold as the circumference of analysis is expanded across the three ecologies. This complex ecology and the myriad of possible circuits, pathways, and relationships disrupt the traditional notion of self, individual purpose, or agency and place mind outside of the skin and into distributed systems. This expansive model of ecology and the play between immanence and levels of scale provide a way into tracing Ned's digital ecologies that produce a basis for gathering publics.

Tracing what happens when complex quasi-objects such as ecologies become entangled requires a method or process for engaging them that is consistent with Bateson's conceptual model. In contrast to informational efficiency and technological determinism, Matthew Fuller extends the notion of media ecologies taken up by Katherine Hayles and Fredrich Kittler into the work of Bateson, Felix Guattari, Gilles Deleuze, and Manual DeLanda (*Media Ecologies* 4–5). Hayles and Kittler extend the concept of ecology beyond an interest in human goals and culture but still use ecology matter-of-factly. Fuller wants to problematize the notion further by stretching it across all levels of scale—mental, social, and environmental. Ecologies for Fuller are "massive and dynamic interrelation[s] of processes and objects, beings, things, patterns, and matter" (2). But since there is no way to ever get a complete view of these larger constellations, Fuller focuses on affordances and the medial drives created through their combined connections and pathways. Following J. J. Gibson and Donald Norman, Fuller sees affordances as "the predispositions, capacity to combine, and inherent forcefulness of objects and organisms" (7). Affordances might be considered the capacity to create pathways along which differences, forces, affects, and ideas are, as Bateson puts it, "transmitted under transformation" (*Steps* 318). The combinations of these affordances create a condition of possibility or a "medial drive" that might be characterized through Bateson's model of change or evolution—continual feedback or folding over into conditions of possibility generates everchanging future movement that coproduces political and aesthetic effects.

Fuller's method for engaging this model of ecology, which he describes as "an inventory of parts," is built more out of Dada and the arts than complexity or systems theory or models of biological ecologies. Complexity theory often looks for general models of complex interactions and processes. But Fuller, perhaps resonating with Latour, looks more for particular engagements with media ecologies and in specific descriptions of these interactions than in the production of general models. Instead of trying to map an entire ecology, his chapters on radio, the camera, or websites build a list of media affordances and ecological traits and then flesh out their interrelations. For Fuller, the fragments in a simple list always begin to coalesce. Such an inventory is a form of speculative writing that opens up spaces within ecologies and suggests possible connections, combinations, and constellations. Fuller writes, "A simultaneous reeling off of information and reeling at the implications of each element making it up provides a compositional drive for the use of lists in developing an account of medial interconnection. Simply enumerating the diverse components that make up a media system allows for speculative work to take place. Parataxis (a sequence of this and that, 'ands') always involves a virtuality that is hypotactic (concepts and things, nested, meshed, and writhing). It puts into place a virtual syntax. How *can* they be connected?" (15). So, for example, he gives a list for his chapter on pirate radio: "Transmitter, microwave link, antennae, transmission and studio sites; records, record shops, studios, dub plates; turntables, mixers, amplifiers, headphones; microphones; mobile phones, SMS, voice; reception technologies, reception locations, DJ tapes; drugs; clubs, parties; flyers, stickers, posters" (15). Each has a layered and interconnected set of affordances that combine to produce thriving and evolving scenes. Their juxtaposition and alignment begin to reveal "patterns, alliances, affinities" that Fuller tries to articulate through his writing (16). The production of these inventories is at root an inventional device, then, to help the circuits or pathways that Bateson describes show up. Such an approach could never account for the complete functionality of the entire system but can promote an engagement with the ecological nature of media.

Collin Brooke's *Lingua Fracta* adds to Fuller's immanent approach a take on the levels of scale within these ecologies and how they interrelate through practice. Brooke provides a more particular model of levels of scale than mental, social, and environmental, which connects more directly to a rhetorical approach to new media.[14] He sees in Fuller's critique of informational and technological approaches a distaste for their prescriptive approaches in favor of descriptions at a larger cultural level. Fuller characterizes his more expansive, nonreductive approach as developing "a network of interpretation, with the unfortunate possible result of a certain arduousness" (qtd. in Brooke 41; Fuller 11). Basing interpretation in copious lists and thick descriptions, for Brooke, has the tendency to emphasize the larger cultural backdrop and the abundance of possible accounts or articulations. Brooke is interested in a more specific sense of scale and a slightly more defined sense of system. He doesn't want a reductive foreclosure but wants more "lightly structured" explanations rather than copious descriptions. To do this he focuses on a revised version of the levels of scale: culture, practice, and code.[15] Culture is the broadest level and includes interpersonal relations, local discourse community, and cultural assumptions or logics of regional, national, or global cultures. Practice, or the middle level of human engagement, focuses on "the strategies and tactics that we bring to bear on new media at the same time that our technologies constrain and empower us" (41)—the practice of producing and designing interfaces, the digital practices made possible by such interfaces, and the practice of particular users that designers didn't intend. Code is not just rules of grammar or programming code but an ecology of and around code: "All of those resources for the production of interfaces more broadly construed, including visual, aural, spatial, and textual elements" (48). Brooke looks for the available means and conditions of possibility from culture and code that go behind and follow from active human engagement and uses the levels as a "light structure" to triangulate analyses of interfaces as a form of practice (52).

The kinds of inventories that Fuller uses combined with the more specific discussions of scale and interface as practice that Brooke develops can begin to show how social ecologies or publics might be formed through digital ecologies. While Felix Guattari's "The Three Ecologies" takes Bateson's levels of scale more in the direction of his work with Deleuze and a critique of psychoanalysis, his discussions of social ecologies illuminate how the interface practices discussed by Brooke extend into the social as an alternative ecological praxis. In response to dominant institutional and economic forces of subject formation, Guattari calls for a kind of curation of personal and social ecologies. He makes the distinction between the individual and subjectivity in order to highlight the "developmental, creative, and self-positioning" aspects of the individual in the process of subjectification (131). Rather than accept the dominant institutional practices and subjectivities, individuals have to "cultivate dissensus" via new forms of social ecology and "articulate themselves across a whole range of . . . interconnected and heterogeneous fronts" (138–39). The breakdown of larger social ecologies dominated by institutions, he argues, will lead to grassroots social ecologies that are affective and pragmatic configurations of human groups in various sizes with their own discursive practices.

Even though the article was originally published in 1989, Guattari recognizes that computer technology will become important for these emerging alternative practices, particularly in response to traditional capitalistic institutions. He predicts somewhat accurately, "Any social ecological programme will have to aim therefore to shift capitalistic societies out of the area of mass media and into a post-media age in which the media will be reappropriated by a multitude of subject-groups" (144). In the context of the current disruption of major record label economic models, digital media allow musicians to curate their own ecologies of practice in order to open pathways for the production of social ecologies around and through music.

To begin thinking about how digital ecologies generate circuits and pathways that allow newer forms of publics to emerge, I took a closer look at Ned's digital practice. In 2011, while Ned was still at USC, I started by creating a simple list of Ned's media ecology at the largest level of scale, the Internet and its digital *culture*. I did a Google search for his name, surfed through the top fifty to sixty hits, and collected an inventory of sites he was on. In addition to his band's main website, he is on: Facebook, Twitter, Myspace, YouTube, Vimeo, WordPress, ReverbNation, Sonic Bids, Indie on the Move, Band Camp, Noise Trade, CD Baby, Amazon, iTunes, Napster, Deal Nay, Scene SC, Vent, Ligg, Bebo, Song Kick, Indaba Music, Eventful, Cayce South Carolina, and Gigzee. During an interview with Ned about these sites and how he uses them, I grouped them into five predominant categories: home and social networking sites, artist and industry sites, consumer sites, public or community sites, and crawler sites.[16] In order to look at *code* as a more specific level of scale, I took a particular interest in one artist and industry site in particular, ReverbNation. After the interview with Ned, I signed up for ReverbNation as a fan and looked extensively at Ned's artist interface and all of the affordances for circuits and pathways made possible by the site and then made extensive lists of ReverbNation's affordances across the main artist interface toolbar—My Home, My Profile, Stats, Shows, Promote, Fan Reach, Widgets and Apps, Press Kits, Earn Money, Distribution, Site Builder, Reverb Store, Resources, Opportunities. That copious workup showed quite clearly the potential for possible pathways and circuits among all of the sites in Ned's media ecology and their multiple affordances. As Fuller suggests, the lists did open up two key points about how Ned's digital *practice* would allow us to think differently about the potential for forging publics through digital circulation.

First, Ned's curation of his own digital ecologies allows him to connect multiple publics and create social ecologies. ReverbNation bills itself as a "music ecosystem" that brings together artists, labels, managers, live venues, and fans, providing digital tools for "web promotion, fan-relationship management, digital distribution, social-media marketing, direct-to-fan e-commerce, fan-behavior measurement, sentiment tracking, web-site hosting, and concert booking and promotion." It allows users to sign up as an artist, fan, manager, record label, or venue, each category having a different interface with different digital tools that correspond to the different user needs. This creates a wide array of affordances and potential pathways for connection within the site itself as well as across wider ecologies. For example, ReverbNation pushes and pulls information across its own site, the artist's website, and Facebook, Twitter, and Myspace. It also has a widget that allows its members to place music content on other web pages that links back to additional content on Reverb-Nation and tracks the circulation of music listening. Ned used ReverbNation mostly to negotiate content across multiple social networking sites, connect to venues to gets gigs, develop and alert a fan base, and to make connections to other artists for shows. He's made connections to other musicians in the area and abroad, and some shows have come directly through ReverbNation connections. Scene SC, Ned's most utilized local site, also affords connections across various publics—fans, artists, promoters, and so forth—but emphasizes local connections more directly than ReverbNation. It has a blog dedicated to the indie scene in South Carolina, it puts on live shows at a local club, and it functions as a booking agent for some of the local clubs. While he was in South Carolina the bassist for Ned's band also interned with the site, writing local show and album reviews. Both sites create pathways that are the digital equivalents to Bateson's cane or axe that facilitate circuits and go well beyond traditional record company promotion to digital circulation.

Second, such connections across publics afford expanded digital circulation that feeds back into the sites and folds over into off-line ecologies and gathered publics—the global digital cultures bleed into the local music scenes. What Pariser describes as a bubble misses both this fold over into publics and the accidental or aleatory connections that forms of digital media other than Google or Amazon still make possible. When I first logged on to ReverbNation and set up my profile as a fan, I listed Columbia, South Carolina, as my home place. Before I even friended Ned, I got an automatic list of shows in town that day. On it, I realized Ned was opening for a group called The Black Lillies. I'd been meaning to see Ned live anyway, so I went. Even though the site labeled The Black Lillies country, a genre I generally don't follow, the show was at a small club I'd already been to and I knew something about the scene. I stayed for The Black Lillies' set, which was phenomenal—expert musicianship and an array of stylistic diversity, from alt-folk to bluegrass to roots country. Reverb-Nation and my initial cursory connection to Ned's online ecology enabled me to go to a show in my off-line ecology that I may have otherwise never gone to. Rather than enclose me in a bubble, the entanglement of online and off-line ecologies opened me up to another sphere on the network that went beyond the traditional genre and subculture that I typically participate in. I haven't continued to follow that genre much, but I have brought a few alt-country artists, including The Black Lilies, into my teaching. And I have continued to follow this local music scene a great deal, which has been made possible in no small part by the potential paths of contagion that digital media and social networking provide for the emergence of *a public* through *a discursive public*. As Fuller puts it, the accretion of all of the minute details and affordances that cut across online and off-line spaces into "crowds, arrays, and clusters" makes a form of "reverberation" of these practices possible across the networks and levels of scale (14).

Such reverberation in and through ReverbNation is possible because of the pathways the site affords: it explicitly connects to other social networking sites so bands can connect to fans, to other distribution sites so bands can sell their tracks, and to a wide range of people—bands looking for gigs, booking agents looking for artists, fans looking for shows to go to. This "reverberation" is a kind of sustained circulation based on ripples and waves through the net-works and pathways that can produce aleatory connections, not just restricted ones. Part of this is done through the kinds of search and filtering protocols that Pariser talks about, but its connection to place and geography over these digital connections makes aleatory connections more likely across genre and venue. Fans in ReverbNation can search for all shows in an area or city, not just ones in a particular genre or at a particular venue. These fans can coalesce as temporary publics at a show with the potential to become long-term fans of the new genre or community around the venue. This doesn't problematize the narrow bandwidth around counterpublics or idiocultures (idiosyncratic or individualistic cultures), but it does problematize the sealed-off nature of the digital in both Warner and Pariser, both of whom draw narrower conclusions than the potentialities and possibilities of digital ecologies warrant. The profiles, songs, gig postings, videos all circulate at different speeds at different times and through different emergent networks depending on who is online, who is searching, or who happens to check their profile or catch the event notice in their in-box or on their newsfeed.[17] These multiple variations can make different kinds of publics possible. With the almost innumerable combinations of pathways created once a site like ReverbNation connects to other sites directly and indirectly through Google searches, the networks of pathways can become so dense that the network logic creates emergent spheres of activity.

By 2013, when Ned was preparing to move to Los Angeles, he'd stopped using ReverbNation altogether. ReverbNation is more about tracking and connecting people from various places across distances who don't initially know each other—its predominant digital features track hits, comments, number of fans, listens/plays, earnings, show opportunities, and e-mail lists. For Ned, its ranking system became more of a limit than an affordance. ReverbNation generates charts for various genre in every city by tracking the number of fans, hits, and plays on ReverbNation and pulling fan info from Facebook and Myspace. But for Ned the ranking seemed contrived and inaccurate because it skewed to people who use ReverbNation. Less credible bands who have one song and never play local shows can be ranked No. 1 on the Columbia charts over more active artists who play more shows and are more well known locally. For Ned, this is a clear disconnect between the digital scene of circulation on Reverb-Nation and local off-line social ecologies. In preparation for the move to Los Angeles, Ned found Sonic Bids to be a better artist and industry site. It allows bands to establish an electronic press kit that can be sent to various promoters and venues, which helped Ned book shows at the Whiskey a Go Go and other venues in Southern California. Perhaps the most important site in relation to his shift in local ecologies was Kickstarter. A demo doesn't go as far as it used to, so Ned felt that he had to have a full, solid, well-recorded album as a promo before moving to Los Angeles and launched a Kickstarter campaign to fund it. For Ned, Kickstarter is the best online experience he has had in terms of creating a social ecology through digital circulation. People, users, and fans want to connect or identify with artists, so his band spent a lot of time on their intro video. It was goofy, quirky, and fun, which were critical aspects to him for cre-

FIGURE 5.1.   Ned and the Dirt's LP *Giants* from its first Kickstarter campaign.

ating these identifications. Along with the intro, the band offered a number of idiosyncratic rewards (for $500 Ned agreed to high five one person every time he saw her at a show).[18] His goal was $5,500 and he received $5,800 to fund the recording, which became the basis for finding a new band in Los Angeles.

Since Ned's move to Los Angeles, I've shifted from his local entanglement of online and off-line ecologies in Columbia to the long tail of his digital ecology, primarily through Facebook. For Ned it's been the most immediately helpful social networking site to connect him to fans, since that is where the majority of people are, but also to bands and musicians. Bands can now book shows through their Facebook pages, taking over one of ReverbNation's affordances, and Facebook event pages are one of the primary ways bands and venues promote shows. Since Facebook has changed the way the individual band page works, pushing the show or event notifications to the side and making them less visible, Ned posts more status updates and on other people's walls to circulate and share. But even at this distance, I've been able to follow when Ned's album was posted on Pandora and Spotify, when he produced a new video for a song from the album, posted a new track for an upcoming new EP, and when his tour is happening and where the band is playing. I managed to catch him live again in 2015 as he made a stop in Columbia on an East Coast swing—a momentary sphere that emerged from the long tail of the network, a happenstance coalescence of Ned's chosen digital practices, the affordances of Facebook's interface, and a tour as an emergent phenomenon where local spheres emerge and decay as the tour progresses temporally.[19] Following Brooke's notion of ecologies of practice, interface is not just about the static page and its affordances, which function more at the level of code. Interface is "a momentarily situated encounter among users, machines, programmes, cultures, and institutions" (*Lingua Fracta* 42). It is the active coproduction of networks in excess of Ned's deliberate strategies and the affordances of social media: they simply contribute to possible pathways and the conditions for future enactments of the whole ecology.

TEMPORALITIES AND CIRCULATION

In order to deal with these publics as emergent spheres of activity, temporality has to be something more than punctuated so that promotion and distribution can be fully let loose into circulation. In his various versions of "Publics and Counterpublics,"[20] Warner has a very particular model for the formation of publics. He proposes seven characteristics needed for publics to coalesce, two of which concern digital practice most directly: circulation and temporality. Warner's sense of circulation is clearly exhibited in Ned's digital practice, since without the circulation of media there is little for a public to gather around. But Warner's particular reading of temporality with regard to new media needs to be revised to account for what seems to be happening in the digital practices of music promotion and the formation of publics. Warner's argument, interestingly, rests on a sense of scale that shuts digital media out of the social. There are three levels of scale at play in Warner's argument: the unified global culture of *the* public sphere; the social world of publics and circulation; the private world of one-to-one dialogue or sender-receiver models of communication. Warner sees traditional practices of print circulation operating at the social level but argues that new media privilege either a larger scale of archival time or a narrow, individualized experience of time that doesn't allow publics to emerge self-reflexively as a distinct public in the social realm. Digital media can in fact function at the social level to coproduce publics, but this process requires some alterations to Warner's sense of time, especially punctuality, in order to make the case. And these alternative senses of time lead to a different sense of publics that I call sphere publics.

Warner's fifth criterion for the formation of publics centers on circulation. Warner writes, "A public is the social space created by the reflexive circulation of discourse" (420). He is arguing against traditional sender-receiver, author-reader models that would focus on a single text or message reaching a single reader in a bounded moment. The distribution of a single text can't create the kind of reflexivity that for him is necessary for a public to emerge. Though he doesn't put it in these terms, it takes a wider ecology to produce a public as "an ongoing space of encounter" (420). The distribution of one song or the publication of one interview is much less likely to generate a sustained space of encounter and thus a broader audience beyond a single reader than the ongoing circulation of multiple texts across and through multiple sites. Warner argues that the potential interaction created by the circulation of multiple texts over time gives a public the ability to be reflexive or recognize itself as a distinct public. Multiplicity provides the opportunity to see a range of differences needed to ground a particular public in distinction to *the* public. Warner writes, "Any position is reflexive, not only asserting itself but characterizing its relation to other positions up to the limits which are the imagined scene of circulation" (420). This larger understanding of circulation is clearly at play in the sustained multiplicity that operates within Ned's digital ecology and the affordances of ReverbNation to cut across various genre as well as roles—artist, fan, manager, venue, label. Both the site and Ned's larger digital ecology establish the range and scene of circulation over time that sustains possible pathways for social connections, allowing people to self-reflexively and collectively identify as fans of an artist as a part of the process and scene of circulation.

Warner's comment about new media comes in his discussion of the sixth criterion for the formation of publics that centers on temporality and punctuality. For Warner, "Publics act historically according to the temporality of their circulation" (421). A sense of time that sees interaction happening in an ongoing "sphere of activity" instead of a timeless, unified culture is critical for the reflexive recognition of a group as a counterpublic. The fact that circulation happens at different rates or speeds allows Warner to distinguish various publics in relation to scenes or spheres of activity. Politics, for example, is more punctual and abbreviated, operating on the temporality of the headline. Academics has longer rhythms and flows, operating on the temporality of the archive, and is thus more detached from politics. Warner argues that "a public can only act in the temporality of the circulation that gives it existence" (421). This means that the more punctual and abbreviated forms of circulation are more historical and thus closer to politics. The longer, more extended flows of academia make specific historical action harder to imagine and enact. This provides the basis for Warner's speculations about new media. Warner writes, "One way that the internet and other new media may be profoundly changing the public sphere, by the way, is through the change they imply in temporality. Highly mediated and highly capitalized forms of circulation are increasingly organized as continuous ('24/7 instant access') rather than punctual" (421). His understanding of punctuality rests on the historical specificity needed for politics and his basis for this argument in print circulation—the regular daily or weekly publication of a newspaper or monthly publication of a magazine. Public discourse can't be narrowed to the scale of one-on-one dialogue or sender-receiver models nor expanded to the scale of a universal culture or archival stretch of time. Therefore, it has to be punctuated through a socially recognized sense of publication that is both indexed and retrievable and anticipatable by the reading public. This punctuated form of circulation of multiple texts and discourses creates the "intertextual environment of citation" that gives a public a sense of "activity and duration" (421).

Warner notes that at the time of his article (2002), the web had little sense of this kind of punctuated citational field that unfolds over time. In his sense of the web at the time, web pages typically aren't punctuated with a publication date, and most websites aren't archived or centrally indexed. The only "reflexive" aspects of the web are hyperlinks and search engines that aren't punctual. In short, either web discourse is too individualized and even narrower than dialogic communication and/or more general and timeless than even the academic archive. It doesn't create the midlevel social ecology that Warner sees as crucial for the formation of publics. He acknowledges that there are exceptions, such as the migration of print serials online, but maintains that the general forms of circulation on the web problematize the formation of publics. For Warner, future change in the infrastructure of the web may mean that the further absence of punctuality will diminish the formation of publics or that some other new form may arise to make it necessary to "abandon 'circulation' as an analytic category" (421). To be fair to Warner, he clearly notes that this is speculation, and it is fair to wonder what new media can do to the print model of public formation. But his work does require a sustained response by digital theorists who are interested in public rhetorics, and there seem to be three potential ways to approach an update to Warner's argument in light of the development of digital media: (1) abandon circulation for newer terms and models; (2) reconceptualize the notion of time and punctuality; and (3) acknowledge a newer form of publics beyond counterpublics.

In "For Public Distribution," Dale Smith and James J. Brown take the first approach, arguing, in part, that newer digital technologies and practices necessitate a move away from print notions of circulation to a networked model of distribution. They write, "Content is no longer circulated via centralized or even decentralized networks. It is now distributed through networks in which each node is both sender and receiver."[21] For them, not only are there many punctual forms online today such as time stamps of blogs and social networking feeds in addition to more and more traditional media outlets, but there is also an entire level of code that facilitates the distribution and archival interconnectedness of discourse online. Dropping circulation in favor of distribution makes sense if the emphasis is on the contrast to print circulation. But looking specifically at Ned's engagement with digital ecologies from the context of music publication rather than print publication leads me to retain the notion of circulation. While traditional print publication is typically described as circulation, traditional record publication is referred to as distribution. Music distribution refers to the traditional corporate channels that lead out from the centralized record company to wholesale distributors and then to chain and independent record stores with official and anticipated release dates. Circulating music online, then, provides a contrasting process to the dominant form of music distribution since it is based on ongoing releases and recirculations from various points of departure.[22] What I refer to as the distributed album—the publication of songs, images, lyrics, and band information that would have traditionally appeared on an album is now spread across various sites and places on the Internet and often posted by various users and even distributed in some cases automatically via technology—is closer to Smith and Brown's notion of distribution than traditional music distribution. But the distributed album is part of the conditions of possibility for circulation through the kinds of networks and pathways made possible through digital ecologies. It isn't just distributed from one point to another (a form of sender-receiver communication models) but is distributed in a network of pathways that opens up its potential circulation and produces spheres of activity. This model of circulation that is decentralized and made possible by contemporary digital ecologies runs counter to major record label economics of distribution and is better characterized by the concept of circulation put forward by Jenny Rice in "Unframing Models of Public Distribution." Rice's model of distribution extends Warner's notion of circulation into a more ecological model where multiple actors circulate and rearticulate discourse and is closer to the kinds of circulation I see around the distributed album and in Ned's ecologies of practice.

However, I think it is important to reconceptualize Warner's notion of time and punctuality to think about how this might be the case and how it can lead to another version of publics. The global sense of time as duration and the momentary sense of time as deixis pulls and spins those levels of scale into the sphere of social ecologies rather than shuts them off from it. In *Network Culture*, Terranova extends her thinking on continents, archipelagos, and islands into the problem of global space in relation to local place (49). Global space is typically considered a centripetal force of attraction or a gravitational pull that draws in local specificity to produce a more homogenous mass culture. But this sense of the centripetal force of continents doesn't account for the centrifugal fluidity of local places, whether digital archipelagos or local and regional cultures. The problem for Terranova is looking at this situation in terms of space rather than time, specifically Bergson's notion of duration. Warner sees the traditional model of print circulation as providing duration. But this is a particularly spatial reading of time based on regular, punctuated moments that can be plotted on a time line. For Terranova, mass homogeneity is no more or less static than local difference, and Bergson's duration accounts for the interrelation of grid-like or networked space and the dynamic movements and circulations of information flows. A grid-like or quantitative notion of space can't account for duration as a qualitative becoming that affects the text, sender, receiver, and overall context at every moment of connection in its movements and circulations. Circulation is not just the distribution of an object through space. This model presupposes a homogenous time (the points in time at which a plane departs and arrives) and a homogenous space (the points along the way where the plane can always be located). For Terranova, "The notion that the Internet annihilates the heterogeneity of times onto a single space can only make sense within such a metaphysical understanding of the space-time relation" (51). This is specifically what Warner does when assuming the Internet will raise and disperse publics up to a generalized, unified, or global culture or close them down to individual nonsocial points on a grid or time line. Assuming that the Internet overcomes or dissolves time and space, as is commonly thought, misses "the *virtuality* of duration, the qualitative change that every moment brings not only to that which moves, but also to the space that it moves in and to the whole into which that space necessarily opens up" (51). The airplane also changes the chemical composition of the atmosphere—it disperses molecules or air, redirects cloud formations, leaves a trail of smoke behind it. It affects passengers, perhaps making them anxious; tires pilots after extended trips; changes the schedules and flight paths of other planes; affects passengers' connecting flights and their stress when they run late. There is a whole ecology here of movement and affect much more along the lines of Bateson's ecology of mind and Guattari's social ecologies than the punctuation of print circulation.

Similarly, the more specific moments of Internet searches and digital connections can actually open up individuals to social ecologies. Circulation as the ongoing play of centripetal and centrifugal forces creates a sense of punctuality modeled on deixis rather than a timed point on a grid or distribution schedule. In "Weblogs as Deictic Systems," Collin Brooke makes this point directly. Deixis has its roots in one of the three types of rhetoric, epideictic, which represents a timeless present tense. Words such as "now" and "then" change meanings depending on the time and space they are delivered. Speaking "now" during an academic talk, writing "now" in an academic article, and reading "now" after the article is published invoke three different immediate circumstances. For Brooke, deictic terms do address a specific time and place and are thus transitory, but they "must also address an audience capable of sharing the reference, and even when the moment has passed, the terms are capable of referencing that moment. . . . There is an immediacy to deixis that functions rhetorically as an invitation to shared experience: we are here, in this place, and now, at this time, and we are connected, however, briefly, through the shorthand of deixis. . . . However tenuous and transitory, deixis evokes the social." Deixis invites the audience to imagine those various possible shared nows of others and connect them to the now of the present reading. Brooke argues that this rhetorical gesture connects a centripetal or inward movement into the particular now of one's reading and the centrifugal or outward and distributed movement of the evoked social space in which the discourse circulates and produces a shared or connected social experience (when writing an academic article, for example, an author focuses inwardly to the more closed logic of the text and also invokes wider circulation and social connections through references to other articles and times).

This double movement circulating on, around, and through an ever-evolving now becomes particularly important for technological systems that are continuously changing and opening up wider spaces for these forms of circulation. As Steven Johnson argues in "Use the blog, Luke," blogs shouldn't be seen as threats to traditional journalism but rather to Google. Blogs don't simply package opinions and news of the day; they help organize the web "tailored to your minute-by-minute needs." The conceptual limit to journalism and individual blog entries is that they are organized around punctual or linear time. The assumption is that once the time has passed, the information is old or less relevant. But many bloggers post on material that is relevant on the timescale of a year or two, not necessarily the day or moment. Johnson writes, "The beautiful thing about most information captured by bloggers is that it has an extensive shelf life. The problem is that it is being featured on a rotating shelf. If there is a time element that I do care about, it's not the just-off-the-wires time of today's news. It's my time. It's what I'm doing right now." A page that is time-stamped two years ago may be relevant to me right now in the context of the project I am working on. A review of a book written two years ago can be timely or have a qualitative importance in the context of a search right now, which does more than simply put the searcher into a nonpublic archival time. It opens onto the social via connections and pathways.

With the exception of live event schedules circulated through sites like ReverbNation that are clearly more punctual and clearly public, this same kind of qualitative duration pulls fans into the social sphere of bands across deictic timescales and digital circulations, actually making these kinds of fan publics even more possible. When I do a web search in 2012, click on a review from 2008 for an album from 1999, such as Refused's album *The Shape of Punk to Come*, I am pulled into the album and band's public via duration and deixis, identifying self-reflexively with the social ecology of the artist and its fans. I've also noticed when teaching a course on the rhetorics of popular music that many younger students are becoming fans of classic rock because the digital archive gives them access to this whole history of music with the same mix of centrifugal and centripetal forces. The archive and search make it possible for them to become a part of those texts' publics even decades later in a way that traditional record label distribution can't. The web is the place that distributes this kind of timeless material in the potentially perpetual now of circulation. And this space of circulation is a social space, a social ecology. Ultimately, this model of circulation and temporality seems much more in line with Warner's model of public circulation as a field of ongoing citation and intertextuality than his print perspective allows him to see. As Terranova notes, a piece of information spreading through networked space doesn't work on a sender-receiver model: "It is also a potential transformation of the space crossed that always leaves something behind—a new idea, a new affect (even an annoyance), a modification of the overall topology. Information is not simply transmitted from point A to point B: it propagates and by propagation it affects and modifies its milieu" (51). This is consistent with Latour's notion of variable ontology and time as a whirlpool or spiral that reaches back to the past and spins out to the future, where the past would not simply be surpassed but revisited, repeated, recombined, reinterpreted and brought closer to the present. Toward the end of his article, Brooke connects this rhetorical and digital phenomenon to the kinds of "small world networks" developed around blogs and social networking sites and the use of networks to develop these spheres of common social activity.

FROM NETWORKS TO SPHERES

The kinds of publics that emerge through digital ecologies of practice don't necessarily fit easily into Warner's categories. They are not *the* public—the people in general or the social totality that make up Habermas's unified, normative, and rational public sphere. They can be *a* public in his initial distinction from *the* public—a direct crowd gathered for an event that is self-reflexive in the sense that it recognizes that it is bounded in a particular place at a particular time for a particular social purpose—but they are also distributed in time and space. This makes them closer to Warner's third sense of public, what I call a *discursive* public—a kind of public that only comes into existence via the circulation of texts but with certain key differences in relation to medium and an expanded sense of circulation. They also wouldn't necessarily fit into *counterpublics*—a special case of discursive publics that are marked by nondominant discursive practices. They can be counterpublics if they are marked against dominant social norms or popular genre, but increasingly digital spaces complicate these boundaries. Sometimes these issues aren't at play at all: no social norm is overtly being countered. And sometimes they aren't in play self-reflexively: digital circulation is so integrated into everyday life that it isn't consciously punctuated and acknowledged as in print circulation but operates via affect at varying distances. Warner notes that there are transitions among his four categories that produce various social effects as the different senses of audience and circulation in each type of public change and respond to rhetorical situations and forms of self-organization. But given the differences in media, I think that a different sense of publics that is more regularly articulated through contemporary digital ecologies is warranted and that Latour's work on the relationship between networks and spheres provides a good beginning point for such an articulation, especially in the context of popular music, where the circulatory cross-pollination among online and off-line networks coproduces emergent, and often temporary, sphere publics.

In "Some Experiments in Art and Politics," Latour provides basic definitions of networks and spheres that he derives from Peter Sloterdijk[23] and begins to work through their connections via Tomas Saraceno's installation art piece, *Galaxies Forming along Filaments, Like Droplets along the Strands of a Spider Web*. The metaphor of the network has come to be applied to everything from technical infrastructures to terrorism and geopolitics. But for Latour the image is ultimately static and "anorexic"—thin lines of connection between narrow points. As Latour says specifically in *Reassembling the Social*, his sense of networks "does not designate a thing out there that would have roughly the shape of interconnected points much like a telephone, a freeway, or a sewage 'network'" (*Reassembling* 129). This "computer network" model can describe connections across long distances and highlight edges and movements along established lines, but Latour wants to flesh out this reductive version of networks through Sloterdijk's spheres and envelopes. Spheres are "complex ecosystems in which forms of life define their 'immunity' by devising protective walls and inventing elaborate systems of air conditioning." Spheres, then, are good at describing local, fragile, complex conditions that network theories can't account for.

Like Terranova, Latour is thinking in terms of globalization, recognizing that theories of globalization don't really have a global view, only views from various local spheres. But these aren't in opposition to networks. They exist through, within, and on networks, and Saraceno provides a model for how this might work. His installation uses elastic connectors to produce a network of intersecting lines across a room—attached to the walls, ceiling, and floor—and two giant spheres made of the elastic connectors in the middle of the room, suspended by the intersecting lines of the connectors. Latour writes, "If you . . . shake the elastic connectors, . . . your action would *reverberate* quickly through the links and points but much more slowly through the spheres. This is not to say that spheres are made of different stuff, as if we must choose between habitation and connection, between local and global. . . . [M]ultiplying the connections and assembling them closely enough will shift slowly from a network (which you can see through) to a sphere (difficult to see through)" (emphasis mine). Just as thin threads can be stitched together to achieve dense cloth, "envelopes" are the walls or quasi-walls that are supported by external connections and lateral links. Latour argues that these envelopes are "made possible only through the double movement of connecting distant anchors and stitching together local nodes." What is important for Latour is that these bubbles or spheres demarcated by the envelopes are in no way independent from the network. They are never self-sustaining, existing without relations and connections to the rest of the world: "The very possibility of having an envelope around a local habitat is given by the length, number, and solidity of the connectors that radiate out in all directions."

In this ecological model, there is no universal, global, or public sphere that contains an entire public—the room is not a sphere. Various spheres and spheres within spheres are ultimately coproduced through Latour's actor-networks—actions, movements, and translations of energy that coproduce social ties and stitch digital networks into envelopes and spheres. For Latour this model shows how there can be many connected local orderings, hierarchies, and spheres within spheres but with no global hierarchy. Every sphere or envelope is inside another sphere or supported by networks of social ties that are constantly being made and remade. Networks are a series of actions and mediations that feed back and coproduce one another as spheres emerge on them through layered and intensive activity. Much more than a set of static nodes and lines, spheres are the emergent properties of networked movements, relations, and transformations.[24] Such a model suggests how sphere publics form through digital networks and produce social ecologies that mix the online and the off-line in ways that Warner doesn't account for. Sphere publics operate at various rates of emergence—are sometimes densely, sometimes loosely connected; sometimes exist primarily online, at other times gather as local events. As Jeff Rice shows in *Digital Detroit*, such events or gatherings are functions of a person's coparticipation. As a writer, he begins with emplacement but "need[s] to travel through the various networked spaces to comprise, for me, Detroit" (45). This is a version of the space enacted through the engagement of an emergent set of potentialities and capacities. Rice writes, "Despite the informational overload I feel as I assemble these items (the citations I noted along with the neighborhoods I pass, the histories I recall, the personal moments I experienced, . . .) they are part of an overall identity I name Detroit. They comprise *my* network" (52). This isn't subjectively egocentric or objectively a city, he argues, but a shifting network particular to an emergent activity that coproduces "more than one way to get to Detroit as well as more than one kind of Detroit" (52). Latour calls this variable process the social; Serres, the emergent relationality of quasi-objects and quasi-subjects. In order to provide one version of what this might look like, I trace the artist Boyfriend and the circulation of her work through digital networks that coproduced a social ecology as a sphere public.

I first came across Boyfriend via Facebook. I'm friends with Mary Hocks, who teaches rhetoric at Georgia State University. I noticed one day that she was friends with a former student at George State, Julie Hawk. My interest is always piqued when I see someone with my last name so I clicked on Julie's profile to find out that she is from northern Alabama, where all of my extended family settled in the early nineteenth century: if there is a Hawk in Alabama, I'm related to that person. I sent a friend request to Julie. It turns out that we are distantly related by marriage through the Atlanta Hawks, where the Alabama Hawks originated before they migrated to Alabama. As I followed her feed, I noticed that she posted a video for Boyfriend. Always on the lookout for interesting music and artists, I clicked on it and spent the next hour or more watching her videos. Boyfriend, it turns out, is Julie's niece. Her father is a songwriter in Nashville and mother is a photographer. She went to UCLA for her undergraduate degree, majoring in creative writing and minoring in film. Not necessarily taking rapping as a serious career option, she made a couple of videos while still in Los Angeles for fun and realized she had a knack for it. The early videos ironically play up the English nerd angle, are full of wordplay, and sport Boyfriend trying on various personae. In one of her earlier videos, "Humblebrag," she most fully takes up the English student persona. With large spectacles and nimble wordplay, she touts her rap prowess, only to shift into full nerd persona by the end of the video and declare herself the "worst rapper alive." These early videos struck an affective chord with me. I spent a number of hours just surfing YouTube, watching them again and again. I passed some of the videos on to a couple of my friends in Columbia and liked Boyfriend's Facebook page so I could follow her progress. Boyfriend had moved from Los Angeles to New Orleans and had quickly connected with the local rap and cabaret scenes and took up the self-imposed challenge to make one video a month for a year. Assuming that this might be the extent of her foray into rap, she continued to try on multiple personae in various videos, always with a playful, ironic and, on occasion, satirical angle. "Period Rap," for example, has her adorning sixteenth-century wardrobes while drinking blood from a goblet. The videos began to circulate and dovetail with live shows she put together in New Orleans and generated some significant attention, enough to warrant a management offer and some small club tours of the Southeast.

Julie began to post status updates on Facebook about the Southeast tour that landed Boyfriend in Atlanta and Savannah but on days during the week that I couldn't attend. Half-joking, half-serious, I bemoaned to Julie in a Facebook message that apparently I would have to get Boyfriend to play in Columbia if I was ever going to see her. Surprisingly, Julie said she'd mention it to Boyfriend. Julie and I then exchanged a few Facebook messages and she sent me an e-mail address for Boyfriend's manager. I corresponded with her manager to set up a show and got promotional photos from a current shoot and new radio-edit tracks over Dropbox. A year earlier I had booked a show at Conundrum Music Hall in Columbia for the sound artists Mind over Matter, Music over Mind (MOM^2), so I contacted Cecil Decker at Conundrum through a Facebook message to set up a show for Boyfriend. I had met Cecil through Tony Stagliano, then a grad student at USC. Cecil was a media arts student and worked in one of USC's computer labs. He also happens to be a sound artist and rapper himself. He'd heard of Boyfriend already and was eager to book the show and also open up for her. His band Autocorrect, a mix of electronica,

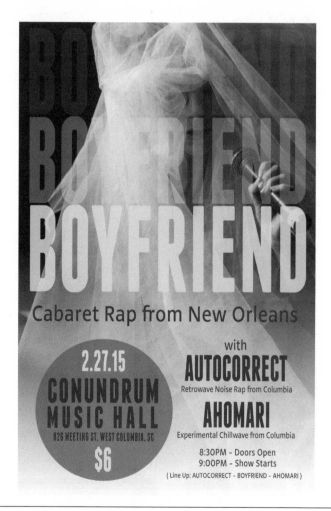

FIGURE 5.2.   Boyfriend poster for her show at Conundrum in Columbia, SC. Photo by Steve Hatley.

noise, and rap, was perfect to play a show with Boyfriend, whose newer tracks draw heavily on electronica as a basis for her raps and performances. I set up a Facebook event page for the show and started circulating a few of her videos, inviting as many friends as possible from Columbia, as did Cecil, who has a much broader connection to the local music scene.

By now Boyfriend's multiple personae were getting refined, shifting from what I would collectively call nerd rap to a more consistent visual style emphasizing the influence of New Orleans burlesque shows that Boyfriend calls cabaret rap, and she had been receiving a great deal of press, perhaps most notable at the time a review in *The Huffington Post*. I posted a few of these articles as well as her SoundCloud page with newer tracks from her then-current EP. One of the images her manager sent me through Dropbox became the flyer for the show, produced by Brian Harmon, who filmed our research in the recording studio and who, along with Tony Stagliano, filmed the show. I posted the flyers around campus and in Five Points, a small bar/restaurant district in Columbia near campus, which includes a record store, music store, coffee shop, skate shop, and head shop. Thanks to Cecil, Boyfriend got a nice write-up in the *Free Times*, the local weekly, and got some of her "radio edit" tracks played on WUSC radio. Overall the show was a success. Conundrum, a small ninety-nine-capacity venue, had over a hundred paying customers for the evening, and a small buzz about the show continued to circulate for a time after the show.

Similar to Ned's case, once the emergent event subsided, I became once again a part of Boyfriend's digital social ecology, primarily through Facebook. Boyfriend's social media strategy aims for forms of affective identification through circulation. The DIY aesthetic of her early videos have given way to very stylized and professionally shot photos that create a consistent mood and fit with both the overall persona and cabaret theme: vintage lingerie, hair in oversized rollers, librarian glasses. This practice and aesthetic creates forms of affective exchange online that feed back through her live performances. Live, Boyfriend often brings audience members onstage for intimate encounters, traverses the crowd to address individual audience members directly, and uses props to facilitate a participatory exchange. At a South by Southwest (SXSW) performance in 2016, for example, she brought cupcakes for everyone in the audience, which generated an impromptu food fight. But the gift exchange works both ways. In an interview with *Atypical Sounds* after

SXSW, she is asked about her attire—a 1950s-style satin bra and panty set with a dressing gown. Boyfriend replies,

> Believe it or not, this was from a fan. . . . I pretty much give everyone gifts at every show; . . . but since it was my birthday I decided to really go all-out. So anyone who came in lingerie received an actual present in a bag. . . . Well, I started receiving gifts as part of the whole exchange and someone handed me this beautifully wrapped [package with] this robe inside of it. She just took it upon herself to make this for me. So then I reached out to her on Instagram, my favorite place, and said "I love the robe, I want something to wear under it." And so she found this vintage pattern, and I sent her my measurements.

Boyfriend's quirky yet cabaret persona is very much a part of a sex-positive, female-empowerment ethos that resonates through the performances and feeds back online. This Facebook post by Jill Ventimiglia in response to Boyfriend's SXSW performance captures some of the affective intensity this generates:

> New day! New eyes! New voice! Hear me roar!! If anyone needs to be empowered because someone push[ed] them around and knocked them down, listen to burlesque rapper "Boyfriend"! I saw her show last night at Cheer Up Charlies and it changed me!! Think Lady on Crack! It was like she was preaching the word right at me. No one can hold me down again!! I'm Jill and I'm amazing and unbelievable!! Love u Boyfriend for giving me much needed musical therapy and helping me through to the other side!! I will be following you around the globe! Gonna try to make the show in New Orleans!!

Boyfriend's live shows emerge as sphere publics—temporary gatherings of coparticipatory feelings that resonate through her social networks (a reverberation that got Boyfriend invited to open for Big Freedia's national tour in late 2015 and early 2016).

The details of this account, of course, highlight the entanglement of online and off-line networks in a whole host of actions, social ties, and feedback loops that enact temporary sphere publics around an event. Neither Pariser's notion of filter bubbles that lock users into conceptual digital islands nor Warner's discursive or counterpublics that are grounded in a conception of print circulation can account for the emergent formations of these publics. Digital bubbles aren't just online shields from others: they are porous spheres that coproduce publics through digital circulation. What Pariser's argument misses is that he assumes the effects of online practice stop at reading. But as is becoming increasingly clear since the 2016 election, the lines among online and offline ecologies overlap considerably, to the point that it is becoming difficult to find mental, social, and environmental ecologies that aren't entangled with the digital. Music in the digital age is such a body multiple—fractured, poly-contextual, and poly-temporal—but held together through circulation. MP3s circulate in an ecology of multiple sites along with images, lyrics, videos, social media posts, and interviews, gathering networks of artists, club owners, label executives, band managers, booking agents, writers, fans, and academics. All of this collective, coordinated circulation picks up speed, amplification, and intensity that drive the emergence and decay of sphere publics. As Boyfriend's circulation increases it starts producing gravity, an attraction that pulls more people into its centripetal and centrifugal forces and generates a strengthening of envelopes as it disseminates social ties.[25] Boyfriend's videos never really sought to persuade me. I was taken up in the circulation of their affective ecology and folded back into it to coproduce one momentary sphere public. I became a part of Boyfriend's *distant public*, affectively charged but not directly active; then I became more active, coproducing a temporary sphere public, a series of online and off-line exchanges that for a time compressed and condensed into *a* public; and finally I spun back out into a *distant public* again out on a long tail of the digital ecology's temporal whirlpool but still connected. Like so many others, I became a quasi-subject for its quasi-object—a version of me for this ecology. The digital network generates an affective "virtual proximity" that creates the potential for an "actual proximity" that can then slow down and settle back into a virtual one.[26] These are the movements of sphere publics that are always temporally entangled, even as far back as the history of my family.

These online-offline sphere publics aren't just temporal but also disrupt a static sense of place through an entanglement of local, translocal, and virtual scenes. In "Consolidating the Music Scenes Perspective," Andy Bennett sees music scenes as actualizing each of these in various combinations: local styles, social relationships, and venues; transregional or global styles and people that can influence local scenes and be reimagined by them; and the virtual spaces online where these people and styles come into relations through a "ritual sharing of information" (230).[27] In the same interview, Boyfriend is asked if she has everything she needs to run her career through New Orleans. Her response is direct and telling: "I sort of resist the narrative of being a 'blank-based artist' because I think anyone who's being realistic knows that you're an internet-based artist, and that physically you might be in one place but you're emailing with people in different places every single day, and you're going to places for meetings, and for sessions. So, could I have stayed in New Orleans and not leave, and become who I've become? No way. But I don't think any-one could stay where they live and become who they're going to become." Whether bourgeois or counter, publics no longer exist solely or simply in a salon or through local zines but arise out of networks to form temporary spheres and disperse back into networks that entangle local, national, and global in any given emergent moment. Ned and Boyfriend circulate through digital networks to coproduce affective feelings, identifications, or relations that end up gathering and enveloping place, space, technologies, and sound into sphere publics. Ned was a sphere that turned into a network; Boyfriend, a network that turned into a sphere. Each is a variable ontology that entangles global and local scales along with past and future temporalities—emergent quasi-objects driven less by issues and more by circulation and the relation-ality it makes possible.

All levels of scale then become immanent, as Bateson tries to show. The global and the local might be different in scale, but they aren't different in kind. Centrifugal and centripetal forces pull them into various spheres of activity—actions and movements that coproduce the pathways or manifold associations and temporarily associate digital spaces and live performances. These collective points of contact, their various lengths of duration, their variable speeds and densities, and their shifting levels of intensity create the spheres of relation as ambient environments through which sphere publics emerge. As Galloway and Thacker make clear in *The Exploit*, it's all Deleuz-ian movement and modulation, which makes the distinction between nodes and lines ultimately break down. Nodes are slowed-down edges; edges, sped up nodes. Or as they put it, "Nodes will be constructed as a by-product of the creation of edges, and edges will be a precondition for the inclusion of nodes in the network. . . . [N]odes are nothing but dilated edges, while edges are constricted, hyperkinetic nodes. Nodes may be composed of edges, while edges may be extended nodes" (99). As products of edges or relations, nodes and their affordances coproduce new relations, and they do so precisely as a function of time: networks ultimately are "sets of *relations* existing in *time*" (33; emphasis mine); networks are "only networks when they are 'live,' when they are enacted, embodied, or rendered *operational*" (62; emphasis mine). And this is precisely why Latour problematizes the notion of static networks and why the dash in actor-network is necessary. Networks are the smaller actions that articulate social ties and provide the condition of possibility for ambience. Ambience is the distant accumulation of these social ties and provides the condition of possibility for other networks. They are both caught in a mirror play of revealing and concealing, constantly being rearticulated and coproduced as the larger coordinated actions of ecologies.

With the shifting economic conditions brought on by new technologies and the diminishing role of governmental institutions, Guattari argues that these new social ecologies will be neither public nor private and will have to confront how to achieve a "universal minimum income" as a human right, not a matter of corporate workforce (145). The digital practices of contemporary musicians are in the process of exploring these possibilities. Guattari even notes that technology may be at the forefront of these experimental ecologies. He writes,

> That hegemony, however, can be challenged, or at least made to incorporate methods of valorization based on existential productions, and determined neither in terms of abstract labor time, nor of expected capitalistic profit. Computerization in particular has unleashed the potential for new forms of "exchange" of value, new collective negotiations, whose ultimate product will be more individual, more singular, more dissensual forms of social actions. Our task . . . is not only to bring these exchanges into existence; it is to extend notions of collective interest to encompass practices which, in the short term, "profit" no one, but which are, in the long run, vehicles of processual enrichment. (146)

This is the type of eco-praxis being enacted online across the globe by artists just like Ned and Boyfriend. It is neither public nor private, given the old definitions of these terms. They are simultaneously mental, social, and environmental in the sense that they engage in a transversal practice that cuts across all three ecologies without becoming a universal or normative synthesis of them or an isolated idioculture separate from them.[28] They are immanent networks connected across all three ecologies that are not generalizable. In short, these new ecological practices operate through networks that are in continual coproduction and circulation at various rates of speed, tension, connectivity, and intensity but always participating in the social practices that bring inventories of parts and levels of scale together into sphere publics.

SIX

RHETORIC AS RESONANCE

RHETORIC IS A COPRODUCTIVE function of circulation in excess of human intention, which collapses rhetoric and persuasion into the rhetorical, a process of world making that extends relationality into future publics. Current work on rethinking rhetoric in excess of human intent runs on a continuum from the prior logical necessity of response to the ambient environs that ground responses to the extended circulations that resonate and continue to enact responses. In *Inessential Solidarity* Diane Davis sets out to establish the concept of rhetoricity as the logically prior grounds for any symbolic action. Rhetoricity is the necessary condition of response as a function of being-in-the-world—the capacity or ability to be affected and persuaded that is prior to language and subjectivity. Davis describes this affective and nonsubjective enaction fairly simply: "As anyone who has irrepressibly tapped her foot to an unfamiliar tune will acknowledge, 'persuasion' frequently succeeds without presenting itself to cognitive scrutiny" (2). Rhetoricity, as this tacit potential to be entrained, grounds being-with, being-for, and ultimately Heidegger's being-there. Humans are thrown into and exist *with* a community of others. The subject emerges in response to this alterity and therefore exists *for* others. And this existence is a function of its futurity, its being-*there* toward its future possibility. As a logically prior condition, rhetoricity is not a choice that humans make but an inescapable exposure to the other that is always present and exceeds individuals. Humans don't choose to respond. They simply are this openness and exposure to others—humans, animals, technologies, sound waves, bacteria, atoms—and respond to them tacitly as an obligation or a rhetorical imperative prior to any cognitive or discursive choice or action.

This recognition pushes questions of epistemology down into ontological grounds and forward toward ontological impacts, the coproductivity of, and thus coresponsibility for, the effects of our responses. This persuasion without a rhetorician isn't simply historically or temporally prior but logically prior. It is the grounding condition of every present enaction and moment of worlding. It is pre-ontological, prior even to ontology, or what Heidegger calls a fundamental ontology: the condition and logical grounds for the emergence of anything at all—an unavoidable relationality. Ultimately, rhetoricity forms a type of community, sans any necessary essence—no predetermined or uncontaminated definition is possible because everything is coproduced through difference and relationality. It is an inessential solidarity that is distributed in both space and time and is at the heart of all rhetorical practice and engagement.

In short, rhetoricity as the grounds for being-with, being-for, and being-there collectively provides a basis for ambience. In *Ambient Rhetoric* Thomas Rickert articulates a Heideggerian ontology of being-with, being-for, and being-there but without the emphasis on rhetoricity as a fundamental ontology.[1] Instead of the logical necessity of relationality, Rickert sees rhetoricity in terms of the relationality of world. For him, "rhetoricity is always the ongoing disclosure of world shifting our manner of being in that world so as to call for some response or action" (xii). World is what is disclosed through human coparticipation as a function of material relations and the responses of all things. It is the material environs plus our enfolded involvements, cares, affects, and anxieties that emerge with and alongside it and help bring it to presence "through our doing, saying, and making" (xii). Importantly, however, ambience puts coparticipants in contact with the entire situation, not just the immediate uses and meanings but all of its materiality and possibility. Ambient environs are not dead matter but live coparticipants in the world and especially in human doing. Cave art, as Rickert argues, isn't just visual representations of animals. It is a function of the acoustic properties of the cave, the reflective properties of the walls as fire light flickers, and the cultural conceptions infused in the ritual practices that archeologists now think happened in places such as Lascaux.

The ensemble of ambient capacities and forces generates attunement. Humans don't decide to attune themselves to the world and aren't simply attuned by other humans. They are being ambiently tuned to their worlds through a constellation of forces, affordances, and practices at all times and fold back into that attunement through their activity. For Rickert, archeologists took so long to come to this conclusion about cave art because the background constellation of forces, affordances, and practices within archeology itself had to shift over time in ways that finally let the cave paintings show up for them as art. As archeology shifted, it attuned the archeologists to engage the world differently: "Ambience, then, becomes a useful distillation of ongoing dynamic shifts in a vibrant, robust, environment that we seek to understand, explain, and work through" (5). This play of forces is never fully disclosed all at once but through a continual shifting of concealed grounds and revealed world—"interpretation is not a subjective activity humans perpetuate on an object but rather an implicit affordance already knit into the nature of things" (16). Archeologists didn't just decide to reveal cave paintings differently but were attuned to them through their own ongoing coparticipation *with* and *for* the materiality of the caves that altered their own futurity or being-*there*. Ambience is the material conditions and affordances that attune humans to the degrees of freedom for human responsiveness.

This coordination, for both Davis and Rickert, is a form of persuasion. Davis models persuasion through psychoanalysis. Early on, Freud used the technique of hypnosis, a series of verbal suggestions that "persuade the patient to become persuadable" (Freud qtd. in Davis, *Inessential Solidarity* 29). Patients drift into a docile state in which they are more compliant. For Freud, the power of suggestibility confirms Plato's fears about rhetoric's "influence without a logical foundation" (Freud qtd. in Davis 29). An idea is aroused in the brain and accepted without any rational consideration. This troubled Freud so much that he gave up the practice because he could find no scientific evidence or logical reasons that showed how or why hypnosis worked. Like rhetoricians in Plato, hypnotists can't account for their own practice or show why it is effective. So Freud gives up persuasion for interpretation, analysts' speech for patients' free association. But even when analysts don't speak, analysands are susceptible to transference—a suggestibility prior to language. Freud sees this same suggestibility at the heart of all social ties and group formations. Any leader, party, ideology, or leading idea could fill the role of hypnotist and function as a unifying figure for transference, an affectability that operates on a model of contagion and a logic of exposure—once exposed to the other, it infects you. Freud's only consolation is that removing the charismatic leader or discrediting the leading idea can break the hypnotic identification. But for Davis, identification is precisely what remains once a leader is disposed. It becomes "persuasion without a rhetorician" (*Inessential Solidarity* 31), an affectivity born of circulation and exposure in the absence of any direct suggestion. Include the phenomenon of countertransference, and this exposure to relationality in excess of rhetors can be its own driving force running through its own feedback. Both Freud and Burke ground their theories of identification on a subject of desire. But hysteria and suggestibility disclose a version of identification without someone to do the desiring, a subject already under the influence of an other. Davis argues that "what suggestibility suggests is a human capacity to be 'directly and immediately' induced to action or attitude by an other, sans all logical foundation and cognitive direction . . . that takes place behind the back and beyond critical faculties" (32). For her, it is impossible to disentangle the unconscious imperative to respond from conscious decisions, or motions from actions, upending Burke's action/motion divide.[2] In short, rhetoricity as a logical condition generates persuasion without a rhetorician.

Again, Rickert extends this sense of persuasion into particular cases, bringing rhetoricity into world. Persuasion without a rhetorician is always coproductive and entangled with "a materialist affectability that sustains our being-in-the-world" (*Ambient Rhetoric* 162). Rickert's primary examples focus on the automobile as a keystone species within contemporary ecologies. The Toronto Islands, just offshore from downtown Toronto in Lake Ontario, are some of the largest urban, car-free communities in North America and only accessible by ferry. In the 1950s the city wanted to make them accessible via bridge or tunnel so city residents could have broader access to the parks and shorelines. But the small number of full-time residents fought the proposals because introducing the car would change their entire way of life. With cars would come the need for roads, parking lots, a gas station, a repair shop, new regulations; they would bring more visitors, which would mean more shops, restaurants, beaches, hotels; and more cars and people would bring more pollution, congestion, accidents, and costs—cascades of material persuasion through the ecology.[3] Rickert develops this ecological take on material persuasion through the speed bump. Not only does a speed bump persuade a driver to slow down through the combined affordances of the speed bump, the car, and their relationality, but the entire ecology of the automobile also gathers language and culture along with it, withdraws into the ambient background, and conditions further relationality. Rickert writes: "The speed bump exemplifies material persuasion, yes, but it equally connects to vibrant networks of relations that are rhetorical to the extent that an originary affect is already built in, awaiting catalysis. . . . We might see the speed bump, [then], less as persuading us to slow down than as organizing the world differently. The bump allows a new way for the world to reveal itself" (208–9). The islanders successfully argued against the car's introduction, but for Rickert the goal shouldn't be to only resist the auto as a present danger but also to open possible new ways of life. The EV1, for him, is an example of this latter rhetorical option. Built by GM from 1996 to 1999, the EV1 electric car was the first mass-produced electric vehicle from a major US automaker after a California state mandate to develop and sell zero-emissions automobiles. Rather than ban cars, California sought to disclose an ulterior world through a different kind of automobile. Even though the EV1 was discontinued once GM and other automakers got the mandate reversed, for Rickert it shows that "persuasion inheres in the environment and infrastructure and not just the attitudes of people" (265). It shows that revealing new conditions for possible futures via material persuasion is a viable option that ambient rhetoric affords.[4]

One consequence of accepting rhetoricity as the ground of ambience is the corresponding acceptance of activity, action, and circulation as vital to ambient rhetoric. Even though Rickert builds from Latour, he ultimately disavows Latour's actor-networks in favor of Jane Bennett's vitalism.[5] But in *Still Life with Rhetoric*, Laurie Gries acknowledges the vital role of movement, activity, and action in Latour and circulation's central role in a materialist sense of rhetoric, not just as ambient conditions but also as revealed rhetorical transformations that coproduce new potential conditions. Her primary case study on the Obama Hope image traces these circulating resonances. It started as an Associated Press photograph that got transformed into a campaign poster with the now iconic color scheme of red, white, blue, and light blue, but it circulated well beyond the poster as a medium and these initial rhetorical situations to transform into multiple variations across multiple media, some of them barely recognizable, that become rhetorical in diverse ways and "alter multiple realities" (8). Through its many remakes—such as the face of *The Big Lebowski* actor Jeff Bridges with the tagline "Abide," the face of George W. Bush with the tagline "Dope," the face of Batman's Joker with the tagline "Joke," or the image of a drone with the tagline "Nope"—Obama Hope exceeded its initial conditions, opened up to a multiplicity of relations, and took on multiple, diverse rhetorical functions: "Protest, critique, satire, parody, advertising, fundraising, branding, education, commemoration, inspiration, entertainment, propaganda, commodification, embodiment, call to action, political enchantment, civic engagement, social and political commentary, environmental/political activism, rhetorical (dis)identification, and touchstone for debate" (281). These functions went beyond being conceptually persuasive to gathering and activating new actants and new networks and, in the process, coproducing multiple future transformations. As versions circulated through a number of Greenpeace campaigns in Berlin, Paris, and Indonesia and through Occupy protests across cities in the United States, for example, they transformed "everyday citizens . . . into active political participants; graphic designers . . . into empowered critics; service workers . . . into important players in a powerful art movement; . . . a senator into the first African American president; . . . and a graduate student into an academic" (293). These human transformations emerge as traces of networks, quasi-subjects for the Obama Hope image as a quasi-object.

Obama Hope as a gathered and gathering force becomes rhetorical through the particular *ways* it circulates, enters into associations, transforms and coproduces consequences, mobilizes relations, materializes change, and reassembles collective existence—in short, through its emerging futurity. This becoming rhetorical requires action to produce revealed traces that emerge from ambient conditions and produce persuasion in excess of a rhetor, and it is why Gries needs actor-network theory as a way into the analysis of circulation. Logical conditions of rhetoricity and material conditions of ambience come to fruition through circulating actions to produce the rhetorical. Gries writes, "By rhetorical, I refer to something's ability to induce change in thought, feeling, and action: organize and maintain collective formation; exert power, etc., as it enters into relation with other things. . . . I resist the notion that something is rhetorical just because it has been intentionally created to persuade and has been delivered to a particular audience. . . . Instead, my understanding of rhetoric is that all things have potential to become rhetorical as they crystalize, circulate, and enter into relations, and generate material consequences" (11). Gries sees these emergent networks of association and coproduction specifically as vitalist. Becoming rhetorical is an "ongoing activation," a worldly activity as a "distributed event, an energetic and generative process in which single things become multiple and vital as they experience rhetorical transformation" beyond the moments of production and delivery (287). Gries is extending the scope of the rhetorical, "whose beginning and ending cannot be easily identified," into "a dynamic network of energy" that "materializes, circulates, transforms, and sparks material consequences" (291).

Gries sees this sense of the rhetorical as material, temporal, and consequential, extending beyond its moments of production and delivery into ripples of affect and effect that leave traces of their consequences. The rhetorical, then, resonates, coproducing unforeseeable, divergent consequences in excess of intent that unfold through a distributed process of circulation. Through circulation, resonance entangles conditions produced by past works, embodiment in present listening practices, and affective impacts on other resonant bodies and ecologies, even in distant futures. In "Composing for Sound: Sonic Rhetoric as Resonance," Mary Hocks and Michelle Comstock treat sound as a material object that is vibrating, embodied, and dynamic, which allows them to develop resonance as a both a literal phenomenon and a metaphorical concept: "Physically, resonance refers to the impact of one vibration on another, the ringing of multiple sympathetic frequencies or tones in (usually) harmonious ways. Metaphorically, of course, we often use the term for a wide range of meaning that indicates our harmony and connection with a text, a place, an idea, or an object" (138).[6] Resonance is the various ways bodies experience vibration and engage the world through a combination of "biology, environment, evolutionary sense processing, and culture" (138). It entangles materiality and meaning, induces shifts in how humans live and dwell in the world, and coproduces ulterior versions of world—a continual making that emerges from the complex activity of the system. Rickert recognizes the enfolded, ecological coproductivity of building and dwelling (a form of disclosure that needs disclosing) but doesn't grant this entanglement to ambience and networks in the form of Latour's actor-networks that aren't simply nodes and lines but instead are complex movements, circulations, and relays that fold back and generate world.[7] Ambience isn't produced without both the logical conditions of response *and* the vital movements, circulations, and relays of those responses that coproduce actor-networks, leaving concealed conditions as well as revealed traces in its wake. World worlds as *way* not just as ground. And the rhetorical emphasizes the way this operates through resonance. The noise of rhetoricity, the ecology of ambience, and the relationality of networks operate in sustained, resonating entanglements to coproduce the emergence of quasi-objects.

This version of rhetoric that emerges as "the rhetorical" is geared less toward conscious rhetorical action that a single artist or rhetor produces, though that of course is a part of the process of composing, and tends more toward a version of Warner's poetic world making inflected with Heideggerian worlding and grounded in circulation—tacit, emergent formations of coordinated activity and dissemination. Any rhetorical intent put into a rhetorical work is going to have an excess of potential persuadability within it and resonant relationality beyond it: a rhetorical work enacts and opens possible relations with a world; ambient relations with that work shift over time and produce new versions of that world; and extended circulation of that work coproduces the resonant conditions for its eventual future relationality, its worlds to come. As a part of the turn toward circulation studies that Gries calls for, I examine John Covach's application of Heidegger to musical analysis to elaborate on the rhetorical work of poetic world making as one avenue for thinking about public rhetorics. Covach argues against musical analyses that see music or aspects of music (intervals, rhythm, timbre) as discrete or abstract objects. Instead, he looks to see how music works in an overall context of other musics—listeners can't fully hear a piece of music without a tacit background experience of the genre that allows the music to show up for them. But music is also experienced in relation to shifting cultural traditions and emerging historical moments that circulate beyond moments of production and reception. Music's sonic, affective power always exists and operates among networks of relations that are densely layered and extend through possible future experiences, thoughts, and actions. Just as music can't be heard without a musical world, publics can't be persuaded without a poetic world that allows persuasion to affect them, an inessential solidarity built through prior relationality and processes of suggestibility. Through this resonant sense of the rhetorical, I argue that the Refused album *The Shape of Punk to Come: A Chimerical Bombination in 12 Bursts* is both an example of and a call to create a public rhetoric through poetic world making—for integrating explicit and tacit worlds as the grounds for future rhetorical transformations. Refused broke up shortly after the release of this, their third, album. But the record took on a rhetorical life of its own in the wake of emerging digital technologies and gained a larger public in excess of authorial intent through the circulating resonance of worlding, listening, and the rhetorical.

WORLDING AND RELATIONALITY

Warner's sense of poetic world making operates as a performative practice in excess of logical argumentation and establishes the social worlds behind publics. In addition to being self-organizing and a function of circulation, poetic world making "must characterize the world in which it attempts to circulate and it must attempt to realize that world through address" (*Publics* 114). Counterpublics can't just be "subalterns with a reform program" that operate on traditional dominant models of rhetoric (119). A counterpublic poetic performs for a particular subaltern audience rather than a dominant one and speaks in the idiom of that potential public. African Americans, Warner notes, will be more likely to speak in a marked vernacular to a group of African Americans. His more extended example is a group of women who started a She-Romp club as a free space to act as rowdy and indecorously as men. The group, explicitly set up to counter public gender norms, was not necessarily oriented toward strangers at the level of *the* public, instead aiming toward a kind of "quasi-public"—a scene of in-group participants but with the potential to affect public gender roles (111). Their quasi-public performances inherently include risk as their world (re)making project circulates toward wider publics of indefinite others. Warner writes: "I cannot say in advance what romping will feel like in my public of She-Romps. Publicness is just this space of coming together that discloses itself in the interaction. The world of strangers that public discourse makes must be made of further circulation and recharacterization over time; it cannot simply be aggregated from units that I expect to be similar to mine. I risk its fate. . . . Counterpublics are spaces of circulation in which it is hoped that the poesis of scene making will be transformative, not replicative merely" (122). Warner recognizes that poetic world making risks potential transformation, not only of the public but also of itself, as the performance disseminates through wider circulation. But this future is not just a social reality; it is also an ontological one. Heidegger's sense of the poetic, of course, isn't tied to the forms of poetry or even the performance of a social world. Poetry in Heidegger is the revealing of a world. Any form of art whether linguistic, visual, rhetorical, or musical coproduces this opening, saying the world through a particular temporal enactment. Poetry in this broader sense is the opening or revealing of a world that is still intimately tied to the concealed equipment that grounds it and establishes its emergence but also opens it to an undisclosed futurity ("Origin" 72–77). The work itself *sets up a world* as part of the grounds for its own understanding, but it also *sets forth the earth* as the world's own deployment and future possibility.

In order to think through how *The Shape of Punk to Come* enacts and risks this futurity, I'll work through Covach's notion of musical worlding, which he develops in relation to traditional models of musical analysis and phenomenology. In "Destructuring Cartesian Dualism in Musical Analysis," Covach juxtaposes his approach to traditional models of musical analysis that are grounded in a subject/object division—the separation that occurs when critics objectify a piece of music as "out there," separated from the subject or listener. Trying to approach the musical piece as a work, or an object, creates certain problems: Is the work a score, a recording, a performance, which performance? Following Husserl's phenomenology, Covach argues that music is no object independent of subjects and their mutual production. But even this approach creates a problem. Husserl's phenomenological method called for bracketing the world and focusing only on the subject's experience of the music, retaining a form of objectifying the work (Covach, "Destructuring" par. 3). A Heideggerian "hermeneutic phenomenology," however, breaks with this tradition and attempts to include the entirety of interpretive context. For Heidegger, Being is not something that can be bracketed: it is the ground for experience and can't be fully accounted for by separating it into objects for rational analysis. In *Being and Time* Heidegger argues that, in their everyday life, humans don't interact consciously with objects but experiences a totality of equipment tacitly within larger environments. Heidegger's point that Covach wants to emphasize is that this tacit ground is more fundamental than the subject/object split that gets bracketed once the object stands out from its ambient environment (par. 9).

For Covach, music critics still tend to bracket music by examining intervals, rhythms, timbres, form, and harmony, as if they are distinct objects operating on universal laws. Theories of tonality, for example, aren't first principles; they derive from certain historical traditions of music that emerge more tacitly and are then abstracted from these musical worlds. An example might be the 1–4–5–1 chord progression that is predominant in blues but not in other styles of music from other periods or places. The progression can't be a universal or objective law of music, only a form that emerged from a particular historical practice (par. 12–13). Theories of tonality don't refer to isolated pieces of music but to how such a piece relates to other pieces in a historical or generic network. What is important for Covach is not that critics can consciously identify the intertextuality or interrelations of such networks of musical pieces to form a theory of style, for example, but that these networks provide the tacit grounds for a listener's ability to actually hear and understand a work prior to any theoretical cut (par. 15). Parents don't understand their kids' music because they don't share their musical world: to parents in the 1970s and 1980s, punk is *literally* noise. A musical world is the product of a person's "cumulative experience of music" but not something consciously acknowledged: listeners could never consciously list all of the musics in their musical world that allow them to hear a particular piece of music (par. 16). A student, then, could never learn a style strictly in the abstract from sheet music. For jazz improvisation in particular, a student must devote hours upon hours to listening to music in the style in order to build a musical world to ground his or her musical practice.

Covach closes with three key points about musical worlding: (1) musical worlds aren't just about the past and just about defined historical traditions—they can incorporate a wide variety of works and future potential works to be written from the conditions of possibility of a given musical world (hence invention comes from this crossing of generic boundaries within one's musical world); (2) a piece of music from this perspective is not an object but a location for gathering together these musics—critics can label these gatherings tonality, form, or harmony, but these are simply cuts from musical worlds; (3) for many styles, rock in particular, the notion of a musical work as an object doesn't make sense—the rock tradition doesn't value the work in the same way that the classical tradition does: a song then becomes a world not a work.

To rephrase Barthes's "from work to text," Covach calls for a turn "from work to world" ("Destructuring" par. 18–20). A particular piece of music isn't an isolated object but a location in which musical, cultural, and material worlds intersect—they gather together in and through that location. This sense of work as world implies the action and activity of networked coproduction and shows up in Heidegger's take on works of art.

Importantly, Covach expands the notion of musical worlding as the necessary tacit musical background needed in order to hear, understand, and interpret a piece of music to this larger notion of art as worlding. In "Musical Worlds and the Metaphysics of Analysis," Covach draws from the later Heidegger rather than the Heidegger of *Being and Time* to address responses to his initial article.[8] In "The Origin of the Work of Art," Heidegger discusses Van Gogh's painting of peasant shoes. Heidegger writes: "On the leather lie the dampness and richness of the soil. Under the soles slides the loneliness of the field path as evening calls. In the shoes vibrates the silent call of the earth, its quiet gift of the ripening grain and its unexplained self-refusal in the fallow desolation of the wintry field. . . . This equipment belongs to the *earth*, and it is protected in the *world* of the peasant woman" ("Origin" 34; qtd. in Covach, "Musical Worlds" par. 6). Covach notes that in this discussion, Heidegger isn't interested in the other paintings of Van Gogh or other impressionist paintings but in the world of the peasant woman. Covach's point is that people can have access to this world precisely because they have the cultural background to understand it and the painting brings them into contact with, or a networked relation with, that world. Music, however, isn't as easily accessible as more figurative forms of visual art. Without musical worlding as a tacit network of past musical experiences, listeners won't be able to gain fuller access to the world of the song (par. 7–8). In popular music, then, musical worlding often works in concert with more visual and lyrical aspects of a song or album, which connect the musical world to the world the artist gathers. Contemporary pop music is rarely experienced as music in isolation from this larger process of worlding that Heidegger identifies.

In a short response, Covach doesn't have the space to expand on Heidegger's point, but a closer look at "The Origin of the Work of Art" sheds more light on worlding as a function of the work of art. Heidegger notes that viewers are not brought into the world of the peasant woman by an actual pair of shoes but by Van Gogh's painting: "In the vicinity of the work we were suddenly somewhere else than we usually tend to be" (35). Heidegger splits this reorientation into two aspects: setting up and setting forth. A work of art *sets up a world* in a way that the pair of shoes doesn't. The shoes are a part of the tacit background environment in which people work and live. The work of art pulls the object out of the tacit background, revealing it to the viewer in the way a broken computer shows up for the writer. But for Heidegger, this revealing isn't simply figural or representational. Rather than represent an object, a work of art sets up a world in a particular historical and cultural context where it gathers the tacit background into a set of relations and reveals that world in the present, holding it open to experience, thought, and action. A Greek temple, for example, doesn't simply house a statue that represents a god. It is by virtue of the temple and the world it opens up that the god exists there in the temple: "This presence of the god is in itself the extension and delimitation of the precinct as a holy precinct. . . . It is the temple work that first fits together and at the same time gathers around itself the unity of those paths and relations in which birth and death, disaster and blessing, victory and disgrace, endurance and decline acquire the shape of destiny for human being. The all-governing expanse of this open relational context is the world of this historical people" (42). The temple as a work of art sets up these relations and makes the world of the gods ontologically possible and disclosed, both physically as well as conceptually. For Heidegger, all art—visual, linguistic, and architectural—performs this function. The enactment of a tragedy doesn't represent the battle of the gods; it *is* the battle: "it transforms the people's saying so that now every living word fights the battle" (43). By "erecting a building, raising a statue, presenting a tragedy at a holy festival" the holy is opened up, made possible, brought into being—"to be a work means to set up a world" (44).

But the work of art doesn't just set up a world by revealing past forces and relations in the present. It also functions to *set forth the earth*. If setting up a world is revealing, setting forth the earth is concealing. If Van Gogh pulls the shoes from their ambient background to reveal the world of the peasant woman, the temple and statue take the stone from its environment and put it back on the earth to establish a new tacit environment through which the world of the gods is enacted. The stone recedes into the material background of the world. Setting forth puts the work of art into material form and folds it back into a material situation as part of the tacit conditions of possibility for present and future action (Heidegger, "Origin" 45). Heidegger notes that these two aspects of the work always go together: the combination of setting up a world and setting forth the earth establishes future paths of possibility that a work in its present relations opens up (48). Their relationship, for Heidegger, is analogous to rest and motion. Only what is in motion can come to rest, and what is at rest has the potentiality for particular paths of motion. The work might seem to be static, but it holds within it potential futures that are activated and made possible once it is set in material relations. Setting up a world and setting forth the earth come together in the present to establish a striving, both conceptually and materially, for these potential futures, making them possible (49). Rest and motion, world and earth, embody a kind of coproduction. Their struggle is not one of opposition in which one overcomes the other but of ongoing struggle that propels forward movement. The combination of world and earth, the revealing of a world through art and the concealing of material possibilities of the earth, creates a striving through their tension and interplay that puts these possible worlds on the path to becoming—"the work is an instigating of this striving" (49).

The function of the work of art as the revealing of worlds and the concealing of ambient conditions for their futurity is at work in the Refused album *The Shape of Punk to Come*. As a work of art, the album *sets up* a world through the way it is placed historically in terms of music traditions; the way the album is situated in the contexts of philosophical works and various textual genre; the way visual elements of the album articulate aspects of its world; the way the lyrics themselves, particularly the song "New Noise," express this rhetorical context and projection. This worlding sets up or reveals the world Refused want their music to be tacitly experienced through: it articulates the world around the musical production and the style of the music itself. Refused rather explicitly attempt to place their album historically relative to musical traditions. The title of the album is clearly a reference to Ornette Coleman's *The Shape of Jazz to Come*. Recorded in 1959, the album was one of the first avant-garde jazz records ever released. The album was considered shocking at the time because Coleman eliminated chord progressions played on individual instruments. Songs would start with a melody, transition into free improvisation, and then return to the melody. The structure was typical for bebop at the time, but there was no underlying chord structure to ground the improvisation, resulting in a much freer, inventive style. The album laid the groundwork, set forth the grounds, for much of the avant-garde free jazz that followed. In his preface to *The Shape of Punk to Come*, included in the liner notes, Patrick T. Daly writes about the creative tension in Refused when writing the album. Punk in the late 1990s was two decades old. Much of the standard structures and tropes had been established. Even though punk had engendered many off-shoots—new wave, thrash metal, post-punk, grunge—punk itself was (again) at a crossroads that revealed the limits of the genre. Some music emerges out of an origin in the paradigmatic conditions, while other music, as works of art in Heidegger's sense, emerges out of the tension exposed by the limits of the paradigm. By invoking Coleman, Refused locates its origin in the latter. This sense of pushing style forward and creating new musical worlds to ground the audience's ability to hear and imagine something new is critical to the rhetorical work of the album, and invoking the world of avant-garde free jazz sets up a context for understanding this projected future.[9]

Refused extend this worlding by implementing a variety of textual genres. Just by including something like a preface in the liner notes, Refused are signaling that they are stepping out of a standard approach to the album. The textual expansion also includes a manifesto in the inner sleeve that is steeped in philosophical texts with references to Marx, Feuerbach, and Thomas Paine. The genre is played out to the hilt, with much anticapitalist ranting against a system that oppresses human creativity in the name of capital gain. The manifesto riffs off of each song, expanding the arguments behind the lyrics into prose. "Turn the knob and wait for the liberating sound of ecstasy and revolution," starts the paragraph for the song "Liberation Frequency." "New forms of work camps are arranged and new ways of hiding the monotonous beat of slavery are being presented," exclaims the paragraph on the track "The Deadly Rhythm (of the Production Line)." The song "Summer Holiday vs. Punk Routine" is presented as a clear shot at punk's appropriation into capitalist accumulation and the resulting musical stagnation that follows. "So reclaim art," they demand. "We need new noise and new voices and new canvases to become something more than the last poets of a useless generation." Daly's preface comments on the thinking behind the album and what led the band to strive for a "revolutionary" theme in both the layout and music. Daly writes, "While in past albums, there were hints of revolution, embedded in the lyrics and layout, in this album, the entire product conveys this suggestion of revolution. The lyrics, music, and layout all merge together to give you something different; something to inspire thought that runs much deeper than what is printed in the lyric sheet." This is a fairly clear attempt to articulate the concept of worlding that operates through the album. Even including a subtitle—*A Chimerical Bombination in 12 Bursts*—suggests the importance of textuality's more central role along with music, lyrics, and images to produce a world in which their music could be, and should be, heard.

Daly's suggestion that their worlding extends to images and layouts is pretty clear with a bit of a closer look. The album cover gathers its world through a collage of four images: musical technologies (the guitar, effects they use); swing kids of the 1940s (one of the music traditions they invoke in the manifesto);

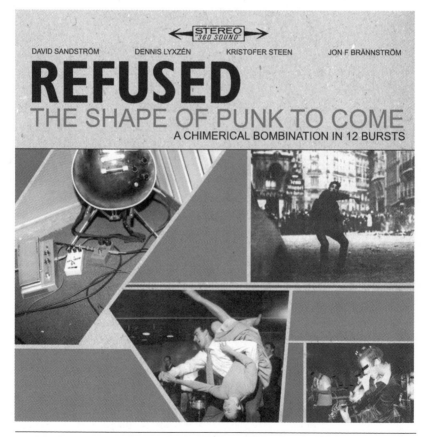

FIGURE 6.1. Refused's *The Shape of Punk to Come* album cover.

youth and worker riots (the historical conditions they open up and build upon); a picture of the band themselves (situated in the lower right quadrant as the culmination of these worlds). The photos in the inner sleeve perform a similar function. Dispersed throughout the manifesto are four photos: a band member with a standup bass, a nontraditional instrument for the genre, invoking Coleman's removal of the piano from *The Shape of Jazz to Come*; a photo of a band member sitting at a typewriter in front of a shelf of books and albums, implicitly composing the manifesto; another photo showing a band member with hand on chin in classical thinking pose; another with a band member hovering over turntables and holding headphones, alluding to future sonic possibilities that the album opens up. The back panel of the inner sleeve shows the band in the studio, in front of a piano, ironically including the instrument Coleman banished, with a poster of John Coltrane on the back wall. The inner sleeve also contains a collage of images and captions that performs similar work with images of factories, musical instruments, political protests, musical traditions, and captions such as "You cannot kill history, Inspiration, Dedication, Motivation, Revolt, Words." The poetic world making of their collages gathers fragments of their musical and social worlds, places the band in this trajectory, and points to the potential future movement and development of their musical worlding.

The general theme of revolution opened up by the record is pointed toward two predominant lyrical themes: political revolution aimed at capitalism and musical revolution aimed at punk rock. The first track on the record opens up with the line, "I've got a bone to pick with capitalism, and a few to break," and launches right into intense guitars and drums. The second track is just as explicit: "I took the first bus out of Coca-Cola city cause it made me feel nauseous and shitty, I took the first bus out of Shell town cause they didn't want me hanging around." The song "The Deadly Rhythm (of the Production Line)" even turns this vitriol toward unions, who are credited with contributing to worker powerlessness and slavery. Refused write, "We will no longer believe that working for you will set us free." The song "Liberation Frequency" calls for taking over the airwaves from corporate control but focuses on music, "What frequency are you getting? Is it noise or sweet sweet music? . . . Who's in charge and what does he say? Is he playing the alternative or does it sound the same old way?" "Refused Party Programme" is more direct in announcing what the band is after: "This is the pulse—This is the sound. This is the beat of a new generation. This is the movement—This is the rhythm. This is the noise of revolution." The track "Protest Song '68" extends this theme. It opens with a slow, quiet guitar intro over which the singer recites Henry Miller: "To sing you must first open your mouth. You must have a pair of lungs and a little knowledge of music. It is not necessary to have an accordion, or a guitar. The essential thing is that I want to sing. Then this is a song, I'm singing." The quote invokes punk's DIY ethic against more academic and technical musical traditions. But when the track breaks into the full song, the DIY ethic gets more detail: "I breathe in and I create—rework the spirit of '68. Fresh meaning to torn ideas—let's bring life to old cliché's. Punch a whole in tradition—yeah, let's listen to the songs of discontent—the chords and the movement." A clear connection between political revolution and musical revolution is being established as the band's primary rhetorical directive.

The song "New Noise" is the first single from the album, and it combines both the indictment of capitalism and the call for new musical styles in the genre of punk. Refused's anticapitalist lyrics contribute to the development of a world in which change and innovation is valued and enacted. The first verse addresses art in the age of capitalism: "It's here for us to admire if we can afford the beauty of it. If we can afford the luxury of turning our heads. If we can adjust that $1,000 smile and behold the creation of man. Great words won't cover ugly actions and good frames won't save bad paintings." Art under capitalism costs money, and no amount of corporate advertising and fashion can save worn-out musical clichés. The pre-chorus indicts the punk movement directly and perhaps all revolutionaries: "We lack the *motion* to move to the new beat." Who is this "we"—the band, the audience, other bands, everyone under capitalism? What is this "new beat," and why can't we move to it? *Hear* it? The second verse is more direct:

> *How can we expect anyone to listen*
> *If we're using the same old voice?*
> *We need new noise*
> *New art for the real people*

Finally the chorus:

> *We dance to all the wrong songs*
> *We enjoy all the wrong moves*

We dance to all the wrong songs
We're not leading

"New Noise" encapsulates the revolutionary ideals of the album, both in politics and art. In order to break the hold of capitalism and the limits of stale genre replication, new styles, new forms of art are needed to set up worlds and the possible futures they might set forth. This worlding enacts a new potential motion, induces this potential striving through a kind of suggestibility or entrainment through exposure to another possible world. It not only responds to current conditions but also sets the conditions for future aesthetic and political response, as Coleman set the grounds through which future avant-garde jazz could be made and heard. But with this worlding comes risk, as Warner notes. There is no determinism in the rhetorical work, only an open relationality and potential futurity.

EMBODIED LISTENING AND TEMPORALITY

In addition to setting up this visual and textual world for the record to inhabit, *The Shape of Punk to Come* also sets up a musical world in which it can be experienced. For Steph Ceraso in "(Re)Educating the Senses: Multimodal Listening, Bodily Learning, and the Composition of Sonic Experiences," listening is a multisensory, multimodal act that includes sight, sound, and touch together. John Dewey considers this combination a "heightened vitality," an aesthetic experience that is "active and alert commerce with the world" (Dewey qtd. in Ceraso 106). This moves Ceraso away from traditional notions of interpretation toward a more immersive and participatory form of embodied experience as the basis for listening. Her primary example is deaf percussionist Dame Evelyn Glennie, who uses visual cues in her performances to affect how audiences perceive sound. Since Glennie can't hear sound with her ears, she experiences its material force with both her body and her eyes. The rhythm and movement of vibrating objects, feet tapping, or heads bobbing offer visual signs of sonic encounters. Glennie builds these connections between sound and vision, or what Ceraso calls "visual listening practices," into her compositions by playing up facial cues or pretending to hit instruments to "contribute to how sound is being experienced by the audience," often making the audience think sound is being made when it isn't (109). This visual-musical relationship comes to the fore in Covach's take on musical worlding. Visual style as a function of cultural context affects how music is heard along with the musical world of the historical period that grounds listening. Rock music, as Covach argues, resists being understood in traditional or objective terms that university music departments value ("Musical Worlds" par. 9) and has always operated on various combinations of the visual and the musical.

Much of the academic analyses of punk outside of music departments, however, has emphasized visual style as the primary mode of counterpublic poetic worlding more than the ambient and embodied aspects of musical worlding. Dick Hebdige's classic *Subculture: The Meaning of Style*, for example, showed how punks in London took everyday objects and commodities and reworked them into a counter-style that provoked the mainstream public and highlighted their class difference. Taking an everyday discarded object like a safety pin and turning it into adornment worn through the cheek, lip, or nose established the subculture against both commodification and middle-upper class norms. The more recent *A Rhetoric of Style* by Barry Brummett likewise focuses on clothing and visual culture. Brummett examines the commodification of counter-styles and their repetition through media and corporate culture but, like Hebdige, downplays musical style as a part of the world of these counterpublics—his only mention of music is that it too can be co-opted (108). This tendency in academic rock criticism reveals the relative ease of understanding the revealed worlding of the work and the difficulty of accounting for its more concealed musical worlding.[10]

But for punk in general, and Refused in particular, musical style is a critical element to poetic world making. In the late seventies, punk music's typical style—simple, loud, fast, sloppy—worked in concert with image and fashion to counter the progressive or classic rock mainstays of the period such as Pink Floyd, Yes, and Led Zeppelin, whose songs were longer, more orchestrated, contained extended solo sections that emphasized individual virtuosity, and employed the most advanced studio techniques and technologies of their time. By the late nineties, Refused are similarly countering established musical styles, but they are responding to different historical grounds and the rigid genre norms of what punk had become through its commodification in the early nineties. So when Refused make statements like, "They told me that the classics never go out of style, but . . . they do. They do. Somehow, baby, I never thought that [we would] too," or "We all need to recognize that style in contradiction to fashion is necessary to challenge the conservatism of the youth cultures placed upon us," it also becomes important to look at their calls for musical revolution in the context of musical worlds, historical transformations, and the dynamic temporality of musical styles.

In his follow up article on musical worlding, "Pangs of History in late 1970s New-wave Rock," Covach uses his approach to musical worlding to analyze two late 1970s groups, Foreigner and The Cars. He argues that while at the time the two were seen as antithetical, from a historical distance and from the perspective of different musical worlds their musical styles were much more contemporary. Covach's analysis is situated in the historical developments of counter-styles. The early rock of the 1950s and 1960s is grounded in simple song structures, clean guitar sounds, and lyrics about love and relationships. Post-Beatles hippie and progressive rock of the 1970s counters with a more modernist and romantic aesthetic. While visually the shorter haircuts and suits of the 1950s and early 1960s gave way to bell-bottoms and long hair, musically virtuosity rather than simplicity was the dominant value—song structures became more complex, technology became more valued as studios evolved and made complex production possible and desirable, and lyrics become more about abstract and utopian themes. As progressive rock becomes more of a mainstream genre, however, the last half of the 1970s sees the tendency to scale back the complex forms and styles of these acts. Bands such as Boston, Styx, and Foreigner are seen as sellouts in some circles but their streamlining of progressive rock into a more mainstream version is still seen by many fans as the height of the classic rock genre, continuing to get airplay today. Punk in the mid- to late 1970s, from the Ramones in NYC to the Sex Pistols in London, counters these trends with a return to simpler song structures, a valuing of poor production, and a DIY approach to musical skill. But just as progressive rock got mainstreamed, so did punk. New wave, while continuing to counter the dominant progressive-turned-corporate rock, is already developing a co-opted form of punk.

It is into these complex historical genre dynamics that Covach situates his analysis. While progressive bands are grounded in a modernist aesthetic, new wave acts such as Elvis Costello and The Cars are grounded in a postmodern, pastiche approach to style; one that presupposes a particular historical and generic situatedness to function rhetorically. Elvis Costello, for example, gathers up a world out of the remnants of rock's past—"the look, names, and instruments in many ways invokes the 1950s and 1960s rock culture" (Covach, "Pangs" 174). Using the name Elvis is a clear reference to a prior moment in the history of popular music; one that was in part ironic given the recent death of Elvis and his later overweight Vegas image. In terms of fashion, the band wore straight-legged pants, narrow ties, short hair, and Costello's horn-rimmed glasses harkened back to the pre-1970s style of Buddy Holly. In the context of the late 1970s, these fashions created a clear counterstatement to the bell-bottoms and long hair of progressive and corporate rock and are meant to influence or set the grounds for how the music is heard. Even Elvis Costello's instruments, a Fender Jazzmaster guitar and Vox combo organ, ran counter to the Gibson Les Paul guitars and Hammond organs of the dominant bands of the day, both visually and sonically. But rather than calling for a return to these times, the style of new wave is making an ironic move to reassemble elements of the past in a new context, to shift the stylistic grounds of the present moment. What Covach wants to investigate is whether there is an aural irony to go along with the visual. How much does the musical world harken back to older styles, participate in the current style, or push forward for a new style?

What Covach finds when he takes a look at two archetypal examples of this moment in the historical development of counter-styles is that musical styles can seem contrary in their initial historical moments but in retrospect can be seen as sharing an ambient musical world. Covach analyzes Foreigner's hit "Feels Like the First Time" (1977) as a benchmark for mainstream music of the day that contrasts with the earlier rock era of the 1950s and 1960s: the synthesizer sounds in the intro invoke then current acts such as Yes and ELP; the 1970s British-influenced blues rock comes through in the more contemporary distorted guitar sounds; the blues turns and ornaments of the vocals are decidedly more polished; and the clean backup vocals have a slick post-Beatles production (Covach, "Pangs" 185). More specifically, Covach notes how Foreigner puts a distinctive structural twist in the song's form to contrast it with the standard AABA model of the 1950s and 1960s—A (verse-chorus), A (verse-chorus), B (bridge), A (verse-chorus) that mostly operates in the same key. "Feels Like the First Time" provides an intro, verse-chorus, verse-bridge1-chorus, bridge2, chorus structure that shifts key on the first bridge, a structural feature that, if it occurred, would typically come after the second chorus in the traditional AABA form (182–84). Everything about the track situates it in the late 1970s and distinguishes it from earlier rock eras.

The Cars's hit song "My Best Friend's Girl" (1978), however, builds a musical intertext that contrasts with Foreigner's attempt to fit squarely into the musical world of the mid- to late 1970s. Rather than distorted guitar, The Cars's track opens with a clean, slightly chorused sound more reminiscent of 1950s rockabilly; the handclaps refer more explicitly to the Angel's "My Boyfriend's Back" and the Beatles's "I Want to Hold your Hand" both from the early 1960s; the lead vocals are more amateurish than Foreigner with hiccups drawn from Buddy Holly (188). All of these establish the difference between new wave and the mainstream rock of the period, reinforcing the visual contrasts that The Cars share with Elvis Costello. Even among these references, however, Covach draws out many aspects of the song more consistent with 1970s mainstream rock. The sonic quality of the production uses all of the current technologies available at the time.[11] Structurally, the song, as many of The Cars's other tracks, doesn't harken back to the 1950s and 1960s standard AABA format, but it looks to complicate that form in ways similar to Foreigner and other groups of the time.[12] And while many Cars songs contain a guitar solo that is shorter, more simple, and melodic than many mid- to late 1970s bands, most of them contain distorted rhythm guitar sounds and power chords much more reminiscent of contemporary 1970s rock.

In terms of musical worlding, Covach notes that the point is not that new wave sends mixed messages, but that the mixed stylistic features of new wave create different meanings based on the musical worlds of their own historical moments *and* their listeners' shifting musical worlds over time. Late 1970s listeners would have been more likely to pick up on the 1950s and 1960s references and read the work as ironic, whereas young listeners today with fewer musical references to the past are much more likely to see classic rock and new wave as a part of the same era or musical world. The worlding strategies of both Foreigner and The Cars are different as rhetorical strategies in their historical moment, but these meanings shift across changing and developing musical worlds of listeners and audiences, revealing their similarities. Foreigner's musical worlding aligns them within the stylistic genre boundaries of its day. The Cars's musical worlding situates them across genre boundaries to produce irony. Covach writes, "But when there are enough new wave songs that cross such boundaries, one tends not to situate each song with regard to earlier music, but rather with regard to each other. Strangely enough, the more new wave songs one knows, the less ironic they seem; this is because the relationships of these songs to one another begin to override the relationships any single one may have to earlier music. At such a point new wave stops being a reaction to hippie music and culture and becomes a distinct music and culture in its own right" ("Pangs" 195). In terms of musical worlding, new wave is consistent between its visual and musical dimensions in the historical context of the late 1970s. But from different historical and individual musical worlds, the rhetorical work gets altered and functions differently in the new assemblage. The musical worlds of The Cars and other new wave groups actually work together, collectively and over time, to produce these shifting, emergent generic formations.

Refused's musical worlding is situated squarely in these kinds of historical references, genre dynamics, and rhetorical complexity. In one sense the music of many new wave artists already participated in a commodification of punk. Punk's musical style in the mid- to late '70s—short songs, simple song structures, noisy production, atonal shouted vocals—is clearly a reaction to progressive rock's epic songs, complex structures, sleek production, and long guitar/keyboard solos. New wave picks up on this musical style but cleans up much of the sound, drawing from the clean guitars of the 1950s and 1960s rather than the noisy barrage of punk, and going for simple, cleaner vocal hooks rather than repetitive shouts. Both punk and new wave react to the typical lyrical content of hippie and progressive rock—"religion, the state, the future of mankind" and "predatory sexual conquest" (Covach, "Pangs" 176). But punk replaces utopia with dystopia, while new wave replaces sexual conquest with dating and romantic love (Joe Jackson's "Is She Really Going Out with Him" or The Cars's "My Best Friend's Girlfriend"). Both are reactions to the post–*Sgt. Pepper's Lonely Hearts Club Band* world of 1970s corporate rock—both see mainstream rock as bloated and overly professional—but their responses at the level of musical style differed. Punk music attacked commercialism; new wave courted it. Rather than oppose corporate rock, new wave wanted to take it over. As new wave artists became pop icons in the early 1980s (Blondie for instance), punk crossed over with heavy metal and became nosier, faster, and angrier. The songs became even shorter and more stripped down in terms of structure, and the lyrical content become more political and aggressive.[13] In response to the appropriation of new wave and the rigid genre conventions of this new crossover "hardcore" punk of the early to mid-1980s, post-punk acts turned the DIY ethic toward a more experimental response to corporate rock. Post-punk bands such as PIL, Cocteau Twins, Chrome, The Replacements, and Fugazi saw nonexpertise as a road to new forms of creativity and innovation and injected more complexity into their musical style and structure. But by the early 1990s these more alternative bands got caught up in their own form of appropriation under the moniker of grunge and pop punk. Nirvana, Green Day, and Blink 182 follow new wave's strategy of stripping down and cleaning up the music.[14] By the late 1990s a clear set of genre conventions for pop punk emerged: simple songs structurally and tonally; catchy, melodic vocal hooks through clean delivery; few to no guitar solos or displays of virtuosity; and sleek professional studio production.

This is the historical and generic context that Refused's music is responding to. They are anticorporate rock just as punk's original core groups of the late 1970s and hardcore groups of the 1980s were, but instead of going for simplicity in response to bloated progressive rock, they are trying to bring complexity back into the genre to counter what punk as a genre had become—simple straight-ahead popular music. Musically, the Refused are developing more complex arrangements. The song "New Noise," for example, complicates the simplistic AABA structures (re)employed by the pop-punk of the 1990s. "New Noise" has an extended intro with clean guitars and ambient keyboard samples; it inverts the typical verse-chorus sequence, and has a bridge section with seven variations on other elements of the song (muted clean guitar, ambient sample breaks, and a variety of heavy accents by the guitars and drums). This counter-style, however, places Refused in the same complex genre dynamics of The Cars. On the one hand, they are injecting difference into their musical worlds that "range from crazy techno beats, clips from radio shows, live recordings of the band itself, and just playing around with a synthesizer" (Neath). On the other hand, their music is squarely connected to certain punk traditions, both tradtions of crossover intensity and post-punk innovation. They mix the guitar sounds and styles of crossover legends, such as DRI (Dirty Rotten Imbeciles) or MOD (Method of Destruction), along with the harsher vocals of underground punk with the experimental desires of post-punk innovators, such as Minor Threat and later Fugazi, by bringing in other instruments (keyboards, turntables, the occasional horn sample), exploring other genres (hip hop, techno), and breaking the simplistic guitar conventions (in the form of jazzy interludes and quirky guitar breaks). Harkening back most directly to Fugazi, who famously turned away from the almost fascist demand to hold to particular genre conventions in the 1980s, Refused struck out to explore the potential for a new musical world.[15] Both of these 1980s precursors are then remixed with the 1990s crossover of metal and dance music to form industrial-techno, which creates the ground for their synthetic work at the level of music. All of these remixed forms contrast with the popular versions of punk that Refused want to counter in their immediate historical context of the late 1990s, leaving some reviewers calling this latest remake of the genre post-hardcore, which fits nicely with Refused's mix of the 1980s styles of hardcore and post-punk.[16]

With all of the effort put into worlding that signals the album to be heard in the context of revolutionary counter-styles, ultimately the album has to contain significant amounts of common musical worlds and recognized genre conventions for the listeners in the late 1990s to be able to hear it as revolutionary. This is the paradox that confronts all forms of musical innovation—too much innovation and no one can hear it; too little innovation and the style stagnates quickly. Keith Negus argues that any "revolutionary" style operates across a continuum of continuities and dialogues that he breaks into three types: genericists, who "accommodate their musical practice and performance to a specific genre style at a particular time and stay with this" (145); pastichists, who "recognize that a new style has appeared or has become popular and so include this in their set as yet another style to be performed as part of a varied reperatoire" (146); and synthesists, who "draw on the elements of an emerging generic style but blend them in such a way so as to create a new distinct musical identity" (145). Refused is aiming toward synthesis in response to genericists, while still operating in the musical world of their genre, which is what allows the significance of their musical responses to show up—this musical worlding is the necessary condition for hearing genre difference and critical for the *collective* development and emergence of a new style or genre over time. The emphasis they place on revolution as a visual and lyrical theme for the album's world functions rhetorically to highlight the synthetic elements their musical world has to offer.

Refused's collective visual, textual, and musical poetic world making sets up or reveals the assembled world in which they want the record to be heard while at the same time sets forth a more tacit musical world that becomes less revolutionary and yet more critical for the evolution of the genre's musical style. How sound produces meaning is a function of how it works in the ever-shifting musical worlds. Just as The Cars's poetic world shifted over time, Refused's album laid the ground for future genre redefinition or rearticulation.[17] As Covach notes, musical worlds aren't just about the past and defined historical traditions—they can incorporate a wide variety of works, including potential future works, as a part of their conditions of possibility and the crossing of generic boundaries they enact; a piece of music from this perspective becomes a location for gathering these temporalities ("Destructuring" par. 18–20). Attunement, in other words, is not just spatial but also temporal. Refused's combination of setting up a world through past references in the rhetorical work and a musical world through present audience affects and responses ultimately *sets forth* potential conditions for how the work will be experienced and responded to by future listeners, even as these responses will be functions of new emerging musical worlds to come.

THE RHETORICAL AND RESONANCE TO COME

The case of Refused so far provides an example of how worlding shifts traditional notions of the work and audience, but it would remain incomplete if it didn't scale out to larger spaces and temporalities of circulation that are vital to an expanded sense of the rhetorical. Refused had no control over the circulation they *set forth* and the impact that it had not only on punk as a genre but also on their own futures. To fully consider these futures means moving beyond Covach's hermeneutic phenomenology to Nealon's hermeneutics of situation as resonant self-organization. In *Spreadable Media* Jenkins, Ford, and Green argue to abandon the viral metaphor because it doesn't account for how media actually spread from person to person. Virality is the tendency of something to spread quickly, widely, and produce multiple versions or remakes. But a work can also spread slowly, operate affectively, and spark imitation without direct remixes. For Laurie Gries, however, both virality and spreadability are forms of circulation. Responses to governor Bob McDonald's call for legislation to make women get transvaginal ultrasounds, for example, circulated and spread more than went viral. Discussions and critiques happened in the Senate; citizens generated petitions; parodies and satires appeared on

TV shows; posts were circulated on Facebook, blogs, and news sites. It just didn't inspire the speed, range, and remakes that Obama Hope did. In addition to the factors that Jenkins, Ford, and Green argue impact spreadability—technological resources, economic structures, attributes of the work, and social networks—going viral is a function of being highly mobile, contagious, replicable, and metacultural. Highly mobile media both spread quickly and over a wide range of space and or time; contagious media trigger affects and influence deeper responses; replicable media inspire both imitations and remakes; metacultural media spark wide forms of response from critique to praise, analysis to reviews, and parody to satire. Combining these two heuristics for spreadability and virality, Gries develops a set of interrelated factors that impact all forms of circulation—technologies, distribution, metaculture, imitation, design, and collectives (Gries 283).[18] These factors open up ways to think through *The Shape of Punk to Come*'s futurity with an eye toward accounting for the ways circulation resonates and becomes rhetorical.

Emerging *technological* changes both enhanced *The Shape of Punk to Come*'s *distribution* and reached its abundance of *metaculture*, which impacted the band's future in ways they couldn't have anticipated. Shortly after releasing *The Shape of Punk to Come* in 1998, Refused embarked on a US tour that witnessed the implosion of the band. Up to that point they hadn't received large amounts of acclaim for their efforts. Like many bands, their third album was something of a do-or-die proposition, and they poured everything they had into the record. But the early dates of the tour showed no signs of shifting reception. Spent energy from writing and recording, conflicts among the band members, and a series of poorly promoted and attended shows in the United States led the band to break up and cancel their tour after playing a house show in the small college town of Harrisonburg, Virginia that had been shut down by police. For most bands prior to this period, these events would have been the end: the label stops promoting the album, record store copies get sent back to the distributor or marked down for the discount bin, reviews and press dry up, and the band fades into the past largely forgotten or at best a footnote. But *The Shape of Punk to Come* has a different story. Emerging technologies in the 2000s—peer-to-peer downloading, iTunes and iPods, blogging and social networking—create the "distributed album," breaking up all of the work's visual, textual, and musical worlding. It is digitized, fragmented, (re) distributed in parts, reconstituted in digital music libraries, burned onto CDs, printed onto new CD inserts. This expanded distribution led to more metacultural responses. The album is blogged about, reviewed online, commented on, and discussed. Videos are circulated, posted on YouTube or Facebook, juxtaposed to album art, lyrics, and liner notes.

Through this process of fragmented distribution and commentary, *The Shape of Punk to Come* is circulated and rebuilt as a unit of discourse. Its world is being constantly reconstituted into variable versions. All of this circulation across the web and eventually social media made *The Shape of Punk to Come* more accessible. Rather than the discount bin, it slowly began to reach and gather more fans, which also sparked more metacultural responses beyond sharing. Reviews started popping up on underground websites as print fanzines started going online, many of which praised the album and rated it either 9/10 or 10/10. And the song "New Noise" started getting rotation on video channels like MTVX and cable radio stations in the early 2000s, three to four years after the band broke up. All of these activities transform the album as single and intentional into a kind of coordinated performance among loosely connected actors and networks that, in turn, transforms both the work and its musical worlds, giving it more power as public rhetoric through self-organized poetic world making.[19]

While it can't be said that *The Shape of Punk to Come* went viral with the speed and replicability of the Obama Hope image, it continues to circulate and by the mid-2000s starts to build a sustained resonance, an affective "suggestibility" that inspires *imitation*. The album is poetic world making in Warner's sense: it "characterize[s] the world in which it attempts to circulate, and it ... attempt[s] to realize that world through address" ("Publics" 422). A work does this not simply through traditional persuasion but through "the pragmatics of its speech genres, idioms, stylistic markers, address, temporality, mise en scene, citational field, interlocutory protocols, lexicon, and so on. Its circulatory fate is the realization of that world." Warner continues: "Public discourse says not only, 'Let a public exist,' but 'Let it have this character, speak this way, see the world this way.' It then goes out in search of confirmation that such a world exists, with greater or lesser success—success being further attempts to cite, circulate, and realize the world understanding it articulates. Run it up the flagpole and see who salutes. Put on a show and see who shows up" (422). In many ways, the album had such a future impact on the genre. Despite being broken up and vowing to never get back together,[20] Refused's continued circulation and resonance influences 2000s-era "screamo" bands who began to sound more like Refused's version of Fugazi. Screamo is a style of hardcore punk-influenced "emo" that began in the early 1990s.[21] But screamo, as the name suggests, employs more aggressive vocals along with more dynamic movements between chaotic noise and melodic guitar, along with vocal lines and shifts in tempo that accentuate these dynamics. Lyrically, emo's romantic relationships give way to issues of politics and human rights that range from more interpersonal acceptance of difference to direct reactions to specific politicians. Other screamo artists begin to draw directly from theorists such as Artaud, Bataille, Nietzsche, and the Frankfurt School. Along with this array of influences, screamo's visual style includes shaggy haircuts, tight T-shirts, denim jackets, and thick-rimmed glasses, harkening back to earlier musical worlds. In the mid- to late 1990s, Refused is clearly opening up this musical world. During this time the term "screamo" makes its way into the more mainstream music press, but it isn't until the mid-2000s that the genre fully arrives in the mainstream. Major label bands such as The Used and Poison the Well were directly influenced by Refused. Refused said, let the world sound like this, and by 2004 many screamo bands did. In retrospect, future listeners might not understand why *The Shape of Punk to Come* became such a classic album because it sounds like other albums of the genre, but this can only be said from a post-2004 musical world. Refused's cultural resonance, in part, made that musical world possible.

But the real force of *The Shape of Punk to Come* is sonic. Something in the *design* of the album's sonic world in addition to its visual, textual, and musical worlds inspired not only imitation but also its material resonance and affective allure. Fans aren't really persuaded by Refused's Marxist position as an argument. They are called and gathered up through the affective feeling of resistance and the analogous sound design and sonic qualities of the record that reinforce it. Musical worlding, in other words, is not just a function of meaning or interpretation but also the situated experience of sound. While many listeners new to heavier musics may experience these sonic textures as noise, Ronald Bogue in "Violence in Three Shades of Metal" argues that only a pure form of deterritorialization can result in noise and what makes any genre of music successful is its ability to navigate the line between noise and music, deterritorialization and reterritorialization, through ongoing movements of variation. Noise is the chaotic overlapping of multiple frequencies that first get narrowed down to fewer identifiable frequencies in sound and then get more formally organized by pitch, rhythm, and structure in music. Music reterritorializes sound waves, putting sound in the patterns of tonal musics. But at the same time, music is also a deterritorializing force that opens sound and music to other nonmusical refrains in a series of movements that function as a becoming-other, connecting them to other networks. Bogue draws on one of Deleuze and Guattari's classic examples, Oliver Messiaen, who reterritorializes bird songs and motifs into his musical compositions. In doing so he notes that "the high pitches, rapid tempos, and peculiar timbres of birdsongs require that he enlarge the intervals between tones, slow the tempos, and find substitute timbres among human instruments" in order to create musical counterparts that ornithologists would likely no longer recognize as bird sounds or songs (97). This is a becoming-other, of both bird songs and music. The musical rendering of the birds' refrains extracts them from their territorial functions and opens them to a field of potential relationality. These aren't simply imitations but sonic analogues, new versions that give new extramusical force to the bird songs and the music. For Bogue, this extramusical force is a musical becoming-other. It is not just a matter of undoing fixed refrains but of engaging and tapping into something distinct from ordinary musical experience. Rather than reterritorialize nature, however, heavy musics reterritorialize an industrial life-world, not imitating industrial machines, or calling attention to them through forms of representation, but producing sonic analogues of their rhythms and timbres. While all musical tones exhibit timbre, these qualities are more central to heavier forms of music and their capacity to affectively envelop their audiences in sound, allowing them to tread a line between noise and music.

Refused's song "New Noise," for example, treads this line between noise and music through variations in tempo (speed), feel (groove), ambience (mood), and of course timbre (sound). Timbre, the quality of a musical note, tone, or sound that distinguishes different sources, operates through qualities such as range—a tone's place on a continuum of noise to identifiable pitch; time envelope—a tone's attack, rise, duration, and decay; tremolo—a tone's modulating changes in volume that have a reverb or chorus effect; intensity—a measurable wave vibration and an affective perception; resonance—the tendency of an object or environment to vibrate at a particular frequency.[22] "New Noise" varies the dynamics of timbre by starting out with a clean guitar on a range toward identifiable pitch and builds through a time envelope of slow duration with guitar ranging toward noise layered in the background underneath the more identifiable pitch. But instead of building to full intensity, the time envelope breaks off and releases the intensity down into tremolo affected keyboard tones and a laid back, less intense groove. Only then do the dynamics shift through an abrupt, short time envelope into full instrumentation that ranges toward noise and peak intensity. The structural and formal dynamics of the song between chorus and verse continues this alteration from full intensity choruses that range toward noise to low intensity verses with mild tremolo that range toward pitch and very short time envelopes between choruses and verses. The mid-section breakdown of "New Noise" starts with electronic tones at low volume and intensity with mild tremolo and angelic voices in the background, which starts another long duration time envelope with low, sustained, resonating bass guitar notes holding it together until drum accents break the low intensity mood and start the build back to full intensity by layering in parts that range toward noise.

Rather than being bowled over with noise, Refused holds the listener in a kind of resonating tension or suspension between noise and pitch, a low vibration intensity and a high vibration intensity, complemented by a dynamic tension between groove and mood, sometimes juxtaposed, sometimes layered. Perhaps the sonic achievement of the song is the controlled noise when the band is at full throttle, noisy enough to communicate all of the intensity they can muster without folding over into fully deterritorialized noise. This is a key part of Refused's sonic rhetoric. The plateaus created through the structures of their songs combine with corresponding timbres that territorialize their listeners by bringing them into a mood through a network of sonic relations. Once that territory is established, they break it off, deterritorialize it, open it to a new refrain or territory that captures listeners in its new mood and level of intensity—an (in)corporeal and rhetorical transformation.[23] For Serres, the grounding multiplicity of noise is "of the possible here and now. It is the intermediary between phenomena, the noise between the forms that come out of it.... [N]oise is always there to invent new music" ("Noise" 57–58). The role of the composer, then, is to "listen to the noises" and straddle the possible "like a living network" (58). But the composer is more like a middle voice, conducting noise into sound and ultimately into song. Noise is the only source of new patterns, and is ultimately the energy that culture parasites.[24]

As *The Shape of Punk to Come* continued to resonate subculturally and pick up steam, above ground print magazines began to run more reviews. Rave reviews were still being written of it over a decade after its release, and its continued circulation is a testament to the album's ability to gather *collectives* over time that enabled it to spread. Over and above its influence on the genre, *The Shape of Punk to Come* set forth a public for Refused's own futurity. By 2010 rumors began to spread across the internet that Refused might reunite. The band's record label Epitaph reposted Refused's old website in anticipation of its reissue of *The Shape of Punk to Come*, but other websites began to quote anonymous sources that the band would reunite and also perform. In the fall of 2011 posters for the upcoming Coachella Festival in 2012 appeared on several sites across the web and included Refused among the lineup. This continued to fuel the now long-awaited and much anticipated reunion rumors. In early 2012 Refused confirmed that they would be playing Coachella and other festivals across Europe. Needless to say, the reception of the summer festival reunion shows was substantial. The Coachella performance was streamed online and the intensity was palpable, both from the band and the crowd, prompting an appearance on *Late Night with Jimmy Fallon* in July, the band's first time on American television. The almost fifteen-year-long slow circulation had started to shift toward viral intensity and ultimately persuaded the band to book their own headlining tour.

After following their case for some time, it almost seemed like fate that their first American date on the headline tour was in Atlanta. The buzz around Columbia, South Carolina was palpable among those into heavier musics, and it was clear a sizable contingency of people would be gathering in Atlanta. They sold so many tickets that the show had to be moved to the field behind the venue, Atlanta's famed Masquerade. Seeing them live brought home the key role of performance in musical worlding. The visceral experience of the sound, the anticipation of the crowd, and all of the qualities of the work's musical worlding were entangled in a becoming-other-together in that moment of embodied listening. The sound waves gathered us in their refrains, the repetitions and diffractions of their patterns, and the timbres held us there, vibrating. Literally our bodies vibrated, resonated tacitly and collectively as the sound waves entangled us in an ulterior collective. Focused and intense, the crowd was gathered as a sphere public through more than a decade of emergent circulation and attuned in the moment by the performance's sonic world.

FIGURE 6.2.   Refused's Dennis Lyxzén live at Coachella in 2012. Photo by
Jason Persse.

In short the band gained worldwide cult status fifteeen years after breaking up. Through a collective self-organized process of activity and response,
Refused emerged bigger than they ever were before they disbanded.[25] After
breaking up at a house show in a small American town, the video for "New
Noise" posted by their label Epitaph records, now as I write, has 2.4 million
hits. And that is just one version in circulation. This is the power that circulation adds to musical worlding, none of which Refused intended with the
production and release of *The Shape of Punk to Come*. Without the possibil-

ity of fully anticipating emerging technologies, the band was left open to the future relationality of the album's circulation. For Latour, Moderns only had an idealized utopian future but never a realistic chance or a looking forward to what he calls their "*prospect*: the shape of things to come" ("Composition Manifesto" 486). Facing a coming crisis, it can seem like there is no future, but Latour argues that these conditions actually reveal many prospects, futures "utterly different from what we imagined" (486). They engender innovation with a sense of consequentiality. As Deleuze and Guattari put it, "The poet ... is the one who lets loose molecular populations in hopes that this will sow the seeds of, or even engender, the people to come, that these populations will pass into the people to come, open a cosmos. ... [I]t may be that the sound molecules of pop music are at this very moment implanting here and there a people of a new type, singularly indifferent to the orders of the radio" (345–46). These shifting assemblages, they argue, are not simply a form of evolution but the results of an open earth that calls the artist to invoke the people, to gather future collectives.

While *The Shape of Punk to Come* didn't go viral like Obama Hope, the album spread and circulated to coproduce a new musical world for its own future reception. Along with emerging technologies, its enhanced distribution enacted the rhetorical prospects of metacultural response, genre imitation, sonic affects, and collective movement. In the wake of emerging digital networked culture, *The Shape of Punk to Come* took on a resonant rhetorical life of its own and reconstituted collective existence. Its circulation through networks in excess of direct rhetorical intent laid the ambient grounds for its own future reception. That ambience doesn't exist without the networked actions of circulation. And the combination of circulation and ambience coproduces another version of *The Shape of Punk to Come* as a quasi-object. Ultimately, the "distributed album" isn't just the circulation of one song or MP3 but multiple parts of the album circulating across and through multiple pathways, platforms, and bodies that make up *The Shape of Punk to Come*'s coproductive ambience.

The rhetorical aspects of this movement are not a function of direct persuasion, the act of persuading another human through language, but a contribution to the tacit conditions upon which future musics, publics, and assemblages are possible and persuaded to gather.[26] The rhetorical is the processes involved in these entanglements. As an adjective "rhetorical" typically modifies a noun, but by using "the rhetorical" as a noun I'm situating rhetoric as an action that modifies, modulates, circulates—a series of vibrations that resonate, speed up, slow down, rearticulate, and invigorate ecologies of composition. The rhetorical inevitably emerges as a coproductive function of networks becoming-ambient and ambience becoming-networked—networks receding into ambient concealment and emerging into disclosure—through movements of material and affective circulation. Gries traces this conception back to a footnote in Wayne Booth's *Modern Dogma and the Rhetoric of Assent*: "There is a sense in which even the lowest animals can be said to intend meanings or to influence the rest of the world rhetorically; I would not even resist defining the universe as essentially rhetorical: it is created, as Whitehead says, in processes of interchange among its parts. Each least particle—whatever that turns out to be—just like the gross beast and 'dead' star, could be defined as a steadily changing 'field of influences,' receiving, processing, and transforming 'information'" (Booth qtd. in Gries 12). While Booth relegates this to a footnote and quickly qualifies it, Gries takes this seriously and sees rhetoric as something that emerges from these fields of influence as it coproduces those fields through actions, activity, and material relations, collectivities that generate multiple agencies, assemble ecologies, and disseminate cascading affects and effects.

Resonance as the result of vibration is distributed through this modulating, circulatory rhetorical ecology. Stefan Helmreich argues that resonance is the transduction of vibration across media, entangling the sonic, haptic, and tactile, and associatively extends into the synchronous vibration of the imagination. Resonance, he writes, "suggests participating in the world, moving in sympathy, working in an empirically attuned embodiment [that] allows us to understand how energy must always be translated through a relay of associations, in order for it to be received at a point distant from its source" ("Transducing" 163). In other words, resonance is a model for turning noise into signal. But this is also a model for spreadability and virality. Tony Sampson, in *Virality: Contagion Theory in the Age of Networks*, argues that biological, viral contagion isn't just a metaphor for how discourse circulates but provides a model for how forces circulate through all kinds of encounters. There is no division between the biological and the social. Their diagrammatic functions are the same—biological viruses and social invention are both ontologically coproductive through force, encounter, and contagion. Vibrations, flows, and radiations circulate and are taken up, imitated, and recirculated. Circulation on this model also blurs the lines between levels of scale. Following Gabriel Tarde, Sampson calls circulation that occurs below the level of individuals micro-imitation—vibratory waves that travel through atoms, genes, cells, and bodies, replicating themselves but also transforming themselves and others through the encounter. The waves generate a connectivity that coproduces collectivities at macro levels as they bubble up to coproduce a social field. Small events build velocity to become contagious vibrating events. Obama's 2008 campaign, for example, taps into micro-relations among voters who already affectively desire change and hope. Voters felt Obama's joy because, even tacitly in his stance and smile, he was mirroring back their own vital force and his imitation amplified it, enabled its virality, and activated the large-scale collective event of the campaign through this resonance.

These forms of circulatory resonance coproduce the rhetorical. In *Vibrant Matter* Jane Bennett writes, "But metal is always metallurgical, always an alloy of the endeavors of many bodies, always something worked on by geological, biological, and often human agencies. And human metalworkers are themselves effects of the vital materiality they work" (60). It doesn't take much to rearticulate this statement from the perspective of the rhetorical: But *rhetoric* is always *rhetorical*, always an alloy of the endeavors of many bodies, always something worked on by geological, biological, and often human agencies. And human *rhetors* are themselves effects of the vital materiality they work. This is the coproductive entanglement of quasi-objects and their quasi-subjects that conditions the emergence of their futurity. No rhetorical act can change the world on its own, but it can contribute to the conditions upon which future change can take place. It coproduces a new set of possibilities, which collectively lays the affective, conceptual, and material grounds through which something could heard, felt, enacted, and composed. Since all rhetorical acts emerge with and through these generative processes that are partially disclosed by the rhetorical act, much of rhetorical and *suasive* force happens in excess of logical arguments that change minds, which makes the rhetorical a matter of resonating acts of emergence that alter potential futures.

CONCLUSION

RESOUNDING

RESOUNDING SENDS ECHOES AND reverberations into the future. As a key term, "resounding" evokes the re-sounding of rhetoric, or bringing sound back to rhetoric after a long detour through print culture, but also establishes resounding as a process of reverberation and resonance that sustains into the future. Reverberation is the diffraction of sound waves or frequencies that resist being absorbed by a body or a wall and bounce back into the room. Resonance is the capacity of a body or wall to more easily absorb a particular frequency and vibrate, in effect amplifying and extending the frequencies that match its own ability to vibrate and reflecting back the other frequencies as reverb. Resonance creates a sustained ringing or repetition of the original tone or frequency to produce a deeper, fuller, more prolonged sound. Resounding evokes a particular way to re-sound rhetoric as the rhetorical, as a form of these kinds of circulations and extended coproductions. In "Conducting Research in the History of Rhetoric" James Murphy defines rhetoric as "the study of means for future discourse" (188). Grammar, he argues, analyzes the structures of language itself, and logic analyzes the validity of argumentative forms, but rhetoric looks forward toward the future uses of those structures and forms and aims its analyses toward those deployments. But in a rare moment for composition and rhetoric, Ede and Lunsford push this a little further. In "Audience Addressed, Audience Invoked" they propose, almost as an afterthought, the concept of eventual audience. For them, it is a reader who might stumble onto the work in the near future that the author didn't address or invoke. But it also suggests a reader who might pull the work off of a bookshelf in some distant future and context that the author can't possibly write for directly or imagine. It is a form of consequentiality that could not have been intended nor prefigured. *Resounding the Rhetorical* uses the sonic as a way into this other eventual mode of materiality, another manner or orientation toward material composition enacted through the ongoing movements of vibrational ecologies and their sustained expansion as quasi-objects.

Ede and Lunsford's classic text "Audience Addressed, Audience Invoked" has been read by almost everyone in the field of composition and rhetoric. It stages the classic debate between addressing a materially real and known audience and writing to their knowledge base and desires, and imagining the audience the author wants the text to invoke and developing textual and rhetorical schemas to create that sense of audience in the reader. They survey the literature as of 1984 to problematize this binary and show how rhetorical situations are clearly more complex than these two options let on. For example, they cite Herbert Simon's book *Persuasion: Understanding, Practice, and Analysis* as establishing a continuum between these extremes based on opportunities for interaction. Between face-to-face audiences that meet regularly over an extended period of time to interact and mass media publics that have little or no contact and maybe no reciprocal awareness of each other, he posits (1) a pedestrian audience that happens to pass a soapbox orator, (2) a passive, occasional audience that comes to hear a lecture in an auditorium, and (3) an active, occasional audience that meets only on specific occasions but actively interacts when they do (161). So for them, both addressed and invoked include drawbacks. Addressed overestimates the role of the reader to determine meaning. Any attempt to fully adopt the audience's position becomes pandering. Invoked overestimates the power of the writer to control readers or address some future "unborn" reader (Moffett qtd. in Ede and Lunsford 164). Attempting to write for a "mythical generic reader" will lose concrete ties to the rhetorical situation (164). In their model, Ede and Lunsford break down more possible subtypes within the larger invoked, addressed categories: invoked audience can include your self, friends, colleagues, critics, a mass audience, future audiences, past audiences, or anomalous audiences (such as fictional characters); addressed audience can include future audiences, mass audiences, critics, colleagues, friends, as well as your self (166). Writers cycle through relations among these audiences in any given composing process.

In their extended example of this more complex situation, Ede and Lunsford discuss their own experience of writing their coauthored article that cycled through a small close-knit audience of an NEH seminar; one author as her own audience as she debated the issues while writing a textbook; each other as colleagues as they began a draft; the editor of CCCs first as invoked audience and then as addressed audience; the outside reviewers as critics; the invoked attendees of CCCCs; the authors they critique; the colleague who gave them feedback; and future readers of CCCs. In their future example, they speculate that maybe someone in speech communication will pick up the article and find it useful, which could prompt them to revise their model. But it is possible to imagine many more variations through the life cycle of an idea, its articulation in a text, and its eventual circulation. What always interested me is this eventuality. They write: "But even this single case demonstrates that the term audience refers not just to the intended, actual, or eventual readers of a discourse, but to all those whose image, ideas, or actions influence a writer during the process of composition. One way to conceive of 'audience,' then, is as an overdetermined or unusually rich concept, one which may perhaps be best specified through the analysis of precise, concrete situations" (168). I'm attracted both to the notion of eventual audiences that will have been materially real and in some cases imaginable and in other cases totally emergent, all of which are equally constitutive of the discourse, and to the recognition that any such analysis has to be of specific material situations and relationships. But the quote is still really about influences on the writer during the process of composing. Moffett puts potential unborn audiences on the table, which calls that into question unless the field takes a broader approach to composition as a quasi-object. Only then would these unknown future readers affect the composing process even if the writer is no longer alive in some futural rhetorical encounter with the work. This more expansive sense of composing complicates their call for addressing audience in specific concrete situations. The concrete situations writers operate in are limited in scope and limited in terms of what the writer can directly effect. The only way to assess such "concrete" futurity is to coparticipate in those emergent processes, analyze their emergent effects in retrospect, and theorize their potential future relationality. Perhaps Moffett suggests such a model in his "spectrum of discourse": researchers and writers engage in processes of recording (the drama of what is happening), reporting (the narrative of what happened), generalizing (the exposition of what happens), and theorizing (the argumentation of what will or may happen) (Moffett qtd. in Ede and Lunsford 164).

While *Resounding* has been primarily concerned with quasi-objects, the coproduction of quasi-objects necessarily carries along with it a number of correlative concepts or phenomena—composition, sound, music, process, circulation, ecology, entrainment, and perhaps most importantly, futurity. The book has been oriented toward eventual futures in two senses, both in the specific case chapters and in the overall movement of the book's model of quasi-objects. The first two theory chapters develop the foundation for this model. Chapter 1 outlines the overall "theory of the quasi-object" derived from a reading of Serres: quasi-objects are relational, parasites are ecological, and noise is vital, living energy that grounds the system in circulation up from noise through ecologies and emerging as relational quasi-objects. Quasi-objects are functions of circulation, coordinated breaks into the circulation of energy that redirect it toward future outcomes through further circulation. Chapter 2, then, turns this systemic order more explicitly into a temporal process by reading it through Deleuze and Guattari's refrain and making parasite the fulcrum, mediator, or assemblage converter of the system.

1. Vital—Deleuze's virtual potential and milieu as an energy source.
2. Ecological—Heidegger's embodied, intuitive, improvisational entrainment and enactment that draws on the milieu's potential to demarcate its territory.
3. Relational—Latour's public that gathers a larger territory and opens back out not only to the milieu but also to potential future relations.

Giving temporality to Serres's model allows the case chapters together to make one large refrain out of the process of recording, performance, and promotion and distribution. Recording draws from the virtual potential in a milieu and transduces or conducts it through performance to create internal organization that opens the assemblage to future relations.

The case study chapters then play out these movements within each chapter, highlighting different aspects of the refrain. Chapter 3 is concerned with vitality, sonic energy and its transduction through the recording process that translates noise into sound. Recording, in general and in research, coproduces new inscriptions and future versions of the object of study. Chapter 4 is concerned with ecology, enaction, and conduction through performance—the human parasite transduces resonance and opens to it new relations. Gesture, in this case, coproduces a new genre. Just because Thomas Stanley doesn't start with and aim for a genre doesn't mean his work can't eventually lead to one, like the collective sound that emerges from their performative gestures. Chapters 5 and 6 are concerned with relationality through promotion and distribution, quasi-objects at two different levels of scale—promotion and distribution create the potential for future publics and audiences. In chapter 5 promotion as circulation rather than distribution coproduces a new emergent public. And in chapter 6 distribution again gives way to circulation as it moves out of the hands of record labels but also artists and into a self-organized, emergent system that sets potential conditions for resonance that coproduces an unanticipated future audience. Within each chapter there is a movement toward futurity, which combines Ede and Lunsford's eventual with Deleuze's emergent event. While I've mostly used future and futurity as analogues, if there is a distinction it might be this. "The future" often connotes some grand future out there ahead of us all that humans have no control over and don't participate in. "A future" more often connotes an outcome, the effect of some process that in many ways humans can recognize and anticipate. But futurity is something both more abstract and more real: it is with us right now as something we are always in the process of coproducing that entangles both anticipatable possibility and unanticipatable potential—it is the futural form of the virtual's potential.

This notion is perhaps best captured in Afrofuturism. In "Further Considerations on Afrofuturism" Kodwo Eshun argues that since Western, imperial Enlightenment has written African American subjectivity out of history and excluded it, the primary historical and cultural response has been to recover it to demonstrate its presence and contributions. These assembled counter-memories, however, ultimately situate the collective trauma of slavery as the founding moment, which leaves African Americans less empowered by being tied to a determining and reductive past. Afrofuturism does not seek to deny counter-memory but to extend it through a reorientation toward potential futures. For Eshun, it is never simply about forgetting this trauma but turning all of the efforts at recovery toward new futures. The future is as treacherous as the past and generates a kind of fatigue that Afrofuturists have a responsibility to fight against so they can fight "towards the not-yet, towards becoming" (289). In the 1980s counter-memory was seen as the ethical response, a commitment to the dead and their experiences. But this lead to counter-futures being coded as unethical and viewed with suspicion, so African intellectuals "ceased to participate in the process of building futures" (289). Eshun argues that scholars, writers, and artists can't leave the future to the futures industry, which circulates information about the future as a commodity—computer simulations, economic projections, weather reports, futures trading speculations, and think-tank policy reports. These futurist projections are dominated by dystopic and negative views of Africa—bad economic projections, weather forecasts of drought and floods due to global warming, medical reports on AIDS, life expectancy forecasts. They are meant to make futures safe for capital but ultimately demoralize Africans. Eshun sees two types of Afrofuturist responses: artistic and vernacular. Contemporary Afrofuturist artists are critical of past-oriented museum traditions by laying them bare, manipulating them, and mocking them via emulation, such as utopian formulations of future nonexistent museums, in order to expose and reframe dystopic futures through new "anticipatory designs" (293). Vernacular expressions, Eshun argues, should be taken as seriously as these high art traditions because they respond to the reductive past and negative future at the level of popular culture—in particular the crossover between science fiction and music.

Mainstream science fiction films and novels are informal parts of venture capital and the futures industry. *The Matrix* and *Minority Report*, for examples, function like product placements for computer-tech industries or R&D departments in the futures industry. Corporate scenarios are predictions of plausible futures, but science fiction is free to deny plausibility and seeks to rewrite reality. Afrofuturist appeals to extraterrestriality, futurology, and techno science fiction operate similarly and are deployed in moments where futures are made difficult to imagine. The Afrofilia of the 1960s and 1970s, for example, is a response to the push back against the civil rights movement. Bob Marley; Sun Ra; Earth, Wind & Fire; and Parliament Funkadelic used the concept album to sustain a shared set of mythological images and icons of extra-terrestrials and space exploration that sought a detachment from the limits of present conditions. Sun Ra's "lifework constitutes a self-created cosmology" based on the confluence of Egyptology and science fiction—the desire to recover lost glories of pre-industrial Africa that European colonialism covered over and project it into an imagined future (Eshun, "Further Considerations" 294). Sun Ra leapfrogs the colonialist and Christian eras to breakup their deterministic hold on new potential futures. More recently, Detroit band Drexciya released the concept album *The Quest* in 1997, which combines a metaphorical, speculative fiction story of slaves thrown into the Atlantic, whose babies were born with the ability to breathe underwater and evolved into a new species, with synthetic, electronic compositions, whose space age sounds create and evoke new moods and subjectivities, and the juridical or cartographic, since the band bought the naming rights to a star as a location in space for this new race (300–301).

In each of these cases of the black vernacular, science fiction and sound coordinate with each other to enact a line of flight toward the potential futurity. Science fiction is not a prediction of a far-off utopia or purely imaginary alternative reality. It is a "distortion of the present" that engineers a feedback loop between "its preferred future and its becoming present"—a mutation put into circulation to produce new ambient grounds (Eshun, "Further Considerations" 290). Similarly, Eshun argues that sound technology disrupts the ability to assign racial identities to sounds and voices. Synthesizers and vocoders create sounds that don't fit stereotypes associated with voice and genre and evoke a future when these boundaries are blurred or nonexistent. For him, this "human-machine interface became both the condition and the subject of Afrofuturism" (296). In *The Rhythmic Event* Eleni Ikoniadou argues that rhythm is the interface between humans and machines. Vibrations, hums, and noises all have variations in rhythm that entangle, attune, and entrain humans with the world. The ability to digitally create rhythms, she argues, introduces a mutation into this entrainment. Like evolution, it injects difference into a system to see what emerges. It creates an openness to futurity whose impact lies in its affective qualities that move bodies via the material forces of resonance and modulation. This is Eshun's *futurhythmachine* (*More Brilliant*). Afrofuturism, then, both thematically and sonically, is a program for the recovery of counter-futures capable of intervening in current politics and reconditioning potential futures. It is not naïve or uncritically celebratory. It is "vernacular futurology" that produces a temporal disturbance—it creates competing futures that "infiltrate the present" and disrupt linear time (Eshun, "Further Considerations" 297).

This kind of concern for futurity shows up in composition and rhetoric primarily in debates over historiography.[1] In "Writing Future Rhetoric" Gina Ercolini and Pat Gehrke make the direct connection between science fiction and Foucault's approach to history. Teleological and utopian predictions, for them, often forestall potential futures that are more transgressive or experimental. They call for writing futures by offering a "mutagenic" space that alters conceptualizations of the past and present through fictional accounts of the future, which adds fissures in a progressive sense of time that they call "fictures" (Ercolini and Gehrke 155). They read science fiction as positing these kinds of as-yet unimagined futures that put the present in question in order to destabilize the future. Orwell's 1984, for example, was not a work that predicted or prescribed the future but functioned as an interruption in his own age. It writes a creative or imaginative fissure into his present in order to change the conditions for potential futures. This is how Ercolini and Gehrke read Foucault's aim of "determining problems and unleashing them" (qtd. in Ercolini and Gehrke 165). Genealogy doesn't determine futures; it opens to such unleashings. The future becomes a site of potential transformation. This kind of work adopts "a fictural relationship to the future . . . by preserving the future's capacity to open questions, problems, and concerns of the present, . . . intervening in the present (through the past) to open up the future. . . . [It] relates to the future as a site of experimentation and open possibility" (170).[2] This is what Afrofuturism seeks. It is also what research does, what improvisation does, and what circulation does, and what artists like MOM[2], Boyfriend, and Refused attempt to do rhetorically and ontologically—they seek to write an eventual future through writing the event.

Writing the event engages in a sense of time that is fractured. In "Writing the Event" Michelle Ballif argues that traditional and revisionary historiography elide the event via narrative and category, forcing it into evidence for a narrative or claim. But the event is purely singular, so the task is to write this singularity, which is both possible and impossible—possible because writers are always in the process of coproducing it, but impossible because they never control it or produce it alone. Writers participate in temporality but do so nonlinearly. This temporality, or fractured time, still has a relationship to a "future to come" (Ballif 247)—a future that can be awaited if the writer remains open to it. The future to come is unknowable in full, but writers must greet this potential future hospitably, welcoming the event. The typical understanding of a messiah functions as a nonevent because it is predicted and certain. The *messianic* means to create and leave a place for him *if* he comes, an open ethical hospitality that sets the conditions for his arrival but accepts if he never arrives.[3] Writers must write as preparation for a future that might or might not come. Such a historiography is performative, ontologically coproducing the event as a rupture in history, narrative, and time. Writing the event asks us to accept and step into these conditions and continually relaunch temporality not as time but as an attunement to the future anterior. In "A Philology for a Future Anterior" Victor Vitanza argues that any logos that posits an assurance of a stable present cannot be trusted. Like Ballif, the event, for him, never takes place in time but in finitude, a rift or break in time. Writing the event is a making of the present but with no subjectivity behind it or necessary effects that come from it. The maker is invented afterward through a faith in grammar that is misplaced onto a false causality. The writer, then, becomes a "quasi-subject" taking on the emergent sensibility of its object under study (Vitanza 180). The writer lives in and is this future anterior, an event that will be completed prior to some future time even though it hasn't been completed yet. For Vitanza, this means that everything writers do now to coproduce the event is already fractured, never fully grounded or "present" in both senses of objective and now. The quasi-subjects and their quasi-objects always will have been toward the future to come. So, history written in the future anterior is history that lies in wait, in anticipation, but is radically open to what will have been (185). It isn't anticipated nor unanticipatable but open in anticipation.

Perhaps Heidegger gets at this sense of temporality most directly but also most poetically. In "On the Origin of the Work of Art" he writes, "The truth that discloses itself in the work can never be proved or derived from what went before. What went before is refuted in its exclusive reality by the work. What art founds can therefore never be compensated and made up for by what is already present and available" (75). Heidegger states pretty clearly that he is not after a direct cause and effect persuasive logic but an emergent one where the work of art emerges from past conditions and then adds to the conditions for what is then possible but is never reducible to or co-terminus with either—that linearity is always fractured.[4] The much debated notion of the fourfold—earth, sky, mortals, and gods—is his poetic heuristic for articulating this sense of temporality as an event. The temple gathers the material conditions such as stone and mortar (earth), the cultural ideals and ritual forms (sky), the people who build and worship (mortals), and the deities that inhabit the temple (gods) to create a particular historical culture through its collective emergence as an event. The temple doesn't represent objects or meanings but brings these things into a gathering as an expression of the world, coproducing new grounds for futurity. In "The Thing" the essence of a jug, for Heidegger, is that it holds and pours water or wine. It has a capacity and potential for use, movement, and action, and its essence is in this action, this becoming or implosion of being and time into an ontological temporality. In performing this capacity, holding and giving, the jug, like the temple, gathers the grapes of the earth, the sun and the rain that nourish the grapes, the humans who make and drink the wine, and the gods evoked through the rituals of drinking—all of which perform an emergent set of relations, opening them to future horizons in every act of pouring. This resonant relationship resounds into the future like the ripples of a wave.

The one constant across the cases that make up *Resounding the Rhetorical* is the ontological presence of sound, resonance, ringing as the ground of composition. Near the end of "The Thing," after his infamous portrayal of the fourfold, Heidegger characterizes the relationship between earth, sky, mortals, and gods as a "staying-appropriating-lighting": each of the four is coproduced through a gathering and holding, an "enfolding clasp of mutual appropriation," and a disclosure of the specific capacities of each while appropriating those capacities for the production of the others (179). In *Inessential Solidarity* Davis sees this appropriation not as a free ethical choice but as a necessary obligation. And rather than simply a mutual appropriation it is a "double deterritorialization": Dasein is both "called into question and into service" (13). Similarly, in *Making Sense of Heidegger*, though he is coming at Heidegger from a more traditionally phenomenological and hermeneutic position rather than an ontological one, Thomas Sheehan argues that at a certain point Dasein has to accept appropriation as a necessary condition and be open to those futurities. Our throwness is not just into the world but also into futurity. The "essence" of Dasein is always *"having to be constitutionally ahead of itself,* . . . being thrown ahead, . . . pulled open, the stretch into possibilities is thrown-*open*-ness" (144). Dasein, along with the worlding of the fourfold, is a deterritorialized, appropriating, and appropriated unfolding toward potential futures.

Heidegger is proposing an emergent logic where the specific manipulabilities and capacities of all things are both utilized and coproduced in the same emergent conditions that they coproduce. Mortals are caught up in this mutual appropriation and emergent self-organization of "world worlding," which cannot be explained through human causes. Heidegger writes, "As soon as human cognition here calls for an explanation, it fails to transcend the world's nature, and falls short of it" ("The Thing" 180). Heidegger calls this mutual, emergent coproduction "mirror-play," and, potentially at least, puts sound at its center. The mirror-play of the four presences the world through a "round dance" that "does not encompass the four like a hoop": the round dance is "a ring that joins while it plays as mirroring" (180). This ring isn't simply round: it is a ringing, a resounding coproductive resonance among the fourfold. Heidegger writes: "Radiantly, the ring joins the four, everywhere open to the riddle of their presence. The gathered presence of the mirror-play of the world, joining in this way, is the ringing. In the ringing of the mirror-playing ring, the four nestle into their unifying presence, in which each one retains its own nature. So nestling, they join together, worlding the world. . . . Out of the ringing mirror-play the thinging of the thing takes place" (180). The "ringing," the resonance, the resounding (perhaps of Derrida's *Glas*) is what joins the fourfold, gathers it in the ontological entanglement of the world—it is an ontological circle not just a hermeneutic one. From this reading, resounding becomes a central image of worlding, coproduction, and middle voice. Sound waves are always a function of world, of differential acoustic processes and temporality—the sustained ringing ripple effect of past, present, and future through the emergent encounter or event, the ontological coproduction of the world as a function of sonic resoundings. This mirror-play between the ontological and the hermeneutic doesn't simply leave us with placing the rhetorical on one side or the other, but it opens the possibility that the rhetorical is aligned with the mirror-play itself, waiting, resonating, resounding.

Taking Ede and Lunsford's suggestion of eventual audiences to frame the book's conclusion makes the third move of the refrain even more explicit. It opens the system back out to future relationality, making the book an example of its content. If writers can't trace the future, even to the small extent that they can the past and present, then what is left? Resounding. Setting off the potential for future resonance with eventual audiences and ecologies. While the book has been focused on composition and finally rhetoric, drawing on examples of sound and music to tease out ulterior aspects of composition, I've largely left writing off the table until now. What would writing the event look like if a writer were to take all of these things into consideration? To that question I can only leave this book as potential evidence. As Audrey Van Mersbergen argues in "The Return of the Addressed," the divide between orality and literacy isn't as stark as Walter Ong and Eric Havelock have suggested. Following Heidegger, she argues that reading a text converts it to sound whether aloud or in the imagination. Just as sound waves fill the space between two speakers, immersing and penetrating them physically with sound, reading allows us to participate in this relation, experience it in the present, hearing "the resonance of the words," feeling "the intensity of address" (251). The Greeks, she argues, didn't separate words in writing from words in speech. Ancient rhetorical discourse still "resonates when we read in modernity," allowing eventual audiences to be immersed in its voice and sound twenty-five centuries later (251).

Resounding has worked to enact the entanglement of composition, sound, music, and rhetoric through such a writing process. In some ways it doesn't look so different—there are chapters and headings and citations and endnotes, not unlike Ede and Lunsford's article. But the linear presentation of the argument belies a centripetal force in all of these divergent materials, drawing them in, gathering them into its orbit, remaking them into a new version as it spins on a constantly changing center, only to sling them back out again through a centrifugal force toward some potential futurity. As linear as the book's structure is, it never fully enacts a theory/application model of criticism because the theories and the objects of analysis continually shift, update, change, and coproduce each other. Theories produce a ground for moving forward but the theories shift when engaging a quasi-object, sometimes becoming enhanced, sometimes falling away, spinning out of orbit, the energy of their waves dissipating. As linear as the book's structure is, in other words, its temporality is emergent and spatially entangled. The book moves back and forth through a series of relays, some that spin back to previous theories, some that spin out to new cases that fold back to rearticulate the virtual model. The entanglement is what is left when the written book, like the recorded album, is in a future reader's hands, ringing, resounding.

NOTES

INTRODUCTION: RE-SOUNDING

1. A number of key authors in composition and rhetoric's sonic turn published articles in this issue, including Bump Halbritter, "Musical Rhetoric in Integrated Media Composition"; Jody Shipka, "Sound Engineering: Toward a Theory of Multimodal Soundness"; and Heidi McKee, "Sound Matters: Notes Toward the Analysis and Design of Sound in Multimodal Webtexts." The early emphasis on meaning in this issue extended through Cindy Selfe's "The Movement of Air, the Breath of Meaning: Aurality and Multimodal Composing" (2009).

2. Goodale is certainly aware of these alternatives. In Goodale's coauthored review essay, the authors write that the object of analysis in sound studies is "vibrations in the air, . . . whether or not [they have] taken on meaning." Scholars in sound studies "do not presume the semiotic, only the affective, . . . the sensation of hearing and feeling" (Gunn el al 476). And while his book takes note of affect (as early as page 3–4), he is still focused on meaning, making a broader argument about sound—that it can be read or interpreted consciously and critically, if not by all listeners then certainly by critics. See also my extended review of Goodale's book in *Philosophy and Rhetoric*.)

3. As Davis notes, *Enculturation* published one of the first special issues on music in

the field in 1999. In the introduction, "Avowing the Unavowable: On the Music of Composition," Thomas Rickert and I work through the notion that composition, like music, operates in excess of meaning and on a model of affective engagement or performative production, starting out with the claim "To confront music is to address the issue of being composed." Christian Smith and I developed a version of this in our contribution to the *Currents in Electronic Literacy* "Writing with Sound" issue "'Digimortal': Sound in a World of Posthumanity." The sound project mixes personal narrative, music criticism, interview, and theoretical analysis in an example of sound writing human embodiment through larger ecological processes.

4. Perhaps one of the best introductions to new materialism is Diane Coole and Samantha Frost's introduction to their edited collection *New Materialisms: Ontology, Agency, and Politics.* It articulates and develops a version of new materialism that understands matter as a form of energy, causality as complex and nonlinear, and corporeality as a function of distributed biological and ecological processes, and provides clear rationales for turning toward new materialist approaches: most other fields have moved beyond classical physics and positivist ontologies, which can't account for emerging problems in the contemporary world such as climate change, GMOs, population growth, and nanotechnologies. The humanities, they argue, must go beyond the methods of the cultural turn in order to develop new forms of empirical investigation to address these problems.

5. For an excellent discussion of how dirt is a function of such processes, see Stacy Alaimo's "Trans-corporeal Feminisms and the Ethical Space of Nature." Dirt is in a constant state of becoming and carries within it the self-replicating agency to turn other bodies such as leaves, twigs, and decaying animals back into dirt.

6. This most generic definition includes animals, computers, and any unintentional rhythmic pulses generated by a variety of natural processes. It is also a definition problematized by experimental composers like John Cage, whose work questions the boundaries among music, sound, and noise—in other words, questions what qualifies as being organized (Sakakeeny 112–24). But for my project, this generic definition establishes a relation between music and sound that plays out at the level of popular music's larger composing processes.

7. Perhaps Steven Katz's *The Epistemic Music of Rhetoric* is the closest book project in our field tackling the relation between music and writing, but his emphasis is much more focused on reception, affect, and reader response than the larger, more material sense of music composition in relation to sound.

8. Even something as seemingly personal or disciplinarily ancillary as Jeff Rice's *Craft Obsession: The Social Rhetorics of Beer* is ultimately about such larger composing processes and their entanglement with quasi-subjects through digital media, rhetoric, and writing.

CHAPTER 1: COMPOSITION AS QUASI-OBJECT

1. In *From Form to Meaning*, David Fleming marks these moments more explicitly with the 1963 publication of Braddock et al.'s *Research in Written Composition*; the 1963 CCCC panel on "New Rhetoric" and the publication of Corbett's *Classical Rhetoric for the Modern Student*; and the gradual rise of the process paradigm from the publication of Rohman's work on prewriting published in 1965, to the 1966 Dartmouth conference that brought American and British educators together, to the work of Emig, Murray, and Elbow in the 1970s (22–23). Part of what Fleming wants to show in his book is that none of these movements were impactful at the time but came to be seen as central touchstones in retrospect as the process paradigm overtook current traditional practices in the 1970s and 1980s. In many ways, I'm making a similar claim for the works on ecology in the 1980s that now in retrospect as the social turn has wound down seem central to the material turn that has emerged in the 2000s (see chapter 4).

2. *Resounding* is in many ways an extension of this argument in that it looks to develop examples of these kinds of ecologies and postprocesses. As Dobrin makes clear in his book, much of what he is after is jumping off from my book, *A Counter-History of Composition*, which drew on, in some respects, his earlier work in eco-composition. Kristopher Lotier notes in "Around 1986: The Externalization of Cognition and the Emergence of Postprocess Invention" that there is a definite distinction between eco-composition, which emphasizes nature and environmentalist rhetorics, and ecological approaches to composition, which is a conceptual or theoretical model for the coproductive nature of composing (379n2). I also make this distinction in *Counter-History*, and Dobrin addresses it in *Postcomposition*.

3. In some ways, the move I am making is more similar to Derrida than to Dobrin, since I don't want to privilege any of the terms. As Michael Syrotinski notes, writing, for Derrida, is "the first of a long series of quasi-transcendental and ever-changing place-holding terms that are all in essence, saying and doing the same thing (*differance, supplement, pharmakon, trace, dissemination, cinders, signature, shibboleth, subjectile, hauntology*, the wholly other, and so on). The ceaseless

movement of this renaming, as Spivak rightly points out . . . itself enacts [Derrida's] refusal to assign priority to any master-word, any master trope" (6). In "Signature Event Context," Derrida flips the speech/writing binary to make "writing in general" the primary term. The absence of author, audience, and context that writing produces is not an inferior degradation of speech, as Plato argued, but instead becomes conceptually primary, showing us more directly how speech, language, and experience are also already grounded in these same absences. After flipping the binary, Derrida ultimately shows how they are all equivalent terms in the face of absence. Dobrin seems to stop at the reversal that privileges writing in general since the field still holds on to composition and rhetoric as functions of presence.

4. I see *Resounding* as a follow-up to *A Counter-History of Composition* not only because it continues to investigate the same kinds of vitalist networked, material, and ecological complexity but also because it continues to follow the inventive "what if?" question *Counter-History* asked: What if we enact *dissoi logoi*—making the weaker argument the stronger—through vitalism? What would that do? How might that impact the field? Similarly *Resounding* asks, What if sound were really central to the field? What would that look like? How might that affect the field's object of study? If it forced us to *really* take Latour's notion of composition seriously for the whole discipline, what would this do? This kind of investigation is a unique feature of the two books and seeks to *open* spaces of inquiry and lines of investigation for composition and rhetoric. It provides just one experiment; an early attempt. The "book" is really an *essai*—"an essay, an attempt, a try, a testing out, a preliminary gesture" (Gaston xvii).

5. Jakob von Uexküll, who is considered the founder of ecology, supposed an infinite variety of worlds for each species of animal that were separate but linked together to produce a functional unity with an environment. Each animal type has a body with specific capacities for functional connections to its environment, or what Uexküll calls "carriers of significance" (Agamben, *The Open* 41, 46). A tick, for example, has the capacity to experience three primary carriers of significance: touch, odor, and temperature. Ticks are eyeless. They find their way to braches by the sensitivity of their skin to light. They have no ears but can smell the butyric acid emitted by mammals. When they smell it, they drop off their perch. If a tick manages to fall onto a mammal, it has an organ that perceives the mammal's precise temperature. In short, the tick is the relationships its carriers make possible (47)—bodily capacities plus ecology. (In addition to Agamben, see Uexküll, *A*

Foray into the Worlds of Animals and Humans, and Hawk, "Vitalism, Animality, and the Material Grounds of Rhetoric.")

6. Serres uses "look" here when *lock* might seem initially the logical term—materially, lock and key fit together through their notches and the wear over time from their enaction. This could, then, simply be a typo. Or, Serres really means look because the tessera is a visual sign—not a representation but a material sign of the other's presence and a sign of the other's coproductive roles in making the tessera what it is in that moment. It is a material trace of the stereospecificity of relations and beings. (See Mailloux's "Archivist with an Attitude" for a productive take on reading typos.)

7. In "This Is What The Internet Sounds Like," Brian Anderson perhaps provides an interesting example or analogy (also posted at *Motherboard* as "Data Centers Are Really Freaking Loud"). We think of the Internet as virtual space, a transmitter of information, or as a network of cables, computers, and satellites. But Anderson writes,

> Big data centers have always had a noise control problem, but it's only now that the relentless din of the cloud seems to be reaching a fever pitch. There is something almost sublime about the sound of data in a holding pattern. It's a digital ambience that fascinates Matt Parker, a British sound artist. Parker recently paid a visit to a medium-sized data center at Birmingham City University-Edgbaston, and rolled tape as the center's server racks and array of hard drives did their thing, emitting a steady white noise. The raw recording is the soundtrack of so much of our lives today, replete with a faulty drive panel that beeps out for help, but nobody's home.

The project is centered on the idea that the everyday practice of computing that we encounter—phones, apps, digital content—is made possible by huge data centers with electricity running through them and hard drives spinning that generate a white noise users never hear but that grounds their enaction.

8. In his introduction to the most recent edition of *The Parasite*, Cary Wolfe notes that noise and quasi-objects are the most cited concepts out of Serres's work (both appear in *The Parasite* and his follow-up book *Genesis*, which foregrounds noise more explicitly). But because of Serres's more poetic writing style that seeks to disrupt linearity and simple systematicity, readers must continually rebuild relationships between these two concepts through their own work, which makes new versions a necessity and feeds more difference, more noise, back into the system. Serres's approach ultimately performs the grounding relationship of

noise to quasi-objects. (See Addy Pross's "Life's Restlessness" for a nice explanation of the movements of evolution and stabilization out of agitation.)

9. See Casey Boyle's article "Writing and Rhetoric and/as a Posthuman Practice" and upcoming book *Rhetoric as a Posthuman Practice*, which relays rhetoric through Gilbert Simondon's version of transduction—an ongoing mediation that produces greater capacities to affect and be affected through movements across the material and semiotic, theoretical and practical, human and nonhuman. Also see David Rieder's *Suasive Iterations* for another take on transduction in relation to media.

10. Sound in the discipline of anthropology has expanded as a subfield and in relation to ethnography, largely in response to Feld's work, but his emphasis on indigenous people's embodied listening practices has also migrated into communication rhetoric scholarship. See Salvador and Clarke's "The Weyekin Principle: Toward an Embodied Critical Rhetoric" and Carbaugh's "'Just Listen': Listening and Landscape Among the Blackfeet."

11. Comically I've used the traditional heavy metal horns as an emblem of Serres's stereospecificity—\m/—(and perhaps one could read the *m* for the fingers as the multiplicity of noise).

12. Consequently, I continue to be mystified by readings of Latour and actor-network theory such as D. Travers Scott's "'Music to Moog By': Gendering in Early Analog Synthesizing in the United States" that cite only secondary sources and claim that ANT upholds the subject/object binary and privileges objects over action—readings that run completely counter to my understandings of Latour and actor-network theory that show fairly clearly they privilege action, movement, circulation, and the emergent coproduction of subjects and objects. In addition to sidestepping primary sources, Scott conflates actor-network theory with object-oriented ontology, ignoring the debates between Latour and Graham Harman in which Latour insists that his work should not be understood as object oriented in Harman's sense. (For more on object-oriented rhetoric, see Barnett, "Toward an Object-Oriented Rhetoric" and "Chiasms: Pathos, Phenomenology, and Object-Oriented Rhetorics." For an interesting example of the mutual coproduction of quasi-objects by humans and nonhumans, see Chen, "Rocks Made of Plastic Found on Hawaiian Beach.")

13. Latour uses terms such as *modern* and *postmodern* not to designate linear historical periods but to stand for argumentative topoi along the continuum of object and subject. To critique him as reducing time to categorical historical periods misun-

derstands his claim what we have never been modern—instead, ontologically, we have always been nonmodern even while we were operating under a modern epistemology. Latour writes, "There has never been any modern world. Still, there are many differences between various productions of collective-things, but they are probably no more than difference of scale like so many loops in a spiral" (18). Reading his use of these terms as distinct historical periods also mistakes Latour's understanding of time as modern and linear rather than a folded spiral and mistakes his sense of history as modern rather than as complex events of coproduction. Latour's thinking on this point comes in direct relation with Serres. In Latour's interviews with Serres published as *Conversations on Science, Culture, and Time*, Serres states that "every historical era is likewise multitemporal, simultaneously drawing from the obsolete, the contemporary, and the futuristic, [and] . . . reveals a time that is gathered together, with multiple pleats" (60). This position echoes Foucault's argument in *The Order of Things* that shows how the modern episteme happens at different times and different places in different disciplines and also Heidegger's collapse of past conditions of possibility and future degrees of freedom into every present revealing of a world. I also read his use of these terms as more akin to Deleuze and Guattari's use of *classical, romantic,* and *modern* in the context of music. These terms are not used as historical periods but as analogs for the three moments of the refrain as an abstract machine. For an extended discussion of this usage, see Ronald Bogue, *Deleuze on Music, Painting, and the Arts* (38–53).

14. In "One More Turn," Latour argues that dialectical models are really no help because they continue to presuppose a distance between object and subject that his model does not. In other words, arguments that claim nondialectical models are still caught in dialectics because third terms such as Latour's "networks" or Victor Vitanza's "some more" synthesize object and subject simply fail to grant the complexity these thinkers are after. Latour makes it clear that he can't be after a synthesis because for him there was never any ontological division to overcome in the first place, only an epistemological presupposition (290). In short, there is no distance to synthesize. The difference emerges *from* his third term as the conditions for these larger scaled distinctions. The addition of multiplicity, multiples, and swirls produces a complexity that can't be reduced to something as simple as a synthesis or a binary. Latour's distinction between the social and the natural emerging out of, collapsing onto, and feeding back through a ground of networks is in no way dialectical or synthetic. "The Junction," Serres writes, "is

no longer a synthesis but a high opening that leads to other openings upstream" ("Noise" 53)—not unlike Vitanza's third move of "some more" is dissemination rather than sublation.

15. This sense of model as relay is a function of both Latour's and Deleuze's use of mediation. In *Negotiations*, in a section titled "Mediators," Deleuze writes,

> Mediators are fundamental. Creation is all about mediators. Without them nothing happens. They can be people—for a philosopher, artists or scientists; for a scientist, philosophers or artists—but things too, even plants or animals, as in Castaneda. Whether they're real or imaginary, animate or inanimate, you have to form your mediators. It's a series. If you're not in some series, even a completely imaginary one, you're lost. I need my mediators to express myself, and they'd never express themselves without me: you're always working in a group, even when you seem to be on your own. And still more when it's apparent: Felix Guattari and I are one another's mediators. (125)

CHAPTER 2: PROCESS AS REFRAIN

1. Ede is essentially doing for process what Robert Connors did for current-traditional rhetoric in *Composition-Rhetoric* and I did for vitalism in *A Counter-History of Composition*. Each retroactive, generic foil produces the conditions for an eventual recovery and rereading.

2. Kent's articles "Beyond System: The Rhetoric of Paralogy" and "Paralogic Hermeneutics and the Possibilities of Rhetoric" inform his book *Paralogic Rhetoric*, which articulates the model of hermeneutic guessing he outlines in the introduction. Paul Lynch's *After Pedagogy* engages *Paralogic Rhetoric* more directly.

3. Kent's strategy is closer to Berlin's social-epistemic rhetoric because it seeks to develop heuristic strategies out of social circumstances rather than through the more social scientific research paradigm of Lauer. See Lauer's book *Invention in Rhetoric and Composition* for a history of such models and an articulation of her own approach (also see Berlin's *Rhetoric, Poetics, Cultures* and Young's "Invention" and "Paradigms and Problems").

4. The problem is Kent's emphasis. His argument depends on both a reductive notion of process and a narrow notion of contingency. For Lynch, "Kent's use of 'guesswork'... is a bit slippery, and it fails to distinguish between shots in the dark and informed hypotheses" (92). His use of emphasis might also be considered willful misreading. Lynch argues that Kent's reading of Dewey is "somewhat cur-

sory," which "leads Kent to make assertions about Dewey that are only half-true" (146n8). I make a similar argument about Kent's reading of Heidegger below. Kent seems to take small pieces of a text or thinker out of context and give them his own spin or emphasis as a standard strategy, one that allows him to build his own theories but significantly shortchanges the thinkers he engages.

5. Phelps is interested in breaking out the "intellectual ecology of composition" (45)—not its institutional ecology. She argues that there is no historical or logical reason that composition has been defined in relation to literature, which distorts and distracts from positive and proper relationships to other disciplines such as linguistics, speech communication, rhetoric, cognitive psychology, philosophy, and potentially a host of other disciplines. Taken out of its institutional secondary status, it is open to any field that impacts on composition as an act or event as an open system. While process didn't disrupt composition's institutional problem, it did "[reposition] composition within the global ecology of knowledge" (45). For Phelps, as long as composition hangs on to process's connections to positivism it will remain too frail a concept to dislodge it from its institutional ecology. But its intellectual ecology is open to an "[exploitation] of its connotations and denotations" (46).

6. For Phelps, the concept of process always carried with it latent contextualist themes, which started to emerge in the 1980s as it started to be understood as a social act and as teaching practices revealed the model's oversimplification. For Phelps, the responses to process in the 1960s and 1970s from vitalist or romantic and rhetorical fronts could not be successful until they confronted the positivism directly and drew upon other contextualist models such as Marxism, poststructuralism, and ethnography (43).

7. In his book *A New Philosophy of Society: Assemblage Theory and Social Complexity*, DeLanda attempts to take Deleuze and Guattari's discussions of assemblages in *A Thousand Plateaus* and build a more extensive theory of assemblages in relation to social networks. And his *Intensive Science and Virtual Philosophy* examines intensive processes in detail with many developed concrete examples.

8. This process is inspired by systems theory and the model of complexity Mark C. Taylor draws from in *The Moment of Complexity*. In his work on complexity in cellular automata in the mid-1980s, Stephen Wolfram classified these movements into four patterns of behavior: structures that don't change, oscillating patterns that change periodically, chaotic activity with no stability, and "patterns that are neither too structured nor too disordered, which emerge, develop, divide, and

recombine in endlessly complex ways" (Taylor 146). Chris Langton discovered that these patterns operated in a regular sequence: order—complexity—chaos—complexity—order.

9. This discussion of Uexküll's work paraphrases his *Theory of Meaning*, which could also be translated as "Theory of Significance." I follow Agamben in *The Open* and use significance to avoid meaning's association with the humans, intent, and conscious interpretation (41, 46). See Uexküll's *A Foray Into the Worlds of Animals and Humans, with A Theory of Meaning*, for the most recent translation, which sides with meaning.

10. Agamben's reading of Uexküll in *The Open* emphasizes capture. See my "Vitalism, Animality, and the Material Grounds of Rhetoric" for a discussion of Agamben's reading of Heidegger.

11. For more on the mechanism versus vitalism debates in the early twentieth century and definitions of vitalism, see Arthur Lovejoy's series of exchanges in the journal *Science*. Uexküll wrote extensively in the early to mid-twentieth century, roughly the time of Bergson's engagement with vitalism and phenomenology and Lovejoy's debates over the meaning of vitalism within the scientific community. For a nice introduction to Uexküll, see Torsten Rüting, "History and Significance of Jakob von Uexküll and of His Institute in Hamburg." Rüting notes that Uexküll was often misunderstood in his time and labeled a vitalist, in the negative, naïve, romantic mystic sense. Even though he was dedicated to developing a proper experimental and epistemological basis for biology, he was critical of positivistic science, which drew him into the mechanism versus vitalism debates of the day. His influence today extends through theories of ecology and the environmental sciences up through the philosophies of Ernst Cassirer and Martin Heidegger to Ludwig von Bertalanffy's development of systems theory. This is one way to read Deleuze's comment about Foucault's work as a "certain vitalism" where life is the capacity to resist force, or a "new vitalism" that defines life as a set of functions that resist death (*Foucault* 93). This is not a naïve vitalism of substance but a complex one, a vitalism of complex relationality and coproductivity.

12. In "Heidegger's 1924 Lecture Course on Aristotle's *Rhetoric*," Daniel Gross argues that Heidegger reads the *Rhetoric* in relation to Aristotle's *Physics*, both of which are fundamentally concerned with bodies being moved in the world. This puts, he argues, animals and humans on the same continuum, and ultimately grounds Heidegger's *Being and Time* in this reading of Aristotle.

13. Similar discussions of Heidegger's tool analysis appear in my book *A Counter-*

History of Composition and in the coauthored introduction to *Emerging Small Tech.* Importantly, also see Sarah Ahmed's "Orientation Matters" where she extends Heidegger's analysis of writing equipment to include the domestic labor that historically grounded philosophical writing and made it possible.

14. In *Counter-History* I followed James Kinneavy's reading of Heidegger's model, which is decidedly different than my reading here. For Kinneavy, fore-structure (as a mental structure) has three subprocesses: fore-having (developing an intention or purpose), fore-sight (imagining something as a unified whole), and fore-conception (grasping the structure of the object in question) (228). My current reading situates interpretation in the context of the tool analysis, which I attempted to achieve in *Counter-History* by arguing that just as the concept of fore-structure grounds interpretation, the concept of dwelling grounds fore-structure.

15. In "Heidegger on Objects and Things," Graham Harman discusses the way Heidegger sets the possibilities for such a view, but ultimately falls back into a human-centered approach. Here I follow up claims in my article "Post-Techne" and *Counter-History* that Heidegger is a proto-posthumanist ("Toward a Post-Techne"; *Counter* 175) to more explicitly address his relationship to humanism and show that Heidegger's position isn't as simple as falling back into human-centeredness; instead, he advocates a human decenteredness even as humans harbor the lion's share of coresponsibility.

16. Historically there have been a number of humanisms—Roman, Christian, Renaissance, German—all of which are grounded in a metaphysics or made to be a ground of metaphysics that predetermines the human ("Letter" 200–202). Humans are not civilized characters (Roman), otherworldly souls (Christian), rational animals (Renaissance), or technical masters (modern). Adding any of these on to the human animal as an object remains in subject/object metaphysics and shuts humans off from Being (204–5).

17. Heidegger notes in "Letter on Humanism" that an appropriate understanding of the "turning," or shift between his early and later works, is a move "from Being and Time to Time and Being," which is not a reversal of his position but a change in explanation and emphasis (208). In *Being and Time*, Heidegger examines Being through a phenomenological analysis of human existence as the temporal and historical experience of Dasein. Heidegger's later work places an emphasis on language and a variety of vehicles through which Being can be disclosed temporally, such as poetry, architecture, and technology. In a fundamental sense, however, the question of Being remains the central question throughout his work as well as

Time's centrality to Being. Arguments that characterize Heidegger as a philosophy of being and Deleuze as a philosophy of becoming—and see this as a categorical difference—fail to understand time, emergence, and becoming as the ground of Heidegger's Being and don't allow for the types of connectivity or potential relation between Heidegger and Deleuze I am attempting to draw together here.

18. Both Heidegger and Deleuze sought to work through the end of traditional metaphysics. Deleuze saw himself as a "pure metaphysician" because he developed general models or abstract diagrams that functioned across diverse material instantiations. But unlike traditional metaphysics, these models or diagrams are not assumed to be ideal forms separate from the world that produce copies in reality. For Deleuze they are abstract but real—virtual models, diagrams, or ideas that function across domains as a real part of the world's actualization. Similarly, Heidegger saw the end of metaphysics and sought to move beyond it into real experience in the world. His model of temporality is a function of how the world works, not an abstract form to be imposed on the world. So even though Deleuze argued in favor of virtual potential over Kant's possible, Heidegger's conditions of possibility are much closer to Deleuze's virtual potential and actual conditions than to Kant's formal conditions.

19. It should be made clear that Latour's use of object-oriented democracy is not the same as others who advocate object-oriented philosophy. Latour uses it in this piece to implicitly make connections between Serres's quasi-objects and Heidegger's things. In a variety of interviews and exchanges, Latour makes it quite clear that actor-network theory and object-oriented philosophy are in many ways opposed; the former is interested in actual assemblages (physics), the latter, in philosophical positions on objects (metaphysics). Graham Harman's *Prince of Networks: Bruno Latour and Metaphysics* stages this difference between Latour's work and Harman's object-oriented philosophy.

20. In *We Have Never Been Modern*, Latour acknowledges a kinship between his position and Heidegger's in that quasi-objects do not belong to nature, society, subjects, or language. But Heidegger does not, for Latour, extend this understanding to modern technologies, science, or politics. In Latour's reading, which is not atypical, Heidegger privileges the Black Forrest or simple premodern modes of life (65). Since Heidegger doesn't see that everything is a function of quasi-objects, not just the premodern, Latour argues that we have never really been modern and forgotten Being, as Heidegger argues. Instead we've always been engaged in emergent, coproductive quasi-objects even when oper-

ating under a modern epistemology (66). But in this later work on the "ding," Latour recognizes, perhaps more directly, how Heidegger's work does extend to all *techne* and all dwelling, as Heidegger argues in "The Question Concerning Technology." This allows Latour to think about Heidegger in relation to more contemporary publics.

21. Oleg Kharkhordin gives an excellent example in "Things as Res publicae: Making Things Public." He discusses the bridge in Novgorord that during the medieval period served both to divide the city and provide a gathering place for deliberating matters of concern. The bridge takes on a life and agency of its own in the history of the city. He emphasizes how the bridge functions as a center point for the convergence of Heidegger's fourfold, assembling Earth, Air, Mortals, and Gods during moments of conflict and division in the city's life.

22. See Heidegger's essay "The Thing" on the distinction between objects and things, the way things gather, and the connection to the concept of the fourfold. Here Latour is arguing that objects, things, and issues are all equally "things" as "das ding," or in Serres's parlance, quasi-objects.

23. Latour's call for openness requires that rhetors include all forms of dissent. In a global, political context this means that we should find ways to include fundamentalism in our political assemblies—we have to include what doesn't even want to be included, even if it runs antithetical to the project of democracy. In their collection, this nod to dissent comes in the form of Rorty's "Heidegger and the Atomic Bomb," where in fine curmudgeonly fashion he chastises them for looking to Heidegger instead of Whitehead, Dewey, or Wittgenstein for their relational philosophy.

24. This is a clear example of the concept of "broken-tool" in Heidegger and elaborated on by Graham Harman in *Tool-Being*. When humans are using a tool it recedes into the ambient background and becomes a part of our tacit fore-having (what Harman calls tool-being). When it breaks, the tool's specific manipulability as a thing in relation to a manifold assignment shows up for our concern.

25. In "The Origin of the Work of Art," Heidegger gives an analysis for Van Gogh's painting of peasant shoes (*Les Souliers*). The shoes belong to the earth, the fields in which the peasants work, the sky under which the grain grows, and the world of the gods and the cultural rituals surrounding cultivation, and the human world of meaning and equipment. The painting doesn't represent objects but brings the human viewer into the gathering that the shoes enact; it is a public expression that connects us to that world and makes it a part of our understanding.

CHAPTER 3: RESEARCH AS TRANSDUCTION

1. Entries in "keywords" collections past and present attest to this attention. See Paul Heilker and Peter Vandenberg's *Keywords in Composition Studies* (1996) and *Keywords in Writing Studies* (2015). Both have entries on research that acknowledge research's variability and contestation and suggesting, in their own way, the productive nature of this multiplicity.

2. In his interview with Foucault, "Intellectuals and Power," Deleuze disrupts the application of theory into practice through the concept of relay, which, not unlike Serres, sets the conditions for others to speak rather than imposing a theory on them. Deleuze writes, "Representation no longer exists; there's only action—theoretical action and practical action which serves as relays and forms networks" (Foucault, "Intellectuals" 206–7).

3. Many scholars in composition and rhetoric have taken up such postcritical methods under the banner of rhetorical invention and historiography (such as Victor Vitanza, *Negation*) and have developed its implications for composition and pedagogical practices with new media (such as Jeff Rice, *Digital Detroit*).

4. There are a number of online sources such as Acoustics 101.com, which has a free PDF booklet by Eric T. Smith (http://www.acoustics101.com/), and "Room Acoustics 101 with Peter Freedman," which gives a quick DIY class on improving room acoustics in a vocal booth (http://www.youtube.com/watch?v=np-dyiowWRQ).

5. Jim notes that a large-scale analog soundboard would cost about $80,000 to $100,000 (and he doesn't have the space for it in his small studio, anyway). So he uses as much physical sound design techniques and analog boutique gear as possible before recording digitally to give the recording a more analog feel and sound. This is a big part of what makes his studio unique compared to a lot of other boutique studios in the Dallas area.

6. In this earlier stage of his career, Latour performs a basic negative deconstruction by flipping the subject/object, human/nonhuman binary to highlight the nonhuman. But he fairly quickly moves on to terms such as *actors*, *actants*, and *actor-networks* (instead of *humans*, *nonhumans*, and *hybrids*), acknowledging as far back as *We Have Never Been Modern* that both subjects and objects emerge out of networks. His emphasis on the nonhuman early on is a rhetorical choice to begin disrupting the human-centeredness of the modern constitution. Karen Barad, however, argues that if we start with the human/nonhuman divide, then we've already missed the point that subjects and objects emerge out of entanglement. She prefers to use the term *inhuman* rather than *nonhuman* to emphasize that

nonhumans such as bacteria are already *in* the human, disrupting any division. Jane Bennett, in the preface to *Vibrant Matter*, notes her discomfort in bracketing the human in favor of an emphasis on the nonhuman but acknowledges this as a rhetorical strategy. Latour and Bennett want to include the "nonhuman" as a first step toward disrupting human centrality, but we can't think of this as where they stop. It is a first move toward entanglement, which then folds over into the coproduction of the human and the dissolution of the divide. For my own choice of terms, I tend toward parahuman, which sees the human as a function of complex processes of ecology and emergence. From this perspective, Deleuze's virtual, Heidegger's fundamental ontology, Latour's actor-networks, Barad's entanglement are all attempts to investigate this space beneath, behind, and within the subject/object divide, which is largely what situates them all in a new materialist paradigm.

7. This necessary entanglement of humans and nonhumans I call the parahuman. Actor-network theory, as Latour notes, is always dealing with "lieutenants"—lieu-tenants, holding place in lieu of something else: figurative-literal, human-nonhuman, conceptual-material all presuppose the other in cascades of translation and circulation. For Latour, this inevitable mediation isn't simply attributing the human to the nonhuman, as some sociologists charge. Anthropomorphism, he argues, is anthropos + morphism; *both* what has human shape *and* what gives shape to humans. The door closer is anthropomorphic in three ways: (1) it has been made by man; (2) it substitutes for human actions; and (3) it shapes human action ("Mixing Humans and Nonhumans Together" 303). This is ultimately a feedback loop of humans and nonhumans that researchers can't ignore. If this is truly the Anthropocene, where collective human action affects the entire Earth, then researchers can't ignore the human impact on nonhumans and the impact of the changing nonhuman world back onto future human worlds. As circulation expands to larger quasi-objects, the coproductive mixing of humans and nonhumans will ultimately come into play. Even though Latour's small door closer example moves from human to nonhuman, left column to right, this is not a necessary movement that centers the human and sees the nonhuman as its "extension"—delegation and translation are always shifting and folding back to produce new grounds for both humans and nonhumans, revealing the division as an epiphenomenon.

8. In *Sonic Persuasion*, Greg Goodale notes the comparable relationship between sound and light through the Doppler effect. Christian Doppler first made this

discovery in relation to light, noting that as light moves toward us it shifts into the higher frequency range of the color spectrum, blue. When it moves away from us, it shifts into the lower frequency range, red. Three years later, Christoph Hendrik Diederick tested the theory on sound with a train, finding that as the train approached, the sound waves shifted into the higher frequencies, and the "rapid movement away from a listener cause[d] sound waves to stretch out, thus lowering their frequency" (118).

9. Older studios, Jim notes, typically used three or more layers of five-eighth-inch drywall, or put up MDF (medium-density fiberboard), or built a wall on each side of both rooms. He then shows us a roll of "barium loaded vinyl." Barium is like lead, which old studios used to use. New studios, apartment builds, office spaces, university classrooms, or even courtrooms will put a layer of this between two five-eighth-inch drywalls for noise abatement. Architects are more sensitive to these issues, and Jim argues that this commercial exigence drove the development of these products that are now used in studios. Jim decided to use Green Glue because it is much easier to handle and easier for contractors to work with—"That's a whole other level," Jim notes. And he thinks it works better at containing sound waves than the vinyl.

10. Jim notes, "The regular window is a liability in some regards. . . . In a more traditional studio approach where you have a control room and tracking room and people looking at each other through two pieces of glass, or some places will put in three pieces, one in the middle and one on each side, they like to slant the windows." If someone is standing in front of a flat plane, the sound will bounce right back at the person. If the window is slanted toward the floor, the sound is deflected away from the person. The regular window keeps his studio looking like a house to provide a degree of comfort for people coming in to record and also for the resale value of the house. Jim shows us where he left another space in the windowsill to install shutters. The shutters would also allow him to vary the acoustic properties, because sound reflects differently off different surfaces, giving him more options to play with by opening and closing the shutters to various effect.

11. Modal response, or modes, is how a structure responds to varying types of vibration. Measuring modal response allows designers to determine the best plan of action for soundproofing a room. The dimensions of the room—width, length, height—dictate the frequency response. Modes are basically multiples of the resonances in the room, called "standing waves," which have mathematical formulas that easily predict the modes of rectangular rooms. So for Jim, it is almost easier

to know what he is dealing with in a rectangular room than a room with splayed walls. Each approach is a trade-off with pros and cons. Jim chose to keep the room a rectangle since it is easier to predict and it maintains the traditional look of a house.

12. Barad gives other light examples: razor blade-shaped slit that produces alternating bright and dark lines; BB-pellet barrier that produces a bright spot in the center of the BB's shadow; and a CD: "The rainbow effect commonly observed on the surface of a compact disc is a diffraction phenomenon. The concentric rings of grooves that contain digital information act as a diffraction grating spreading white light (sunlight) into a spectrum of colors" (80)—perhaps not unlike Jim's use of diffusers in the recording studio, and perhaps not unlike Deleuze's virtual, white light contains the potential for all of the colors that are actualized once a prism breaks into it and diffracts or induces this virtual potential.

13. Clinton Davisson and Lester Germer, for example, generated this result for electrons in 1927, which was confirmed in 1974 by Eisberg and Resnick (Barad 82, 418n15).

14. In one version of the wave-particle debates, Broglie-Bohm models posit that particles have definite locations and properties but are guided by some form of "pilot wave." A wave travels through both slits and produces the diffraction pattern, but the particle only travels through one slit, propelled by the wave. While this model was first proposed by Louise de Broglie in the 1920s, and developed further by David Brohm in the 1950s, it garnered further support in 2005. Emmanuel Fort conducted an experiment to see how oil droplets combine or merge as they fall into a tray of oil as the tray vibrated. When the vibrations reached a certain frequency, ripples began to form around the droplets, and the droplets began to be self-propelled, surfing on their own waves. Fort characterized this as a "dual object, . . . a particle driven by a wave" (qtd. in Merali). Fort has since shown that such waves can guide these droplets through a double-slit experiment, mimicking the quantum realm at the classical level, especially when grounded in noise—the vibration of the tray of oil. Vibrations and waves are the ground of materiality, not particles. In quantum theory, entanglement is action at a distance, measuring a particle in one location and being able to predict how its changes in qualities affect another particle at another location. Researchers can predict this action at a distance mathematically, but they don't really know how it works. In the pilot wave model, action at a distance is produced through waves. Recently the notion of pilot wave gravity has been proposed for the unification of general relativity

and quantum mechanics at the level of scale of planets and solar systems (see MacDonald).

15. Also see Barad, *Meeting the Universe Halfway*, for more on these issues (88, 416n2, 419n25–26, 28.)

16. From the drum kit there are multiple sources and multiple frequencies and multiple microphones. Engineers want to manage the diffraction, making sure that the sound waves are arriving at the mic both at the peak or trough of the waves so that they are in "time alignment." As already discussed, if one is positive and the other negative, they will cancel each other out and be out of phase. Distant mics, such as the ones Jim has in the bathroom, don't contribute greatly to the problem. Direct mics versus overhead mics produce the most phase issues.

17. There are three basic types of mics: dynamic, condenser, and ribbon. Dynamic mics are moving coil mics, which are just miniature speakers in reverse—they have a voice coil, and the air is moving the coil that sends out a low voltage and thus need the preamp. Condenser mics use a capacitor to convert sound waves into electrical energy and require external voltage, such as a battery, in order to work. A ribbon microphone uses a thin aluminum film of electrically conductive ribbon placed between the poles of a magnet to produce a voltage. (See also "Blumlein Stereo Microphone Technique," https://www.youtube.com/watch?v=psclm-3HTF4g).

18. Jim has a variety of preamps and equalizers. Since there are a number of different models out there with "various sonic textures and characteristics, it is good to have a number of different flavors." Jim has an API, a Germanium, and a Neve preamp. The API is the most simplistic—four channels with only a gain knob and four buttons to manipulate the sound. The Germanium is a transistor-based preamp that has a knob for feedback that allows him to vary the sonic texture. The Neve 1073 is a two-channel mic preamp with equalization on it that is an emulation based on an old circuit design from Neve. He also has an API 500v series EQ with no preamp. API is the company that invented the unit in the late 1960s. The 500 series is a universally standard format, so multiple companies can make EQs, compressors, mic preamps, and other dynamics processors that are all compatible. For this recording, Jim has the five toms coming out of the preamp and over to the API EQ; the snare is coming into a different channel on this EQ; and the inside and outside mics on the kick drum each have separate channels on this EQ. Then he is routing the signal out of that and over to a compressor for more dynamics processing.

19. As with almost anything, there are a number of software programs for studio-level digital audio. On the one hand, each one has its particular characteristics and does some things better than others. On the other hand, they all ultimately do similar things. Jim uses Nuendo, which is a higher-end version of Cubase SX. Jim used Cubase back in the 1990s and got used to that interface, so he uses Nuendo for the comfort level. But there are also things that it does better than some of the other software: it has more intuitive editing features, does some things faster than ProTools, and does some things ProTools can't. For example, Nuendo can click and drag to perform some editing applications, whereas ProTools users have to hold down a key combination and hold down the plus and minus keys. But ProTools is the industry standard. It's what all of the major studios have, so it's better from a compatibility standpoint. Jim bought a license for ProTools to be able to work with people who bring in files from other studios. He also has Logic for that reason. Logic is less expensive since Apple bought it and can be downloaded easily from the app store, so a number of people use it. It is also an upgrade based on GarageBand, Apple's free program. People start learning in GarageBand and get used to it, so they simply upgrade to Logic.

20. Jim's control board is a "digital console" with ninety-six digital channels or tracks. And even though the manual board doesn't have ninety-six channels, he can "bank" or "page" through the channels in groups with buttons on the console: 1–24, 25–48, 49–72, 73–96. The Nuendo software, as with many digital recording programs, has an unlimited numbers of tracks available. Most of the programs now at least go up to 256 tracks. With all of the drum tracks, scratch bass, guitars, and vocals, Jim is working with twenty-two tracks that he highlights with colors so he can distinguish the waveforms more easily in the interface. He has his own color code that he uses for each drum—kicks are red, toms are blue, orange for overheads, and light blue for room and bathroom mics. Green is for scratch bass, yellow for scratch guitar.

21. With two stereo faders on the console, Jim can control the volume to the "Grace Design" M904 monitor controller, which is the remote control for the unit behind the workstation where the signal comes out of the computer sound card and back to a DAC. The unit controls the mix, going from digital to analog and out the control room speakers. It can manage multiple digital and analog sources. He has a CD player hooked up to it also and can hook an iPhone up to the controller. It also has high-end boutique digital-to-analog converter that takes the AES (Audio

Engineering Society) output of the digital console and makes it analog to drive the monitor speakers.

22. Jim has a number of converters: a sixteen-channel A→D, and two sixteen-channel D→A: Big Ben, AD16X, DA16X, DA16X (in that order on his rack of effects). The Big Ben is a "master clock" that reduces "jitter," or the undesired deviation of a signal from the ideal timing.

23. Jim points out that one of the advantages of the digital plug-ins is multiplicity. When engineers have an analog unit, they can only use it on one thing at a time. When they buy the plug-in, they can use it as many times as their computer and DSP power setup allows. That's definitely an advantage or affordance of the digital technology, so it is a trade-off. Analog purists might not want to use it multiple times if it doesn't sound right. But if the sound is close to the analog, then the plug-in is worth using because they could never have ten analog units. Jim pulls up the digital (SPL brand) "transient designer" as an example. Each digital version has attack, sustain, and gain knobs doing the same thing. These are highly useful on the drums. The drummer in this session has five toms, but the analog rack unit only has four channels. So Jim uses the analog rack unit for the kick and snare and the digital version for the toms. He's also committed to the settings when he is tracking with the rack unit, whereas with the digital unit he can always go back and change the digital settings.

24. There are countless plug-ins on the market, but Jim uses Universal Audio—power plug-ins that run off of a DSP card inside the computer that runs all of the plug-ins from UA—because it makes the best emulations of the analog processers and attempts to model this nonlinearity. Some plug-ins try to capture the characteristics of the circuitry of the analog units through a "convolution process" where they run an impulse through the circuit and try to capture its waveform and then impart that digitally into the plug-in to create the same tone. But there are both static and dynamic characteristics of the analog devices that this particular digital modeling technique doesn't capture, though they have been getting better at it over the years. Universal Audio, however, tries to produce digital models of the circuits themselves—each particular transistor, capacitor, resistor, transistor, and the transformer of the analog unit. The characteristics of these circuits are nonlinear and ultimately unpredictable, making them hard to model (transformers in particular are very nonlinear).

25. For more on amp electronics, see Rozenblit, *Beginners Guide to Tube Audio Design*;

Hunter, *The Guitar Amp Handbook*; Blencowe, *Designing Value Pre-amps for Guitar and Bass*; Fliegler, *Amps! The Other Half of Rock and Roll*.

26. The recording studio discloses all four of John Law and Vicky Singleton's types of multiple objects—regions, networks, fluid objects, and fire objects. All of the specific technologies function as regions along with their stabilizing networks. The studio itself is perpetually under construction, and all of its technologies are adaptable fluid objects that slowly change and evolve. And bursts of sound energy function like fire objects that reveal and conceal complex discontinuities the studio attempts to capture and record (see "Object Lessons").

27. Feminist theory and research methodology on positionality inform science and technology studies in Europe fairly explicitly; the work of Annemarie Mol and Vicki Singleton are particularly prominent examples. Barad brings their work and its emphasis on ontology to a broader range of culturally oriented feminist research in the United States.

28. Early on, however, Gries acknowledges that she characterizes her methodological approach as a remixing of Spinuzzi's work with Louise Wetherbee Phelps, Jenny Rice, and others in the spirit of Ulmer's approach to method, which in her words is "using theory to invent new forms and practices" (xv).

CHAPTER 4: COLLABORATION AS COORDINATION

1. While Ede and Lunsford revisit this work in their collection *Writing Together: Collaboration in Theory and Practice* (2012), it is still very much centered on their human-human collaboration in the production of texts. And while Kennedy and Howard's chapter on collaboration in Tate et al.'s *A Guide to Composition Pedagogies* (2014) attempts to update the concept in terms of digital technologies, it is still within the context of pedagogical methods for student authorship.

2. Even though Maureen Daly Goggin's entry on collaboration in Heilker and Vandenberg's 1996 *Keywords in Composition Studies* opens with the claim that collaboration is "not a unified object but rather . . . a variety of pedagogies and practices, each grounded in somewhat different and often conflicting epistemological and ontological assumptions," this insight, along with her conclusion that collaboration is grounded in "multiple social contexts (e.g. writing classrooms, disciplines, professions), innovations in technology, . . . and competing philosophies and rhetorical ends," is not taken up by the field at large. Her entry overviews work in the

field from the 1940s up through 1992 (only one citation is from 1994), but the term *collaboration* is absent from the second edition, 2015's *Keywords in Writing Studies*, which updates work in the field post-1996.

3. Cooper notes that Greg Meyers had already made this connection between writing and its potential evolution in ecological contexts in his 1985 article "The Social Construction of Two Biologists' Proposals" (Cooper 367). But today scholars generally recognize Richard Coe's "Eco-Logic for the Composition Classroom" from 1975 as one of the first pieces in the field to articulate a need for thinking ecologically in composition.

4. For example, her collaborative book with Michael Holzman's *Writing as Social Action*, which includes "The Ecology of Writing" as its initial chapter, often gets referenced with an emphasis on the social, and her other chapter in the book, "Why are We Talking About Discourse Communities?" seems to get more attention.

5. There is a sense in which this argument in *Resounding* is an extension of the logic in 2007's *A Counter-History of Composition*. In *Counter-History*, I examine conversations in the late 1970s and into the 1980s surrounding vitalism and its relegation to the margins of the field, to the point of its almost complete exclusion. The movements of the social turn engendered a particular reading of vitalism that positioned it against the social paradigm. Through that book I tried to tease out a counterhistory of the concept by connecting it to models of emergence, ecology, and complexity. While ecology was perhaps more visible in the 1980s than vitalism, the social turn in composition dominated the decade of the 1990s and, if nothing else, took up the field's attention to the exclusion of these ulterior models.

6. In addition to Cooper and LeFevre being primarily read in terms of the social, Phelps's book never really gets fully addressed either, partly because it is detailed, complex, and difficult to pin down to a blurb that can easily circulate, and partly because it doesn't fit neatly into the paradigm of the social turn. For example, Schilb's critique of Phelps in his *Contending with Words* chapter, "Cultural Studies, Postmodernism, and Composition," mostly contests her continued emphasis on the self, which Schilb sees as phenomenological, romantic, and hermeneutic and thus out of step with the social turn, which emphasizes, for Schilb, a more complex Marxist orientation to social and cultural contexts. And more recently in *Situating Composition*, Lisa Ede references Phelps as well but with just one paragraph noting that she problematizes the theory/practice divide and calls for

their mutual coconstitution but that her "analysis remains at a fairly high level of abstraction" (123). The implication here is that she remains too theoretical in her attempt to bring philosophy, educational theory, cognitive science, and hermeneutics together through composition as a crossroads of theory and practice (though we could easily read Ede as similarly erring on the side of practice; for Phelps, writing theory *is* compositional practice). In *The Practice of Theory*, Michael Bernard-Donals gives Phelps more sustained engagement but notes a similar phenomenon. In his chapter on Phelps, he argues that her challenge to the field—to become a "macrodiscipline" at the juncture of the human and natural sciences—"went largely unmet" and was reviewed with responses from "hostility" to "utter incomprehension" (131). But while he recognizes that her challenge is daunting, "There are good reasons to pay close attention to Phelp's project" (131). Her aim is to critically examine "the ways language and social practice function in the material world" (131). This connection to materiality is crucial and, I would argue, positions her and the field of composition to take up an ecological conceptual view and methodical practice.

7. This resurgence of the concept of ecology begins with Margaret Syverson's *The Wealth of Reality: An Ecology of Composition* (1999) but explodes over the next dozen years: Kristie Fleckenstein's *Embodied Literacies* (2003) turns Bateson's ecology of mind toward an ecology of embodied meaning, image, and word; Clay Spinuzzi's *Tracing Genres through Organizations* (2003) turns genre theory and activity theory into an analysis of genre ecologies; Cynthia Haynes's "Writing Offshore" (2003) deploys an ecological metaphor of a ship at sea to rethink composition as a contingent practice in relation to the movement and force of waves; Jenny Rice's "Unframing Models of Public Distribution" (2005) turns rhetorical situation toward Deleuzian rhetorical ecologies; my *A Counter-History of Composition* (2007) links ecology to a history of vitalism and complexity; Collin Brooke's *Lingua Fracta* (2009) turns the rhetorical canons toward media ecologies; Sid Dobrin's *Postcomposition* (2011) turns his prior work with ecocomposition toward complexity; Jeff Rice's *Digital Detroit* (2012) enacts ecology through Latourian networks; Thomas Rickert's *Ambient Rhetoric* (2013) thinks ecology through ambience and Heidegger; and Laurie Gries's *Still Life with Rhetoric* (2015) extends Jenny Rice's approach to circulation and traces the rhetorical ecology of a visual meme.

8. Up to this point, no one has extensively read collaboration in relation to ecologies and the material turn. William Duffy's recent piece, "Collaboration (in) Theory" (2014), recognizes the fact that collaboration as a key concept in the field drops

out in the 1990s because of a particular take on the social paradigm, but his solution is to rework the social turn rather than embrace ecology as a function of the material turn. Jay Jordan's "Comment and Response" with Brian Ray makes the same assessment: Duffy's argument is more in line with Davidson and Thomas Kent and aims for the "collaborator's enhanced perception" in order to develop "an even sharper human ability" (391).

9. To answer these questions, Syverson concludes that composition and rhetoric would need a larger and more complex sphere of inquiry as its "unit of analysis" (2, 24). Like Phelps, she argues that this new object of analysis would have to draw on various disciplines such as biology, physics, computer science, cognitive science, economics, and philosophy in order to even approach "a comprehensive theory of composing as an ecological system of interrelated structures and processes that are at once physically or materially, socially, psychologically, temporally, and spatially emerging in codependent activities" (25). The value of expanding our "unit of analysis" to ecological systems, for her, is that "it compels us to ask a better set of questions about the dynamic relationships among writers, readers, and texts and drives us toward a deeper understanding of composition" (206).

10. Despite its promise, Syverson argues, the short length of an article and the emphasis on social interactions through ideas, purposes, interpersonal interactions, cultural norms, and textual forms keeps Cooper's "The Ecology of Writing" within the social turn.

11. Enaction ultimately subverts Burke's action/motion divide that still grounds much of composition and rhetoric as well as speech communication. Many in this ecological and material turn in composition and rhetoric are working to problematize this divide that places human subjects as the seat and cause of action upon objects. (See also my "Toward a Post-Techne.")

12. For Bennett an actant can be an entity, a constellation, or a force: a region, a fluid network, or a fire object (Law and Singleton, "Object Lessons"). Following Latour and actor-network theory, then, Bennett sees an actant as anything that modifies other actors through a series of trials that can be listed through some experimental or experiential protocol. In a sense, then, all actors are actants, or at least potential actants, given various scenarios or conditions. And what distinguishes actants from actors is the emphasis on being able to be listed, which is important for method and methodology. All actors are mediators, but actants are mediators that can be seen as such and listed through methodical description.

13. Law in *Aircraft Stories* and Mol in *The Body Multiple* both emphasize coordina-

tion as a key aspect of connecting multiple versions of their objects of study. Law emphasizes the brochure and MoI, medical files: the former articulates various aspects of the TRS-2 aircraft across multiple inter- and intra-institutional groups; the latter articulates various versions of atherosclerosis across the hospital, lab, and clinic. While both emphasize textual accounts, Syverson and Bennett give us a different version of coordination, more explicitly material and systemic. But ultimately these are differences on a continuum rather than differences in kind.

14. For more on complexity, see William Rasch's *Niklas Luhmann's Modernity*, particularly his discussions of noise injecting difference into a system and autopoiesis as a form of coproductive syncing.

15. For more on Borgo's extension of these practices of improvisation, see his "The Ghost in the Music, or the Perspective of an Improvising ANT" and "Embodied, Situated, and Distributed Musicianship" in which he discusses how coordinated systems jointly cause behavior at other levels and how creativity is an emergent function of these systems. For more on his use of complexity theory in *Sync or Swarm*, see my "Stitching Together Events" and "Embodying *Heurisis*." Also see Jennifer LeMesurier's discussion of "complex sensory environments" that embody and distribute memory through performance ("Mobile Bodies").

16. For more on the move from interpretation to postmeaning, see Jeffrey Nealon's *Post-Postmodernism*. For more on improvisation from this kind of Deleuzian perspective, see Eugene Holland, "Studies in Applied Nomadology." And for more on improvisation as a form of "composition in performance," see Jeremy Gilbert's "Becoming-Music."

17. For more on Gregory Ulmer's reading of conduction, see his *Teletheory* and *Heuretics* and my brief discussion of his development of its three connotations (*A Counter-History*, 248).

18. In composition and rhetoric, gesture is commonly discussed as something that supports speech, is represented in writing, or remediated in digital media. Gilbert Austin's nineteenth-century treatise *Chironomia* outlines a system for noting emphasis and hand gestures. Johanna Wolfe's article "Gesture and Collaborative Planning" shows how writing groups rely on gesture to operate as well produce common representations of group documents. Michael Schandorf's "Mediated Gesture" breaks down how nonverbal gestures are transposed into new media spaces. Sean Morey's *Rhetorical Delivery and Digital Technologies* examines media art in relation to gestural actions and networks of delivery and feedback. And Cory Holding's "Rhetoric of the Open Fist" goes back to John Bulwer's *Chirolo-*

gia and reads it in terms of relational moves that ground persuasion in sensations among bodies, arguing that gestures "communicate, attitudinize, and forge pathways" in ways that are "inevitably improvisational" (416). I am most interested in extending this latter line of thinking.

19. Gesture studies is an emerging field of research (see the International Society for Gesture Studies, for example). Holding characterizes much of this work as interested in labeling actions as deliberate expressions, still very much a field focused on humans and meaning. But Vilem Flusser's recently translated collection of essays, *Gestures*, examines gesture from a more Heideggerian take on phenomenology, showing how worlds are expressed through a wide range of gestures. Speaking, painting, telephoning, photographing, shaving, or listening all the way up to mass manufacturing express a particular relation between the world and the body that gestures. This gets closer to how gesture itself is embodied and articulates worlds in the context of composition writ large. And most applicably, Erin Manning's *The Minor Gesture* gets directly at these issues, in particular the chapter "Weather Patterns, or How Minor Gestures Entrain the Environment."

20. When the waves hitting each mic are out of phase, the sound is hollow. In-phase waves sound more present and compact. Jim notes that today companies have developed variable phase tools that allow engineers to shift the phase to various points—90 degrees, 70 degrees, and so on. But for him when it gets to that point, engineers really need to get back into the room and start moving mics around to find the best natural sound. "But I didn't have to do that," he notes, "because I've done it enough times now that I can get it right or close enough."

21. In addition to checking the phase, Jim is adjusting the sound of the kick drum. He is reaching down with his left hand and flipping the phase while adjusting a knob on a small box on the top right corner of the console. Jim explains, "So this is a transient designer, it allows you to dry up the kick drum, it's got sustain and attack, it's like a gate but not really a gate. It's like an envelope follower." As he is twisting knobs, he illustrates: "I can give it more point, or attack, or I can dry it up. Now if I bypass it, hear how it is kind of undefined? It's loose." He clicks it back in. "Gives it some dynamic front. . . . A little more snap." The Transient Designer is the name of the module in the rack to the right of the mixing board. He swings over to another rack on the left of the board, the API 500V EQ. There are channels for the kick drum that he is adjusting. He's working the EQ on both the inside and outside mics for the kick drum. There are innumerable microadjustments like this as engineers are preparing to record.

22. Jim notes that it is a limitation of the headphone setup that he has—only a single mix is sent to the headphone mixer, and while there are multiple channels on it, each one can only adjust the volume and tone of the overall mix, not individual tracks. Bryan pitches the possibility of running his headphones through his Digitech unit, which is what he does at home. Jim explains, "That would be the solution, I guess, if you had a headphone amp that would take a stereo input and one more input, which would be the digital input and you could boost more [of your guitar]." Jacob notes that he has a headphone amp, a Fire studio, and a Mackie (audio mixer), and they can sort something out. David, Jim's brother, is around for the session and notes, "You could take the headphone into the Mackie so that would be stereo, and then Bryan's dry signal out and into the Mackie and then he can boost the shit out of it if he wants." On the next night, Bryan brings his gear and attempts to set it up as a workable solution, a long process that sets off a whole separate ecology to be composed that included user manual schematics from Digitech and a host of additional cables.

23. Recording is all about versioning on a number of different levels. There are, of course, various takes of different parts and the various versions of a song that get laid down. But there are also the versions of amps, effects, and even software. At one point, the computer crashes and all the faders on the board physically drop to zero. Jim talks about the fact that all the different software packages have their bugs. This one slows or drags and crashes. And every time a different version of software comes out, Jim has to learn the new version. And at another point, Bob and David have a discussion about the fact that the best amp tubes were developed by the Russian military in the 1980s. David notes that the tubes he uses to build Naylor amps are versions of those tubes (6L6 50w). Bob explains that in the 1980s the Americans went to transistors, but the Russians kept advancing tube technology, so that's why now everyone uses tubes modeled after the Russian military. And the studio itself is in a constant state of building and updating. This is all emergent preinscription as a form of composition: recording as a tangle of multiple versionings.

24. In the late 1960s, producers manually had to turn the tape reels around where track 2 was now on track 22 in order to play a track backwards. Jimi Hendrix and Eddie Kramer were pioneers in creative uses of these techniques. Hendrix had to learn how to play a part forward that would sound right backwards, or learn to play the part backwards so they wouldn't have to flip the tape. Today, a couple of clicks can get a similar effect, though it doesn't always sound like the old tape versions

of the technique. And in the late 1970s, Pink Floyd was famous for extending and elaborating on studio techniques by "performing" its mixes with multiple people at the console. Each turn expanded the ecology of performance to include more actors and actions.

25. The technology and Digital Audio Workstations in particular have allowed lesser-quality musicians to create music because these tools can extend a performance beyond what those persons are capable of doing. It's often up to the artist or producer to accept the technologies and use them or to shun them. Obviously, different artists and producers have to draw the line somewhere. If a client is paying a producer to be the engineer and they are producing, that line is up to them. Of course, this can be very controversial. There has been a backlash in certain genres such as rock and folk and among certain circles of producers. But for some genres such as pop and hip-hop, it is a nonissue. For Jim, rock used to set the boundaries for the uses of technology, but now it is hip-hop. "They are using these technologies in creative ways that most people aren't." Since Jim mostly works with rock and folk clients, he tries to only use the technology for its convenience (and space and price) and keep as much analog sound and natural performance as possible. Jim notes that he doesn't always let the artist know how much he is manipulating a performance. Sometimes he does it just to get a performance done faster, sometimes because that is genuinely the only way to get the best performance.

26. This is precisely the kind of thing we wanted the research project to capture through video—traces of these actions that compose networks and gestures that enact ecologies. In *Internet Invention*, Gregory Ulmer writes about the capacity of video to record a moment like this and loop it over and over. It allows us to see the world differently than any other culture before us. It produces a new kind of affect, with only the potential to become a new kind of meaning (168).

27. Luke argues that Bobby uses the turntable as an instrument rather than something he is just pressing play on and listening to. Instrumentalists take little pieces or snippets of music they've learned on the instrument—scale or a riff or a chord—and apply that to the particular musical situation. Bobby is using the same snippets from records as the raw source material and adding the manipulation to it. But "he had to listen to those records and had to learn what those sounds are and build up a repertoire in his head of music that he has at his disposal to use in a musical situation."

28. Thomas has a particular take on technology that is open to a technology's affor-

dances and particularity, learning all its little quirks and how to work with, through, and around them. He isn't interested in chasing the latest software packages and synth modules. Instead, he wants to explore the untapped possibilities of older gear. People abandon only slightly outmoded technologies before they have explored all of their affordances or conditions of possibility. Thomas says, "My goal is a novel result, so I need something that will create a novel sound." And that's why he wants to go back to forgotten or discarded technologies. As Luke puts it, "We're unpacking the expectations of those instruments and using them in our own personal way … finding ourselves within those instruments."

29. Thomas sees all of this as a part of composition that prepares him to have a "conversation." Luke explains:

> The conversation is just group improvisation in general. One of the main buzzwords you hear is conversation. Everybody in the group is working with their own instrumental and conceptual parameters and having a discussion with energy, with musical energy, with sound, using their particular instruments. … When you are performing in that vein you are performing in front of an audience and performing in a space so all of that becomes part of the composition and process when you are talking about improvised music in a group setting. It's a conversation plus an interaction with the people around you, with the environment, with your own instruments, with the audience, and with the whole vibe you are creating.

30. In "Consolidating the Music Scenes Perspective," Andy Bennett defines the "translocal" as "the way . . . young people appropriate music and stylistic resources in particular local contexts while retaining a sense of their connectedness with parallel expressions of musical taste and stylistic preference occurring in other regions, countries, and continents" (229). Novak pushes this to disrupt the bounded space of the local by showing how it is circulation itself that places a genre, not the specific or literal local.

31. Keith Negus argues that any "revolutionary" style operates across a continuum of three approaches to genre: *genericists*, who take up "a specific genre style at a particular time" and rarely if ever waver; *pastichists*, who see that a new style has become popular and "include this in their set as … another style to be performed" along with other genre; and *synthesists*, who "draw on the elements of an emerging generic style but blend them" with elements of other genre to create "a new distinct musical identity" (145–46). Negus's typology, however, is focused on pop-

ular music. The avant-garde, on the other hand, is grounded in a conception of anti-genre: synthesis isn't enough to become revolutionary. The new is created through *attempts* to reject all genre.

32. In "Is Pop Music?," Greg Hainge's distinction between pop and music in many ways mirrors the genre and anti-genre distinction in the context of Deleuze. He argues that pop and especially Muzak emphasize the territorializing aspects of the refrain, which organizes sound waves (music) and light waves (art). Pop intensifies its territory, capturing listeners in the capitalist mode of consumer (42). Music, on the other hand, pushes, extends, disrupts the forms of refrains beyond themselves to enact intensity and affect for deterritorialization. The refrain, of course, includes both movements, often simultaneously and in superposition. The refrain is the coordination among the birds, trees-twigs-leaves, light, and so forth through a repeated series of actions, movements, and gestures that are always in process. In short, the refrain is a quasi-object that produces compositions.

CHAPTER 5: PUBLICS AS SPHERES

1. The term for "public sphere" Habermas uses in German is *offentlichkeit*, which includes public, publicity, and public sphere in its associative network of meanings. When translated in English as "public sphere," it loses some of these additional meanings and propels certain critiques among English readers of the abstract and spatial limits of the term *sphere*. But for Habermas all three still emphasize the social space generated through communicative action—a public as a body of people, publicity as a mode of print circulation, and the social spaces in which these people enact and engage these discourses. The bourgeois public sphere exerted independence on all three levels and engendered the normative and bracketed characteristics that he continues to value.

2. In *After the Public Turn*, Frank Farmer draws a brief genealogy of the term *counterpublics*, from Ockar Negt and Alexander Kluge's proletarian public sphere, to Rita Felski's feminist counterpublic sphere, to Nancy Fraser's subaltern counterpublics, to Warner's queer counterpublics (14–18). Much of composition and rhetoric draws from Fraser and Warner but most recently, especially in relation to digital media and circulation, Warner.

3. The work cited throughout is the abbreviated version of Warner's essay that

appeared in *QJS*. See also Warner's book *Publics and Counterpublics* and his excerpted chapter of the same title in the journal *Public Culture*.

4. Warner doesn't use the term *discursive* directly. For him, these characteristics hold for publics in general. I use the term to distinguish it more directly from "the," "a," and "counter" publics. The term *discursive* highlights his emphasis on circulation and the potential shifts between and among the different types of publics—for example, a discursive public can at some point gather and become *a* public; a counterpublic can be constituted discursively at a distance and in public performance.

5. Farmer draws on Emily Donnelli's distinction between micropublics, protopublics, and counterpublics as a framework for looking at this kind of specificity in composition pedagogy's public turn. The writing class can be a micropublic, where students see the class as part of the larger public and defined and circumscribed by it; a protopublic, where the classroom is a space for practice or preparatory work in anticipation of moving into larger publics; or a counterpublic, where the class "introduces students to the notion of multiple, contending publics" (9). For simplicity I'm combining the first two, but there are a range of approaches within this general scheme, including composition's engagement in community literacy and service learning projects to aid micropublics.

6. Farmer sees in this kind of activity a role for bricolage. Following Levi-Straus, he notes that older senses of the term *bricolage* emphasized human movements, especially in terms of sports and hunting—a kind of bodily circulation and activity—while more contemporary definitions draw out the "radically flexible handiwork" central to craft as well as craftiness, using tools and materials ready to hand toward some more immediate and emergent purpose (32). Farmer sees this work explicitly in punks' reuse of commodities to develop a counterstyle—a safety pin through the cheek worn as jewelry or a garbage bag as a shirt—along with an identity that both signified and lived out an alternative way of being and a new social arrangement at the edges of dominant culture. Farmer's version of this bricoleur, the citizen bricoleur, is an activist that tacitly comes to understand how these kinds of cultural publics are "made, unmade, remade, and made better" through the scraps of material and methods left over by dominant structures and practices (36).

7. Farmer considers a cultural public "any social formation established primarily through texts, whose constructed identity functions, in some measure, to oppose and critique the accepted norms of the society in which it emerges" (56). It looks both to organize its own culture while at the same time doing it publicly. Counter-

publics especially are oppositional in relation to the other; have a marginal, subaltern, or excluded status; and produce identity through circulation. As Nathan Crick notes in his *RSQ* review, Farmer, as least in this work, sees these marginalized positions as necessarily good without addressing the possibility that counterpublics can also come from the other side of the political spectrum—"Neo-Nazi counterpublics, local militia counterpublics, anti-vaccine counterpublics, Holocaust denier counterpublics, Islamic State of Iraq and Syria (ISIS) counterpublics" (190). All of these kinds of counterpublics can be enhanced and extended through digital circulation.

8. In addition to "Unframing Models of Public Distribution," where she examines the affective ecologies of the Keep Austin Weird campaign, see also "Executive Overspill," where she argues that rather than being dissuasive, Bush's mispronunciations, slips of the tongue, and awkward bodily quirks create an affective environment that reflects his populism and serves as the ground and content of his persuasiveness, which anticipates Trump's rhetorical effectiveness quite well. Ultimately, these are more expansive situations where rhetoric circulates in rhetorical ecologies beyond sanctioned political spaces and engenders various alternative publics.

9. Rice draws on a combination of Foucault and Warner for her version of subjectivity: the subject does not preexist discourse, apparatuses, and enactment; and the subject is created through acts of circulation in processes of poetic world making. Rather than a self-present consciousness or something solidified over time, it is "an articulation of multiple narratives, practices, and apparatuses that coalesce at any given moment" (*Distant Publics* 44). We enact and embody multiple subject positions in any given moment through discourses and apparatuses that precede and exceed us but which we articulate or enact in particular ways in particular moments. Public subjectivity refers to the roles we inhabit when we speak and act about public matters in relation to others, "a process of interfacing with others" or being-in-the-world (45). For example, being a "pro-choice parent" for Rice "emerges whenever I act in relation to these multiple claims that are circulating in public" (45). "Pro-choice parent" exists through webs of discourses, images, affects, and histories that have been "circulating for ages" (45). All of which, a la Warner, says "let a public exist" and "let it have this character, speak in this way, see the world this way" (Warner, qtd. in Rice 45).

10. Jeffrey Grabill's "On Being Useful" puts forward another version of actor-

network theory in relation to rhetorical publics, focused on assembling publics and supporting performances. But by in large it is more human-centered and less focused on circulation than Rice.

11. Kazys Varnelis's coauthored collection *Networked Publics* is perhaps a case in point. Mizuko Ito, author of the introduction, takes the notion of networked publics mater-of-factly. See also Jenkins and Thorburn's *Democracy and New Media* for more on the notion of digital media in relation to publics. These works open a wider potential for both media and publics than Warner acknowledges.

12. Terranova is following the work of Steve Lawrence and Lee Giles, who developed a virtual geography of continents, archipelagos, and islands—megaclusters around the dominant media sites, smaller interlinked ideological clusters, and the isolated islands of government and military sites closed off from public view. Importantly, as I will discuss later, she attributes a different sense of time to this phenomenon than Warner.

13. See Pariser's TED talk entitled "Beware Online 'Filter Bubbles'" (based on his book *The Filter Bubble*). See also Ravi Somaiya's "How Facebook Is Changing the Way Its Users Consume Journalism." But rather than being primarily digital or conceptual phenomena, these digital practices fold over into physical spaces and impact the emergence of publics. In "Weblogs as Deictic Systems," Collin Brooke argues that without the capability to constantly update mass amounts of information that technologies such as Twitter and Amazon provide, many of the sites' corresponding human acts would not be possible (a particular book, for example, might never be bought, read, acted upon, recirculated without Amazon recommendations). These technologies function as actors to collate data in ways that ground and enable human communication and action beyond an individual human scale and disperse it across fields of both human and nonhuman actors. Quasi-objects are informational as well as physical, both of which are fundamentally material: both informational and physical objects can be "sensed, made use of, and . . . make other elements or compositions tangible" (Fuller 2).

14. Brooke's brief history of uses of ecology adds more thinkers in composition and rhetoric to Fuller's usual suspects: Marilyn Cooper (writing ecologies), Margaret Syverson (complexity theory), Andruid Kerne (interface ecology), Karen Burke LeFevre (ecologies of invention), Clay Spinuzzi (genre ecologies) (37–41, 44, 51).

15. But Brooke is fairly quick to point to the differences between Clay Spinuzzi's

macro-, meso-, and microlevels of scale and his approach to ecologies of practice. Brooke doesn't see culture, practice, and code in terms of size as distinct categories: the smallest code necessarily embodies/enacts all three levels (51–52). In this way he is closer to Bateson's integration of scale and immanence.

16. Home and social networking sites are the band's main website and typical social networking sites used across the culture—Facebook, YouTube, Twitter. Artist and industry sites have exploded since the compression of major labels and the separation of indie labels from traditional means of promotion and distribution. Sites such as ReverbNation, Band Camp, Sonic Bids, Indie on the Move allow bands to post audio files, develop digital press kits, book shows, and submit materials to record companies. Consumer sites are interfaces that allow fans to buy MP3s as individual songs or complete albums and download them directly: everything from Amazon and iTunes to Napster and CD Baby. Public or community sites, such as Scene SC, are mostly participatory or user-generated sites and are often geared toward local scenes, but college radio and public access TV also can play key roles. Finally, crawler sites such as Bebo, Song Kick, Eventful, and Gigzee either pull information on shows and live events from specific sites such as Facebook and ReverbNation or crawl the web for show information to post on their own site.

17. I see this broader sense of reverberation in relation to the concept of rhetorical velocity put forward by Jim Ridolfo and Daniel DeVoss in "Composing for Recomposition" and reworked in *The Available Means of Persuasion* by David Sheridan, Jim Ridolfo, and Anthony Michel.

18. Amanda Palmer, who has a TED talk on crowdsourcing a music career, asked for $200,000 and got $1.5 million. Artists get to keep this excess, which goes straight into their account via Amazon or PayPal. Palmer used the excess money to tour and added a certain price goal that would allow her to tour Europe. She also kept adding more rewards (house parties, getting naked, drawing on her). Palmer is also well known for getting naked on stage in response to a review that focused only on her looks, so these antics aren't just about generating attention and funding. They also function as a political voice and mode of credibility as the basis for identification.

19. Personal networks should also be taken into account. Ned's stepmother is Kiya Heartwood, guitarist and singer-songwriter from the 1980s band Stealing Horses, which was on Arista Records and worked with Clive Davis. She fronted folk duo Wishing Chair and is currently in the band Pie Tramps in Austin with Christa Hill-

house, former bass player for 4 Non Blondes. Heartwood gives Ned a lot of industry advice on navigating these ecologies.

20. Again I cite here from the abbreviated version published in the *Quarterly Journal of Speech*.

21. This quote is from an earlier draft of their now-published chapter, so there is no page citation. Their argument is a little more complex than the version I have here, but for my purpose, which is aimed less toward civil society and more toward social ecology, it allows me to make the distinction between distribution and circulation. In many ways this chapter is getting at their viral "events" and chapter 6 is getting at their sense of "archives" that have been hacked into for further circulation.

22. See *Networked Publics* (8–10) for a brief discussion on different economic models online such as niche markets and the long tail. See also John Hartley's "The Frequencies of Public Writing" for more on time and technology with regard to publics.

23. See Sloterdijk's "Foreword to the Theory of Spheres" for an introduction to his larger works on spheres. Also see Latour and Sloterdijk's lectures at Harvard, originally delivered Feb. 17, 2009, and later published in *Harvard Design Magazine*.

24. In their introduction to the collection *Public Modalities*, Daniel Brouwer and Robert Asen briefly assess the advantages and disadvantages of various metaphors for theorizing publics—spheres, networks, publicity, screen, and culture—and advocate for the use of modalities. While their version of modality resonates with my project in that they advocate multiplicity, movement, and activity, their emphasis on a fairly human-centered version of *techne* and the scholar as critical arbiter, "who discerns the values implicated in particular engagements and judges their progressive or regressive qualities" (21), stands in contrast to my interest in examining these movements in public life and the role of writers, researchers, and participants in coproducing these movements. In many ways I follow their suggestion earlier in the introduction to think about how spheres, networks, publicity, and screens can function together in the emergence of particular music-oriented subcultures.

25. Warner recognized that since counterpublics operate without institutional support, they would be self-organized through the circulation of texts and therefore operate through an economics of attention. Publics would "commence with the moment of attention, [and] must continually predicate renewed attention, and cease to exist when attention is no longer predicated" (*Publics and Counterpublics* 88). Less punctuated forms of circulation that mix text, sound, image, and video

all operate to enhance this continued call for attention, which is perhaps not so ironically exemplified in Boyfriend's video for the song "Attention," but rather than cease to exist, the public shifts into a different mode.

26. The association and collapsing of virtual and actual proximity can actually pose problems for some counterpublics. Any public, as Warner notes, is a function of stranger sociability, eventual audiences that writers aren't addressing or invoking (Ede and Lunsford). Lois Keidan, in "The 'Underground' Arts Scene Is Now Just a Click Away from the Easily Offended," notes an uptick in complaints, outrage, and even protests over experimental arts performances that she attributes to the increased accessibility of once-hidden-away arts scenes that could operate only in relation to their specifically addressed audiences. "The problem with the internet," she writes, "is that the underground arts scene—that safe space where risk, dissent and difference are possible—is now only a click away." Events pages and online notices often circulate in aleatory pathways that performers and promoters can't control, so people end up attending performances that offend them because they aren't really for them. Sphere publics aren't isolated at all, as Pariser suggests: all of their tentacles out into networks make them even more porous and open to relationality and sociality.

27. Some authors in popular music studies refer to this phenomenon as "glocality" or the "glocal." In *Exploring Networked Worlds of Popular Music*, Peter Webb characterizes it as "when a global flow is modified by its contact with the local and made to conform to local conditions in a creative way" (116). This is clear in the global circulation of hip-hop and its various instantiations in places such as Germany, Ghana, Korea, or Palestine, sometimes picking up on the marginalized and anti-establishment ethos of its American origins in response to local conditions, at other times taking up its appropriated and commercialized American version and combining it with local pop culture. In *Sound Tracks*, Connell and Gibson argue that the terms *glocal* and even *glocalization* are still too spatial and "reify the status of geometric space over the dynamic conditions under which space is actively constructed . . ." (16). With the concept of sphere publics, I attempt to articulate a version of the combined spatial and temporal aspects of these dynamics.

28. In "Idioculture," Marc Perlman's review of the book *My Music* based on the Music in Daily Life Project, he characterizes idioculture as analogous to a fingerprint, signature, or voice in terms of its particularity but grounded in an individual's specific listening across genre borders that is too diverse to be a subculture.

CHAPTER 6: RHETORIC AS RESONANCE

1. Davis is arguing that rhetoricity interrupts our "appropriation of the world" (*Inessential Solidarity* 57). It demands a response and puts us in an ethical dilemma, and ultimately, it is a driver of change. Rickert's version of worlding doesn't address this contestation as directly or extensively. Davis is trying to recognize and account for the coresponsibility, coproductivity, and entanglement necessitated by rhetoricity because it not only coproduces our world but also disrupts it. While Rickert deals with both revealing and concealing, his reading of rhetoricty as relation via world doesn't allow him to account for this disruption in the same way. In part the difference is in Davis's emphasis on Levinas. For Davis, it is Levinas that really brings this ethical demand to and for the other to the foreground, adding on to Rickert's more exclusively Heideggerian reading (*Inessential Solidarity* 107, 110).

2. The capacity of suggestion is like the ability of language to induce motion in people. It is directly suasive and defies the presumed distance between self and other, evading deliberation and critical assessment, and upends theories of relationality grounded in respresentation. But ultimately rhetoricity shows that there is a grounding difference, always a distance, always the necessity for an ethical response to the other. Persuad-ability is the grounding obligation prior to any self, prior to any Dasein that is "my own." Courtship as a model for persuasion that is "one's own" shows that once persuasion at this level succeeds it dies, full identification erases difference. But seeing persuasion as the ground for worlding shows that difference, alterity, is not only necessary for persuasion but also an ongoing necessity, one that never fully resolves (Davis 171).

3. Rickert's definition and sense of ecology follows this logic. An ecology is "things and forces joined together in dynamic co-existence sustainable over time" (248). Ecology literally means dwelling-logic, "a comprehensive science of an organism's relation to its environment, with environment here being where one dwells" (248–49). It is a continual corresponding to the overall conditions through "feedback loops that emerge within circulating, sustaining activities and material interactions" (249). Feedback loops create degrees of freedom that allow for dynamic self-organization and a sustainable ecology.

4. Rickert acknowledges that both of his key examples fail from a certain perspective. Both are essentially "preparatory" (261, 265). The islander's response was largely reactionary. Arguing against the car on ambient grounds opens a way for thinking and dwelling in those terms, but it doesn't enact a new way of life. The

EV1 also failed to bring about a new way of life with and through the automobile, but at least it attempted to build this world. Both, then, are ultimately preparatory conditions for this potential future way of life.

5. In a number of places, Rickert pulls back from Latour, reading him as extending Burke's dramatism, simply extending the social drama to include nonhumans (208), or reading Latour's parliament of things as a function of a reductive notion of representation (238). Rickert reads the parliament of things as a "deficiency," simply a matter of "bringing all the elements" to the table (266), and reads *dingpolitik* as seeing "everything is as it is, available for assembly and reassembly but still already there" (267). But as I've argued since chapter 1, through a reading of Latour and actor-network theory from a basis in quasi-objects, there is an inherent coproductivity built into the system. Nothing is *ever* simply as it is since it is always in the process of being coproduced through the circulatory actions and encounters of a variable ontology. Affordances matter, but they are constantly being remade as they are incorporated into new actants that build new associative networks and gather new conditions for new futurities.

6. As Casey Boyle Notes in "Pervasive Citizenship through #SenseCommons," Gilbert Simondon recognizes that resonance is not just about homeostasis. Resonance "describes how components function together and not how those components reach some teleological end of balance" (273). Instead it produces a "saturation of relations that then leads to new problematics" (275).

7. For more expanded readings of Latour, see Lynch and Rivers's collection *Thinking with Bruno Latour in Rhetoric and Composition*. In the introduction, for example, they note that activities in Latour's "nondiscursive components of persuasion . . . intensify and redistribute rhetoric," so that "the world can be productively understood as a *rhetorical machine*" (5). Similarly, Jeff Grabil's "On Being Useful: Rhetoric and the Work of Engagement" connects the activity and movement of association and assemblage in Latour to "the rhetorical": "The study of the rhetorical, therefore, is the study of particular kinds of associations that are actively created and re-created. The rhetorical is and creates particular kinds of connection" (195).

8. See Cochrane's "The Ideal Four Minutes and Thirty-Three Seconds" and Smoliar's "Musical Objects."

9. Another potential association in the intertextual network could be H. G. Wells's *The Shape of Things to Come*, which speculates on future world historical events from 1933 until the year 2106. Wells's novel offers predictions for a Second World

War, the development of the League of Nations, the rise of socialism, and the creation of a global state, all from his vast historical knowledge and research as well as his readings of Marx and his utopian outlook. While it is highly likely that Refused know this work given the other types of works and associations they are gathering, their emphasis on advancing musical style makes the Coleman association more direct. In a more general sense, however, all three works—Wells's, Coleman's, and Refused's—not only attempt to articulate or reveal the conditions for possible futures but also to fold back into those conditions and become a part of that striving futurity.

10. In associating the visual and textual with revealed and the musical and sonic with the concealed, I'm taking certain liberties with Heidegger. Every work of art as a whole reveals and conceals. There will still be concealed aspects to the visual art and revealed elements of the music. But in general the visual and textual elements of the work will be more consciously accessible to the average listener than the more technical aspects of the music. The basic punk fan, because of his or her musical world, will be able to note differences in style but generally won't be able to articulate them as an academic like Covach or trained musician could. Rhetorically speaking, in terms of poetic worlding, I think this is in part why Refused put so much into the explicit elements of worlding around the record.

11. Roy Thomas Baker, who also produced Queen and later Foreigner, produced The Cars's album and gives it a (then) contemporary sleek sound (Covach, "Pangs" 190). No attempt to go back to earlier equipment is made, as with the Whites Stripes' more recent attempts to reiterate the sounds of the '50s and '60s.

12. "My Best Friends Girl" includes an intro and breaks up the verse-chorus sections with short bridges that complicate the traditional form. The Cars song "Just What I Needed" even further complicates the standard structure with an introduction, an interlude or bridge after the first verse (instead of a chorus) in the first A section, and a verse-chorus pair + interlude for the second A section. A verse-chorus-chorus structure follows the interlude and then repeats to the end. Covach notes that these structures were already there in the demo tapes before Baker came in to produce ("Pangs" 190).

13. For more on "crossover," see Steve Waksman's *This Ain't the Summer of Love: Conflict and Crossover in Heavy Metal and Punk*, which walks the line between insider and academic to show how these two subcultures worked with and against each other to define a sense of genre and cultural identity in response to the arena rock that emerged out of the 1970s.

14. For a concise history of punk in relation to these aestheic and economic issues, see Stacy Thompson's *Punk Productions: Unfinished Business*. Thompson looks at the New York, London, DC, LA, and Berkley scenes, emphasizing the DIY ethic with regard to comidification and counterpublic economics.

15. See Andersen and Jenkins's *Dance of Days: Two Decades of Punk in the Nation's Capital* for more on Minor Threat, their transformation into Fugazi, and the musical contexts they were countering.

16. Neoteric, in his review, works to find a name for the genre Refused is developing, claiming that "Without this album, I'd doubt there would be a lot of what has become post-hardcore." Others, he notes, have tried labeling the band "industrial hardcore" because of the use of synthesizers. This attempt to name the genre that is emerging out of their work is testament to the effects Refused had on the collective evolution of punk and the album's current underground status as a punk classic.

17. For more on sonic worlds and listening, see Salome Voegelin, *Sonic Possible Worlds: Hearing the Continuum of Sound*, which proposes an approach to investigating works across genre and times.

18. In "Composition and the Circulation of Writing" John Trimbur emphasizes the economic factors that show up in Jenkins et al., drawing on Marx's *Grundrisse* for a model of how circulation materializes contradictory social relations between exchange value and use value with an eye on expanding public forums open to the writing classroom. Gries, on the other hand, focuses more on technologies, attributes, and networks.

19. In a world of iPod rotations and Spotify mixes of various tracks, musical worlds—in the larger sense of musical worlds as the ground for the ability to hear that Covach is after—are built out of databases that contain a wide variety of genres. But the type of poetic world making that comes from the collective work of an album is still critical. In his review Kyle Neath writes, "*The Shape* . . . is an album that absolutely must be listened to as one whole piece of work. . . . Each song flows into one another through a masterfully produced string of effects." Similarly AtomicGarden writes, "I literally get goose bumps whenever I'd listen to the CD all the way through." These are vital aspects of contemporary affective rhetorics that are produced through ciruclation and attention. Even though formats such as the LP and CD come and go, the album as a unit of discourse is still very powerful rhetorically and *more* able to forge publics through this process of fragmenta-

tion and circulation than ever before. The album is extended beyond the lifetime of a typical record of the past.

20. After the band broke up, vocalist Dennis Lyxzen posted a blistering open letter on their label's website titled "Refused Are Fucking Dead." By 2006 the band released a documentary by the same title about the last year of the band's existence. It included live performances of almost all of the songs from *The Shape of Punk To Come* and two of their official music videos ("Rather Be Dead" and "New Noise"). The documentary reinforced Lyxzen's statement while at the same time contributed to the emerging mythos around the band and the album.

21. Emo—a more subdued and emotional subgenre of punk with confessional lyrics—emerged as a subgenre of post-hardcore in mid-1980s Washington, DC. Where Fugazi took a more progressive route out of early hardcore, bands such as Rites of Spring and Embrace were influenced more by new wave or indie rock without becoming as commercial. However, in the early 1990s emo's sound and meaning shifted into more pop-oriented versions such as Jawbreaker and Sunny Day Real Estate. By the mid-1990s, numerous emo acts had formed across the United States and some independent record labels began to specialize in the genre. Emo became mainstream by the early 2000s with the platinum-selling bands such as Jimmy Eat World and Dashboard Confessional.

22. Timbre helps distinguish different sources such as voices, string instruments, wind instruments, and percussion instruments, even when they have the same pitch and volume. When the average person hears the same note played at the same volume on a horn and a piano, it is fairly easy to identify which is the horn and piano, even though it isn't very easy to put language to that difference. Bogue writes: "The language of timbre, of course, like the language of tastes and smells, is crude at best, but whether one can precisely name the word or not, one can easily discriminate a basic feel to the sound" (100). Here I'm repurposing traditional musical and sonic terminology for some language to help distinguish basic timbres within the song.

23. As Gries puts it, "incorporeal transformation occurs when an entity experiences a transformation in identity, sense of purpose, position in society, or relations even as its body may not go through significant change on the outside that can be easily detected" (63). Matthew Fuller, following Deleuze and Guattari, sees both the incorporeal (language) and corporeal (bodily) transformations as aspects of materiality. Fuller argues that objects are informational as well as physical, both

of which are fundamentally material: both informational and physical objects can be "sensed, made use of, and . . . make other elements or compositions tangible" (2). Sound carries this dual functionality and has the ability to change a body incorporeally and corporeally at the same time. Through movements of (de)territorialization, a listener's relationality to others is materially and functionally altered.

24. Also see Cary Wolfe's intro to *Parasite* (xiii), and William Paulson's *The Noise of Culture*.

25. Not every album is going to experience this kind of futurity, but there was something in the combination of the emergent conditions and the qualities of the work itself. Another group from the 1990s, Failure, have almost an identical story. Their third album, 1996's *Fantastic Planet*, was make or break: produce a success or get dropped from the record label. The band put everything they had into the record, writing, producing, and recording it themselves. Their subsequent tour lasted longer than Refused's, but tensions among the band members and slow initial sales led to a breakup in 1997. And like Refused, this third record in retrospect turned into a classic over time. In 2003 the band A Perfect Circle covered the song "The Nurse Who Loved Me" from *Fantastic Planet*, giving it a more sustained profile, but the album's continued circulation online enabled it to find new audiences as the musical times started catching up to the record. Seven tracks from *Fantastic Planet* appeared on their 2006 best of collection *Essentials*, and in 2009 the website JustPressPlay hailed *Fantastic Planet* the third best album of the 1990s and the song "The Nurse Who Loved Me" #10 on their top 100 songs of the 1990s. Like Refused, Failure reunited in 2014 for a tour and new record. But neither band's reunion follow-up albums, Failure's *The Heart Is a Monster* nor Refused's *Freedom*, have lived up to their fans' expectations. *Freedom*, for example, attempts to work the dynamics of *The Shape of Punk to Come* in terms of song writing, but it doesn't capture the overall sonic qualities of the classic album. The guitar sound ranges more toward pitch than noise, and the record ultimately loses its intensity. It's too over-produced and not enough of the songs enact the classic dynamic displayed on *The Shape of Punk to Come*.

26. Whether Refused persuaded anyone to adopt their politics is not really the question. Michael Horvath asks in his review, "Is music still politically motivating? Can it be? While I would like to believe that it is still possible, it also seems that it is very difficult." It is difficult because of the paradox of capitalist appropriation—

if a work circulates enough to have wide political impact, then it has likely been appropriated by capitalism. So Horvath concludes: "*The Shape of Punk to Come* is only as important as the person who listens to it." It is not important whether the album makes money or creates new leftists. Refused are successful in contributing to the conditions of possibility for future recordings, styles, and perhaps even politics by circulating and being listened to. Being taken up and listened to opens up those lines of flight for others to build upon and redeploy through moments of attention.

CONCLUSION: RESOUNDING

1. In *The Future of Invention* John Muckelbauer develops the logical relation between invention and futurity, but work such as Eshun's and Ercolini and Gehrke's is more interested in the pragmatic aspects of futurity. Much of *Resounding* has been interested in both theorizing futures, as Moffett suggests, and examining how this plays out in particular cases.

2. This experimental orientation is vital. In "Digital Empathy" Trisha Campbell attempts to develop empathy through imitating and then speaking through the voice of an other via digital technologies, risking misrecognizing the other for the chance of more empathy and identification. She grounds this risk on John Rajchmann's call for an "experimental relation to the future." Rhetorical practices and pedagogies can't be givens that foreclose on potential outcomes. Any new insights or practices will only come from experiments "as yet unmade, that provoke us to think or imagine in new ways" (qtd. in Campbell). Such a challenge, Margaret Syverson acknowledges, will be fraught with difficulties. The process of developing "entirely new disciplinary ways of seeing, thinking, and sharing knowledge" will generate many failed attempts, but to fail to attempt is the greater evil, leaving composition and rhetoric to only reiterate the already known failed attempts (Syverson 27). Composition and rhetoric must make such attempts as an ongoing process of experimentation if it is ever going to think more in-depth about complexity and futurity.

3. For more on the messianic, see Walter Benjamin's "On the Concept of History" and "Paralipomena to 'On the Concept of History.'"

4. In an endnote on thrownness, translator Albert Hofstadter makes it clear that our chance thrownness into a particular set of historical conditions is coupled with

the projection of possibility that might emerge from those conditions. Humans have the potential to understand their situatedness and project possible outcomes from their enactions. This is not a cause and effect plan, but the opening and recognizing of possibilities, emergence set in motion (Heidegger, "Origin" 71–72).

WORKS CITED

Agamben, Giorgio. *The Open: Man and Animal*. Stanford, CA: Stanford UP, 2004.

Ahmed, Sarah. "Orientation Matters." *New Materialisms: Ontology, Agency, and Politics.* Ed. Diane Coole and Samantha Frost. Durham, NC: Duke UP, 2010. 234–257.

Alexander, Jonathan. "Glenn Gould and the Rhetorics of Sound." *Computers and Composition* 37 (2015): 73–89.

Alaimo, Stacy. "Trans-corporeal Feminisms and the Ethical Space of Nature." *Material Feminisms*. Ed. Stacy Alaimo and Susan Hekman. Bloomington, IN: Indiana UP, 2008. 237–264.

Andersen, Mark, and Mark Jenkins. *Dance of Days: Two Decades of Punk in the Nation's Capital*. New York: Akashic Books, 2001.

Anderson, Brian. "This Is What The Internet Sounds Like." *The Creator's Project* 5 May 2014. 13 June 2014. http://thecreatorsproject.vice.com/blog/this-is-what-the-internet-sounds-like.

Anderson, Erin. "Toward a Resonant Material Vocality for Digital Composition." *Enculturation* 18 (2014): http://enculturation.net/materialvocality.

AtomicGarden. Rev. of Refused: The Shape of Punk to Come. *PunkNews* 15 July 2001. http://www.punknews.org/review/364.

Austin, Gilbert. "Chironomia." *The Rhetorical Tradition: Readings from Classical Times to the Present*. 2nd ed. Ed. Patricia Bizzell and Bruce Herzberg. New York: Bedford St. Martin's, 2000. 889–897.

Ball, Cheryl, and Byron Hawk. "Letter from the Guest Editors." *Sound in/as Compositional Space: A Next Step in Multiliteracies*. Special Issue of *Computers and Composition* 23.3 (2006): 263–398.

Ballif, Michelle. "Writing the Event: The Impossible Possibility for Historiography." *RSQ* 44.3 (2014): 243–255.

Barad, Karen. *Meeting the Universe Halfway: Quantum Physics and the Entanglement of Matter and Meaning*. Durham, NC: Duke U P, 2007.

Barnett, Scot. "Chiasms: Pathos, Phenomenology, and Object-Oriented Rhetorics." *Enculturation* 20 (2015): http://enculturation.net/chiasms-pathos-phenomenology.

Barnett, Scot. "Toward an Object-Oriented Rhetoric." *Enculturation* 7 (2010): http://enculturation.net/toward-an-object-oriented-rhetoric.

Bateson, Gregory. *Steps to an Ecology of Mind*. 1972. Chicago: U of Chicago P, 2000.

Benjamin, Walter. "On the Concept of History." *Walter Benjamin: Selected Writing Vol 4, 1938–40*. Ed. Howard Eiland and Michael Jennings. Cambridge: Belknap Press, Havard UP, 2003. 389–399.

Benjamin, Walter. "Paralipomena to 'On the Concept of History." *Walter Benjamin: Selected Writing Vol 4, 1938–40*. Ed. Howard Eiland and Michael Jennings. Cambridge: Belknap Press, Havard UP, 2003. 400–411.

Bennett, Andy. "Consolidating the Music Scenes Perspective." *Poetics* 32 (2004): 223–234.

Bennett, Jane. "The Agency of Assemblages and the North American Blackout." *Public Culture* 17.3 (2005): 445–465.

Bennett, Jane. *Vibrant Matter: A Political Ecology of Things*. Durham, NC: Duke UP, 2010.

Berlin, James. *Rhetoric, Poetics, Cultures: Refiguring College English Studies*. 2nd ed. West Lafayette, IN: Parlor Press, 2003.

Bernard-Donals, Michael. *The Practice of Theory: Rhetoric, Knowledge, and Pedagogy in the Academy*. New York: Cambridge UP, 1998.

Blencowe, Merlin. *Designing Value Pre-amps for Guitar and Bass*. Merlin Blencowe, 2009.

Bogue, Ronald. *Deleuze on Music, Painting, and the Arts*. New York: Routledge, 2003.

Bogue, Ronald. "Rhizomusicosmology." *SubStance* 66 (1991): 85–101.

Bogue, Ronald. "Violence in Three Shades of Metal: Doom, Death, and Black." *Deleuze and Music*. Ed. Ian Buchanan and Marcel Swiboda. Edinburgh: Edinburgh UP, 2004. 95–117.

Borgo, David. "Embodied, Situated, and Distributed Musicianship." *Sound Musicianship: Understanding the Crafts of Music.* Ed. Andrew Brown. Cambridge Scholars Publishing, 2013. 202–212.

Borgo, David. "The Ghost in the Music, or the Perspective of an Improvising ANT." *The Oxford Handbook of Critical Improvisation Studies.* Vol. 1. Ed. George Lewis and Benjamin Piekut. Oxford UP. 2016. 91–114.

Borgo, David. *Sync or Swarm: Improvising Music in a Complex Age.* New York: Continuum, 2007.

Boyfriend. Interview. *Atypical Sounds.* 1 Apr. 2016. http://atypicalbeastsagency.com/atypicalsounds/love-your-boyfriend/.

Boyle, Casey. "Pervasive Citizenship through #SenseCommons." *RSQ* 46.3 (2016): 269-283.

Boyle, Casey. *Rhetoric as a Posthuman Practice.* Columbus: Ohio State UP. 2018.

Boyle, Casey. "Writing and Rhetoric and/as a Posthuman Practice." *College English* 78.6 (2016): 532–554.

Brooke, Collin. *Lingua Fracta: Toward a Rhetoric of New Media.* Cresskill, NJ: Hampton Press, 2009.

Brooke, Collin. "Weblogs as Deictic Systems: Centripetal, Centrifugal, and Small-World Blogging." *Computers and Composition Online* (Fall 2005): http://www.bgsu.edu/cconline/brooke/brooke.htm.

Brouwer, Daniel, and Robert Asen. Introduction. "Public Modalities, or the Metaphors We Theorize By." *Public Modalities: Rhetoric, Culture, Media, and the Shape of Public Life.* Ed. Daniel Brouwer and Robert Asen. Tuscaloosa, AL: U of Alabama P, 2010. 1–32.

Brown, Steven D., "Michel Serres: Science, Translation and the Logic of the Parasite." *Theory, Culture and Society* 19.3 (2002): 1–27.

Bruffee, Kenneth. "Collaborative Learning and the 'Conversation of Mankind.'" *College English* 46 (1984): 635–652.

Brummet, Barry. *A Rhetoric of Style.* Carbondale, IL: Southern Illinois U P, 2008.

Byrne, David. *How Music Works.* San Francisco: McSweeny's, 2012.

Campbell, Trisha. "Digital Empathy: A Practice-Based Experiment." *Enculturation* 24 (2017): http://enculturation.net/digital_empathy.

Carbaugh, Donal. "'Just Listen': Listening and Landscape Among the Blackfeet." *Western Journal of Communication* 63.3 (2009): 250–270.

Cecchetto, David. *Humanesis: Sound and Technological Posthumanism.* Minneapolis: U of Minnesota P, 2013.

Ceraso, Steph. "(Re)Educating the Senses: Multimodal Listening, Bodily Learning, and the Composition of Sonic Experiences." *College English* 77.2 (2014): 102–123.

Chen, Angus. "Rocks Made of Plastic Found on Hawaiian Beach." *Science Magazine* 4 June 2014. 13 June 2004. http://news.sciencemag.org/earth/2014/06/rocks-made -plastic-found-hawaiian-beach.

Cochrane, Richard. "The Ideal Four Minutes and Thirty-Three Seconds: Response to John Covach." *Music Theory Online* 1.1 (1995): http://mto.societymusictheory.org/ issues/mto.95.1.1/mto.95.1.1.cochrane.tlk.html.

Coe, Richard. "Eco-Logic for the Composition Classroom." *CCC* 26.3 (1975): 232–237.

Coleman, Ornette. *The Shape of Jazz to Come.* 1959. Atlantic/WEA, 1990.

Comstock, Michelle, and Mary E. Hocks. "The Sounds of Climate Change: Sonic Rhetoric in the Anthropocene, the Age of Human Impact." *Rhetoric Review* 35.2 (2016): 165–175.

Connell, John, and Chris Gibson. *Sound Tracks: Popular Music, Identity and Place.* New York: Routledge, 2003.

Connors, Robert. *Composition-Rhetoric: Backgrounds, Theory, and Pedagogy.* Pittsburgh: U of Pittsburgh P, 1997.

Coole, Diane, and Samantha Frost. "Introducing the New Materialisms." *New Materialisms: Ontology, Agency, and Politics.* Ed. Diane Coole and Samantha Frost. Durham, NC: Duke UP, 2010. 1–43.

Cooper, Marilyn. "The Ecology of Writing." *College English* 48.4 (1986): 364–375.

Cooper, Marilyn, and Michael Holzman. *Writing as Social Action.* Portsmouth, NH: Boyton, 1989.

Covach, John. "Destructuring Cartesian Dualism in Musical Analysis." *Music Theory Online* 0.1 (1994): http://mto.societymusictheory.org/issues/mto.94.0.11/mto.94.0 .11.covach.art.

Covach, John. "Musical Worlds and the Metaphysics of Analysis." *Music Theory Online* 1.1 (1995): http://mto.societymusictheory.org/issues/mto.95.1.1/mto.95.1.1.covach .tlk.html.

Covach, John. "Pangs of History in late 1970s New-wave Rock." *Analyzing Popular Music.* Ed. Allan Moore. New York: Cambridge UP, 2003. 173–195.

Crick, Nathan. "Public Intellectuals, Both Real and Unreal." *RSQ* 46.2 (2016): 176–193.

Davis, Diane. *Inessential Solidarity: Rhetoric and Foreigner Relations.* Pittsburgh: U of Pittsburgh P, 2010.

Davis, Diane. Introduction. *Writing with Sound.* Special Issue of *Currents in Electronic Literacy* (2011): https://currents.dwrl.utexas.edu/2011.html.

DeLanda, Manuel. *A New Philosophy of Society: Assemblage Theory and Social Complexity.* New York: Continuum, 2006.

DeLanda, Manuel. *Intensive Science and Virtual Philosophy.* New York: Continuum, 2002.

Deleuze, Gilles. *Foucault.* Foreword by Paul Bove. Minneapolis: Minnesota UP, 1988.

Deleuze, Gilles. *The Logic of Sense.* Ed. Constantin V. Boundas. Trans. Mark Lester with Charles Stivale. New York: Columbia UP, 1993.

Deleuze, Gilles. "Mediators." *Negotiations.* New York: Columbia UP, 1995. 121–134.

Deleuze, Gilles, and Felix Guattari. *Anti-Oedipus: Capitalism and Schizophrenia.* Foreword by Michel Foucault. Minneapolis: U of Minnesota P, 1983.

Deleuze, Gilles, and Felix Guattari. *A Thousand Plateaus: Capitalism and Schizophrenia.* Trans. Brian Massumi. Minneapolis: U of Minnesota P, 1987.

de Laet, Marianne, and Annemarie Mol. "The Zimbabwe Bush Pump: Mechanics of a Fluid Technology." *Social Studies of Science* 30.2 (2000): 225–263.

Dobrin, Sid. Introduction. *Writing Posthumanism, Posthuman Writing.* Ed. Sid Dobrin. Anderson, SC: Parlor Press, 2015. 3–18.

Dobrin, Sid. *Postcomposition.* Carbondale, IL: SIUP, 2011.

Dreyfus, Hubert. *Being-in-the-World.* Cambridge: MIT, 1995.

Duffy, William. "Collaboration (in) Theory: Reworking the Social Turn's Conversational Imperative." *College English* 76.5 (2014): 416–435.

Edbauer, Jenny (see also Rice, Jenny). "Unframing Models of Public Distribution: From Rhetorical Situation to Rhetorical Ecologies." *RSQ* 35.4 (2005): 5–24.

Edbauer, Jenny (see also Rice, Jenny). "Executive Overspill: Affective Bodies, Intensity, and Bush-in-Relation." *Postmodern Culture* 15.1 (October 2004): http://pmc .iath.virginia.edu/text-only/issue.904/15.1edbauer.txt.

Ede, Lisa. *Situating Composition: Composition Studies and the Politics of Location.* Carbondale, IL: SIUP, 2004.

Ede, Lisa, and Andrea Lunsford. "Audience Addressed, Audience Invoked: The Role of Audience in Composition Theory and Pedagogy." *CCC* 35.2 (1984): 155–171.

Ede, Lisa, and Andrea Lunsford. *Writing Together: Collaboration in Theory and Practice.* New York: Bedford/St. Martin's, 2012.

Ercolini, Gina, and Pat Gehrke. "Writing Future Rhetoric." *Theorizing Histories of Rhetoric.* Ed. Michelle Ballif. Carbondale, IL: SIUP, 2013. 154–171.

Erlmann, Veit. "Resonance." *Keywords in Sound.* Ed. David Novak and Matt Sakakeeny. Durham, NC: Duke UP, 2015. 175–182.

Eshun, Kowdo. "Further Considerations on Afrofuturism." *CR: The New Centennial Review* 3.2 (Summer 2003): 287–302.

Eshun, Kowdo. *More Brilliant Than the Sun: Adventures in Sonic Fiction*. London: Quartet Books, 1998.

Farmer, Frank. *After the Public Turn: Composition, Counterpublics, and the Citizen Bricoleur*. Logan, UT: Utah State UP, 2013.

Feld, Steven. "Acoustemology." *Keywords in Sound*. Ed. D. Novak and M. Sakakeeny. Durham, NC: Duke UP, 2015. 12–21.

Fleckenstein, Kristie. *Embodied Literacies: Imageword and the Poetics of Teaching*. Carbondale, IL: SIUP, 2003.

Fleckenstein, Kristie, Clay Spinuzzi, Rebecca Rickly, and Carole Papper. "The Importance of Harmony: An Ecological Metaphor for Writing Research." *CCC* 60.2 (2008): 388-419.

Fleming, David. *From Form to Meaning: Freshman Composition and the Long Sixties, 1957-1974*. Pittsburgh: U of Pittsburgh P, 2011.

Fliegler, Ritchie. *Amps! The Other Half of Rock and Roll*. Hal Leonard, 1993.

Flusser, Vilem. *Gestures*. Minneapolis: U of Minnesota P, 2014.

Foucault, Michel. "Intellectuals and Power: A Conversation between Michel Foucault and Gilles Deleuze." *Language, Counter-Memory, Practice*. New York: Cornell UP, 1977. 205–217.

Freedman, Peter. "Room Acoustics 101 with Peter Freedman." YouTube. 15 Oct. 2009.

Fuller, Matthew. *Media Ecologies: Materialist Energies in Art and Technoculture*. Cambridge: MIT, 2005.

Galloway, Alexander, and Eugene Thacker. *The Exploit: A Theory of Networks*. Minneapolis: U of Minnesota P, 2007.

Gaston, Sean. Introduction. *Reading Derrida's Of Grammatology*. Ed. Sean Gaston and Ian Maclachlan. New York: Continuum, 2011. xiii-xxvii.

Genosko, Gary. "A Bestiary of Territoriality and Expression: Poster Fish, Bower Birds, and Spiny Lobsters." *Canadian Review of Comparative Literature* 24.3 (1997): 529–542.

Gilbert, Jeremy. "Becoming-Music: The Rhizomatic Moment of Improvisation." *Deleuze and Music*. Ed. Ian Buchanan and Marcel Swiboda. Edinburgh: Edinburgh UP, 2004. 118–139.

Goodale, Greg. *Sonic Persuasion: Reading Sound in the Recorded Age*. Champaign, IL: U of Illinois P, 2011.

Goodman, Steve. *Sonic Warfare: Sound, Affect, and the Ecology of Fear*. Cambridge: MIT, 2010.

Goggin, Maureen Daly. "Collaboration." *Keywords in Composition Studies*. Ed. Paul Heilker and Peter Vandenberg. Portsmouth, NH: Boyton/Cooke, 1996. 35–39.

Grabill, Jeffrey. "On Being Useful: Rhetoric and the Work of Engagement." *The Public Work of Rhetoric: Citizen Scholars and Civic Engagement*. Ed. John Ackerman and David Coogan. Columbia, SC: U of South Carolina P, 2010. 193–207.

Gries, Laurie. *Still Life with Rhetoric: A New Materialist Approach to Visual Rhetoric*. Logan, UT: Utah State UP/UP of Colorado, 2015.

Gross, Daniel. "Heidegger's 1924 Lecture Course on Aristotle's *Rhetoric*: Key Research Implications." *Philosophy and Rhetoric* 50.4 (2017): 509–527.

Guattari, Felix. "The Three Ecologies." *New Formations* 8 (1989): 131–147.

Gunn, Joshua, Greg Goodale, Mirko Hall, and Rosa Eberly. "Auscultating Again: Rhetoric and Sound Studies." *RSQ* 43.5 (2013): 475–489.

Habermas, Jurgen. *The Structural Transformation of the Public Sphere: An Inquiry into a Category of Bourgeois Society*. Cambridge: MIT, 1989.

Hainge, Greg. "Is Pop Music?" *Deleuze and Music*. Ed. Ian Buchanan and Marcel Swiboda. Edinburgh: Edinburgh UP, 2004. 36–53.

Halbritter, Bump. *Mics, Cameras, Symbolic Action: Audio-Visual Rhetoric for Writing Teachers*. Anderson, SC: Parlor Press, 2013.

Halbritter, Bump. "Musical Rhetoric in Integrated Media Composition." *Computers and Composition* 23.3 (2006): 317–334.

Harman, Graham. "Heidegger on Objects and Things." *Making Things Public: Atmospheres of Democracy*. Ed. Bruno Latour and Peter Weibel. Cambridge: MIT, 2005. 268–271.

Harman, Graham. *Prince of Networks: Bruno Latour and Metaphysics*. Melbourne: Re. Press, 2009.

Harman, Graham. *Tool-Being: Heidegger and the Metaphysics of Objects*. Chicago: Open Court, 2002.

Hartley, John. "The Frequencies of Public Writing: Tomb, Tome, and Time as Technologies of the Public." *Democracy and New Media*. Ed. Henry Jenkins and David Thorburn. Cambridge: MIT, 2003. 247–270.

Hawk, Byron. *A Counter-History of Composition: Toward Methodologies of Complexity*. Pittsburgh: U of Pittsburgh P, 2007.

Hawk, Byron. "Curating Ecologies, Circulating Musics: From The Public Sphere to Sphere Publics." *Ecology, Writing Theory, and New Media: Writing Ecology*. Ed. Sid Dobrin. New York: Routledge, 2012. 160–179.

Hawk, Byron. "Embodying *Heurisis*: Tagmemics, Complexity, and Flow." *JAC* 33.3–4 (2014): 723–732.

Hawk, Byron. "Reassembling Post-Process: Toward a Posthuman Theory of Public

Rhetoric." *Beyond Post-Process*. Ed. Sid Dobrin, J. A. Rice, and Michael Vastola. Utah State UP, 2011. 75–93.

Hawk, Byron. Rev. of *Sonic Persuasions: Reading Sound in the Recorded Age*, by Greg Goodale. *Philosophy and Rhetoric* 47.2 (2014): 219–226.

Hawk, Byron. "The Shape of Rhetoric to Come: Musical Worlding as Public Rhetoric." *Pre/Text* 20.1-4 (2010): 7–42.

Hawk, Byron. "Stitching Together Events: Of Joints, Folds, and Assemblages." *Theorizing Histories of Rhetoric*. Ed. Michelle Ballif. Carbondale, IL: SIUP, 2013. 106–127.

Hawk, Byron. "Toward a Post-Techne: Or, Inventing Pedagogies for Professional Writing." *TCQ* 13.4 (2004): 371–392.

Hawk, Byron. "Toward a Rhetoric of Network (Media) Culture: Notes on Polarities and Potentiality." *Mark C. Taylor and Emerging Network Culture*. Special Issue of *JAC* 24.4 (2004): 831–850.

Hawk, Byron. "Vitalism, Animality, and the Material Grounds of Rhetoric." *Communication Matters: Materialist Approaches to Media, Mobility, and Networks*. Ed. Jeremy Packer and Stephen Wiley. New York: Routledge, 2012. 196–207.

Hawk, Byron, and Christian Smith. "'Digimortal': Sound in a World of Posthumanity." *Writing with Sound*. Special Issue of *Currents in Electronic Literacy* (2011): https://currents.dwrl.utexas.edu/2011/digimortalsoundinaworldofposthumanity.html.

Hawk, Byron, and David Rieder. Introduction. "On Small Tech and Complex Ecologies." *Emerging Small Tech: Technologies at the Intersection of Cyberculture and New Media*. Minneapolis: U of Minnesota P, 2007. ix-xxiii.

Haynes, Cynthia. "Writing Offshore: The Disappearing Coastline of Composition Theory." *JAC* 23.4 (2003): 667–724.

Heidegger, Martin. *Being and Time*. Trans. John Macquarrie and Edward Robinson. New York: Harper/Collins, 1962.

Heidegger, Martin. "Building, Dwelling, Thinking." *Poetry, Language, Thought*. New York: Harper and Rowe, 1971. 143–161.

Heidegger, Martin. "Letter on Humanism." *Basic Writings*. Ed. David Farrell Krell. New York: Harper and Rowe, 1977. 193–242.

Heidegger, Martin. "The Origin of the Work of Art." *Poetry, Language, Thought*. New York: Harper and Rowe, 1971. 15–78.

Heidegger, Martin. "The Question Concerning Technology." *The Question Concerning Technology and Other Essays*. New York: Harper Torchbooks, 1977. 3–35.

Heidegger, Martin. "The Thing." *Poetry, Language, Thought*. New York: Harper and Rowe, 1971. 163–182.

Heidegger, Martin. "The Way to Language." *On the Way to Language*. New York: Harper Collins, 1982. 111–136.

Heilker, Paul, and Peter Vandenberg, eds. *Keywords in Composition Studies*. Portsmouth, NH: Boyton/Cooke, 1996.

Heilker, Paul, and Peter Vandenberg, eds. *Keywords in Writing Studies*. Logan, UT: Utah State UP, 2015.

Helmreich, Stefan. "Transducing." *Experience: Culture, Cognition, and the Common Sense*. Ed. Caroline Jones, David Mather, and Rebecca Uchill. Cambridge: MIT, 2016. 162–167.

Helmreich, Stefan. "Transduction." *Keywords in Sound*. Ed. David Novak and Matt Sakakeeny. Durham, NC: Duke U P, 2015. 222–231.

Herndl, Carl, and Scott Graham. "Getting Over Incommensurability: Latour, New Materialisms, and the Rhetoric of Diplomacy." *Thinking with Bruno Latour in Rhetoric and Composition*. Ed. Paul Lynch and Nathaniel Rivers. Carbondale, IL: SIUP, 2015. 40–58.

Hill, Bobby. Personal Interview. 6 Dec. 2013.

Hocks, Mary, and Michelle Comstock. "Composing for Sound: Sonic Rhetoric as Resonance." *Computers and Composition* 43 (2017): 135–146.

Holding, Cory. "Rhetoric of the Open Fist." *RSQ* 45.5 (2015): 399–419.

Holland, Eugene. "Studies in Applied Nomadology: Jazz Improvisation and Post-Capitalist Markets." *Deleuze and Music*. Ed. Ian Buchanan and Marcel Swiboda. Edinburgh: Edinburgh UP, 2004. 20–35.

Horvath, Michael. *Rev. of The Shape Of Punk To Come*. Kevchino. 12 May 2010. http://www.kevchino.com/review/refused/shape-of-punk-come/1575.

Hunter, Dave. *The Guitar Amp Handbook: Understanding Tube Amplifiers and Getting Great Sounds*. 2nd ed. Backbeat Books, 2015.

Ikoniadou, Eleni. *The Rhythmic Event: Art, Media, and the Sonic*. Cambridge: MIT, 2014.

Jenkins, Henry, and David Thorburn, eds. *Democracy and New Media*. Cambridge: MIT, 2003.

Jenkins, Henry, Sam Ford, and Joshua Green. *Spreadable Media: Creating Value and Meaning in a Networked Culture*. New York: NYUP, 2013.

Johnson, Steven. "Use the blog, Luke." *Salon* 10 May 2002. http://www.salon.com/technology/feature/2002/05/10/blogbrain/index.html.

Katz, Steven. *The Epistemic Music of Rhetoric: Toward the Temporal Dimension of Affect in Reader Response and Writing*. Carbondale, IL: SIUP, 1996.

Keidan, Lois. "The 'Underground' Arts Scene Is Now Just a Click Away from the Easily

Offended." *The Gaurdian* 17 Jan. 2015. http://www.theguardian.com/stage/theatre blog/2015/jan/17/underground-art-mainstream-culture-outrage-sex-morality.

Kennedy, Krista, and Rebecca Moore Howard. "Collaborative Writing." *A Guide to Composition Pedagogies*. 2nd ed. Ed. Gary Tate, Amy Rupiper Taggart, Kurt Schick, and H. Brooke Hessler. New York: Oxford UP, 2014. 37–54.

Kent, Thomas. "Beyond System: The Rhetoric of Paralogy." *College English* 51.5 (1989): 492–507.

Kent, Thomas. Introduction. *Post-Process Theory: Beyond the Writing-Process Paradigm*. Ed. Thomas Kent. Carbondale, IL: SIUP, 1999. 1–6.

Kent, Thomas. "Paralogic Hermeneutics and the Possibilities of Rhetoric." *Rhetoric Review* 8.1 (1989): 24–42.

Kent, Thomas. *Paralogic Rhetoric*. Lewisburg, PA: Bucknell UP, 1993.

Kharkhordin, Oleg. "Things as Res publicae: Making Things Public." *Making Things Public: Atmospheres of Democracy*. Ed. Bruno Latour and Peter Weibel. Cambridge: MIT, 2005. 280–89.

King, David. Personal Interview. 7 Aug. 2013.

King, Jim. Personal Interview. 6 Aug. 2013.

LaBelle, Brandon. *Background Noise: Perspectives on Sound Art*. London: Bloomsbury Academic, 2006.

Lanham, Richard. *The Economics of Attention: Style and Substance in the Age of Information*. Chicago: U of Chicago P, 2006.

Latour, Bruno. "An Attempt at a 'Compositionist Manifesto.'" *New Literary History* 41 (2010): 471–490.

Latour, Bruno. "The Berlin Key, or, How to do Things with Words." *Matter, Materiality, and Modern Culture*. Ed. Paul Graves-Brown. New York: Routledge, 2000. 10–21.

Latour, Bruno. "From Realpolitik to Dingpolitik or How to Make Things Public." *Making Things Public: Atmospheres of Democracy*. Ed. Bruno Latour and Peter Weibel. Cambridge: MIT, 2005. 14–41.

Latour, Bruno. "Mixing Humans and Nonhumans Together: The Sociology of a Door-Closer." *Social Problems* 35.3 (1988): 298–310.

Latour, Bruno. "One More Turn After the Social Turn: Easing Science into the Non-Modern World." *The Social Dimensions of Science*. Ed. Ernan McMullin. Notre Dame UP, 1992. 272–292.

Latour, Bruno. "Some Experiments in Art and Politics." *E-flux* 23 (March 2011): http://www.e-flux.com/journal/view/217.

Latour, Bruno. "Spheres and Networks: Two Ways to Reinterpret Globalization." *Harvard Design Magazine* 30 (Spring/Summer 2009): http://www.bruno-latour.fr/articles/article/115-SPACE-HARVARD-09.pdf.

Latour, Bruno. *Reassembling the Social: An Introduction to Actor-Network Theory.* New York: Oxford UP, 2005.

Latour, Bruno. *We Have Never Been Modern.* Cambridge: Harvard UP, 1993.

Lauer, Janice. *Invention in Rhetoric and Composition.* West Lafayette, IN: Parlor Press, 2004.

Law, John. *After Method: Mess in Social Science Research.* New York: Routledge, 2004.

Law, John. *Aircraft Stories: Decentering the Object in Technoscience.* Durham, NC: Duke UP, 2002.

Law, John, and Vicky Singleton. "Object Lessons." *Organization* 12.3 (2005): 331–355.

LeFevre, Karen Burke. *Invention as a Social Act.* Carbondale, IL: SIUP, 1987.

LeMesurier, Jennifer. "Mobile Bodies: Triggering Bodily Uptake through Movement." *CCC* 68.2 (2016): 292–316.

Lotier, Kristopher. "Around 1986: The Externalization of Cognition and the Emergence of Postprocess Invention." *CCC* 67.3 (2016): 360–384.

Lovejoy, Arthur. "The Meaning of Vitalism." *Science* 33.851 (1911): 610–614.

Lovejoy, Arthur. "The Import of Vitalism." *Science* 34.864 (1911): 75–80.

Lovejoy, Arthur. "The Meaning of Driesch and the Meaning of Vitalism." *Science* 36.933 (1912): 672–675.

Lynch, Paul. *After Pedagogy: The Experience of Teaching.* Urbana, IL: NCTE, 2013.

Lynch, Paul, and Nathaniel Rivers. Introduction. *Thinking with Bruno Latour in Rhetoric and Composition.* Carbondale, IL: SIUP, 2015. 1–19.

MacDonald, Fiona. "Mind-Bending New Approach Could Explain Our Solar System's 'Random' Patterns." *Science Alert* 10 Feb. 2018. https://www.sciencealert.com/mind-bending-new-theory-of-everything-suggests-there-s-a-hidden-force-that-controls-our-universe.

Mailloux, Steve. "Archivist with an Attitude: Reading Typos, Reading Archives." *College English* 61.5 (1999): 584–590.

Manning, Erin. *The Minor Gesture.* Durham: Duke UP, 2016.

Massumi, Brian. "Undigesting Deleuze." *Los Angeles Review of Books* 8 Nov. 2015. https://lareviewofbooks.org/essay/undigesting-deleuze/.

McKee, Heidi. "Sound Matters: Notes Toward the Analysis and Design of Sound in Multimodal Webtexts." *Computers and Composition* 23.3 (2006): 335–354.

Merali, Zeeya. "What Is Really Real? A Wave of Experiments if Probing the Root of Quantum Weirdness." *Nature* 20 May 2015. http://www.nature.com/news/quantum-physics-what-is-really-real-1.17585.

Meyers, Greg. "The Social Construction of Two Biologists' Proposals." *Written Communication* 2 (1985): 219–245.

Miller, Carolyn. "Genre as a Social Action." *QJS* 70 (1984): 151–167.

Mol, Annemarie. "Actor-Network Theory: Sensitive Terms and Enduring Questions." *Kölner Zeitschrift für Soziologie und Sozialpsychologie* 50 (2010): 253–269.

Mol, Annemarie. *The Body Multiple: Ontology in Medical Practice.* Durham, NC: Duke UP, 2002.

Mol, Annemarie. "Ontological Politics: A Word and Some Questions." *Actor Network Theory and After.* Ed. John Law and John Hassard. Oxford and Keele: Blackwell and the Sociological Review, 1999. 74–89.

Morey, Sean. *Rhetorical Delivery and Digital Technologies.* New York: Routledge, 2016.

Muckelbauer, John. *The Future of Invention: Rhetoric, Postmodernism, and the Problem of Change.* Albany: SUNY, 2008.

Murphy, James. "Conducting Research in the History of Rhetoric." *Publishing in Rhetoric and Composition.* Ed. Gary Olson and Todd Taylor. Albany: SUNY, 1997. 187–95.

Nealon, Jeffrey. *Post-Postmodernism: or, The Cultural Logic of Just-in-Time Capitalism.* Stanford: Stanford UP, 2012.

Neath, Kyle. Rev. of Refused: *The Shape of Punk to Come. Warpspire* 2006 Feb. 15. http://warpspire.com/reviews/music-2/refused-the-shape-of-punk-to-come/.

Negus, Keith. *Popular Music in Theory: An Introduction.* Hanover, NH: UP of New England, 1996.

Neoteric. Rev. of Refused: *The Shape of Punk to Come. Sputnik Music* 27 April 2006. http://www.sputnikmusic.com/album.php?albumid=411.

Nordstrom, Susan Naomi. "Not So Innocent Anymore: Making Recording Devices Matter in Qualitative Interview." *Qualitative Inquiry* 21.4 (2015): 388–401.

Novak, David. *Japanoise: Music at the Edge of Circulation.* Durham, NC: Duke UP, 2013.

Novak, David, and Matt Sakakeeny. Introduction. *Keywords in Sound.* Durham, NC: Duke UP, 2015. 1–11.

Palmer, Amanda. "The Art of Asking." *TED* Feb. 2013. http://www.ted.com/talks/amanda_palmer_the_art_of_asking.html.

Panzner, Joe. *The Process That Is The World: Cage/Deleuze/Events/Performances.* New York: Bloomsbury, 2015.

Pariser, Eli. *The Filter Bubble: What the Internet is Hiding from You*. New York: Penguin Press, 2011.

Pariser, Eli. "Beware Online 'Filter Bubbles.'" *TED* Mar. 2011. http://www.ted.com/talks/eli_pariser_beware_online_filter_bubbles.html.

Paulson, William. *The Noise of Culture: Literary Texts in the World of Information*. Ithaca, NY: Cornell UP, 1988.

Perlman, Marc. "Idioculture: De-Massifying the Popular Music Audience." *Postmodern Culture* 4.1 (1993): http://pmc.iath.virginia.edu/text-only/issue.993/review-7.993.

Phelps, Louise Wetherbee. *Composition as a Human Science: Contributions to the Self-Understanding of a Discipline*. New York: Oxford UP, 1988.

Powell, Katrina, and Pamela Takayoshi, eds. *Practicing Research in Writing Studies: Reflexive and Ethically Responsible Research*. New York: Hampton Press, 2012.

Pross, Addy. "Life's Restlessness." *Aeon Magazine* 29 Apr. 2014. http://aeon.co/magazine/nature-and-cosmos/stability-how-life-began-and-why-it-cant-rest/.

Rasch, William. *Niklas Luhmann's Modernity: The Paradoxes of Differentiation*. Stanford, CA: Stanford UP, 2000.

Ray, Brian, and Jay Jordan. "Comment and Response: Triangulating Translingualism." *College English* 78.4 (2016): 387–393.

Refused. *The Shape of Punk to Come: A Chimerical Bombination in 12 Bursts*. Epitaph/Burning Heart, 1998.

Rice, Jeff. *Craft Obsession: The Social Rhetorics of Beer*. Carbondale, IL: SIUP, 2016.

Rice, Jeff. *Digital Detroit: Rhetoric and Space in the Age of the Network*. Carbondale, IL: SIUP, 2012.

Rice, Jenny. *Distant Publics: Development Rhetoric and the Subject of Crisis*. Pittsburgh: U of Pittsburgh P, 2012.

Rice, Jenny (see also Edbauer, Jenny). "Unframing Models of Public Distribution: From Rhetorical Situation to Rhetorical Ecologies." *RSQ* 35.4 (2005): 5–24.

Rice, Jenny (see also Edbauer, Jenny). "Executive Overspill: Affective Bodies, Intensity, and Bush-in-Relation." *Postmodern Culture* 15.1 (October 2004): http://pmc.iath.virginia.edu/text-only/issue.904/15.1edbauer.txt.

Rickert, Thomas. *Ambient Rhetoric: The Attunements of Rhetorical Being*. Pittsburgh: U of Pittsburgh P, 2013.

Rickert, Thomas, and Byron Hawk. "Avowing the Unavowable: On the Music of Composition." *Enculturation* 2.2 (1999): http://enculturation.net/2_2/intro.html.

Rickert, Thomas, and Michael J. Salvo. "The Distributed *Gesamptkunstwerk*: Sound,

Worlding, and New Media Culture." *Computers and Composition* 23 (2006): 296–316.

Ridolfo, Jim, and Dànielle Nicole DeVoss. "Composing for Recomposition: Rhetorical Velocity and Delivery." *Kairos* 13.2 (2009): http://www.technorhetoric.net/13.2/topoi/ridolfo_devoss/index.html.

Rieder, David. *Suasive Iterations: Rhetoric, Writing, and Physical Computing.* Anderson, SC: Parlor Press, 2017.

Rozenblit, Bruce. *Beginner's Guide to Tube Audio Design.* Audio Amateur Publications, 1997.

Rorty, Richard. "Heidegger and the Atomic Bomb." *Making Things Public: Atmospheres of Democracy.* Ed. Bruno Latour and Peter Weibel. Cambridge: MIT, 2005. 274–275.

Rotman, Brian. *Becoming Beside Ourselves: The Alphabet, Ghosts, and Distributed Human Being.* Durham, NC: Duke UP, 2008.

Rüting, Torsten. "History and Significance of Jakob von Uexküll and of his Institute in Hamburg." *Sign Systems Studies* 32.1–2 (2004): 35–72.

Ryder, Phyllis Mentzell. "Multicultural Public Spheres and the Rhetorics of Democracy." *JAC* 27 (2007): 505–537.

Sakakeeny, Matt. "Music." *Keywords in Sound.* Durham, NC: Duke UP, 2015. 112–124.

Salvador, Michael, and Traceylee Clarke. "The Weyekin Principle: Toward an Embodied Critical Rhetoric." *Environmental Communication* 5.3 (2011): 243–260.

Sampson, Tony. *Virality: Contagion Theory in the Age of Networks.* Minneapolis: U of Minnesota P, 2012.

Schandorf, Michael. "Mediated Gesture: Paralinguistic Communication and Phatic Text." *Convergence* 19.3 (2012): 319–344.

Schehr, Lawrence. Preface and Introduction. *The Parasite.* By Michel Serres. Baltimore: Johns Hopkins UP, 1982. vii–x.

Schilb, John. "Cultural Studies, Postmodernism, and Composition." *Contending with Words: Composition and Rhetoric in a Postmodern Age.* Ed. Patricia Harkin and John Schlib. New York: MLA, 1991. 173–188.

Scott, D. Travers. "'Music to Moog By': Gendering in Early Analog Synthesizing in the United States." *Technoculture* 3 (2013): http://tcjournal.org/drupal/vol3/scott.

Selfe, Cindy. "The Movement of Air, the Breath of Meaning: Aurality and Multimodal Composing." *CCC* 60.4 (2009): 616–663.

Serres, Michel. *Genesis.* Trans. Geneviève James and James Nielson. Ann Arbor: U of Michigan P, 1995.

Serres, Michel. "Noise." *SubStance* 12.3 (1983): 48–60.

Serres, Michel. "Theory of the Quasi-Object." *The Parasite*. Trans. Lawrence Schehr. Baltimore: Johns Hopkins UP, 1982. 224–234.

Serres, Michel, and Bruno Latour. *Conversations on Science, Culture, and Time*. Trans. Roxanne Lapidus. Ann Arbor: U of Michigan P, 1995.

Sheehan, Thomas. *Making Sense of Heidegger*. New York: Rowman and Littlefield, 2015.

Sheridan, David M., Jim Ridolfo, and Anthony J. Michel. *The Available Means of Persuasion: Mapping a Theory and Pedagogy of Multimodal Public Rhetoric*. Anderson, SC: Parlor Press, 2012.

Shipka, Jody. "Sound Engineering: Toward a Theory of Multimodal Soundness." *Computers and Composition* 23.3 (2006): 355–373.

Shipka, Jody. *Toward a Composition Made Whole*. Pittsburgh: U of Pittsburgh P, 2011.

Shipka, Jody. "Transmodality in/and Processes of Making: Changing Dispositions and Practices." *College English* 78.3 (2016): 250–257.

Simmons, W. Michelle, Kristin Moore, and Patricia Sullivan. "Tracing Uncertainties: Methodologies of a Door Closer." *Thinking with Bruno Latour in Rhetoric and Composition*. Ed. Paul Lynch and Nathaniel Rivers. Carbondale, IL: SIUP, 2015. 275–293.

Sirc, Geoffrey. *English Composition as a Happening*. Carbondale, IL: SIUP, 2002.

Sirc, Geoffrey. "English Composition as a Happening II, Part One." *Pre/Text* 15.3–4 (1994): 266–293.

Sirc, Geoffrey, and Steph Ceraso. "Digital Lyrical." *Writing with Sound*. Special Issue of *Currents in Electronic Literacy* (2011): https://currents.dwrl.utexas.edu/2011/digital lyrical.html.

Sloterdijk, Peter. "Foreword to the Theory of Spheres." *Cosmograms*. Ed. Melik Ohhanian and Jean-Christophe Royoux. New York: Lukas and Sternberg, 2005. 223–240.

Sloterdijk, Peter. "Spheres Theory: Talking to Myself about the Poetics of Spheres." *Harvard Design Magazine* 30 (Spring/Summer 2009): http://www.gsd.harvard.edu/research/publications/hdm/back/30_Sloterdijk.pdf.

Smoliar, Stephen. "Musical Objects: Response to John Covach." *Music Theory Online* 1.1 (1995): http://mto.societymusictheory.org/issues/mto.95.1.1/mto.95.1.1.smoliar.tlk.html.

Smith, Dale, and James J. Brown. "For Public Distribution." *Rhetoric, Writing, and Circulation*. Ed. Laurie Gries and Collin Brooke. Logan: Utah State UP, 2018. 208–224.

Smith, Eric T. *Acoustics 101: Practical Guidelines for Constructing Accurate Acoustical Spaces*. Indianapolis: Auralex Acoustics, 2004.

Somaiya, Ravi. "How Facebook Is Changing the Way Its Users Consume Journalism." *New York Times* 26 Oct. 2014. http://www.nytimes.com/2014/10/27/business/media/how-facebook-is-changing-the-way-its-users-consume-journalism.html.

Spinuzzi, Clay. "Losing by Expanding: Corralling the Runaway Object." *JBTC* 25.4 (2011): 449–486.

Spinuzzi, Clay. *Tracing Genres through Organizations: A Sociocultural Approach to Information Design.* Cambridge: MIT, 2003.

Stanley, Thomas. *The Execution of Sun Ra.* Shelbyville, KY: Wasteland Press, 2014.

Stanley, Thomas. Personal Interview. 6 Dec. 2013.

Stanley, Thomas. "Unless we can develop a generation . . ." Facebook. 15 Nov. 2013.

Stanyek, Jason, and Benjamin Piekut. "Deadness: Technologies of the Intermundane." *The Sound Studies Reader.* Ed. Jonathan Sterne. New York: Routledge, 2012. 304–324.

Stewart, Luke. Personal Interview. 6 Dec. 2013.

Stone, Jonathan. "Listening to the Sonic Archive: Rhetoric, Representation, and Race in the Lomax Prison Recordings." *Enculturation* 19 (2015): http://enculturation.net/listening-to-the-sonic-archive.

Syrotinski, Michael. "Origins: 'The Most Original and Powerful Ethnocentrism.'" *Reading Derrida's Of Grammatology.* Ed. Sean Gaston and Ian Maclachlan. New York: Continuum, 2011. 5–10.

Syverson, Margaret. *The Wealth of Reality: An Ecology of Composition.* Carbondale, IL: SIUP, 1999.

Taylor, Mark C. *The Moment of Complexity: Emerging Network Culture.* Chicago: U of Chicago P, 2001.

Terranova, Tiziana. *Network Culture: Politics for the Information Age.* Ann Arbor, MI: Pluto Press, 2004.

Thaiss, Chris, and Terry Zawacki. *Engaged Writers and Dynamic Disciplines: Research on the Academic Writing Life.* Portsmouth, NH: Boynton/Cook, 2006.

Thompson, Stacy. *Punk Productions: Unfinished Business.* Albany: SUNY, 2004.

Trimbur, John. "Composition and the Circulation of Writing." *CCC* 52.2 (2000): 188–219.

Uexküll, Jakob von. *A Foray Into the Worlds of Animals and Humans, with A Theory of Meaning.* 1934. Trans. Joseph O'Neil. Minneapolis: U of Minnesota P, 2010.

Ulmer, Gregory. *Heuretics: The Logic of Invention.* Baltimore: Johns Hopkins UP, 1994.

Ulmer, Gregory. *Internet Invention: From Literacy to Electracy.* New York: Longman, 2003.

Ulmer, Gregory. *Teletheory*. New York: Routledge, 1989.

Ulmer, Gregory. "The Object of Post-Criticism." *The Anti-Aesthetic: Essays on Postmodern Culture*. Ed. Hal Foster. Seattle, WA: Bay Press, 1983. 83–110.

Van Mersbergen, Audrey M. "The Return of the Addressed: Rhetoric, Reading, and Resonance." *Rhetoric Review* 16.2 (1998): 242–252.

Varnelis, Kazys, ed. *Networked Publics*. Cambridge: MIT, 2008.

Ventimiglia, Jill. "New day! New eyes! New voice! Hear me roar!!" Facebook 18 Mar. 2016, 11:32am..

Vitanza, Victor. "A Philology for a Future Anterior: An Essay-as-Seminar." *Theorizing Histories of Rhetoric*. Ed. Michelle Ballif. Carbondale, IL: SIUP, 2013. 172–189.

Vitanza, Victor. *Negation, Subjectivity, and The History of Rhetoric*. Albany: SUNY, 1996.

Voegelin, Salome. *Sonic Possible Worlds: Hearing the Continuum of Sound*. New York: Bloombury, 2014.

Waksman, Steve. *This Ain't the Summer of Love: Conflict and Crossover in Heavy Metal and Punk*. Berkeley, CA: U of California P, 2009.

Warner, Michael. *Publics and Counterpublics*. Cambridge: Zone Books, 2002.

Warner, Michael. "Publics and Counterpublics." *Public Culture* 14.1 (2002): 49–90.

Warner, Michael. "Publics and Counterpublics (abbreviated version)." *QJS* 88.4 (2002): 413–425.

Webb, Peter. *Exploring Networked Worlds of Popular Music: Milieu Cultures*. New York: Routledge, 2007.

Weisser, Christian. "Subaltern Counterpublics and the Discourse of Protest." *JAC* 28.3–4 (2008): 608–620.

Wells, H.G. *The Shape of Things to Come*. 1933. New York: Penguin Classics, 2006.

Wilson, Greg, and Carl Herndl. "Boundary Objects as Rhetorical Exigence: Knowledge Mapping and Interdisciplinary Co-operation at the Los Alamos National Laboratory." *JBTC* 21.2 (2007): 129–154.

Wolfe, Cary. Introduction. "Bring the Noise: *The Parasite* and the Multiple Genealogies of Posthumanism." *The Parasite*. By Michel Serres. Trans. Lawrence Schehr. Minneapolis: U of Minnesota P, 2007. xi–xxviii.

Wolfe, Johanna. "Gesture and Collaborative Planning: A Case Study of a Study Writing Group." *Written Communication* 22.3 (2005): 298–332.

Yarbrough, Stephen. *After Rhetoric: The Study of Discourse Beyond Language and Culture*. Carbondale, IL: SIUP, 1999.

Young, Richard. "Invention: A Topographical Survey." *Teaching Composition: Ten Bibliographic Essays.* Ed. Gary Tate. Fort Worth: Texas Christian UP, 1976. 1–44.

Young, Richard. "Paradigms and Problems: Needed Research in Rhetorical Invention." *Research and Composing: Points of Departure.* Ed. Charles Cooper and Lee Odell. Urbana, IL: NCTE, 1978. 29–47.

INDEX

Note: Page numbers in *italics* indicate figures.

RESOUNDING THE RHETORICAL

PITTSBURGH SERIES IN COMPOSITION, LITERACY, AND CULTURE

David Bartholomae and Jean Ferguson Carr, Editors